ROME AND THE DISTANT EAST: TRADE ROUTES TO THE ANCIENT LANDS OF ARABIA, INDIA AND CHINA

Rome and the Distant East

Trade Routes to the Ancient Lands of Arabia, India and China

Raoul McLaughlin

BLOOMSBURY
NEW DELHI • LONDON • OXFORD • NEW YORK • SYDNEY

BLOOMSBURY INDIA
Bloomsbury Publishing India Pvt. Ltd
Second Floor, Building No. 4
DDA Complex LSC, Pocket C – 6 & 7
Vasant Kunj, New Delhi 110070
www.bloomsbury.com

BLOOMSBURY, Bloomsbury Academic India and the
Dianalogo are trademarks of Bloomsbury Publishing Plc

First published in India 2021
First published 2010

This edition published with permission from Bloomsbury Publishing Plc,
50 Bedford Square, London, WC1B3DP, UK

British Library Cataloguing-in-Publication Data
A catalogue record for this book is available from the British Library.

Library of Congress Cataloging-in-Publication Data
A catalog record for this book is available from the Library of Congress

ISBN: 978-93-89391-57-2

For sale in the Indian subcontinent only

Typeset by Pindar NZ, Auckland, New Zealand
Digitally Printed and bound in India by Replika Press Pvt. Ltd.

For my parents William John McLaughlin
and Elizabeth Terry McLaughlin

Acknowledgements

This book is based on a doctoral thesis completed at Queen's University Belfast in 2006. When I was looking for a place to study Eastern trade I applied to many universities, but none could accommodate a subject so broad and ambitious. This work could only have been written in Belfast and I greatly appreciate how I was allowed to follow my academic interests under constructive direction and encouragement. I would like to thank my doctoral supervisor Dr John Curran, for without his guidance and support I would not have had the opportunity to investigate this subject. I would also like to thank Professor Brian Campbell and Dr Colin Adams for agreeing to be my doctoral examiners and acknowledge how much I have benefited from their advice.

I was educated at Lagan College in Belfast, the first cross-community integrated school to be established in Northern Ireland. The college was founded with the aim of giving young people the opportunity to understand and respect all cultural and religious backgrounds without the divisions of race or social class. I have come to realize how skilfully the teaching staff, led by the principal Dr Brian Lambkin, promoted this ethos among us, without ever discouraging independent thought or undermining the social, or political, views of each individual. I have remained in contact with my school friends throughout my time at university. I especially thank Jenny Kirkwood for helping me with modern language translations and Mawuli Amoaku for offering me the opportunity to visit China.

The early stages of my doctoral research were paid for by the Northern Ireland Department of Education and Learning, but I have funded subsequent study from my own resources. Queen's University Belfast has hosted both my undergraduate study and my postgraduate research. I greatly value my university and I respect the skills and attitudes of its people, who have never discouraged me or disparaged my ideas. In Belfast, Ancient Historians are able to study in the same department as Social Anthropologists and Modern Historians. In this environment, history has a global context and the study of distant cultures has a distinct value. Doctor John Curran and Professor David Whitehead have given me the opportunity to teach tutorial classes in Republican Roman and Classical Greek history at the university. This experience has been invaluable and my position at Queen's has given me access to library resources and research materials that I would not otherwise have been able to acquire. This has permitted me to pursue my studies long enough to complete this book.

I would like to acknowledge my fellow ancient historians Chris McCoubrey and Jonathan Eton. They have offered me practical help and because they are scholars of the Roman military, our conversations have always been lively and interesting.

In particular Jonathan Eton has read early versions of my manuscript and has been able to provide valuable constructive criticism. Shaun McDaid is studying modern Ulster history, but he has always offered me support. Claire Rush, who has a background in Irish history, has also obtained rare books on my behalf and for this I owe her a debt of gratitude. As a student of Social Anthropology Gemma Wieberg uniquely understands the complexities of human society and I have valued her insights.

This book is dedicated to my parents William and Elizabeth McLaughlin. They have had to accept that turning my doctoral research into a book has meant financial hardship and my father has worked beyond retirement age to offer me assistance. I must thank my brother Leon for taking the time and trouble to draft my maps and check my ancient references. My whole family, especially my sister Thayna, have given me immeasurable support and encouragement.

To all the above, I acknowledge receipt of your kindness and consideration. Without you this book would not have been possible.

Raoul McLaughlin
Belfast
June 2009

Contents

Illustrations

9 A Roman mosaic showing how hunters captured tiger cubs (*Hunt Mosaic*, Antioch): 'India produces the tiger which has tremendous swiftness. The hunter lies in wait to seize the tiger cubs, and then escapes on the fastest horse because, as soon as the female finds her lair empty, she springs into pursuit' – Pliny the Elder in his *Natural History*.

10 A classical bust depicting a subject of the Roman Empire who adopted Buddhist beliefs (Museo Nazionale Romano).

Abbreviations

AE	*L'année épigraphique*.
BE	Bagnall, R. S. and Helms, C. and Verhoogt, A. M. F. W. (2000–), *Documents from Berenike*. Bruxelles: Fondation Égyptologique Reine Élisabeth.
CIL	*Corpus Inscriptionum Latinarum*.
CIS	*Corpus Inscriptionum Semiticarum*.
EI	*Epigraphia Indica* (produced by a variety publishers).
IG	*Inscriptiones Graecae* (Berlin 1873–).
IGRR	*Inscriptiones Graecae ad Res Romanas Pertinentes*.
ILS	*Inscriptiones Latinae Selectae*.
Inv.	Cantineau, J. and Starcky, J. and Gawlikowski, M. (eds) (1930–), *Inventaire des inscriptions de Palmyre*. Beirut, Paris, Damascus.
O. Mich.	Greek Ostraca in the University of Michigan Collection.
O. Petr	Ostraca in Professor W. M. Flinders Petrie's Collection at University College, London.
OGIS	Dittenberger, W. (1903–1905), *Orientis Graeci Inscriptiones Selectae*.
P. Lond.	Kenyon, F. G. and Bell, H. I. (1893–), *Greek papyri in the British Museum*. London, British Museum Department of Manuscripts.
P. Mich.	*Greek Papyri in the University of Michigan Collection*.
P. Tebt	Grenfell, B. P. and Hunt, A. S. (eds) (1902–), *The Tebtunis Papyri*. London.
P. Vindob.	Vindobensis Papyri, Austrian National Library, Vienna.
RES	Clermont-Ganneau, C. S. (eds) (1900–), *Répertoire d'épigraphie semitique*. Paris, Imprimerie nationale.
SB	*Sammelbuch griechischer Urkunden aus Ägypten*.
SEG	*Supplementum Epigraphicum Graecum*.

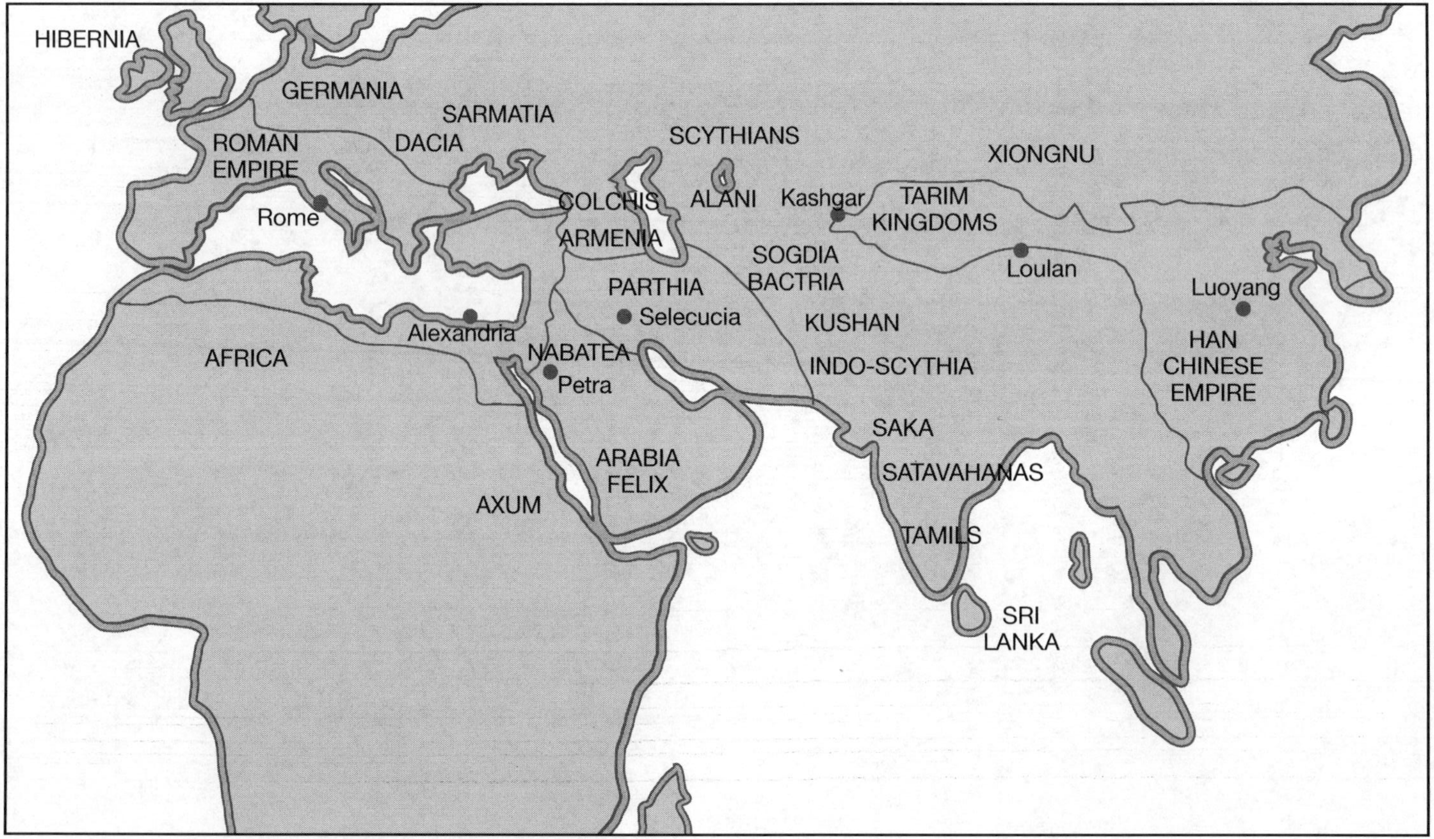

The empires and territories of the Ancient World (first century AD).

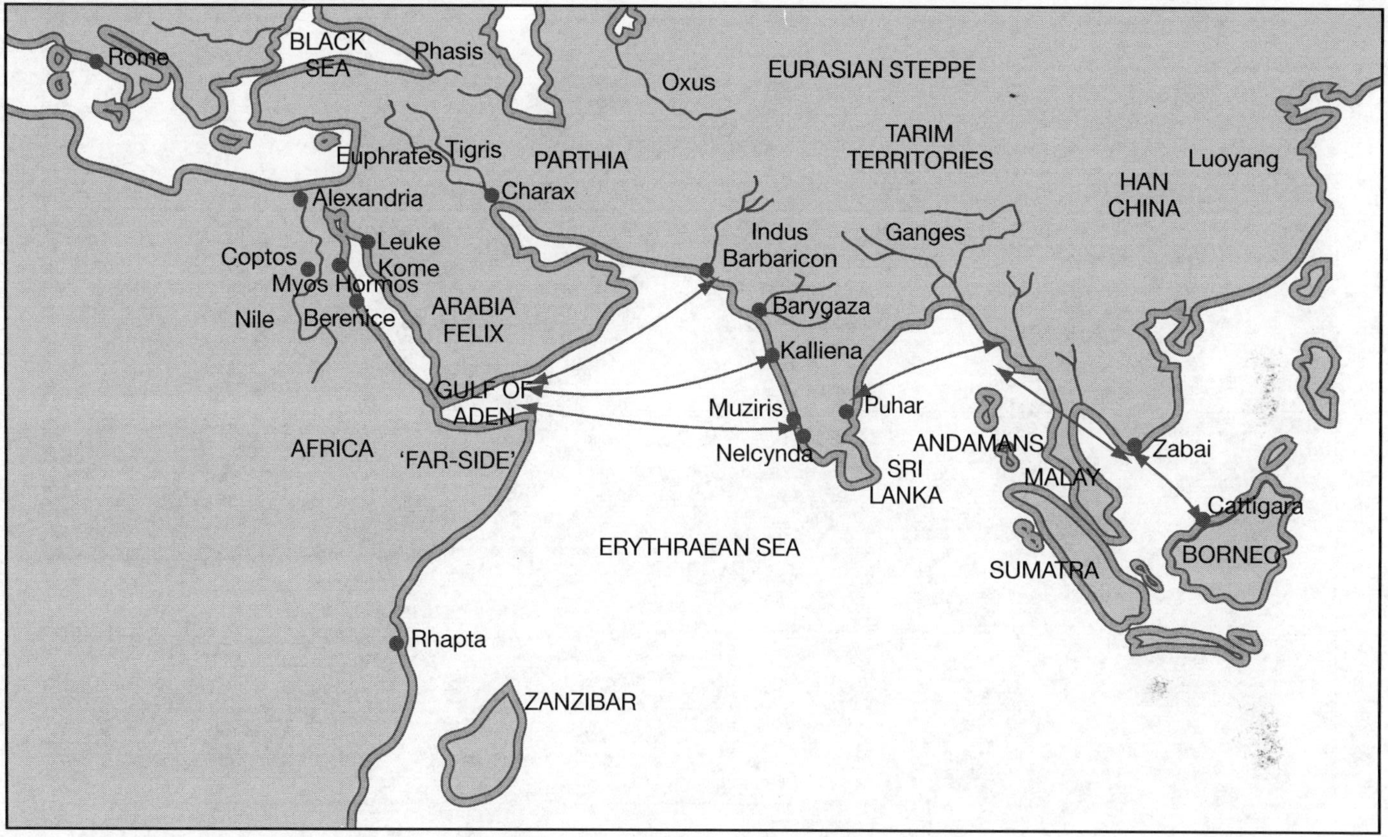

The Indian Ocean (first century AD).

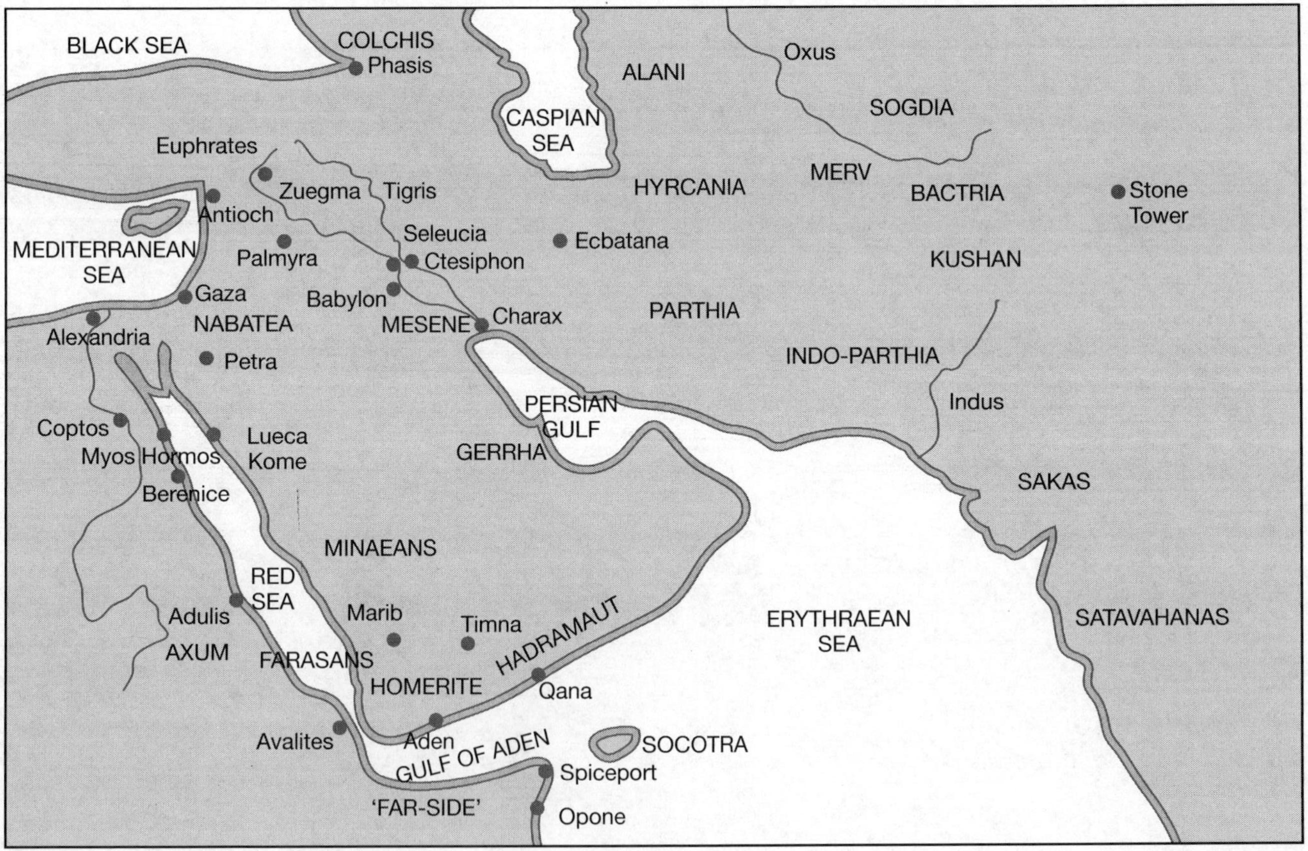

The Middle East (first century AD).

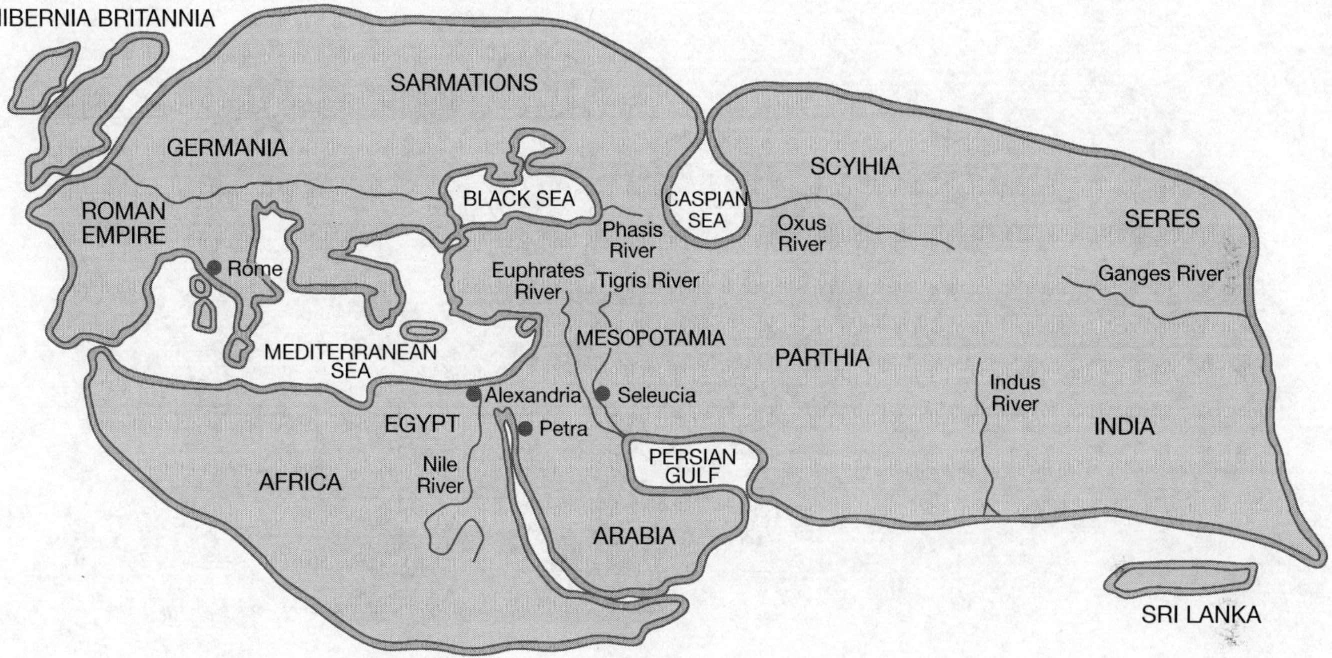

Strabo's world view (early first century AD).

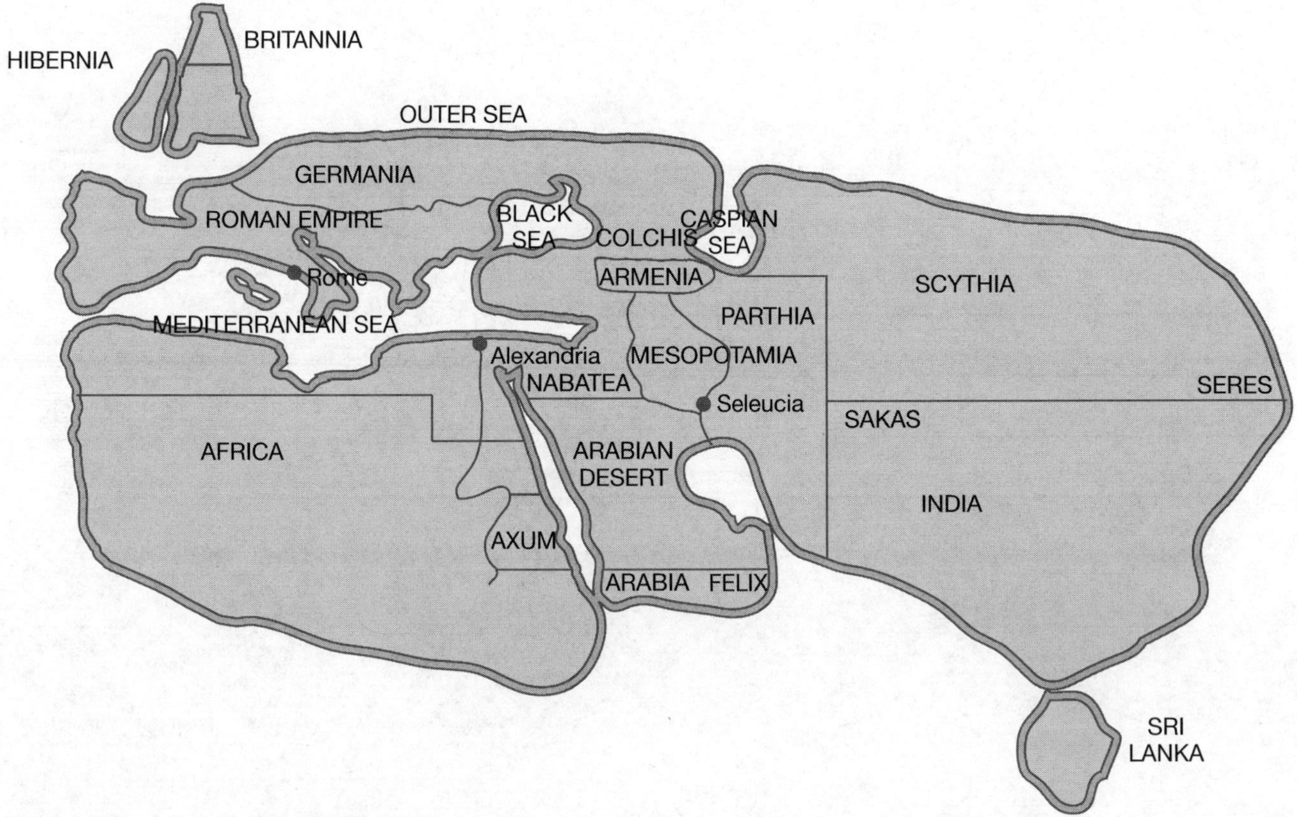

Pliny's world view based on details in his *Natural History* (mid first century AD).

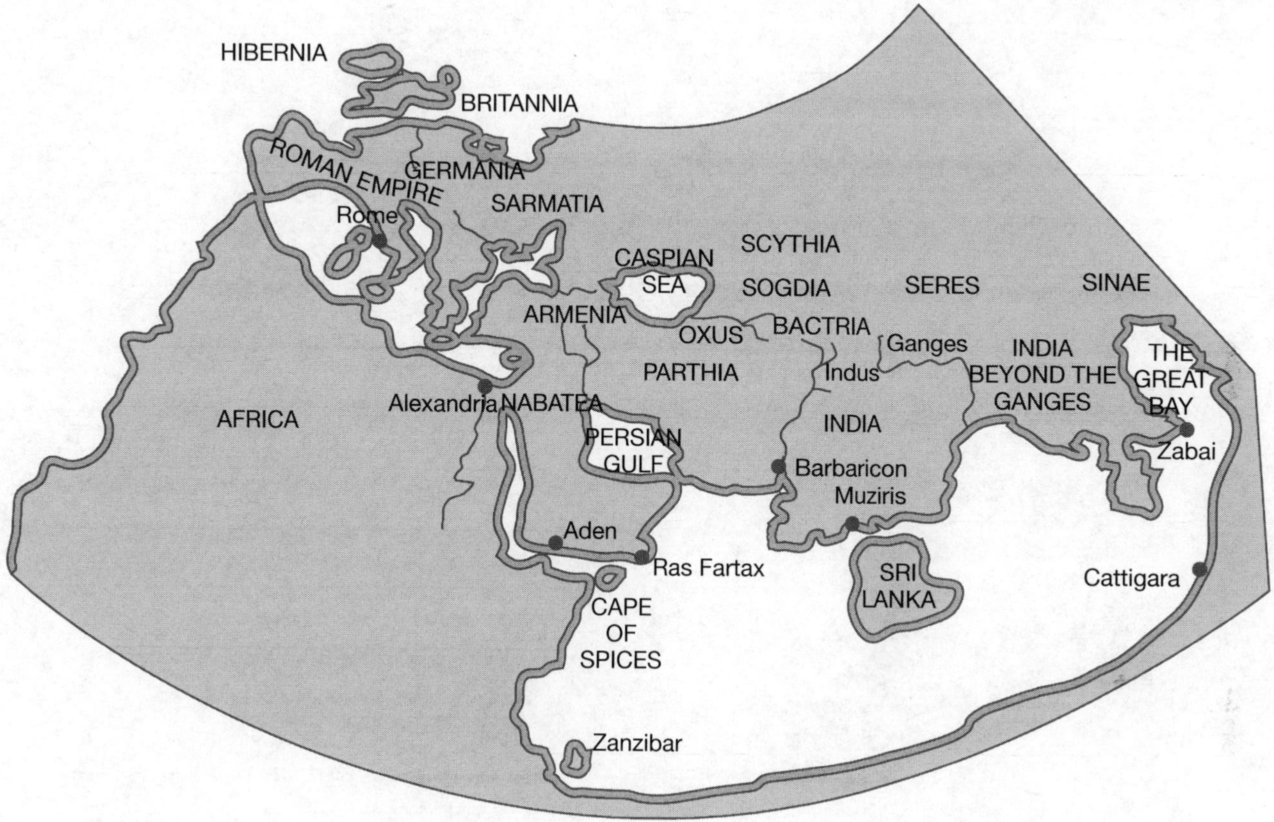

Claudius Ptolemy's world view (mid second century AD).

Introduction: Rome and the Distant East

In the closing years of the Republican era, the Romans completed their conquest of the remaining Mediterranean kingdoms. Yet few in that Empire appreciated the scale of the ancient world they inhabited. Far beyond their frontiers, across the immense inhospitable territories of Inner Asia, lay the vast expanse of Han China. Previously unknown to the Romans, China had for almost two centuries governed a population and domain that equalled Rome at the height of its power. Although the Romans remained only dimly aware of China, the Han maintained ambitions in the distant West and as time progressed they drew together reports of Rome. They regarded this distant equal with increasing fascination and made ambitious plans for contact.

Driven by new commercial fashions, trade goods moved in increasingly large quantities between China and Rome. However, the hostile kingdoms that lay between the two great empires jealously guarded the commercial profits of this traffic and blocked almost all direct communications between the Roman and Chinese civilizations. To the east of the Roman Empire, lay the Parthian Realm, the formidable rival to Rome that stretched across Persia from Mesopotamia and Iran to the outer edge of India. The presence of the Parthians denied Roman subjects access to the vital overland caravan routes that connected across Iran and led onwards to India and China. Nevertheless, by the close of the Republican era, the Roman Empire had gained possession of Mediterranean territories bordering the Red Sea, and as market opportunities improved, greater numbers of Roman subjects began to use this region to reach the Indian Ocean and explore the distant East.

Source accounts from the classical texts reveal how, in ancient times, these distant trade routes connected the eastern territories of the Roman Empire to the faraway lands of Arabia, India and China. Ancient evidence indicates that after the conquest of Egypt, a variety of exotic goods from the distant East became increasingly available to Roman society. The ancient testimonies also describe the operation of trade ventures undertaken by Roman subjects who, compelled by profit, travelled far beyond the Empire's eastern frontiers and confronted great dangers to acquire valuable spices, prized silks and costly aromatics.

The sources reveal how Roman merchants sailed from the Egyptian Red Sea ports on distant ocean crossings to explore the commercial opportunities offered in the far-off territories that encircled the Indian Ocean. By the early first century AD Roman merchants routinely sailed as far as Tamil India and through these trade connections imported into the Empire a vast range of exotic materials including spices, fabrics and gemstones.

On these distant trade voyages Roman merchant ships would visit African markets in Ethiopia and Somalia to acquire valuable local products including exotic slaves and precious aromatics. Roman merchants also became frequent visitors to Eastern bazaars in the territories of southern Arabia where they would receive precious stocks of frankincense and myrrh harvested in the surrounding regions. As this aspect of trade developed, merchants from the Arabian kingdoms began to send great camel caravan trains northward through the vast desert expanse of Arabia to reach prosperous markets in Palestine and supply Roman society with further stocks of this costly incense.

The ancient accounts also provide evidence for the operation of distant overland trade routes that crossed Asia to supply Roman markets with a further range of exotic Eastern products. Mesopotamia was an ethnically diverse region and Parthia did not have absolute authority over their small communities and kingdoms. Merchants from the Roman Empire could therefore cross freely from Syria into Mesopotamia to visit the great Greek and Persian cities that existed in the fertile territories near the Tigris and Euphrates river systems. There they found Eastern goods that had reached Mesopotamia through maritime trade routes extending across the Persian Gulf to northwest India. Mesopotamia also offered further commercial possibilities for Roman merchants. It was at the edge of major caravan routes that stretched across the Iranian territories of the Parthian Realm to reach distant sites in Inner Asia and, ultimately, China.

Although China remained remote, classical authorities had from the earliest stage of their history appreciated the scale and significance of ancient India. Modern interest in Rome has tended to emphasize the importance of Western Europe, but India has always been significant in classical knowledge of the ancient world. In the fifth century BC the Greek historian Herodotus records tribute lists from a Persian Empire that extended from Egypt and Asia Minor, across Iran to the outer edge of India. Although the Persians controlled only the Indus region, this eastern terminal of their realm provided their king, Darius, with almost a third of his total tribute revenues.[1]

By the Roman era, the growth of international trade permitted greater connections between these distant civilizations and India was arguably even more significant to the classical world. 'They say that India forms one-third of the whole earth and that its populations are innumerable – and this is certainly possible.'[2] These are the words of the Roman writer and commander Gaius Plinius Secundus, better known as Pliny the Elder. Pliny served as an adviser to the Emperor Vespasian and in the first century AD composed one of the most extensive surviving studies of the ancient world. Elsewhere in his encyclopaedic work, Pliny considers the development of Roman trade voyages across the Indian Ocean and justifies his inclusion of this new material with the comment, 'This is an important matter since India drains more than fifty million sesterces a year from our empire'.[3] To place this export figure in context, a sum of 50 million sesterces was larger than the annual tribute that Caesar imposed on Gaul following his conquest of this productive territory.[4]

These ancient statements regarding the distant East become significant when modern scholars propagate the grand imperial claims of Roman 'world rule'. The real ancient world was far larger than either the Roman Mediterranean or the fringe territories of northwest Europe. Any well-informed Roman appreciated that Rome only governed a small portion of the earth, and that beyond the eastern frontiers, there existed sophisticated kingdoms that could rival their Empire. Evidence of these distant powers was on display in the markets of their popular urban centres which offered the products of Arabia, Persia, India and the Far East, to keen Roman customers. These eastern kingdoms often sent representatives to the Roman Emperor and their rulers would have, with justification, regarded themselves as equal to their Roman counterparts.

The Romans perhaps felt uneasy about what lay beyond their eastern frontiers. Rome depended on Egypt to feed its vast population, but Egypt was also the gateway to the Indian Ocean and the outer limits of its enormous expanse remained unexplored. With almost no provocation Augustus had launched a Red Sea fleet of 130 warships against Arabia, to conquer the peninsula with an army to seize their wealth.[5] The city of Aden was sacked during these hostilities and although the conquest failed, a precedent had been set.

As merchants further explored the distant East, Roman authorities realized the ancient world did not end at the limits of India as their Greek predecessors, and their Republican ancestors, had imagined. By the first century AD trade contacts had expanded to reach the Malay Peninsula and reports began to arrive of the even more distant territories beyond. Consequently, Roman authorities had good reason to feel awed by the scale of the inhabited world. Yet they also appreciated how these new contacts enabled unprecedented communications between the most distant territories known to Roman society. As Seneca observed, 'What after all is the space that lies between the furthest shores of Spain and India? Only a few days travel if a ship is blown by a favourable wind'.[6]

It was through their most distant maritime contacts with India that the Romans first began to receive confused accounts of another significant power in the Far East. This was China, the true source of the silk fabrics that had already become popular fashion amongst prosperous Roman consumers. As Roman trade with the distant East steadily expanded, direct contacts between these two great imperial civilizations seemed inevitable.

The Roman philosopher and statesman Seneca, tutor of the Emperor Nero, was sufficiently interested in the distant East to compose a book on the subject of India.[7] This work has not survived into modern times, but statements in his prolific studies seem ominous, especially as the first rumours regarding China were reaching Rome during Seneca's lifetime. Criticising mankind's capacity to cause harm to foreign nations, Seneca warns that even Rome might one day find itself victim to a distant imperial power as yet unknown. He muses, 'What if some ruler of a great nation, at present unknown to us, increased by good fortune and ambitious to expand the boundaries of his realm, is at this very moment fitting out a fleet to send against us?'.[8]

In the ancient world, the struggle for supremacy was not always decided by invasion and war. In lands remote from Rome, imperial agents were using economic strategies to bring foreign peoples into positions of subservience. In the Far East, the Han set in motion subtle long-term schemes to undermine their foreign enemies and damage any ability to resist, or make war, on China. The Han encouraged a market for Chinese foodstuffs and fashions amongst foreign peoples including the Xiongnu hordes of the Mongolian Steppe. The eventual aim was to make these populations dependent on Chinese foods and manufactured goods so that these items could be withheld, or offered in diminished amounts, to inflict economic damage on these foreign communities. A Han official outlined how this strategy should be implemented, advising, 'Every large border market we establish must be fitted with shops . . . and all shops must be large enough to serve between one to two hundred people . . . The Xiongnu will then develop a craving for our products and this will be their fatal weakness'.[9] The Xiongnu were beguiled through thousands of trade exchanges that collectively reduced their resources and weakened their economic independence. As another Han official reported, 'A piece of plain Chinese silk can be exchanged with the Xiongnu nomads for articles worth several pieces of gold. By these means we can reduce the resources of our enemy'.[10] With calculated foresight the Han slowly, but surely, gained an economic stranglehold over their most dangerous opponents.

In the Roman Empire the new fashion-driven demand for costly silk fabrics caused growing concern. In a speech before the Senate in AD 22, the Emperor Tiberius drew attention to the effect this unchecked consumerism was having on the Roman economy, 'Our wealth is transported to alien and hostile countries because of the promiscuous dress worn by men and women – especially women'.[11] But no effective measures were taken to restrict the trade and in the following decades escalating fashion demands encouraged the export of ever greater quantities of Roman wealth to the distant East. These issues concerned Seneca who was aware that the wealth of the Empire was being conveyed to some far-off people who were not yet revealed to Roman merchants, nor had they announced their intent to the government in Rome. He concludes ominously, 'these silks are imported at vast expense from nations unknown to us even through trade'.[12] Pliny also identifies the 'Silk People' as one of the main participants in the eastern haemorrhage of Roman bullion and accuses them of orchestrating a trade where the eastern peoples, 'take 100 million sesterces from our empire every year – so much do our luxuries and our women cost us'.[13] This figure is equivalent to perhaps one-eighth of the total Roman expense budget. By this era it may already have been too late to restrict the trade, as the Roman Empire became increasingly reliant on the customs revenues received from taxing the commerce created by the incoming Eastern goods.

The Romans had good reason to receive rumours of China with apprehension. Seneca was a member of the imperial court during the reign of Claudius when a Sri Lankan king sent a party of ambassadors to establish the first diplomatic contacts between the Sinhalese kingdom and the Roman state. Pliny was a young military officer serving in Germany at the time of these events, but he later wrote an account of this episode, suggesting that the Roman elite were awed by this unexpected encounter. Previous classical authorities had known very little about the Sinhalese kingdom before this dramatic diplomatic overture and there had been popular speculation that Sri Lanka might have been the tip of a vast unexplored continent – an *alter orbis* – that matched the scale of the Eurasian landmass.[14]

The appreciation that Rome was only a small part of the ancient world has relevance for Roman ideology, especially the assertion made by the imperial elite that their empire had authority over the whole earth. In practice, this authority could not have been military and Seneca hints that the Roman claim to world recognition was achieved by the peaceful dealings of merchants, not through the military might of legionaries. He protests, 'we have been given the winds so that the wealth of each region might become common, and not to carry legions and cavalry, or bring harmful intent to other peoples'.[15]

This latter statement by Seneca offers a more accurate and perhaps more authentic appraisal of the Roman achievement in its ancient context. At the height of Roman power, subjects of the Empire were frequent visitors to trading centres as far west as Hibernia, while in the distant East great commercial fleets routinely sailed from Roman ports in Egypt to coastal markets in India and beyond.[16] The Romans never achieved a global conquest, but Roman rule was able to foster a commerce that had a far greater influence over the ancient world and its resources, than imperial armies could ever have hoped to acquire by coercive force. Perhaps Rome's global achievement would be better assessed through the accomplishments of merchants and measured by the range and scale of their activities.

By studying Roman involvement in Eastern trade, this book places the Roman Empire more firmly within its genuine ancient context. This investigation challenges how Western scholars have traditionally presented Rome and its achievements. Notably, there is still a convention within established scholarship to consider the Roman Empire largely on the basis of its direct political and military sphere of influence, confining studies within narrow academic boundaries. These perceptions need to be confronted and this can be achieved by studying ancient evidence concerning how trade connected and financed the ancient world. Finally, I believe that international commerce is the key to explaining the remarkable economic success of the imperial system that created and sustained the early Roman Empire.

PLAN OF THE BOOK

The study presented in this book is a scaled-down enquiry into the operation of Rome's Eastern commerce. The book is based on my doctoral research completed in 2006 entitled 'Roman Trade with India and the Distant East'. I believe that one of the main issues limiting the study of Eastern commerce is the absence of accessible books on this subject.

This is the first book to comprehensively consider Rome's Eastern trade, but a study on this scale cannot deal adequately with the range of evidence that exists on this topic. I have therefore concentrated my study on the development of Eastern contacts up to their period of greatest significance. The sources used are taken from ancient texts that are difficult for the non-specialist to acquire and I have therefore provided translations whenever possible. I have also directed my discussion towards evidence that can be used to challenge existing views of the Roman economy and traditional attitudes to the ancient world.

Chapter One introduces the main evidence for Roman involvement in Eastern commerce. This includes a review of the main classical texts, an introduction to the archaeological evidence, and a discussion of the ancient works surviving from the

Indian and Chinese civilizations. Chapter Two looks at the maritime trade routes that led from Roman Egypt across the eastern oceans to India and the distant East. Chapter Three considers the gulf trade routes and desert caravan trails, that brought incense from southern Arabia north into Roman territories. Chapter Four examines the evidence for the overland trade routes that crossed Persia to connect with the so-called silk routes of Inner Asia.

The last two chapters of this study consider the political and economic context of the Roman Empire. Chapter Five examines the evidence for diplomatic contacts between Roman government and the distant powers that ruled India and China. The final chapter considers the significance of Eastern commerce to the Roman economy. The first part of this chapter looks at the fashion-driven consumption of Eastern merchandise in Roman society and considers how trade ventures to the distant East were funded. The final section investigates the revenues that Rome received from Eastern commerce and looks at how these funds financed the Empire. This discussion introduces an alternative model for the Roman economy, explaining how the Empire functioned during its period of greatest prosperity.

For the purposes of this book, the term 'Roman' describes the territories of Syria, Palestine, Egypt and Arabia that were within the Empire or under the rule of its client kingdoms. In these discussions the term 'distant East' or 'remote East' refers to territories beyond the Roman frontiers. This includes the Parthian Realm, southern Arabia, East Africa, India, Inner Asia, the Far East and China.

In referencing ancient works I have given the title that is most likely to be known to non-specialists. In the footnotes, I have listed texts in the order they can be read to make sense of the issue. In most cases, I have limited references to the most recent arguments concerning the subject and listed works where further academic details can be found. I believe that Eastern commerce is a worthy subject area for future historical inquiry. Though I personally do not have the opportunity to continue this research, I can create the context that future scholars can use to further explore this fascinating subject.

1

Ancient Evidence for Eastern Contacts

The evidence for Eastern commerce is extraordinary, especially as the Greek and Roman sources are supplemented by various written accounts produced by other ancient civilizations. For example, the earliest Tamil literature describes contact with a foreign people called the *Yavanas* who many believe were subjects of the Roman Empire.[17] Historical records have also survived from ancient China and they record the activities of a foreign people from a great power in the distant West called *Da Qin*.[18] Leading Sinologists identify *Da Qin* as the Roman Empire.[19]

Added to this written testimony is an increasing range of ancient evidence recovered by archaeological finds. These include inscriptions from ancient monuments, texts scratched on pottery fragments known as *ostraca*, and papyri documents from Roman times that have been preserved in the arid environment of Egypt. Ancient sites associated with Eastern trade both within and beyond the Roman frontiers, have also been subject to recent investigation and have provided further important material evidence for the conduct and significance of Eastern commerce.

THE PERIPLUS OF THE ERYTHRAEAN SEA

Classical accounts provide the most extensive and credible evidence for the operation of Rome's Eastern trade, and among these texts a short pamphlet referred to as the *Periplus of the Erythraean Sea* holds a uniquely important position.

The *Periplus* is a merchant handbook consisting of 66 concise paragraphs written in a straightforward style of Greek that was popular in the Roman era.[20] In this important document the unnamed author offers practical information about trade voyages from Roman Egypt to ports of call in east Africa, southern Arabia, and the western coasts of India. This systematic catalogue of trade contact makes the *Periplus* the most detailed and comprehensive surviving account of Roman involvement in Eastern commerce.[21]

One of the unique features of the *Periplus* is that it was written by someone who had direct experience of the distant East and clues in the text suggest that the author was a Greek-speaking businessman from Egypt who had visited India on past trade missions.[22] The author was probably a trusted authority who wrote the report to inform contemporaries about the condition of Eastern commerce, probably for the benefit of speculators who wanted to invest in the trade, or perhaps for less experienced merchants who were considering undertaking the voyage themselves.[23] The *Periplus* is also remarkable because it is one of the few surviving classical sources to have been written by a merchant. Most historical accounts from the Roman era were written by members of the learned social elite who tended to idealise the aristocratic business of landholding and regard merchants as social inferiors. This makes the pragmatic testimony of the *Periplus* even more compelling as a source for ancient practices.

The author of the *Periplus* collected details from different trade voyages and assembled this information into long itineraries that catalogued commercial opportunities along the eastern coasts. Above all else, the interest of the author is directed towards items that could be exchanged at the various ports of call and so lists commodities exported through trade and the Roman goods that could be exchanged in return. On occasion the author also provides details about the quantities of certain goods traded and offers information on the true origins of products, when the merchant dealers exporting the goods were only intermediaries in a wider commerce.

The *Periplus* also contains elements of a maritime manual and a navigational aid with the author offering significant information on sailing routes, marine hazards, landmarks, safe anchorages and useful supplies.[24] This additional detail combines to create a vivid account of the commerce, revealing the concerns of merchants and the many dangers they routinely encountered on these ambitious trade voyages.

The *Periplus* describes characters and events that would date the work to around AD 50. First, the author mentions that an Arabian monarch named Malichus was ruling the Nabatean kingdom and inscriptions from this region reveal that Malichus was in power between AD 40 and AD 70.[25] Second, the author describes northern India before AD 65 when invaders from Central Asia, called the Kushan, were still confined to Bactria, and Gandhara was ruled by minor Indo-Parthian kings.[26] The third piece of evidence is more complex, as the *Periplus* describes an era when the Gujarat region of India was under the control of a king who the author names as 'Manbanos', but the Indian texts call 'Nahapana'.[27] When the *Periplus* was written, Nahapana had just captured territory in the Satavahana Realm to the south of his kingdom, including the important Buddhist monastery at Nasik.[28] Inscriptions from Nasik suggest that Nahapana controlled the region for less than 11 years and scholars have assigned a date of AD 66 for the latest Saka inscription at the site.[29] This suggests that the Saka occupation described in the *Periplus*, could not have begun much earlier than AD 54. Interestingly, the author of the *Periplus* was unaware of events late in the reign of the Claudius when a Roman freedman discovered a new sailing route to Sri Lanka and brought back important new information concerning the island.[30] This suggests that the *Periplus* was written shortly before AD 54 when Claudius was succeeded by Nero.

The *Periplus of the Erythraean Sea* is the only merchant *Periplus* that has survived from antiquity, but at any one time there were probably dozens of these accounts circulating amongst the Greek and Roman businessmen of Alexandria. It is likely that these reports would have been regularly updated and amended as new information became available and further trading opportunities were realized. These guides would have been written by trusted authorities and passed on to select contacts in the business community. Eastern trade was bewildering in its complexity and Roman businessmen needed some form of reference to plan possible market destinations and respond to likely foreign demands. Some trade decisions would have to be made during the voyage as Roman merchants picked up Eastern cargoes at foreign ports to exchange at more distant markets. An up-to-date trade *Periplus* would be invaluable as Roman traders needed to know which Arabian goods were in demand at Indian ports and what other foreign shipping was visiting particular markets. These elaborate trade systems required the type of detailed guide that can be found in the pages of the *Periplus*.

The *Periplus* offers the economic historian an unparalleled insight into distance trade. No other surviving Roman text offers this kind of detail on commerce and the possible strategies behind various trade dealings. If the *Periplus* had not survived, then the study of Eastern commerce would be limited to a few vague and disparate references in the remaining sources. The *Periplus* not only offers a context for all other source accounts, but it also explains archaeological finds that would otherwise remain obscure. The work is unique and has justifiably occupied a central position in almost all modern inquiries into Eastern trade, including my own studies.[31]

THE GEOGRAPHY BY STRABO

About AD 23, a Greek named Strabo completed a geographical study of the known world. Strabo was someone who sought acceptance in Roman society and certain passages of his work demonstrate an underlying approval of the imperial system.[32] He was primarily a historian, and although his version of the history of the world has not survived, the style of his geography reflects his interest in the past.[33] This work contains important information about trade in the eastern Roman Empire and the lands beyond its frontiers.

Strabo was born sometime between 64 BC and 50 BC, in the Pontic city of Amaseia on the southern coast of the Black Sea.[34] His family were Hellenic aristocrats and as part of his education Strabo visited a number of Greek intellectual centres in the eastern Mediterranean.[35] Strabo also resided in Rome before spending several years in Alexandria in the 20s BC, where he developed a friendship with Aelius Gallus. Gallus was one of the first Roman governors of Egypt and Strabo joined his entourage of 'friends and soldiers' to tour around the new province.[36] Strabo returned to Rome shortly after 20 BC and continued to live in the imperial capital, probably until his death in AD 23.[37] It was during this latter period of his life that he composed his geography.[38]

The *Geography* written by Strabo is a substantial, all-encompassing study that collects together ethnographic and political information about the ancient territories known to Greek scholars.[39] Strabo compiled his work from well-known accounts written by traditional Greek and Roman authorities, but he also occasionally added contemporary details concerning recent developments.

The historical information that Strabo collects on Persia and Arabia is of significant value for understanding conditions in these regions. However, his consideration of India relies heavily on respected Greek sources from the time of Alexander the Great and his immediate successors.[40] As a consequence, Strabo provides almost no information regarding events in India during his own era. This is significant, because when Strabo wrote his geography, there would have been thousands of

Roman subjects travelling to India every year. These people had accurate contemporary knowledge of the distant East and Strabo would have encountered them as he walked through the busy streets of Alexandria. However, like other members of the Roman elite, he would have regarded merchants and sailors as his social inferiors. This prejudice excluded contemporary accounts from the type of formal study favoured by the literary classes. Indeed Strabo advises his readers:

> Regarding those merchants who now sail from Egypt . . . as far as the Ganges, they are only private citizens and they are of no use regarding the history of the places they have seen.[41]

It was perhaps true that the traders who sold their goods at the merchant bazaars in Alexandria beguiled wealthy buyers with exaggerated stories about their exotic voyages and the incredible creatures they had seen.[42] This 'sales patter' helped to hype the prices of Eastern goods, but it also meant that authorities like Strabo had difficulty accepting any merchant testimony as entirely credible.[43]

In the Augustan era, members of the Roman government probably had a far more extensive understanding of contemporary India than Strabo, or the surviving sources, would suggest. Strabo mentions that ambassadors from various Indian kingdoms were sending embassies to the Emperor Augustus, but, although Strabo had friends amongst the Roman elite, he was clearly not privy to the exchanges of information that occurred between the Emperor and these prestigious foreign visitors.[44]

Despite its failings, Strabo's *Geography* remains an immensely valuable source of information on Eastern trade in the early Roman era. His survey-like overview of contacts and conditions across the eastern frontiers is indispensable, especially as these outlying territories often receive little mention in the other surviving texts. His approval of Roman imperialism also compels him to comment on how the Empire had benefited these eastern regions by accommodating commerce, or improving security. All these details provide valuable evidence about how the formation of the Augustan Empire fundamentally altered the classical world. Strabo's *Geography* therefore holds an important position in any comprehensive study of Eastern trade.

THE PEUTINGER MAP

A further remarkable document, often referred to as the *Peutinger Table*, reveals Roman perceptions of the world in a map-like display that includes a final segment representing India. The *Peutinger Table* is believed to be a medieval copy of a decorative Roman map, dating to around AD 300. It is relevant for the study of Eastern commerce because it displays important locations in the distant East and outlines significant overland contact routes.

The map is drawn and coloured on parchment and represents the ancient world as a long linear diagram that is less than a third of a metre tall, but stretches to a length of almost seven metres.[45] In the design of the map there has been almost no attempt to represent the true shape of coastlines or countries but important settlements are marked on the document along with various geographical features. Sites represented in the work are connected by coloured lines which are probably travel routes based on overland itineraries used by traders, armies or administrators. A further fascinating feature of the map is the appearance of an Augustan temple in southern India.[46]

The *Peutinger Map* has too many errors and inconsistencies to have been a functional document used for serious overland travel. For example, the Italian town of Pompeii appears on the map, despite its destruction by the eruption of Vesuvius in AD 79. Conversely, the city of Constantinople features prominently, although the city was not founded until the early fourth century AD. This work was probably designed for public exhibition, possibly as some form of state propaganda.[47] The map would visually emphasize the scale and achievements of the Roman Empire, representing the reach of its classical civilization. This would explain why the map depicts a Roman temple in India, a detail which the mapmakers must have found in some earlier classical record. It is therefore likely that the map was compiled by Roman intellectuals using various earlier sources and itineraries to create a large schematic display.

The *Peutinger Map* is an eccentric puzzle of ancient information and any interpretation of the document still remains difficult. The schematic plan of the work can be confusing for the modern viewer and marked locations in outlying territories are sometimes difficult to identify with known ancient sites. General courses recorded on the map can be traced with some confidence, but their significance is often obscure. For instance, it is not clear who was using the ancient routes marked in the sections of the work portraying the distant East and what the original information on these connections may have been. Despite these concerns the *Peutinger Map* is a unique source and this important document will have great significance in future studies of Eastern commerce.

ISIDORE AND THE PARTHIAN STATIONS

The *Parthian Stations*, written by an author called Isidore, is a brief text of unique interest to academics studying Eastern trade. The work gives a short itinerary of sites leading eastward through the Parthian Realm in what many scholars have interpreted as an important overland trade route.[48] Little is known about Isidore, but he seems to have belonged to a Greek community that lived in the Mesopotamian city of Charax, near the head of the Persian Gulf.[49] The text that forms the so-called *Parthian Stations*, is the only surviving extract from a handbook written in Greek that apparently described conditions in the Parthian territories. The surviving itinerary consists of nineteen short paragraphs, many of which are no more than sentences stating distances and providing an occasional pertinent fact about certain locations.

In the *Parthian Stations*, Isidore outlines a route from Zeugma, at the edge of Roman Syria, down the Euphrates River and across the Iranian Plateau to the very limits of Parthian administration.[50] Interestingly, there is no reference in the work to commerce and no indication that the main route outlined through Parthia would lead onwards to either India, or through the lands of inner Asia to reach China. Isidore lists urban centres that probably housed caravan stations, but these sites may also have been included because they functioned as military bases, or because they were important points on official communication routes used by Parthian administrators.

Scholars have suggested that Isidore may have been mapping a military campaign route through Parthian territory, perhaps for the benefit of Roman commanders.[51] This is feasible because early in his itinerary he includes the phrase, 'from this point the forces cross over to the Roman side'. Isidore also shows an interest in the political and military character of sites along the outlined route, occasionally mentioning whether or not a particular location was fortified, or if the local population could be considered 'Greek' and therefore by implication, pro-Roman.[52]

A chance comment by Pliny the Elder could indicate that Isidore was an agent for the Roman government. Pliny writes:

> Charax was the birthplace of Dionysius who is the most recent writer to have dealt with the geography of the world. He was sent to the East by the Emperor Augustus to write a full account of this region. This occurred shortly before Gaius Caesar travelled into Armenia to take command against the Parthians and the Arabs.[53]

It could be that Dionysius wrote under the name Isidore, but it is also possible that Roman authorities used a number of Greek informants to gather intelligence about possible invasion routes through Parthia. The work by Isidore could therefore be the remains of a strategic document produced for the imperial government.[54]

The *Parthian Stations* may date to the Augustan era, but Isidore probably used earlier sources to compile his study. A reference in the work to the city of Alexandropolis being on the eastern frontier of the Parthian Realm is likely to be anachronistic. One theory is that Isidore's report is somehow derived from an official Parthian document, perhaps a survey conducted by Mithridates II in around 100 BC.[55] Although its date and purpose is obscure, the *Parthian Stations* remains an important text for understanding travel routes through ancient Persia, and consequently deserves significant notice in the study of Eastern commerce.

PLINY AND THE NATURAL HISTORY

Pliny the Elder's encyclopaedic *Natural History*, offers important details concerning the use of Eastern products in Mediterranean society, as well as the distant trade ventures undertaken by Roman subjects to acquire these exotic commodities. The *Natural History* is a remarkably complex document and although it provides a uniquely fascinating insight into the mindset of the Roman governing elite, the information it contains is often difficult to interpret and assess.

Pliny was born in northern Italy in around AD 23, but at a young age he was sent to be educated in Rome where he had the opportunity to witness popular events involving members of the imperial court.[56] On reaching adulthood he served with the Roman army in Germany and was involved in a number of military campaigns.

He was then appointed to the office of procurator in Hispania Tarraconensis, where he served in the period between AD 72 and AD 74.[57] Tarraconensis was the largest division of Roman Spain and in the mid first century AD the territory was a major producer of the Empire's new gold reserves. Pliny probably developed his academic interest in mining and bullion production during this period.[58]

Pliny may have held the position of Procurator in other provinces before returning to Rome, where he served as an advisor to the Emperor Vespasian. In Rome, he would have attended meetings where Vespasian consulted his cabinet about state administration and the operational business of the Empire.[59] Pliny developed an academic interest in naval matters and late in his career he was given the prefecture of the Roman fleet at Misenum in the Bay of Naples. He held this post until his dramatic death in AD 79 when he was asphyxiated by volcanic gases while trying to rescue civilians fleeing the eruption of Vesuvius.[60]

In addition to his official duties Pliny pleaded cases in Roman law courts and was a prolific writer on various subjects. He published a tactical work on cavalry manoeuvres drawn from his experiences in Germany, a biography of his patron Pomponius Secundus, and a 20 volume history of Rome's German wars.[61] However, Pliny's only surviving work is the *Natural History* which he compiled during the period when he was serving as a procurator and an advisor to the Emperor.[62]

The *Natural History* is an enormous and unwieldy collection of eclectic knowledge. In 37 dense volumes it deals with numerous aspects of the natural world and man's relationship to nature, divided into sections considering topics like geography, plants, animals, medicines and metals.[63] In discussing these subjects Pliny assembled classical accounts from a wide range of respected Greek and Roman authorities. Consequently, many sections of his study read as a compendium of traditional accounts rather than an enquiry into contemporary conditions.

The material that forms the *Natural History* is only loosely assembled into topics and reading the book the modern scholar encounters, 'detail juxtaposed with detail, parataxis, particularity, multiplicity, and self contradiction.'[64] Pliny's discussions are also full of embellishments, anecdotes and colourful descriptions. He offers numerous accounts of wonders, curiosities, monstrosities and other *mirabilia*, often with little critical or authoritative comment.[65] When Pliny does offer his personal viewpoint it is often in the form of a moralising judgement or an amusing comment.[66] When Pliny was writing the *Natural History*, Roman government was receiving important contemporary detail about the distant East from imperial agents, overseas merchants and distant ambassadors.[67] Yet Pliny generally withholds this information because it does not suit his chosen genre which emphasized the need to make sense of traditional classical accounts.

Though modern scholars find the *Natural History* challenging, there is much to recommend the work. Pliny spent a lifetime in the service of the Roman Empire, upholding its authority in the provinces and managing its power near the centre of imperial government.[68] He clearly intended that his study should be of value to the Roman ruling class and the work is dedicated to Vespasian's son Titus, who was a renowned military commander and heir to the Empire.[69] Pliny's attitudes to established 'knowledge' therefore make the *Natural History* an exceptionally important document for understanding the interests of Roman society and the cultural attitudes of its governing elite.[70] The *Natural History* and its controversies will consequently perform a significant role in all future studies of Eastern trade.

THE GEOGRAPHY BY CLAUDIUS PTOLEMY

About AD 139, an Alexandrian Greek named Claudius Ptolemy completed a geographical study of the world. He concentrated on how mathematical information, including distances and coordinates, could be used to create accurate maps.[71] This work is the only study of world cartography that has survived from classical antiquity and it reveals how greatly commerce had increased Roman knowledge of the distant East.

Claudius Ptolemy was living in a city were Indian merchant princes were regularly seen at public gatherings, but he preferred to deal with academic texts, rather than investigate the realities of the ancient world through direct inquiry. Ptolemy received his data from scientific treaties rather than personal experience and most of his information is taken from a study compiled by a near-contemporary named Marinos of Tyre. Marinos managed to acquire detailed merchant reports similar to the *Periplus of the Erythraean Sea*, but describing the next generation of trade contacts. This included a work written by an entrepreneur named Alexandros, who described even more advanced Roman trade voyages into the distant East.[72] Using this information, Ptolemy was able to list dozens of new commercial settlements that had risen to prominence in Roman trade dealings with India and the lands beyond. Ptolemy occasionally reveals his sources when he mentions articles of trade in his catalogues of Eastern coordinates.

Ptolemy was not concerned with descriptive reports of peoples and regional histories. Consequently, his *Geography* is mostly a vast compendium of data formed into long lists of site names and coordinates. Yet the work also contains a series of essays dealing with aspects of scientific cartography and in these studies Ptolemy outlines how his figures for latitudes and longitudes could be used to create geographical 'impressions' of various world regions.

There are clear problems with Ptolemy's data and the approach he used to create maps of the distant East. Ptolemy designates Eastern trade centres as 'emporiums', 'villages', 'cities' or even 'metropolises', but he never adequately explains this terminology. Significantly, Ptolemy also restructured some of his data to make it fit flawed theories regarding the shape of the Asian landmass. For instance, Alexandros and the author of the *Periplus* knew that India formed a triangular shape and that its coast ran from north to south, yet Ptolemy remained convinced by the traditions of Greek geography and decided to ignore this peninsula shape. He therefore restructured his coordinates to flatten the southern Asian coast.

Despite these failings, the maps that can be constructed from Ptolemy's data are still impressive. His work suggests that by this era, Roman merchants were reaching Malaysia and classical authorities were aware that the distant East occupied far more than two-thirds of the known earth. Ptolemy's account also reveals that the Romans had knowledge of Chinese territories in the most distant regions of the orient.

REMAINS FROM ROMAN EGYPT

In ancient times, the two most important Roman ports for Eastern trade were the Egyptian towns of Berenice and Myos Hormos which lay on the upper coast of the Red Sea. The ruined remains of these towns are still visible on the desert landscape and the sites have recently been excavated by archaeologists who have unearthed impressive new evidence that reveals the conduct of their Eastern trade business.

A collection of ancient texts scratched on pottery fragments have been discovered at Berenice. These *ostraca* have been identified as public records that were removed from a nearby customs building sometime before AD 70 and dumped in the dry sandy soil of an ancient rubbish pit.[73] The records are pottery tokens that served as official permits, probably issued at the Nile city of Coptos after export duties had been paid on cargo sent across the Egyptian desert to the Red Sea ports. The passes served as tax receipts shown to authorities at Berenice to confirm that the goods being loaded onboard ship had been charged the proper dues at Coptos.[74] These remarkable records provide vital detail about ancient loading operations at the port and are incredibly important to future discussion of Eastern commerce.

The texts recorded in the Berenice *ostraca* follow a standard formula and are set out as a correspondence between state officials. In a typical example a customs officer named Rhobaos writes:

> Rhobaos to those in charge of the customs gate, greetings. Let Psenosiris son of Leon pass with eight *italika* of wine for loading.[75]

The surviving texts concentrate on wine cargoes and other assorted goods, but do not document some of the main Roman exports recorded in the *Periplus*. This was probably because certain custom officials were charged with monitoring particular cargoes. The surviving *ostraca* therefore represent only one department at the port and there were probably several other customs officers at Berenice in charge of other goods such as bullion and coin, fabrics, base metals and glassware.[76] Cargoes would have been broken down into smaller consignments for transport to and from trade vessels. Consequently, the Berenice *ostraca* cannot be used to reveal the possible size of Roman ships or their cargo capacities.[77]

A collection of *ostraca* called the *Nicanor Archive*, provides further valuable information about the caravan transport operations that supplied the Red Sea ports during the Roman era. The *Nicanor Archive* was found at Coptos and consists of transport receipts from a small family-run company that was active from AD 6 to AD 62.[78] This company held important contracts to deliver monthly food supplies to Roman garrisons stationed in the desert. The head of this business was a Greco-Egyptian called Nicanor who owned a small caravan that probably numbered at least thirty-six camels.[79]

It seems that Roman businessmen hired Nicanor to transport their cargoes across the desert, and when these goods arrived safely, their agents at the ports would issue an *ostraca* receipt to acknowledge delivery. Nicanor, or the member of his extended family who was making the delivery, would then return to Coptos with the receipt. This receipt could then be used to verify that the delivery had been made exactly as agreed. There are 88 *ostracon* in the *Nicanor Archive* stating the member of Nicanor's family who transported the goods, the quantity and type of freight conveyed, the delivery destination, the name of the individual who received the consignment, and the date when these dealings were concluded.[80] The *Nicanor Archive* therefore provides valuable information about the identities and activities of Roman businessmen who were operating at the Red Sea ports.

A large stone inscription, referred to as the *Coptos Tariff*, also provides crucial information about the travellers who were crossing Egypt's Eastern Desert in the Roman era. The text, which dates to around AD 90, once stood in some prominent public location at Coptos and it records tolls to be paid by travellers leaving the city for the Red Sea ports. People were taxed according to their occupations and the inscription also records tolls to be paid on pack animals and other unusual transports such as funeral possessions.[81] As this desert crossing was the main route to the Red Sea ports, this text indicates the many occupations involved in Roman trade voyages to the distant East.

Other remarkable evidence for this traffic comes from the desert itself, where travellers occasionally rested along the caravan routes at small rock shelters that offered temporary refuge from the glaring sun or sand-gritted winds. At many of these stopping points travellers carved their names into the rockface, thus leaving a permanent record of their journeys across the desert and providing historians with fascinating information about the people who journeyed to Red Sea ports, then travelled onwards to destinations such as India.[82]

Egyptian papyri documents recovered in the modern era are a further important source of information on Eastern trade, especially when they record business arrangements. One of the most intriguing documents available to this study is a fragmentary loan contract called *P. Vindob. G 40822*, also known as the *Muziris Papyrus* because it records details about a cargo consignment brought back from Muziris onboard a Roman merchant ship called the Hermapollon.[83] The text lists arrangements for the transfer of this Indian cargo across the Eastern Desert and north along the Nile to warehouses in Alexandria. The text is significant because it provides important details about the values of Eastern cargoes involved in this extensive commerce.

New archaeological discoveries in Egypt are continually adding evidence to the study of Eastern trade. In the future, this information will offer greater insights into the organization and scale of Rome's overseas trade business. The time will come when all detailed studies of the Roman Empire and its ancient economy will be required to take this important evidence into account.

CARAVAN INSCRIPTIONS FROM PALMYRA

The vast ruins of ancient Palmyra, including the remains of great temples and large administrative buildings, are still visible in the Syrian Desert. In the rubble of the ancient stonework, hundreds of fragmentary classical columns mark where broad avenues once led through the centre of the city.[84] In ancient times, Palmyrene dignitaries and merchants set up statues, or other sculptured offerings, to commemorate individuals who had performed some noteworthy service to the city or its inhabitants. These monuments were placed amongst the stone architecture of the city and were set in prominent locations along public thoroughfares and market squares. Large numbers of these statues were destroyed or defaced in later centuries in acts of iconoclasm, but the accompanying inscriptions have survived.[85]

Many of the Palmyrene inscriptions commemorate individuals who assisted caravans from the city on their commercial ventures east into Mesopotamia. Consequently, they offer important information about the organization of caravan ventures, the destinations of these trade missions, the titles of individuals who enabled or assisted the expeditions, and even incidents such as banditry that had affected the merchants.[86] The commemorative inscriptions from Palmyra are written in a form of Aramaic unique to the city, but these dedications are often duplicated in Greek. The inscriptions that document caravan ventures date from AD 19 to the 260s AD and there is a marked concentration of texts from the second century.[87] The dedications indicate the frequency of trade, but they might also reflect the popularity of certain epigraphic fashions in the city.

Carved reliefs have been found in the ruins of ancient Palmyra and they provide important visual evidence for the appearance of the city's inhabitants. These sculptures show dignitaries and merchants, dromedary camels and even the sea-going ships that Palmyrenes operated in the Persian Gulf. Many of these carvings are from funerary monuments and the ruins of tower-like tomb structures which exist on the outskirts of the ancient city. A tax-law inscription has also been recovered from Palmyra and this important text, dating to AD 137, reveals how tariffs were imposed on goods entering the urban markets.[88] This evidence further reveals how distance commerce can be considered within the wider context of regional production and localized trade.

ROMAN COIN EVIDENCE FROM INDIA

As part of their trade dealings with the distant East, Roman merchants exported vast amounts of gold and silver coinage to ancient India. In recent times sizable quantities of Roman coins have been found in India and these hoards can be used to indicate the development of Eastern trade and gauge its possible impact on imperial finances.

There have been close to 80 reported Roman coin finds documented in India. Most of these discoveries were made in the southern regions of the subcontinent and documented cases have ranged from single finds to large hoards containing hundreds of coins. Almost all of the Roman finds consist of high value gold or silver coins and it is rare to find hoards where these precious metals are mixed together.[89]

Many of the documented Roman hoards were discovered during a period in the nineteenth and twentieth centuries when India was part of the British Empire. During this era, interested antiquarians often worked with English administrators to try to recover recently unearthed Roman hoards. In most cases they could only seize a small fraction of the coins, but in many instances they were able to gather important information about the finds, including helpful detail about the scale and condition of the discoveries. Scholars estimate that from the Roman hoards recovered, around 5,400 denarii and 800 aurei still exist in various modern collections.[90] However, a far larger number of coins have disappeared from the records and are not available for study.

The Roman coin hoard evidence from India presents a uniquely complex numismatic puzzle for modern researchers and it is therefore a challenging subject for non-specialists to comprehend. Despite these difficulties, coin evidence is vitally important to any modern study that seeks to understand the progress and significance of Rome's Eastern trade.

BUDDHIST INSCRIPTIONS FROM ANCIENT INDIA

The Roman merchants who visited India found large populous kingdoms, with long-established traditions of craftsmanship and urban culture.[91] Inscriptions from ancient India commemorate gifts to Buddhist monasteries by craftspeople and traders who were associated with various commercial guilds. These texts offer important information about the economy of ancient India and they also record the involvement of Roman subjects in Eastern trade networks.

Some of the most interesting ancient inscriptions from India come from the hilly terrain of the western Deccan. In this region Buddhist monasteries thrived in the mountain passes used by merchants on inland journeys to the great cities of central India. The Buddhist communities received the patronage of visiting merchants and took advantage of the local terrain to begin carving their rock face surroundings into elaborate facades. Natural cave systems were also excavated to create complex religious facilities with decorative pillars and meditation cells.[92] These rock-cut structures were modelled on the freestanding wooden buildings that existed at Buddhist monasteries across ancient India. The Deccan sites therefore offer a unique glimpse into the distant past and the inscriptions they preserve provide a remarkable record of ancient practices.

The inscriptions found at the Deccan sites record devotional acts of patronage and are written in a popular form of Sanskrit known as *Prakrit*. A small number of these texts mention funds given to the monasteries by new converts to Buddhism who seem to have been merchants from the Roman Empire.[93] This evidence is fascinating and will certainly become significant in future enquiries into distant Roman trade.

THE ANCIENT TAMIL LITERATURE

Ancient Tamil literature contains epic narrative poems dating from the first centuries AD. These epics describe a time when Roman subjects were visiting the Tamil lands on distant trade ventures and they provide unique evidence about the activities of Romans in ancient India.[94] This literature offers an important insight into the operation of early Tamil society and cannot be omitted from any serious study of the ancient world.

The Tamils viewed the Romans as exotic foreigners and referred to them as *Yavanas*. The name was ultimately derived from the ancient term *Ionian*, which originally denoted the Greeks of coastal Asia Minor, whom the Persians called the *Yauna*.[95] By the time the name reached India it had become *Yavana* and was applied to anyone who was Greek, or had a classical identity that appeared outwardly Hellenic. Consequently, when the Tamils first encountered Roman merchants from the Empire, who spoke mainly Greek, they labelled them *Yavana*.

Most of the Tamil references to *Yavanas* appear in a collection of narrative poetry known as *Sangam* literature which deals with heroic themes such as love and war.[96] Tamil literature was originally bardic poetry so these idylls were passed down through the oral tradition until late antiquity when they were committed to writing. By the seventh century AD they were collected into the large anthologies that have survived into the modern era.[97]

The Tamil verses were composed to glorify patrons and so were never intended to be a historical record. As a consequence, the description of Tamil society contained is often incidental to the wider narrative. Although the settings and events are recounted in a highly descriptive manner, some information is conveyed in stock phrases and stereotyped expressions. The Tamil accounts contain no mention or discussion of Rome as a political state. Instead the *Yavanas* appear as background characters, mentioned in a few descriptive passages. Yet the information provided by these accounts is remarkable and the Romans are described as craftsmen, mercenaries and visiting merchants arriving on extraordinary ships.

ARCHAEOLOGY BEYOND THE EMPIRE

There have been significant new archaeological discoveries in the distant East that will transform the current understanding of Roman commerce. Important ancient sites have recently been rediscovered in India and now await full investigation. Three Roman shipwrecks have also been identified on the seabed below the ancient sea lanes that crossed the Indian Ocean.

The most important of these recent discoveries could be the large Roman shipwreck recently found off the Red Sea coast of Quseir in Egypt. This trade vessel sank near the ruins of the ancient Roman harbour at Myos Hormos, probably during the Augustan era. The discovery of Campanian wine amphorae on the seabed indicates that the freighter was carrying Italian cargo on an outbound expedition when it sank in unknown circumstances.[98] Another Roman wreck has been found further down the African side of the Red Sea near the Shab Rumi Reef on the coast of Sudan. Little is known about this vessel, but it was carrying a cargo of Coan-style wine amphorae, suggesting another outbound expedition that somehow ended in tragedy.[99] Both wrecks will reveal substantial information about the quantities and types of durable cargoes selected for Roman export to the distant East.

A further Roman shipwreck has been investigated by divers off the coast of Bet Dwarka in northwest India. The wreck belongs to a large freighter and sizeable sections of the hull have been preserved deep in the seabed sediment, where the vessel sank some 5,000 kilometres from Roman territory. Investigations have been limited, but the cargo seems to have included amphorae containers as well as circular lead ingots intended for the Indian market.[100] This wreck will provide significant information about the modifications made to the Roman freighters that sailed this distant ocean. It could also offer valuable new details about the crew and equipment carried onboard Roman ships on these dangerous voyages.

The Tamil trade port of Muziris held an important position in Roman trade with India and recently a team of archaeologists have identified a site that they believe could be the ancient city. This discovery was made by a geoarchaeologist named K. P. Shajan, using satellite imagery to trace the course of the ancient Periyar River. He then followed this forgotten route on foot, trekking through backwaters and undergrowth, until he found the remains of a vast, long-abandoned settlement that matched literary accounts of ancient Muziris. A team of international researchers, including a classical archaeologist named Roberta Tomber, are currently investigating this ancient site. They have already uncovered significant Roman finds, including amphorae fragments from Mediterranean wine shipments.[101]

The early Tamil literature describes how Roman merchants built large residences at the busy city port of Puhar, on the southeast coast of India. Yet these sources also describe how the ancient city was submerged beneath the sea in a powerful tidal flood.[102] Modern divers operating off the Coromandel Coast have found the sunken ruins of ancient Puhar on the seabed and these discoveries confirm that some catastrophic event in the distant past had overwhelmed the city.[103] This unique site will provide great challenges to future marine archaeologists but the findings may offer further remarkable insights into ancient world trade connections.

THE SOGDIAN LETTERS

During the first few centuries AD, a people from Inner Asia called the Sogdians developed a trade presence in the Tarim kingdoms of Central Asia and established various merchant communities in ancient China. Sogdian merchants organized caravans to bring Chinese goods to their homeland city of Samarkand and arranged trade ventures to send products from Inner Asia, east, to markets in China. In 1907, the famous British explorer Aurel Stein discovered a small collection of Sogdian letters in the remains of a ruined watchtower that had once stood on the ancient Chinese frontier near Dunhuang.[104]

The five Sogdian letters were written in a complex form of ancient Iranian script that remains difficult to translate. Some of the letters are personal correspondence and others are mainly concerned with business matters. The letters are addressed either to community leaders in Samarkand or Sogdians residing in the Tarim kingdoms on the caravan routes to their homeland. The Sogdian letters mention conditions in China after a series of devastating invasions by horsemen raiders from the Asian Steppes. The raiders were Xiongnu and these details would date the documents to about AD 313.[105] Something happened to the Sogdian merchant entrusted with the responsibility of delivering the letters. He either hid them in the tower or perhaps a soldier on the Chinese frontier decided to confiscate the documents, fearing they contained information that might be strategically valuable to their Xiongnu enemies.

The *Sogdian Letters* offer significant insights into the activities and concerns of ancient caravan merchants on the Silk Roads of Inner Asia. They indicate how Chinese goods would have reached Roman territories and this evidence needs to be included in any comprehensive study of Eastern commerce.

RECORDS FROM ANCIENT CHINA

In the late first century AD, the Han Empire launched a major series of military campaigns to regain control over the Tarim kingdoms of Central Asia. Generals were sent west to complete the task and gather important information about countries in the distant West. These reports were sent back to the court of the Chinese Emperor to be entered into the official records. Testimonies from visiting ambassadors were also recorded. These sources informed the Chinese government that a new power had emerged in the distant West that was equal in size and importance to the Han Empire. Han agents in Central Asia dubbed this place *Da Qin*, meaning 'Great China', and details from their accounts indicate that this 'other China' must have been the Roman Empire.[106]

Court records from ancient China have not survived in their original form, but they are accurately preserved in later texts.[107] In late antiquity Chinese scholars made extensive use of the Han records to compile detailed histories about their past. The best evidence for *Da Qin* therefore comes from a fifth century work called the *Hou Hanshu*, also known as *The Later Han Histories*. This work contains a chapter called the 'Western Regions' which was compiled from court records and the reports of leading generals who had campaigned in Central Asia. These correlated accounts were submitted to the Han Emporer about AD 125.

Records also exist from the Chinese States which succeeded the Han Dynasty in AD 220. A particularly important work from this era is the *Weilue*, or *Brief Account of the Wei Dynasty*, written by a contemporary Chinese scholar named Yu Huan. A chapter in the *Weilue* called 'Peoples of the West' has survived because it was faithfully quoted in later Chinese accounts. This *Weilue* chapter is significant because it updated earlier information about the Roman Empire and discussed overland routes leading from China to the distant West. References to Mesopotamia in the work suggest that it was based on reports collected between AD 116 and AD 165.[108]

The Chinese records provide uniquely important information about the ancient conditions and politics of Central Asia. They also reveal the types of Roman goods reaching the Far East through overland trade routes and distant voyages across the Indian Ocean. Some of the Chinese accounts mention the arrival of strange visitors in China who were possibly subjects of the Roman Empire.

The ancient Chinese records are credible and compelling. It is fascinating to read how another politically advanced ancient civilization viewed the Roman Empire. Given their significance, Chinese accounts must be examined in any serious discussions of Roman trade and they will certainly have a significant place in future considerations of the ancient world economy.

CONCLUSIONS

Any historian investigating Eastern trade has to take account of a wide range of diverse source evidence from very different ancient civilizations. There are also archaeological remains to consider, including coin evidence from Indian hoards, and this detail provides further interpretive challenges to this study. This makes any examination of Eastern commerce an extremely complex and demanding task.

With the classical sources, it is important to recognize how genre and social attitudes affected how ancient information was recorded and presented. Evidence of Roman trade detailed in the written accounts of other ancient cultures should also be considered with appropriate caution. Doubts and concerns regarding the surviving sources can be discussed and expressed in endless debates, but in many cases the most credible way to determine the legitimacy of an ancient source is to compare its testimony with the evidence provided by other texts or material remains.

In my view, a comprehensive exploration of Eastern trade can only be made within an historical study that involves ancient evidence from all the available sources. A greater understanding of how Eastern trade operated, based on a wider context of evidence, will also help historians to more informatively appraise the validity of any sources containing details that may at first appear 'suspect'. All of the above sources combine to give the scholar a complex and fascinating glimpse of ancient multi-cultural co-operation.

2

Roman Egypt and the Sea Routes to India

In the surviving ancient records, the sea voyage from Egypt to India is the best-attested trade route between the Roman Empire and the distant East. Every year thousands of Roman merchants sailed the Red Sea to visit important markets in Africa and Arabia. These trade sailings often led them onwards across the ocean to India and the Bay of Bengal. This commerce was an important phenomenon and as the Roman merchant fleet that reached India numbered more than a hundred vessels, thousands of tons of Eastern cargo was imported into Alexandria every year. The commercial opportunities presented by this trade possibly determined the economic fortunes of the Roman Empire.

Eastern trade has a long history stretching far back into the distant past. From the time of the Pharaohs, the Egyptians had contacts with eastern territories on the outer fringe of the Red Sea. By the third millennium BC, Arabian aromatics had acquired a special significance in Egyptian religious ceremonies. Archaeological remains and hieroglyphic texts from the Old Kingdom era reveal that incenses were burned on Egyptian temple altars and used in important funerary customs, including mummification. The later Pharaohs established harbours on the Red Sea coast and Queen Hatshepsut, who ruled from 1473 to 1458 BC, sent a seaborne expedition to a distant land called 'Punt', somewhere beyond the outer fringes of the Red Sea to bring back these precious substances. Her funerary temple near the Valley of the Kings has wall paintings and reliefs showing this distant expedition taking Egyptian personnel as far as northern Somalia in the search for these exotic goods.[1]

In the sixth century BC, Egypt was conquered by the Persian king Cambyses and under Persian rule the region became part of a diverse empire that stretched from the eastern Mediterranean to the frontiers of India. Representatives from Greek communities in Anatolia would have encountered other subject peoples including Indians from the distant East at the Persian court in Babylon. When the Persian King, Darius, who ruled from 522 to 486 BC, tried to establish new routes of communication across his empire, he reconstructed a canal linking the Nile to the Red Sea. Darius then sent ships to explore the sea-routes that led around Arabia into the Persian Gulf. He commemorated his achievements in Egypt with inscriptions carved into granite *stelae*.[2] Darius also sent a Greek sailor named Scylax to the Indus territories on a mission to discover and explore a sea-route from India to Egypt. This voyage into the virtual unknown took nearly 30 months to complete and as a result Darius bombastically claimed to have 'opened' the Indus territories to Persian shipping.[3] These extraordinary events demonstrated the possibilities of maritime contacts between far-off lands, but trade continued to be localized and distant commerce remained a remote prospect.

In the late fourth century BC, the Macedonian King, Alexander the Great, conquered the vast Persian Empire and brought Greek rule as far as Bactria in Inner Asia. On reaching India in 326 BC, Alexander sent a Greek fleet under the command of an admiral named Nearchus, on an exploratory voyage from the Indus coast back to the Persian Gulf. Nearchus re-explored the route that Scylax had followed nearly two centuries earlier.[4] After Alexander's death his empire was divided between his leading generals and each founded a new ruling dynasty in the territories that were formally the vast Persian Empire. The Ptolemies ruled in Egypt, while the lands of Persia and the Near East came under the control of the rival Seleucids. The Seleucids soon established new arrangements with Indian kings who supplied them with war elephants to use as an intimidating, if unpredictable, force in their western conflicts.[5]

The physical and psychological impact of battle elephants was considerable. With their loud trumpeting and unusual odour they struck fear into the horses of enemy cavalry. The Ptolemies could not allow the Seleucids to maintain this advantage in their Near Eastern wars and by the third century BC they were sending out military expeditions to capture African forest elephants in the territories to the south of Egypt. To facilitate these hunting operations the Ptolemies created and restored ports on the Red Sea shore and built ships to further explore the Ethiopian coast. Soon elephant hunting-stations were established on the eastern coast of Africa with Ptolemaic guards dispatched to protect the large transport ships called *elephantegoi* which brought the captured animals back to Egypt.[6]

The African elephants were off-loaded at a Red Sea port called Berenice. They were herded into giant corrals surrounded by deep v-shaped ditches that are still traceable on the outskirts of the ancient port. From Berenice it was a journey of nearly two weeks across the Eastern Desert to reach river ports on the Nile Valley. At various stopping places on these routes the animal handlers and their guards left evidence of their journeys by scratching graffiti images of their elephants on the natural rock shelters.[7] At the Nile ports the elephants were transferred on to large river barges and taken downstream to Alexandria in preparation for battle training.

These operations unintentionally created a vital transport infrastructure that would protect and facilitate future distance commerce. Also, as a by-product of their elephant-hunting expeditions, the Ptolemaic government began receiving vast amounts of ivory which it sold for profit in the eastern Mediterranean. An inscription from the Aegean mercantile island of Delos indicates that by the mid-third century BC this ivory so saturated Mediterranean markets that it caused a significant fall in prices.[8]

In this era, Greek merchants began to operate at the Red Sea ports, trading with communities in coastal Ethiopia and making the first tentative commercial voyages to southwest Arabia. As Red Sea trade became better established, other Mediterranean peoples became involved in these distant commercial voyages. A remarkable second-century papyrus records a Greek-Egyptian trading venture to Africa involving investors from Veii in central Italy and Marseilles in southern France.[9] Despite advances, conditions were still not ideal for the full development of this commerce. Many of the goods brought back from these early trade ventures were appropriated by the Ptolemaic government and officials in Egypt forced merchants to sell their cargo to the state at artificially low prices.[10]

About this time, classical authorities became aware that the island of Socotra, near the Horn of Africa, had become a major centre for Indian and Arabian commerce.[11] Agatharchides reports:

> In these islands it is possible to see merchant vessels at anchor. Most come from the place where Alexander established an anchorage on the Indus River.[12]

This market centre was probably at the furthest reaches of the Ptolemaic trade routes, but the development of this commerce was soon to permit direct contact between Egypt and India.

THE SEA ROUTE TO INDIA

Strabo describes how the Ptolemaic government first received accurate information about a maritime trade route to India.[13] In 118 BC a Ptolemaic navy patrol scouting the Gulf of Aden discovered the remains of a strange ship and rescued a starving Indian sailor from its wreckage. They took the lone survivor to the court of Ptolemy VIII Euergetes II to recover from his ordeal. The man quickly learned Greek and informed the Ptolemaic court that his vessel had been blown off course on a trade sailing from India. He offered to act as guide for any Greek sailors willing to return with him. Euergetes was enthusiastic about this prospect and planned a mission to establish direct contacts with India. A Greek explorer named Eudoxus of Cyzicus was appointed as chief officer and under the direction of the Indian as pilot, he sailed to northwest India.[14]

This first contact was probably considered more of a diplomatic exchange than a commercial mission and Eudoxus was furious when Ptolemaic officials confiscated all the valuable goods he had brought back from India. King Euergetes claimed that the mission was a royal enterprise and therefore the Eastern cargo was a 'gift'. Within a few years Euergetes had died and Eudoxus was sent by his successor Cleopatra III on a second voyage to India, this time on a larger ship. On his return, Eudoxus tried to conceal some perfumes and precious stones, but Cleopatra discovered his theft and once again he was deprived of his valuable Eastern cargo. Eudoxus now recognized the profits he could make by supplying Mediterranean markets with Indian goods. He also realized how the Ptolemaic regime was hindering the development of this trade by their confiscations and compulsory purchases. Eudoxus became obsessed with the idea that it was possible to avoid Egypt and reach India by sailing directly from Spain around the coasts of Africa. On his second attempt to discover this route, he set out along the unexplored coasts of western Africa and was never heard of again.[15]

Eudoxus had demonstrated that there was a viable sea route from Egypt to India, but it seems that only a few Greek ships dared to travel this far into the distant East during the final decades of the Ptolemaic era. Most Greek merchants sailed only as far as the city port of Aden on the coast of southwest Arabia where they could acquire Indian goods from visiting Eastern traders. The *Periplus* reports:

> In earlier times Aden was once a full-fledged city. It was called "Prosperous" because vessels from India did not go to Egypt and ships from Egypt came only this far. Ships did not dare to sail to the places beyond Aden and for this reason the city used to receive cargoes from both [Egypt and India].[16]

Strabo also confirms that Ptolemaic trade activity was largely confined within the Gulf of Aden, writing:

> In these earlier times, not even 20 vessels would dare to sail into the Gulf of Aden far enough to glance outside these straits.[17]

Voyages beyond Aden carried the threat of storm and shipwreck far away from friendly shores, and with the endemic menace of piracy in these distant waters, merchants were risking their lives as well as their valuable cargoes. By the late Ptolemaic era, a few enterprising Greek merchants were evidently reaching India, but these contacts were still minimal, as Strabo writes:

> Under the Ptolemaic kings only a few vessels would sail to India and carry back Indian merchandise.[18]

Evidence of these distant ventures comes from the Pan Temple at El-Kanais in Egypt's Eastern Desert. Here a man named Apollon recorded his incense offering of 'Indian myrrh' for the safe return of his father.[19] Perhaps Apollon was the son of an entrepreneur engaged in one of these dangerous early trade ventures to Arabia, or beyond.

THE END OF THE PTOLEMAIC KINGDOM

In 31 BC, at the decisive sea battle of Actium, the Roman general Octavian defeated the joint forces of his rival Mark Antony and the Ptolemaic Queen Cleopatra VII. In a last desperate effort to evade capture, the doomed Cleopatra arranged for some of her surviving Mediterranean galleys to be dragged across the Suez isthmus and lowered into the Red Sea. From there she planned to escape to the distant East and so brought a large force of royal attendants and a great sum of wealth.

Perhaps Cleopatra planned to settle in northwest India, out of reach of her Roman enemies. The scheme was thwarted when Nabatean Arabs, incited by the Romans, and with old scores to settle, attacked and burned her gathering fleet. Thus ended Cleopatra's last hope of escape and removed the prospect of an exiled Ptolemaic court being established in the distant East.[20] Despite her failure and impending capture by the Romans, Cleopatra still planned to send her young son Caesarion to India with several trusted advisers and a large amount of wealth. Heir to the Ptolemaic regime, he was also the natural son of Julius Caesar and an ongoing threat to Octavian who was only Caesar's son by adoption.[21]

As her urgent schemes were conducted with secrecy, later authorities were uncertain how far Cleopatra's plans had progressed. Caesarion possibly reached

Berenice, and waited for the trade winds that would take him east to the safety of an Indian court. The youth never arrived as he was deceived and killed by Roman sympathizers.[22] Thus ended the Ptolemaic dynasty and with Egypt subdued, the Romans now claimed unopposed dominion over the entire Mediterranean.

THE ROMAN EXPANSION

With the defeat of Cleopatra and the capture of Alexandria, Egypt finally became a full Roman province. Octavian now established himself as the first Emperor of Rome and adopted the name 'Augustus'. From the onset of his rule Augustus had important plans for Egypt. Using the Roman army as a massive labour force, the new regime rapidly repaired irrigation canals and transport infrastructures, thus restoring the essential agricultural economy that the Ptolemies had allowed to fall into serious disrepair.[23] By building on the administration of the former Ptolemies, the Romans were able to create a substantial bureaucratic system in Egypt that dealt with the logistics of grain production and its subsequent transportation. The results were remarkable and Josephus suggests that by the mid first century AD, the province was supplying the city of Rome with almost a third of its annual grain needs.[24]

The Romans rapidly moved in to exploit the valuable natural resources available in Egypt's Eastern Desert, including its ancient gold and emerald mines. The State-organized building projects in Rome required vast quantities of suitable stone so the new regime increased activity at Mons Porphyrites and Mons Claudianus, where convicts quarried decorative porphyry and granite. As a result of these projects the Roman army had to improve travel conditions along the desert roads that connected sites in the Eastern Desert with the Nile Valley. This was crucial because the Nile formed the main conduit for communication and travel throughout ancient Egypt.[25]

In ancient times, the roads that crossed the Eastern Desert were little more than track-ways cleared of rubble and intermittently marked by cairns to guide caravans between desert stations.[26] In the Ptolemaic era, travellers had made the journey mostly by night, trudging alongside camels that carried their water provisions. During the excessive heat of day, travellers who had not reached a desert station would try to find some suitable rest at any available natural rock shelters.[27] The merchants who trekked these routes had reason to be fearful as roving bandits would lie in wait to ambush them and take their valuable goods.

The new Roman regime was not prepared to accept any threat that disrupted overland communications. The Roman army upgraded the desert routes to the Red Sea ports by installing additional watering stations to facilitate travel. They also built military outposts to protect desert traffic from bandits and hostile nomads.[28] These new forts that guarded the caravan routes were called *phrouroi* and their garrisons sent out military patrols to protect and monitor passing traffic. The improved caravan stations were called *hydreumata* and were large fortified complexes equipped with wells, water cisterns and other vital amenities to accommodate passing travellers.[29] These early improvements were concentrated on the desert route that led from the Nile city of Coptos to the closest Red Sea port of Myos Hormos. Strabo reports:

> In previous times the camel merchants travelled by night, using the stars as their guide, just as sailors do. They also carried water with them when they travelled. But now the Romans have built *hydreumata* by digging to great depths and they have constructed cisterns for rainwater which is normally scarce.[30]

Archaeologists have surveyed these desert routes and examined the ruins of the ancient stations. Their investigations have revealed that the Roman military also constructed dozens of solid platform watchtowers on the hills flanking the desert roads to the Red Sea ports. These towers were built within sight of one another to oversee caravan traffic crossing the desert and their sentries would have signalled nearby *hydreumata* when an approaching caravan was sighted, or when bandit marauders were seen in the vicinity.[31] These new protective measures greatly improved the confidence of the merchants who travelled the desert routes to and from the Red Sea ports.

Soon after Egypt was secured, Augustus ordered preparations for the Roman invasion of Arabia which began in AD 26. The governor of Egypt, Aelius Gallus, constructed a fleet of 80 war galleys and 130 transport vessels near the northern Red Sea port of Clysma.[32] It is not recorded what happened to these transport ships after the failed invasion, but this ambitious scheme must have established major shipbuilding facilities and supply lines on the Red Sea coast.

Strabo, who was living in Egypt during this era, confirms the impact these projects had on Eastern commerce. Writing of events in 26 BC he recalls:

> When Gallus was the prefect of Egypt, I accompanied him along the Nile River as far as Syene and the frontiers of Ethiopia. There I learned that as many as 120 vessels were sailing from Myos Hormos to India.[33]

This suggests that, within only a few years of Roman rule, over a hundred extra merchant vessels were annually reaching India. In a further passage, Strabo indicates an accompanying increase in Greek trade contacts with east Africa.[34] He adds:

> At this present time large fleets are sent as far as India and the extremities of Africa from which the most valuable cargoes are brought to Egypt.[35]

This trade increase was partly as a consequence of new economic conditions in the Mediterranean markets.[36] Augustus captured vast quantities of bullion treasure from Ptolemaic Egypt and this wealth was quickly released into the Mediterranean economy where it enriched Roman society and caused rapid price inflation.[37] This made it easier for merchants to borrow money for commercial enterprises.[38] There was a corresponding 'revolution' in Roman social customs as privileged subjects of the Empire scrambled to spend their increasing wealth on acquiring exotic Eastern luxuries.

In its final decades the Ptolemaic kingdom had been little more than a regional power with a failing infrastructure, but under Roman authority, Egypt was brought into an Empire that controlled virtually all of the Mediterranean territories and ruled over a population approaching 50 million people.[39] Under the new *pax augusta*, merchant communities were no longer beset by damaging regional conflicts that destroyed livelihoods and disrupted trade. The Roman regime also abolished Ptolemaic measures controlling the sale of Eastern imports, so interested merchants were free to sell their imported goods to any market of the Roman world that could afford the high commercial prices.[40]

These market conditions were unprecedented and occurred at a time when the Romans had constructed Red Sea shipyards capable of building and refitting hundreds of military vessels, including transport ships. Private contractors now found a commercial use for these facilities and the profits that poured into the Eastern trade business allowed merchants to rapidly outfit and construct large numbers of new freighters. Greco-Roman merchants were now in a position to undertake better financed and more adventurous trade voyages far into the distant East.[41]

Under Roman authority Egypt's trade with the distant East increased, not only in scale and intensity, but also in geographical scope.[42] By the end of the Augustan era, a few adventurous Roman merchants were sailing as far as the Ganges to reach distant territories that Greek authorities had formerly believed to be at the very edge of the known world. Strabo writes:

> As for the merchants who now sail from Egypt up the Nile and along the Arabian coasts as far as India, only a small number have ever sailed as far as the Ganges.[43]

The Roman Empire therefore achieved something that no other ancient regime could manage. By abolishing anachronistic legislation, providing increased security, and unintentionally boosting commercial markets, they had brought the Greek Mediterranean into full commercial contact with India. From now on, people and resources could move in great numbers between these distant economies in a commerce that connected at least half the population of the ancient world.

ROMAN PORTS AND DESERT TRAFFIC

By the first century AD the routine of Eastern trade was well established. From Alexandria it took twelve days sailing south along the Nile River to reach Coptos, almost 650 kilometres distant from Alexandria. The city was a major river port and an important commercial clearing house for Eastern goods arriving across the desert from the Red Sea ports. As a consequence, Coptos functioned as a base for trade associations, transport firms, and served as the headquarters of the various government representatives who monitored and taxed the flow of import and export commodities.[44]

Anyone crossing the Eastern Desert had to pay a tariff at Coptos, receiving in return a travel permit that would be inspected at military installations along the route. These passes raised revenues, allowed officials to monitor traffic, and ensured that any armed civilians using the roads were on legitimate business. Nearing the time of embarkation, the desert roads would be filled with various types of personnel travelling to the Red Sea ports. The Coptos Tariff records:

> [this is] how much is to be paid in tax:
> For a helmsman of the Red Sea, eight drachmas;
> A ship's lookout, ten drachmas;
> A guard, five drachmas;
> A sailor, five drachmas;
> A shipbuilder's servant, five drachmas;
> An artisan, eight drachmas.[45]

Under Roman rule, Myos Hormos and Berenice became the two most important Red Sea ports in the Eastern trade.[46] Journeys from Coptos to these towns were made by camel, carrying trade goods and supplies across the busy desert routes. Myos Hormos was approximately 180 kilometres distant from Coptos and it took six or seven days to make this journey.[47] Berenice lay further south at the very edge of Roman territory. Consequently, the desert crossing was longer and it took almost 12 days to travel by caravan the 370 kilometres to this port.[48] Roman merchants returning from the distant East would follow these same trade routes, crossing the Eastern Desert and loading their Eastern cargo onto barges at Coptos to be taken by river north to Alexandria and the Mediterranean.

The transport operations managed by caravan firms continued throughout the year and it seems that private guards were hired to protect companies of travellers from bandits. The larger caravans probably contained hundreds of men and animals, including scores of drivers and dozens of guards.[49] Under the Romans, Berenice became an important administrative centre and at its height, the town would have needed almost 2,000 camel loads of routine supplies per month, just to equip its inhabitants with essential foods and materials.[50]

Skilled craftsmen making the journey to the ports would have been required for ship construction and maintenance. Indian society also sought Roman artisans for their foreign expertise, so subjects of the Empire could travel east to make their fortunes. According to early Christian tradition, the apostle Thomas found employment in India, where his carpentry skills were sought for the construction of a royal palace.[51] The Tamil poems also speak in admiration of these Roman craftsmen.[52]

In the time of Augustus, Myos Hormos seems to have been the main port for embarkation to the distant East. The shorter desert crossing meant that it was cheaper to deliver outbound goods to this port than send them to Berenice. Early Roman investment in the Myos Hormos route probably ensured that this road had greater facilities and was more secure for travellers. Strabo describes the large harbour at Myos Hormos with a 'winding entrance'. These port facilities were substantial, as Gallus was able to land his large transport fleet at the port after his failed Arabian campaign.[53]

In the Augustan era, harbour facilities at Berenice may have been relatively poor by comparison with Myos Hormos.[54] Strabo stresses that waters around this port were not very favourable for shipping. He writes that Berenice has a 'coast roughened by reefs and submarine rocks and most of the time it is subject to tempestuous winds'.[55] Harbour facilities at Berenice fell into serious disrepair during the later Ptolemaic era and Roman authorities were slow to restore the port.[56] Strabo therefore describes Berenice as 'a site' with convenient landing places, rather than 'a harbour'.[57]

Ships had to wait in port for months until seasonal conditions made Eastern trade voyages possible. Consequently, outbound loading operations at the Red Sea ports were not urgent. By contrast, on the return from a trade voyage the offloading of Eastern cargo would have been a rushed operation, as merchants scrambled to deliver their retail goods to Alexandrian markets in the shortest possible time. This meant that when the Roman cargo fleets returned from the distant East, the facilities at Myos Hormos were greatly overburdened. In response, many merchant vessels opted to offload their Eastern cargoes at Berenice, even though this port had no operational harbour and it was a greater distance from Coptos. Strabo reports:

> Berenice has convenient landing places . . . and at present Indian and Arabian merchandise as well as African goods are brought to the port via the Red Sea. They are then transported to Coptos, the emporium [on the Nile] which receives these cargoes.[58]

In this era, ships offloading at Berenice probably sailed north to the more sheltered port of Myos Hormos once their cargo operations were concluded. This sailing would have taken at least five days, so most Roman merchants returning from the distant East expected to reach Coptos about the same time, whatever port they chose for their disembarkation.[59]

Harbour facilities at Berenice were probably restored during the reign of Tiberius, and evidence suggests that there was greater government investment in the port during the period from AD 14 to AD 37. Cartouches at the temple of Khem in the town centre do not mention Augustus, although they do list his successors beginning with Tiberius.[60] With the harbour repaired, Roman ships could find long-term shelter at the port and remain there for outbound loading operations.

Twelve of the 30 receipts in the *Nicanor Archive* that mention Berenice are dated to the reign of Tiberius and most refer to transport operations occurring after AD 26. This era also saw an increase in caravan traffic travelling the desert routes to Myos Hormos. Three pieces of graffiti from the Augustan era have been identified on this road, compared with ten graffiti firmly dated to the Tiberian period, and a further seven probably belonging to this era.[61] The evidence may be circumstantial, but it suggests a significant expansion in the volume of Eastern trade.

Ostraca records found at Berenice indicate how the restored port operated as a base for outbound trade voyages. These custom passes indicate that produce from markets right across the Mediterranean were being amassed at the town for export to the distant East. The most frequently mentioned cargo is wine, including Italian, Laodicean, Rhodian, Aminaean, Ephesian and Kolophonian, as well as local Egyptian varieties repackaged in used amphorae.[62] The number of amphorae being loaded aboard merchant ships varied in size from large consignments of nearly 50 containers to small deliveries of several amphorae. Dozens of these deliveries would be packed onboard vessels as they waited at dock. The ships were also loaded with provisions including supplies such as beets and onions.[63] Medical drugs termed *pharmakoi* appear several times in lists of goods delivered to the Red Sea ports by the Nicanor firm and these may have been ship provisions.[64] The *ostraka* passes also record that ships were loaded with small jars containing a compound of water and quince-flavoured honey. These concoctions were rich in ascorbic acid and were probably crew rations that would have prevented outbreaks of scurvy.[65]

During the first century AD the Roman military continued to construct additional facilities along the road from Coptos to Berenice. By the time of the Flavian Emperors, substantial fortified installations existed on this route and these could accommodate very large caravans. Pliny writes:

> They make the journey from Coptos to Berenice by camel. There are watering points placed at intervals along the route . . . there is an old *hydreuma*, called Troglodyticum, where there is a fort which accommodates 2,000 people . . . the greater part of the journey is made at night because of the heat and the days are spent at these stations.[66]

Desert garrisons also became larger. For example, the Apollonis station probably accommodated at least 215 soldiers.[67] These garrisons sent out an increased number of military patrols to police the desert roads, perhaps escorting the merchant caravans as they passed through their particular jurisdiction.

By the mid first century AD, Berenice and Myos Hormos shared equally important roles in Eastern trade. The *Nicanor Archive* mentions deliveries to Myos Hormos almost as often as it records goods sent to Berenice. By this era, the larger commercial companies were maintaining agents and facilities at both ports.[68] The Egyptian businessman Paminis sent one of his sons into each town to manage his extensive Eastern trade interests.[69] Writing in this period, the *Periplus* simply states that both sites were 'designated' ports for Eastern commerce and makes no distinction between them.[70]

Excavations carried out at the desert ruins of Myos Hormos reveal how the port had developed by this era.[71] In this arid landscape, most of the supplies necessary for survival had to be brought into the site by sea, or hauled across the Eastern Desert. Myos Hormos was a business town and much of the population would have been temporary residents engaged in facilitating or conducting commercial operations. In the beginning, the town was a collection of basic, but functional, buildings constructed from field stones, mud brick, reef coral chunks and salvaged timbers. Most of these buildings served as temporary dwellings, workshops or makeshift storage places.

Excavations have revealed that harbour facilities at Myos Hormos were extended during the Augustan era. Sand was taken from nearby quarry pits to the shore to reclaim land from the edge of the lagoon.[72] As part of the new harbour construction, thousands of Roman amphorae were closely packed together in dense upright positions to create an artificial foreshore. This landing feature was more than 60 metres long and must have been built to receive ships and manage their cargo operations.[73] Archaeologists have identified larger buildings near these harbour facilities that could be the remains of government facilities or the warehouses of wealthy trading firms.[74] An enclosure was also found on the outskirts of the port that may have been a *caravanserai* for housing large numbers of camels in preparation for the desert treks to Coptos.[75]

Investigations suggest that Berenice was a far more substantial town. Although many of its facilities were built from relatively crude local materials, there were also more significant stone buildings at the site. These well-built structures probably belonged to the Roman administration or to wealthy business firms who operated headquarters and needed warehouses.[76] Near the city centre there was a sizable temple dedicated to the Egyptian god Khem, and around the site were shrines devoted to a range of Greco-Roman deities. Artefacts recovered from the site indicate that some of the inhabitants of Berenice enjoyed a higher level of prosperity, with more elaborate buildings than those found at Myos Hormos. These finds include decorative marble slabs imported from Roman Anatolia, fragments of elaborately woven floor carpets and carved furniture. The discovery of household pets buried with collars indicates that life in this desert town may not have been as austere as is often imagined.[77] Excavations have not yet revealed the extent of the harbour facilities at Berenice, although several sea walls and a pier built from boulders have been investigated by archaeologists.[78]

During this era, the ancient canal linking the Nile to the Red Sea remained in a serious state of disrepair. It was only re-excavated on the orders of the Emperor Trajan who was in power from AD 98 to AD 117.[79] The re-opening of the canal allowed barges to sail from Alexandria directly to Clysma. From Clysma, sea voyages could be made south to Myos Hormos and Berenice, where specialized ocean freighters waited to receive their Roman cargoes. This canal route provided Roman businessmen with a cheaper way to send bulky Mediterranean goods to the Red Sea ports. Many passengers would have preferred this water journey to the arduous desert crossing. Lucian reveals how the re-opening of the canal made travel from Alexandria to India far more convenient. He describes how a student, sent by his wealthy father to study in Alexandria, was persuaded to undertake the voyage on impulse without informing his guardians. He writes:

> The young man cruised up the Nile as far as Clysma, and as a vessel was just putting out to sea, he was persuaded to join others in a voyage to India.[80]

On outbound journeys this supply route avoided the expense and inconvenience of overland desert transport.[81] However, the upper regions of the Red Sea are subject to persistent northerly winds, making return sailings to Clysma difficult and time consuming.[82] Consequently, many merchants returning from the distant East continued to offload their Eastern cargoes at the traditional ports and use the conventional desert routes to rapidly convey their goods to Alexandria.[83]

MERCHANTS AND PERSONNEL

Egypt's Eastern commerce attracted interest from right across the Roman Empire. The trade soon involved a wide variety of businessmen, merchants, investors and commercial agents. People from a very diverse range of ethnic, social and cultural backgrounds would have freely intermingled in this vibrant international commerce.

The *Nicanor Archive* alone reveals the existence of about 20 trade firms, at least

25 businessmen and close to 30 commercial agents.[84] Many transport firms and shipping personnel also made their livelihood from facilitating this commerce, along with craftsmen and mercenaries, who found employment with various business operatives.

The *ostraca* and the desert graffiti, indicate how Greeks and Egyptians were heavily involved in Eastern trade operations. These people performed a vital and diverse range of roles; anything and everything from camel drivers to wealthy businessmen. In Egypt, wealthy Romans operated their commercial dealings mostly through trusted agents who were slaves or freedmen, and these business networks offered a practical and discreet way to invest in commerce. The people who looked after the business interests of rich Roman patrons often had Greek or Egyptian names.[85] There were also prosperous Egyptian entrepreneurs who worked for their own interests, like Parthenios, son of Paminis, who occasionally employed the Nicanor firm. Parthenios was wealthy enough to leave a temple inscription at Coptos in AD 32, which recorded an expensive dedication to the deities Isis and Cronos.[86]

Greek-Egyptians were also operating overseas in the distant East, either for their own interests, or as business agents for wealthy entrepreneurs. A Roman census preserved in a poll-tax register records how a Greek-Egyptian man from the Arsinoe district of Egypt was visiting India in AD 72, presumably on some long-term overseas business.[87] Often it is difficult to determine the 'ethnic' identity of the Hellenized businessmen documented in the surviving texts. For example, a Greek inscription from Coptos, dated to AD 70, records that a merchant named Hermeros, son of Athenion, visited the city and made a dedication to the goddesses Isis and Hera. Hermeros reveals that he was a resident of the south Arabian trade emporium of Aden and he was either a Hellenized south Arabian, or a Greek who had been absent from the Roman Empire for a considerable time.[88]

Roman citizens from across the Empire were also prominent in Egypt's Eastern trade. The *Nicanor Archive* mentions at least seven Roman citizens who owned commercial businesses in Egypt and had representatives at the Red Sea ports.[89] The Berenice *ostraca* also include the names of more than ten Roman citizens who were active at the port, either for administrative or commercial reasons.[90] A Berenice official named 'Andouros' probably came from the western Empire, possibly from the Spanish town of Andura. In 2 BC a Roman citizen named Gaius Numidius Eros carved Latin graffiti onto the rock face of a natural grotto on the road from Berenice to Coptos. Eros probably came from the eastern Mediterranean and he writes that he had just returned from India.[91]

The Italian district of Campania was a major exporter of wine to Egypt both for regional consumption and for further export to the distant East. It seems that Italian businessmen were quick to realize the market opportunities offered by the expansion of Eastern trade.[92] Archaeologists have found plaster amphorae plugs at Coptos that were stamped with the names of wealthy Roman businessmen and these entrepreneurs were probably wine dealers from the western territories of the Empire who had 'labelled' their delivery batches.[93] The name 'G. Norbanus Ptolem.' appears on several plaster plugs and he may be the same Gaius Norbanus who hired the Nicanor firm to deliver goods to Myos Hormos.[94] A wealthy Roman businessman named Varus also had trade interests in a number of Red Sea merchant ships and is mentioned several times in the Berenice *ostraca*. An example reads:

> Herak to Drakon, son of Peisipmous Koud – let pass Peteasmephis son of Horos with six *koilopomata* for loading onto the (ships) of Varus.[95]

The measurement *koilopomata* denotes a wine consignment and Varus could have owned a small commercial fleet.

The most interesting evidence concerning this trade comes from an Egyptian temple in Medamoud, where an inscription reveals the activities of two wealthy Roman businesswomen from Alexandria. The women made an expensive dedication to the temple in celebration of the goddess Leto during the mid second century AD. The Greek inscription reads:

> Aelia Isidora and Aelia Olympias, who are distinguished matrons, Red Sea ship owners and merchants, together with Apolinarios the captain of the fleet of Olympias and Isidora, set up this dedication to the greatest goddess Leto.[96]

Isidora and Olympias referred to themselves *matronai stolatai* meaning that they had more than three children, owned property and were legally entitled to conduct their own business ventures without a male guardian. They also described themselves as *naukleroi* and *emporoi* indicating that they were ship-owners or financial backers as well as merchants. The women also possessed Roman citizenship and the name 'Aelia' indicates that they acquired this status under Hadrian. Apolinarios was evidently the commander of the small Red Sea merchant fleet owned by the women.[97]

South Arabian traders also formed notable groups among the merchants who operated in Roman Egypt. Pottery sherds scratched with Himyaritic and Sabaean writing have been found at the Red Sea ports and a few rare examples of Minaean graffiti have also been identified on the desert routes between Myos Hormos and Coptos.[98] Remarkably, at least two Minaean inscriptions found in southern Arabia also mention trade expeditions to Roman Egypt.[99]

In the early second century AD, Dio Chrysostom wrote a speech in praise of Alexandria which mentions how Indian peoples could be seen amongst the crowds that thronged the city.[100] Many of these Indians would have reached Egypt onboard their own trade vessels. Significant amounts of Indian pottery have been found at the Egyptian Red Sea ports and this indicates the presence of well established foreign communities at these Roman towns.[101] Matting woven in a northern Indian style has been recovered from one of the rubbish pits at Berenice and a number of brailing rings found at this site were attached to small fragments of Indian-made cotton sails.[102] Indian literature refers to trade voyages into the distant West, but the surviving accounts are generally too vague to be helpful about these ancient contacts with Rome.

It is difficult to positively identify merchants from northwest India in the textual records from Roman Egypt. In the second century BC, the Hellenic rulers of Bactria invaded northwest India and for a time a number of small Greek kingdoms existed in these territories. Consequently, many northern Indians visiting Roman Egypt may have been familiar with Greek and possibly adopted Hellenic names in their trade dealings. One example is a man with the Greek name 'Sophon' who left graffiti at the Pan Temple on the desert road from Berenice to Edfu. Sophon asked the god in Greek for a safe journey, but referred to himself as an 'Indos'. This Sophon could have been a Hellenized Indian trader visiting Egypt for commercial purposes, or he could have been a Mediterranean Greek working for the Ptolemies as a mahout or elephant keeper, a position that had also acquired the title 'Indos'.[103] The same Pan Temple has several drawings of elephants that indicate its use as a resting place during the Ptolemaic era, so it seems the ethnic identity of Saphon must remain speculative.[104]

Due to their distinctive cultural character, the Tamils from southern India are easier to identify in the Egyptian archaeological record. Graffiti in the Tamil-Brahmi script has been found on pot sherds at Myos Hormos.[105] This pottery is marked with names like 'Cattan' and 'Kanan', who were possibly the leaders of prosperous Tamil clans involved in Roman trade. The discovery of Indian sailing materials at the Red Sea ports could also be connected with these Tamil trade ventures.

THE MERCHANT SHIPS

The classical sources currently provide the best evidence for the appearance and scale of Roman freighters sailing from Egypt into the distant East. These trade ships were large by Mediterranean standards and would have dwarfed most other vessels sailing in the Indian Ocean. Writing in the early third century AD, the Greek author Philostratus has an Indian character describe the Roman merchant ships that traded with his country. The Indian reports:

> The Egyptians construct ships for our ocean and they send them to sea to exchange Egyptian goods for Indian wares . . . The Egyptians build these ships on a scale whereby one of their vessels is equivalent in size to several of those used by the other races.[106]

Roman vessels involved in Eastern commerce would have been at least 75 tons burden and scholars suggest that most ships would have reached sizes of up to 500 tons.[107] However, a large proportion of the ship's feasible cargo capacity would have been used for crew quarters and provision holds.

Archaeologists excavating Myos Hormos discovered that architectural supports in the remains of ancient buildings had been salvaged from decommissioned ships. They identified beams with dowel holes, iron nails and pitch, as well as planking pockmarked with barnacle impressions.[108] It seems that residents of the ancient port salvaged wood from ocean-going craft to help construct facilities in the town and these remains have offered important information about the construction of Eastern freighters.

Most ancient ships were built as a skeletal wooden framework with the keel acting as a spine for a 'cage' of wooden ribs. The hull planking was then attached to this frame. By contrast, large Greco-Roman freighters were built by first constructing the external hull. The planks of this hull were joined together with mortise-and-tenon joints along their edges, to rigidly lock the sections into position. The result was a very sturdy self-supporting hull to which further strengthening timbers and internal frames would be attached. Planks found at Myos Hormos with mortise-and-tenon joints confirm that these techniques were used on Eastern freighters. This skilled method of shipbuilding bore a closer resemblance to cabinet making than regular ship carpentry and created an incredibly robust hull.[109]

The ancient wood recovered from Berenice includes a tropical hardwood called teak. This wood has been found in beams up to three metres long.[110] Teak is excellent for ship construction, being durable, weather resistant and easily worked. It is native to southern Asia, so Roman shipbuilders must have been receiving this wood through Indian trade dealings. The *Periplus* records how large Indian vessels were delivering a variety of vital shipbuilding materials, including teak and copper, to the Persian Gulf ports.[111] It is likely that similar arrangements existed to supply the Roman shipyards in Egypt. Mediterranean shipbuilding materials were also being brought across the Eastern Desert and the *Coptos Tariff* records tolls to be paid on masts sent to the Red Sea ports.[112]

Greco-Roman freighters could be outfitted at Myos Hormos where there was a ship repair yard near the edge of the lagoon. There were various workshops in the area and lead sheets were strewn across the site, verifying that the Roman ships involved in Eastern trade must have had protective lead-lined hulls.[113] This lead-lining was used below the waterline to protect the ship from tiny marine creatures that would otherwise degrade the hull by boring into the vessel.[114]

Philostratus reports that Roman merchant ships sailing to India had the bulwarks of their hulls raised to a great height and had extra compartments placed on deck. He writes:

> They rib the sides of the ship with bolts to hold the vessel together, and they raise its bulwarks and its mast to a great height, and they construct several compartments on the timber beams which run across the vessel.[115]

Extending the hull far above sea level would have ensured that the deck was not swamped by tall ocean waves. The crew would also be sheltered from the frequently gale-force winds of the monsoon. Some Mediterranean warships had high bulwarks in the form of collapsible wooden ramparts. To prevent boarding by hostile forces bulwalks could also have been added to Red Sea freighters for protection from pirate attacks. On Mediterranean ships, crew and passengers often slept on deck under canvas, but on Eastern voyages passengers would not want to linger on a deck exposed to the severe weather conditions of the monsoon ocean sailing.[116] Extra deck cabins and compartments were probably added as additional berths, or to accommodate further cargo. Roman freighters would also have carried small ship-to-shore vessels onboard and these light craft would have been vital at Eastern ports which did not have adequate docking facilities for larger ships.[117]

In Mediterranean waters large merchant ships were elaborately decorated and many vessels had goose-neck ornaments carved on their sternposts. These figure-heads were symbolic of the Egyptian goddess Isis, the protectress of sailors. This same custom was followed by Romans involved in Eastern trade. Tamil poets describe nightfall on the Indian coastline and mention the *Yavana* 'swan lamps' that illuminated Roman ships with their clear, bright lights.[118] The *Perumpanarruppatai* reports:

> It shone as though it was a swan-lamp seen on the timbers of the *Yavana* ships and it sparkled like the distant star that heralds the dawn.[119]

Lucian provides further details about the decorate features to be seen on the largest Roman vessels. He writes:

> Behold the lofty [goose neck] stern with its gradual curve, and its gilded beak, balanced at the other end by the long rising sweep of the prow. And the prow had figures of the ship's name-sake goddess Isis on either side. As to its other ornamental details, it had paintings and a scarlet topsail.[120]

Details on the mainsail of a ship shown on the Torlonia Relief suggest that some trade vessels had detailed images from Greek and Roman mythology painted on their sails. The Tamil sources also refer to *Yavana* statues and the Indians may have first seen these objects as carved or painted decorations on Roman ships.[121]

In the Mediterranean, Roman merchant ships were fitted with a large square main sail which was placed mid-ship, while an additional smaller sail called an *aremon* was often positioned near the prow.[122] According to Philostratus, the masts of Eastern freighters were raised to greater heights. The enlarged mainsail probably gave these vessels more wind-driven power in the Red Sea and greater speed on their ocean crossings to India. Archaeologists at Berenice found a small graffiti image of a freighter scratched on a pottery fragment and this sketch suggests that large pennants were attached to the mastheads and end beams, high above the decks of these ships.[123] Excavations at Myos Hormos have also recovered the remains of rigging removed from Roman vessels. This includes large wood and horn brailing rings used to secure ropes and facilitate the raising and lowering of sails.[124] Indian cotton was probably used for the sails of some Roman freighters and fragments of this fabric have been found at the Red Sea ports, still attached to Mediterranean style rigging equipment.[125]

Remarkably, there is nomenclature evidence for some of the Greco-Roman vessels that sailed to the distant East. The *Muziris Papyrus* records that a merchant ship called the 'Hermapollon' was involved in trade voyages to Tamil India during the mid second century AD.[126] In Greek mythology, Hermes was a messenger deity who travelled at great speeds and was associated with the crossing of boundaries. Hermes was therefore widely adopted by merchants as protector for their business and wellbeing. It is therefore perfectly appropriate that a monsoon-driven ship that sailed great distances between ancient cultures should be named in honour of this deity. As the Greek sun god Apollo also travels daily through the heavens, beginning his outbound journey in the East, he makes a suitable addition to the name.

An *ostracon* found in a rubbish pit at Berenice records the name of another

Roman trade vessel called the 'Gymnasiarchis'.[127] The gymnasium was central to Greek cultural identity and in the classical world the gymnasiarchs who supplied these institutions with oil and wine were respected benefactors. Perhaps the owner of the trade ship Gymnasiarchis was a Greek businessman who used his commercial profits in these acts of patronage. A name meaning 'Greek benefactor' had appropriate connotations in the Eastern trade, as Roman merchant ships carried the productive wealth of the Mediterranean overseas to distant foreign lands.

CREW AND GUARDS

A man calling himself Severus, son of Moschion, left an inscription on the desert route leading from Edfu to Berenice. Severus describes himself as a *naukleros*, suggesting that he was a captain of a large merchant ship.[128] The captains of these Red Sea freighters commanded a large group of skilled professionals and they were tasked with keeping both crew and cargo safe on their hazardous missions into the distant East.

Philostratus describes the variety of personnel found onboard Roman freighters sailing to India. He writes:

> The [Roman businessmen] set several pilots onboard the ship and subordinated them to the oldest and wisest man. They also post several officers on the prow and set skilled sailors to man the rigging.[129]

The *Coptos Tariff* confirms the description given by Philostratus by mentioning helmsmen, sailors, lookouts, guards and pilots.[130] Some of the pilots may well have been African, Arabian or Indian sailors, who were familiar with various regional waters passed through on route. It was well known that Eudoxus was guided by an Indian mariner and he later consulted Ethiopian pilots familiar with the coastal waters around East Africa.[131] It is likely that Roman freighters carried a permanent staff of carpenters, sail-makers and shipbuilder's servants, in case repairs were needed during these long voyages.

The passengers travelling aboard Red Sea freighters would have included merchants and business agents from a variety of Roman territories, including wine dealers from Italy. Some Roman businessmen could have owned or hired entire merchant ships and staffed these vessels with their own business agents. However, the owners of most freighters probably hired out cargo space to a number of different merchants who might have taken passage onboard the ship.[132] Many Indians and Arabians who did not have their own trade vessels, probably travelled onboard Roman ships carrying their own merchandise.

Throughout antiquity, India was renowned in the classical world for its wondrous sights and remarkable religious practices. The first century philosopher Apollonius of Tyana was said to have travelled to India to investigate its unique belief-cultures and other Roman subjects may have been drawn to the east for similar reasons.[133] Passengers onboard Roman trade ships might therefore have included sightseers like the Alexandrian student persuaded to take timeout from his studies to make the voyage.[134] A later classical account recalls how a Theban lawyer became disillusioned with his profession and escaped to find solace in India.[135]

Nonetheless, the voyage to India was perilous and ancient accounts indicate how great the threat of piracy was in the Eastern seas. The *Periplus* reports that the eastern coast of the Red Sea was inhabited by a 'vicious people' who 'plunder any ships that stray from their course' and 'enslave anyone who they rescue from shipwrecks'. The author therefore recommended that ships avoid this shore on journeys down through the Red Sea and put on extra speed in sailing past this 'fearsome' region.[136] Philostratus records that Roman ships sailing to the distant East carried mercenaries onboard to protect the vessel from pirate raiders. He writes:

> In the crew of this ship there is a detachment of armed men. It is necessary to equip the ship in this manner to protect it against the savages of the Red Sea who live on the eastern coast. They always lie in wait to attack and plunder ships on the high seas.[137]

Pliny also reveals that these mercenaries formed special teams of archers on Roman freighters bound for India. He writes:

> The voyage [to India] is made every year, with companies of archers onboard, because these seas are greatly infested by pirates.[138]

Merchants involved in Eastern trade were extremely wealthy and they could certainly have hired large teams of well-equipped mercenaries to protect their precious investments. For example, the single cargo mentioned in the *Muziris Papyrus* was valued at around nine million sesterces.[139] By comparison, in the first century AD, the total annual pay of an entire Roman Legion was only about 12 million sesterces.[140]

THE VOYAGE TO INDIA

The voyage from Egypt to India was a huge undertaking. For Roman subjects, these voyages meant weeks at sea in hazardous conditions more extreme than anything encountered in the relatively calm waters of the enclosed Mediterranean Sea. Those who sailed across the Indian Ocean were driven by the powerful monsoon winds and their vessels would be travelling for thousands of kilometres into the East. This crossing would take crew and passengers far from the sight and safety of land.

Roman ships sailing to the distant East followed a strict seasonal timetable to exploit favourable weather conditions in the Red Sea and Indian Ocean. The *Periplus* reports that the proper time to leave Egypt for India was in July and this allowed ships to sail through the Red Sea using northerly winds that blow steadily through this region during the summer months.[141] It was a distance of approximately 1,200 kilometres, a 30 day sailing, from Egypt to the Arabian port of Ocelis near the entrance to the Red Sea.[142]

Vessels leaving the Red Sea entered the Gulf of Aden in August at a time when the southwest monsoon was beginning to blow across the Indian Ocean. Some Roman vessels followed the Arabian coast as far as the trade port of Qana, while others sailed along northern Somalia to visit African markets as far as Cape Guardafui. Merchants could spend several weeks visiting trade sites along these coasts, taking onboard further supplies and exchanging Mediterranean goods for local merchandise. Some of this merchandise would be destined for markets in India, or even further East. Roman traders therefore dealt in the trade surplus from African and Arabian territories, as well as merchandise drawn from across the Mediterranean.

On early Eastern voyages, ships from Egypt had followed the Arab and Persian coasts to reach India. But as trade contacts increased, Greek pilots soon realized that these voyages could be shortened in time and distance by direct passage across the ocean.[143] These trade routes were adopted and developed as Greek pilots began to learn about the true shape and position of the Indian and Arabian coasts.

Greek geographers such as Eratosthenes and Strabo did not accept that India formed a triangular peninsula and portrayed this landmass as a flattened horizontal coast running eastward towards the edge of the world. Once Greek mariners became aware that the Indian coast was orientated north–south, then they could undertake direct crossings from Arabia without fearing they would miss India and get lost in the vast encircling world ocean.[144] The *Periplus* retells a story about the mariner who supposedly discovered the first ocean crossing:

> The pilot Hippalus was the first person to discover the direct route to India on the high seas. He gave thought to the location of the ports and the shape of the sea and realised that the *etesian* (monsoon) winds came from the sea and blow seasonally . . . This wind is called 'Hypalos' after this navigator.[145]

Pliny describes further stages in the development of sea crossings that made the journey to India shorter and 'safer'. New routes had been adopted to exploit increased trade opportunities in distant markets, or avoid stretches of coast that became subject either to piracy or threatening regional conflicts.[146] As these routes offered a faster passage, Pliny cynically remarks, 'the desire for gain brings India ever nearer'.[147]

By AD 50 some Roman ships were crossing from Arabia and the Horn of Africa, to sail straight to northwest India. Others headed directly to the southern Tamil lands.[148] The *Periplus* reports:

> Some [ships] leave directly from Qana and some go from Cape Guardafui. Those bound for the Malabar Coast hold out with the wind on the quarter for most of the way. Those bound for Barygaza and Scythia also set out . . . on the high seas and bypass the coastal bays.[149]

The northern voyage covered a distance of more than 1,700 kilometres, while the southern sailing crossed over more than 2,600 kilometres of open ocean. Pliny describes the voyage from the Red Sea to the Tamil lands:

> The most advantageous way of sailing to India is to set out from Ocelis. With the Hippalus blowing it is a 40 day sailing from there to Muziris, which is the first trading station reached in India.[150]

Throughout the voyage to India, Roman freighters would have tried to remain together, sailing within sight of each other in small fleets. Thus they could offer mutual support to repel coastal pirates as they sailed through the gulfs. When on the high seas, continued proximity was necessary in case another ship in the group became damaged while hundreds of kilometres from land. If the mast of a lone ship snapped in gale-force winds, or its wave-pounded hull fractured, the crew would have a limited chance of survival out at sea in the storms of the Indian Ocean.

The coastal trade sailing through the Gulf of Aden would have been a leisurely three week voyage, but the direct crossing to India would have meant over two weeks on the open ocean travelling at wind-driven speeds approaching six knots.[151] The southwest monsoons that blow seasonally across the Indian Ocean are perhaps the strongest and most persistent winds on the planet. During this season, wind velocity over the open waters can average 30 knots with gusts frequently reaching gale-force ferocity.[152] Roman ships began their voyage to India at a time when these winds were reaching their greatest force. The robust hull construction of Greco-Roman ships allowed these freighters to take full advantage of these extreme sailing conditions on their voyages into the distant East.[153] The voyage was turbulent and dangerous, but these direct crossings were faster than any coastal sailing. The *Periplus* therefore concludes, 'The crossing with these winds is hard going, but shorter and absolutely favourable'.[154]

The Roman ships who reached Tamil India would have sailed more than 5,000 kilometres from the edge of their Empire. Altogether, the Roman voyage from Egypt to India would have taken at least 70 days, and when they reached their first destination in India it would have been almost three months since the travellers had left Alexandria. Roman freighters therefore reached western India in early September when the monsoon winds were quietening down. By this time, coastal traffic was resuming as Indian and Arabian craft waited until the strongest of the southwest winds had abated before making their own Eastern sailings.[155]

The return sailing to the Red Sea was not attempted until the onset of the northeast monsoon in early November. This gave Roman merchants almost eight weeks to explore the markets of ancient India. Roman ships visiting the Malabar Coast would delay their return sailing until December, meaning that Roman merchants who travelled directly to this region would spend up to four months in the Tamil lands.

INDO-SCYTHIA

The Indus territories became known to the Greeks as 'Indo-Scythia' after horse-riding warriors from Central Asia migrated into these regions and conquered the existing nobility. By the time of the *Periplus*, these small kingdoms had come under the control of minor Indo-Parthian warlords who were frequently at war with each other and in conflict with their eastern neighbours. The most important trade emporium in Indo-Scythia was Barbaricum which lay near the estuary of the Indus and served a great inland capital called Minnagara.

The *Periplus* vividly describes the coastal approach to Barbaricum:

> The northern seaboard of Scythia is very flat and through it flows the Indus, the mightiest of all the rivers along the Indian Ocean. It empties such a great volume of water into the sea that from far off – even before you reach land – you meet its lightly-coloured waters. Those coming from the sea know that they are approaching land near the river because they see eels emerging from the depths.[156]

Roman ships would moor at Barbaricon to have their trade cargoes transferred upriver to the metropolis at Minnagara. Arriving at these markets, Roman merchants would have traded with various Indian dealers and mingled with visiting Arabs and Persians.

The *Periplus* describes Roman goods sent to this region and begins its list of cargo with fabrics, including good quantity clothing without adornment, multi-coloured textiles and printed cloth. The Romans also offered Mediterranean coral, green peridot gemstones, fragrant storax potions, glassware, silverwares, and Roman money. Pliny confirms that Roman coral was highly prized in Indian society and early Sanskrit texts also mention coral from 'Romaka'.[157] The *Ratnapariksa* describes the magical properties of this desirable product:

> Good coral is tender, smooth and shining and has a beautiful red colour. In this world it procures richness and gains; gives women marital bliss; destroys corruption and illness, and wards off perils such as poison.[158]

The Romans also sent wine to Barbaricon in 'limited quantity'. Amphorae fragments have been found at dozens of Indian archaeological sites, but quantities tend to be quite small compared with local pottery types.[159] Roman merchants also offered traders at Barbaricon some of the African and Arabian frankincense they had acquired on their outbound voyage.

The Indo-Scythian markets offered Roman traders a range of specialized plant products including nard, a herb called 'costus', an aromatic gum called bdellium, and a drug called 'lycium'. These Indus territories were connected to the silk routes of Inner Asia and Minnagaran markets supplied Roman merchants with silk materials and exotic animal furs such as mink and sable. Roman traders also received indigo dyes and various precious stones including turquoise gems and vivid blue lapis lazuli.[160]

During this era, the Han Empire began to re-assert its authority over Inner Asia. As a consequence, the Chinese government began to receive strategic information about the resources of northwest India. It is interesting that these reports focused on the rare goods produced and trafficked through this territory and the Chinese accounts draw particular attention to Roman connections. The *Hou Hanshu* states:

> Tianzhu (northwest India) produces elephants, rhinoceroses, turtle shell, gold, silver, copper, iron, lead, and tin. To the west, it communicates with the Roman Empire. Precious things from Rome can be found there, as well as fine cotton cloths, excellent wool carpets, perfumes of all sorts, sugar loaves, pepper, ginger, and black salt.[161]

The report suggests that Roman goods were being trafficked from Indian ports north into Central Asia along the same trade routes that conveyed silks from these regions down to Barbaricon. Roman exports were therefore supplying market demands in Central Asia, as well as enriching the bazaars of northwest India.[162]

THE SAKA KINGDOM

The sailing from Barbarikon south to Barygaza was almost 900 kilometres, and on the voyage Roman ships would leave Indo-Scythia and cross over into the Saka kingdom which controlled the Gujarat territories of western India. In the time of the *Periplus*, the Saka lands were incredibly wealthy and produced great stocks of grain, rice, sesame oil, ghee and cotton.[163]

The coast approaching Barygaza was hazardous and the *Periplus* describes choppy seas turbid with eddies and violent whirlpools. The author warns:

> There are sandbanks and a succession of shallow eddies reaching a long way from land. Frequently, with the shore nowhere in sight, vessels will run aground and if caught and dragged further to shore they will be destroyed.[164]

Skilful pilots knew their ships were approaching these treacherous stretches from the black eels they saw in these waters.

Barygaza lay on the Narmada River, over 50 kilometres inland from where it flowed into the Cambay Gulf. Roman pilots knew that they were approaching this coast when they spotted small golden-yellow eels in the waters around their ships.[165] The Cambay Gulf was extremely hazardous for Roman shipping, for sailings through its waters involved passage through rock-strewn reefs surrounded by dangerous currents. There were few natural landmarks on the shoreline to guide ships through the maze of concealed sandbanks near the mouth of the Narmada River.[166] Consequently, the Saka kings sent out local fishermen on long rowboats to meet the Roman freighters and tow them through the hazards of the gulf. On reaching the Narmada River, the Roman ships would be taken upstream to deep water pools where they could anchor in relative safety.

The Narmada River stretched deep into central India, and acted as an important communication route for the conveyance of merchandise across the Indian peninsula. The *Periplus* records that Barygaza owed much of its prosperity to its trade links with a large inland city called Ozene, which lay on a major tributary of the Ganges River.[167] This market sent large quantities of cloth and quartz fragments to the Saka kingdom. Barygaza was also connected to important Indian cities lying south of Saka territory. The *Periplus* reports that wagons loaded with precious stones and cottons arrived at Barygaza from the city of Ter which was thirty days distant.[168] Barygaza also had extensive maritime trade links with the Persian Gulf and with the Tamil lands in the far south.[169]

When describing this part of India, the *Periplus* twice mentions local legends involving Alexander the Great. Alexander never visited this part of India, but the activities of the later Indo-Greeks were enough to convince visiting Romans that the great conqueror had indeed reached Barygaza. The *Periplus* reports:

> In the area there are still preserved to this very day signs of Alexander's expedition, ancient shrines and the foundations of encampments with huge wells.[170]

Roman traders could also acquire Greek souvenirs from the money dealers at Saka markets. The *Periplus* reports that old drachmas issued in past centuries by the Indo-Greek rulers Apollodotus and Menander could be found in the region.[171]

Mediterranean wines were important in Roman trade dealings with the Saka kingdom. Italian wine head the lists of Roman imports into Barygaza, along with Laodicean wines from Asia Minor. Also on the list are Arabian wines that Roman merchants acquired at trade stops on the outbound voyage.[172] The prominence of wine in Roman exports to India encouraged jokes in the Empire about Indian drunkenness. Lucian writes:

> Owing to climate, when the Indians try strong drinks like wine, they immediately become drunk and they are driven twice as mad any Greek or Romans would be.[173]

Romans were also sending various basic materials to the Saka markets including raw glass, copper, tin and lead. The Roman shipwreck from Bet Dwarka provides evidence for this trade with its cargo of circular lead ingots.[174] Roman traders visiting Barygaza also offered a wide variety of plain clothing, printed fabrics and multicoloured girdles. Some of these clothes would have been specially manufactured within the Empire to co-ordinate with fashion styles popular in India.

Along with these bulk goods, Roman traders also dealt in coral and peridot gems. Other trade goods included pungent storax potions, fragrant yellow sweet clover, a white chemical powder called antimony sulphate, and a red mineral called realgar.[175] These specialized substances would have found various uses in Indian drug remedies, fabric dyes and perfumed potions.[176] The Romans were also exporting cheap unguent, but faced with local competition, the market for this product seems to have been limited. Towards the end of this list of trade goods the *Periplus* mentions that Roman gold and silver coinage could be exchanged at some profit against the local Indian currencies.[177]

The Saka royal courts in India were major consumers of expensive goods. Roman dealers fully exploited this commercial opportunity and sent high-value merchandise to Barygaza 'for the king'. This included precious silverware, slave musicians, beautiful girls for concubinage, fine wines, expensive clothing and choice unguents. This elite slave trade could explain why ancient Sanskrit drama presents Greek characters onstage amongst the attendants of Indian Kings.[178]

Barygaza exported a range of Eastern trade goods that reached the Saka kingdom from across India. Roman traders dealing with the port received nard, costus, bdellium and lycium that came from Indo-Scythia. Fabrics were a major export from the Saka kingdom and Roman merchants at Barygaza would have received all kinds of cotton cloth, as well as silk materials that had been brought from Central Asia. At Barygaza, Roman merchants could also acquire ivory and different types of precious stones including onyx and agate. The region also offered supplies of long pepper, which was a relatively rare and costly spice used mainly in Roman medicinal remedies.[179] All this Eastern merchandise would have been crammed within the Roman cargo holds in preparation for the continuing voyage south along the western coast of India.

While Roman ships remained in the Narmada River, they were highly vulnerable to tidal floods and the crews had to be continually vigilant.[180] Roman captains would have been anxious to leave the confines of the river. The *Periplus* warns:

> The flood tide can arrive at night. Sometimes this happens when the tide is just beginning to come in and the sea is still calm. People near the mouth of the river hear a rumble like an army heard from a great distance. Then after a short while the sea races over the sandbanks with a loud hiss.[181]

The *Periplus* vividly describes the warning signs when sections of the seabed became visible and new stretches of the coast were revealed by the withdrawal of the sea. Then, 'the sudden inrush of the flood tide surges up the river and a concentrated mass of seawater is driven headlong upstream for many miles against the natural flow'.[182] The experience was terrifying and inexperienced crews who did not have their ships secured with sufficient restraining anchors could run aground on sandbanks or even capsize. Even skilled mariners struggled to control their ships in these hazardous conditions. The *Periplus* warns that, 'if ships cannot be stabilized they will be pulled downward by the ebb and will tilt over on their sides. Then when the flood suddenly returns they will be swamped by the first wave of the flow – because so much power is generated by the inrush of the sea'.[183]

THE SATAVAHANA REALM

The author of the *Periplus* describes the voyage from Barygaza south along the Konkan Coast of the Deccan Plateau. The *Periplus* reports:

> Beyond Barygaza the coast heads south . . . inland there are many barren areas, great mountains, and wild animals of all kinds including leopards, tigers, elephants, enormous serpents, hyenas, and all types of monkey. There are a great many populous nations from here to the Ganges.[184]

The hilly terrain of the Western Deccan contained numerous inland market centres connected by a wide network of overland trade routes. This region was ruled by the Satavahana dynasty whose authority stretched across the Deccan Plateau to the eastern coasts of India.

In their early trade dealings with this region, Roman merchants sent wines and cheap bronze artefacts to the Satavahana markets. Excavations at an ancient residential structure near Kolhapur have unearthed a cache of at least ten classical bronzes, including figurines, vessels, strainers and mirrors. These items were relatively commonplace in the Roman provenances and were exported to India as antiques.[185] It is interesting that the Kolhapur examples were manufactured in Campania, suggesting that Italian merchants were collecting together and exporting old classical bronzes as a profitable sideline to their wine business.[186]

By the time of the *Periplus*, the Saka king Nahapana had seized control over large parts of the Western Deccan. His conquests included the main Satavahana trade port of Kalliena, which lay on the Ulhas river system. This conflict severely disrupted overland trade reaching the port and the new Saka governor of Kalliena began forwarding incoming Roman ships north to Barygaza. These Roman freighters were given a guard of Saka war-vessels, probably because enemy raiders had begun targeting any vessels bringing supplies or wealth into the occupied regions.[187]

The closure of Kalliena lasted just over a decade as an inscription from Nasik reveals that the Satavahana had reclaimed their lost territories by the late 60s AD.[188] In the aftermath, Kalliena must have resumed its position as the major trade port for the Western Deccan, exporting large amounts of cotton fabrics, coloured onyx and beasts for the Roman games.[189]

Details about Satavahana trade contacts are revealed in Prakrit inscriptions found at Buddhist cave structures in the Western Deccan. The inscriptions mention generous donations by *Yavanas*, who were probably Greek and Italian merchants from the Roman Empire. These *Yavana*s resided at nearby towns and conducted their trade business with guilds of Indian traders and local craftsmen.[190] They would probably have forwarded most of the merchandise they acquired to their colleagues when they visited Kalliena. The Romans referred to in the inscriptions seem to have been wealthy converts who adopted self-consciously Buddhist names to better integrate into their new Eastern faith.[191]

Yavana inscriptions have been identified at monastic sites at Karle, Nasik and Junnar.[192] At Nasik some of the votive texts refer to the activities of *Raumakas* which may be a Prakrit rendition of the Latin word 'Romanus'.[193] Many of the Romans at Karle paid for pillars in the *caitya* relic chamber and the inscriptions reveal that a community of *Yavana*s were living at a nearby trading settlement called Dhenukakata.[194] Among this group was a particularly prosperous Roman devotee referred to as *Indragnidatta*. Sometime after AD 110 he donated substantial funds to the Buddhist community and paid for an entirely new hall of worship to be established at the monastery.[195]

It is considered unusual that the occupations of these *Yavana*s are rarely mentioned in the votive inscriptions. This was possibly because the Indian communities understood that the *Yavana*s in this region were predominantly dealers and merchants engaged in distance trade.[196] A number of Roman portrait busts from the Empire show prominent individuals with the composure of philosophers and their hair styled in the manner of Buddhist holy men.[197] These images could depict wealthy Roman businessmen who had adopted Buddhist beliefs in India before returning to live in the Empire where they continued to practice their Eastern faith.

THE CHERA CHIEFDOM

Roman ships travelling to ports in northwest India could continue their voyages south to reach the distant Tamil territories.[198] Pliny suggested that a voyage along this western coast of India could take up to 40 days and nights, but the ships that visited Barygaza and Kalliena probably spent longer travelling the 2,000 kilometre stretch of coast from the Indus to the Tamil lands.[199] Many Roman ships also sailed directly from the Gulf of Aden to southern India, thereby avoiding the shipping hazards and regional conflicts that afflicted the northern coasts.

When the Romans first reached this distant region three rival Tamil dynasties were ruling large swathes of territory in southern India. The Cheras controlled a large part of the Malabar Coast, while to their south the Pandyas ruled the peninsula down as far as Cape Comorin. Beyond these territories were the Cholas who controlled a large stretch of the eastern peninsula including the Coromandel seaboard. These Tamil chiefdoms were engaged in a continual struggle for supremacy over contested lands and resources.

The Tamil population had distinct traditions and customs that were very different from the kingdoms in the rest of India. Early Tamil society was tribal, with powerful regional chieftains ruling over trade ports. Most of the ports had begun as large fishing villages where territorial produce could be collected and exchanged. Heroic Tamil poetry describes episodes in this remote past and reveal how these settlements became more urbanized and commercial as a response to developing trade contacts.

The *Periplus* describes the voyage south from the Western Deccan to the Tamil lands. The first Tamil trade stations reached on this route were Naura and Tyndis. These sites began as busy fishing villages with some trade, but as commerce developed, pirates began to operate in the region.[200] These sea raiders became a serious threat to Roman shipping and as a consequence Roman merchants began to head directly for the more southerly Tamil ports of Muziris and Nelcynda.[201]

Many Roman ships making the direct voyage to the Tamil lands avoided the pirate coasts by making a landfall somewhere close to Muziris. The ancient town was situated on the Periyar River about three kilometres inland. In the final stages of these ocean crossings, Roman lookouts anxiously watched for signs that their ship was nearing the Malabar Coast. The *Periplus* reports:

> Vessels coming in from the open ocean get an indication that they are approaching land from the eels that emerge from the depths of the sea to meet them. These eels are black in colour but they are short with dragon-shaped heads and blood-red eyes.[202]

The *Periplus* reveals how Muziris became the main trade port for the Chera chiefdom. The author explains that this large settlement owed its prosperity to foreign commerce, including shipping arriving from northern India and the Roman Empire.[203] Black pepper from the Tamil hills was brought to the port by local producers and stacked high in warehouses to await the arrival of Roman merchants. As the shallows at Muziris prevented deep-hulled vessels from sailing upriver to the port, Roman freighters were forced to shelter at the edge of the lagoon while their cargoes were transferred upstream on smaller craft.[204]

The earliest Tamil poetry recalls Roman trade activity at ancient Muziris and these passages reveal the importance of gold as an exchange item to acquire black pepper. The *Akananuru* refers to:

> Rich Muziris, the place where the large and well-crafted ships of the *Yavanas* come with gold and leave carrying pepper.[205]

It seems the Tamil elites regarded their contacts with the Roman traders as a form of gift exchange rather than straightforward commercial dealings. The *Purananuru* therefore describes Muziris:

> They are bringing ashore in small boats the "gifts" of gold brought by the large ships and crowding the port in the turmoil created when sacks of pepper are piled up high in the surrounding buildings. Here [the Chera prince] Kuttuvan presents to visitors, the rare products of the mountains and the seas.[206]

In this era, most Roman ships did not sail further than the Mannar Gulf which separates India from Sri Lanka. Consequently, the western Tamil ports became significant as the furthest destinations on Roman trade voyages into the distant East. Hundreds of Roman subjects must have spent months in this region awaiting favourable conditions for return sailings to the Empire. This could explain why the *Peutinger Map* records the existence of an Augustan Temple at ancient Muziris.[207] Greeks and Romans were obligated to perform certain religious observances before major sea voyages and these rituals could have been conducted at this temple.[208]

Visiting people from the Roman Empire brought Christianity to India during this early period of contact. Eusebius describes how a Christian theologian named Pantaenus travelled to India sometime before his death in AD 200. Pantaenus was surprised to find that a form of Christianity was already being practiced in India. Eusebius reports:

> It is said that Pantaenus visited the Indians and that he found that among them there were people who already knew about Christ through the Gospel of Matthew. Tradition suggested that the apostle named Bartholomew had preached to these Indians and that he had left them the writings of Matthew in Hebrew letters, which they still preserved.[209]

This report is credible because ancient evidence suggests significant and prolonged Roman involvement in ancient India. As mentioned before, there is a tradition that the disciple Thomas travelled to India during the first century AD.

It seems that some Roman merchants remained at Tamil settlements throughout the year to make arrangements on behalf of colleagues who arrived seasonally on the trade ships. These agents conducted trade dealings with local inhabitants and maintained facilities like the Augustan Temple for visiting Roman personnel. The *Periplus* records that special consignments of grain were sent to places like Muziris and scholars suggest that these deliveries were intended for resident Romans who needed something to supplement the local diet of rice.[210]

When Pliny wrote about Eastern trade, Muziris was no longer a favoured location in Roman trade dealings with the Tamils. Pliny describes how pirates were encroaching on the port and the awkward loading operations were causing difficulties. He writes:

> Muziris is not a desirable port of call on account of the neighbouring pirates. It is not especially rich in merchandise and furthermore the offloading facilities for shipping are distant and cargoes have to be brought in and carried out on smaller boats.[211]

Muziris faced even greater problems in this era when the Pandyan elite directed their hostilities towards this rival trade port. An episode in the Tamil poetry records how a Pandyan prince succeeded in sacking Muziris. The *Akananuru* recalls how:

> It is suffering like that experienced by the warriors who were mortally wounded and slain by the war elephants. Suffering that was seen when the Pandyan prince came to besiege the port of Muziris on his flag-bearing chariot with decorated horses.[212]

In another passage the same Pandyan prince appears triumphant on a battle elephant after sacking the port. The *Akananuru* recalls:

> Riding on his great and superior war elephant the Pandyan prince has conquered in battle. He has seized the sacred images after winning the difficult battle for rich Muziris.[213]

This description of the Pandyan attack appears just before the mention of Roman ships arriving at the port. Scholars have therefore suggested that the prince sacked Muziris so that the Romans would have to trade with the Pandyan territories instead.[214] This episode is impossible to date, but the attack seems to have succeeded in diverting Roman trade wealth away from the Chera chiefdom. The Tamil sources offer no information regarding the fate of the Roman Temple at Muziris, or what kind of 'sacred images' the Pandyan prince removed from the port.

TRADE WITH THE TAMIL PORTS

The trade port of Nelcynda was only about 90 kilometres south of Muziris, but it was ruled by the rival Pandyan chiefdom. Roman ships could easily visit both these Malabar ports on a single trade voyage to the Tamil lands. Consequently, the *Periplus* decided to offer a joint account of Roman trade dealings with this region.[215]

In this era, Tamil society lacked the type of prosperous, large-scale urban markets that could sustain substantial craft and trade communities. As a consequence, many local resources were concentrated in the hands of tribal elites who acquired and distributed commodities according to kin-based redistribution networks. These leaders tended to interpret foreign trade as 'gift exchange' and Roman merchants had to resort to bullion payments in their dealings.

The list of Roman exports to the Tamil lands begins with the phrase, 'there is a market here mainly for a great amount of our money'.[216] As the Tamil poets speak of Roman traders bringing gold, it is likely that this exported cash contained large amounts of imperial aurei. In this era the Tamils had no commonplace currency and they began referring to these Roman coins as *cirupuram*, using a word that denotes the nape of the neck. This is likely to be a reference to the image of the Roman Emperor which was usually presented as a profile bust.[217] As well as bullion, Roman traders also offered the Tamils peridot gemstones and prized Mediterranean corals. Further specialist trade goods included mineral powders such as grey antimony sulphide, red realgar and yellow orpiment.

Roman merchants provided the Tamils with fabrics, including multi-coloured textiles and plain clothing. There was also a demand in the Tamil lands for large quantities of cheap raw materials including glass, copper, tin and lead.[218] Pliny indicates the scale of this traffic when he repeats the Roman view that, 'India has no copper or lead, so the country procures these metals in exchange for precious stones and pearls.'[219]

Wine appears last in the list of Roman goods offered to the Tamil regions, but it may have been traded in significant quantities.[220] The best indication of Roman wine exports to India comes from excavations carried out at the ancient Tamil port of Arikamedu. This site is on the east coast of India, but the *Periplus* suggests it received regular supplies of Roman goods from the Malabar ports. Almost all the amphorae fragments found at Arikamedu belonged to common Mediterranean table wines similar to the types enjoyed by Roman soldiers at military camps in Gaul.[221] These wines were only remarkable for having relatively high salt contents and this would explain why they were also favoured for Eastern export. The salt ingredient would have acted as a preservative and helped to ensure that the wine did not spoil on the long voyage to India.[222]

Over half of the 400 amphorae sherds found at Arikamedu came from Italian wine vessels and the significance of Italy in Eastern trade is confirmed by other accounts. When the Roman satirist Persius mentions how Italian goods were being sent to India to acquire peppercorns, he alludes to wine exports. He writes:

> Here is someone who barters beneath the rising sun. He hands over the produce of Italy for wrinkled pepper and pale cumin seed.[223]

The earliest Tamil references to the Romans also mention their exotic foreign wines. For instance, the *Purananuru* imagines some Tamil heroes relaxing in luxurious surroundings:

> They live each day with pleasure and increasing joy. The women with shining bangles pour into their beautiful decorated gold cups, the sweet cool wine brought by the superb *Yavana* ships.[224]

Wines that were cheap and mundane in the Roman Empire became costly luxuries in India that were worthy of the Tamil elite.

Many of Coan-style sherds found at Arikamedu had volcanic 'black-sand' particles in their ceramic composition. This indicates that these containers were being made at pottery kilns near Pompeii. The eruption of Vesuvius in AD 79 caused immense damage to the vineyards in southern Campania and the nearby pottery kilns ceased their mass production of amphorae.[225] This dealt a serious blow to Roman merchants trading in Italian wines. They were probably forced to increase their export of other goods to compensate for the reduction in wine stocks.

Tamil references to sacks of black pepper accumulating at Muziris indicate the significance of this spice to Roman trade. In the *Periplus*, pepper heads the list of goods offered at the Tamil ports and the cargo holds of the returning Roman ships were crammed full with this spice.[226] Indian communities were astonished by the insatiable Roman demand for pepper and they even began referring to the spice as *Yavanapriya* meaning 'passion of the Yavanas'.[227]

Pearls of 'fine quality' appear second on the list of Tamil exports to the Roman world. This confirms Pliny's suggestion that pearls and precious stones were a significant exchange item in the trade. As the Pandyan chiefdom controlled large pearl fisheries on the Mannar Gulf, a considerable quantity of pearls was offered for exchange at Nelcynda.[228] The *Periplus* records that the Tamils also supplied Roman merchants with 'all kinds of transparent gems' as well as diamonds and sapphires.[229] There were beryl mines in the inland Coimbatore district and these aquamarine gemstones were gathered in large amounts by the Tamils to supply Roman traders.[230] Other Tamil products included elephant ivory and supplies of fine hawksbill turtle-shell that fishermen and traders acquired from the Lakshadweep Islands lying off the Malabar Coast.[231]

By the time of the *Periplus*, the Tamils had established extensive trade links with territories on the east coast of India and the Bay of Bengal. As a consequence, they were able to supply Roman merchants visiting the Malabar ports with Chinese silks received from the Ganges and large amounts of a cinnamon type-leaf called 'malabathron'. Tamil traders also visited the eastern ports of India from where vessels sailed across the Bay of Bengal to reach a distant land called 'Chryse'. Through these contacts with Malaysia, or perhaps the Andaman Islands, the Tamils were able to acquire fresh quantities of tortoiseshell to supply increasing Roman demands at the Malabar ports.[232]

THE PANDYAN CHIEFDOM

The Pandyan port of Nelcynda was situated 19 kilometres inland on the Pambiyar River and had significant advantages over its rival Muziris. The Tamil poetry describes how the ancient settlement contained large dwellings protected and encircled by a strong defensive moat.[233] Nelcynda was distant from the pirate coasts and its site on the Pambiyar River could accommodate large Roman freighters. This was important for offloading operations, and access to the river also gave Roman ships a place to dock sheltered from the most violent coastal storms.

The *Periplus* indicates that Roman ships coming up the Pambiyar River were still comparatively light with cargo and therefore able to pass safely upstream to Nelcynda over shallows and sandbanks on the riverbed.[234] However, on the return journey, Roman ships would be heavily laden with cargo and would lie too deep in the water to cross over these same sandbanks. Roman freighters would therefore shelter in the Pambiyar River until the time came to receive their cargo, they would then sail downstream to a small settlement called Bacare at the mouth of the river.[235] Cargo from Nelcynda would be sent down to Becare on small craft to be loaded aboard Roman freighters as they waited near the estuary. These arrangements seem to have been very effective and Pliny calls Nelcynda the 'more serviceable port'. He also describes how Tamil people conveyed the pepper harvests to Nelcynda in canoes made of hollowed-out tree-trunks.[236]

As a Pandyan port, Nelcynda had access to a much greater range and volume of trade resources than Muziris. The Pandyan not only controlled pearl fisheries, but they also dominated the sea lanes that passed between southern India and Sri Lanka. This gave the dynasty greater access to goods moving from eastern India across to the Malabar ports and greater opportunities to traffic in products from Sri Lanka.[237]

In the time of the *Periplus*, the Roman ships that reached Nelcynda would have sailed onwards to reach a final destination in Pandyan territory called 'The Strand'. This was a large sheltered bay near the Palk Straits where the Roman freighters gathered to await the return sailing to Egypt.[238] The journey took Roman vessels south past a settlement called Comar inhabited by Indian holy men, then past the Colchi pearl fisheries that were worked by convict labour.[239] As they waited at the Strand, cotton garments from the inland Pandyan capitol of Uraiyur were brought down to the bay to be loaded onboard ships.

The re-assembled merchant fleet would remain at the Strand until November when the return monsoon winds began to blow across the Indian Ocean. According to Pliny, most ships would delay their departure until December so that the last Roman vessels would leave India before mid-January.[240] These ships would call again at the Tamil ports to pick up any Roman merchants who had decided to remain in these settlements during the autumn months. With their exotic cargoes secured aboard, the Roman freighters were ready to begin the ocean voyage that would return them to the Empire.

The return sailing with the northeast monsoon would have been much calmer than the outbound voyage and as the Romans left the Tamil coasts, they would have seen Indian vessels preparing for their own trade voyages to the distant West. The *Silappatikaram* recalls these ventures, made during the gathering monsoon:

> The broad-rayed sun ascends from the south and white clouds start to form in the early cool season. Now it is time to cross the dark bellowing ocean and the rulers of Tyndis dispatch vessels loaded with eaglewood, silk, sandalwood, spices and all sorts of camphor.[241]

It was a journey of over 5,000 kilometres back to Roman Egypt and on the return sailing the merchant ships fully loaded with valuable Eastern cargoes would sit low in the water. The voyage would take more than two months to complete and the passengers that returned safely would have spent almost nine months of the year away from home in the pursuit of wealth, or adventure.

BEYOND THE STRAITS OF PALK

Roman merchant ships sailing to India in the Augustan era were generally more compact. These smaller craft could carefully navigate the treacherous shoals of the Straits of Palk to reach the eastern coasts of India.[242] However, such were the dangers that by the time of the *Periplus*, these routes were only sailed by specialized Indian craft that had shallow hulls and were highly manoeuvrable in the difficult waters of the Strait. These local ships routinely carried goods between the Indian coasts and Pliny records that they could carry large amounts of cargo.[243]

The *Periplus* explains how these trade operations were organized. Indian ships picked up Roman goods at the Malabar markets and brought these cargoes through the Straits of Palk to the Coromandel ports. Once there the goods would be exchanged with local traders and forwarded to further territories across the Bay of Bengal. Some of this cargo would be taken on ocean-going catamarans that travelled as far as the Ganges and Malaysia.[244] The *Periplus* explains:

> There is a market on the eastern coast for all the [Roman] trade goods sent to the Malabar seaboard. Generally speaking, these Eastern ports all year round receive the [Roman] cash that has come to the Malabar Coast from Egypt, as well as most kinds of goods produced in the Malabar districts.[245]

In this era, goods from Sri Lanka were readily available in the Tamil markets.[246] These Sinhalese products included large amounts of ivory, tortoiseshell, pearls, transparent gems and cotton garments.[247] There was therefore little need for the Romans to deal directly with the Sinhalese and, as Roman merchants did not visit the island, they knew very little about the geography of this enigmatic land.

The *Periplus* indicates that Roman merchants were being seriously misled about the size and position of Sri Lanka, perhaps by Tamil dealers anxious to preserve their position as middlemen. The author of the *Periplus* had heard that the island was oriented east–west and was so large that it almost reached the shores of East Africa.[248] There were also popular reports that only the northern parts of this Sinhalese landmass were 'civilized'.[249] As a result, no Roman ships were prepared to attempt a sailing around the Sinhalese shores to reach markets on the east coast of India.

A breakthrough in Roman contacts with the Sinhalese came soon after the *Periplus* was written. Pliny describes how a Roman freedman was blown off course on an Arabian trade voyage and, after a 15 day ocean crossing, made landfall in Sri Lanka.[250] The contact revealed that Sri Lanka had a civilized government and the island landmass could be circumnavigated in ambitious new trade voyages. The information brought back to the Empire therefore suggested impressive new trading possibilities with the Sinhalese.

By the time Ptolemy compiled his geography, Roman merchants were visiting two emporia on the Sinhalese coast to acquire stocks of rice, honey, ginger, beryls and amethysts.[251] Roman ships were also sailing around the island to reach eastern India and sailors had a range of Greek nicknames to describe the distinctive landmarks seen on the Sinhalese shores.[252] Ptolemy also had information on numerous tiny islands in the seas around Sri Lanka and this suggests that Roman ships had begun making ocean crossings from the Gulf of Aden directly to the Sinhalese coast.[253]

The *Periplus* mentions just over 20 trade sites in India, but when Ptolemy compiled his geography, some 60 emporia were operating between Barygaza and the Ganges delta.[254] By this era the small pearl fishing settlement of Colchi had developed into a major emporium replacing Nelcynda as the main Pandyan trade port for Roman contacts. Ptolemy also reveals that the nearby religious settlement at Comar had become a 'metropolis' and the Tamil literature vividly describes this city as a busy market centre that received both regional produce and goods from the Ganges.[255]

Pliny knew that the Pandyan chiefs ruled their territory from a distant inland capitol called Madura and Tamil literature describes this city as a large urban complex of palaces, temples, poetry academies and lofty mansions.[256] The city also had assembly points for market bazaars and was surrounded by protective ramparts with towers, fortified gates and a deep moat.[257] Most Roman merchants would have dealt with Indian traders at the coastal ports rather than travel inland to places like Madura. As Dio Chrysostom comments, 'Those who go to India travel there in pursuit of trade and they mingle mostly with the people of the coast'.[258]

Each year thousands of Roman mercenaries would have arrived in India as professional guards and these armed men would have accompanied Roman merchants onshore to ensure that no harm came to their employers.[259] Some of these mercenaries found employment with the Pandyan princes and travelled inland to Madura in the hope of making their fortune. There could not have been many of these Roman guards in Pandyan service, but they would have fought in battle for their Tamil employers. As reward for their services they would have received valuable gifts such as pearls, gold and precious stones. The Pandyan princes used their Roman mercenaries mainly as high-profile soldiers and elite bodyguards.[260] Teams of these mercenaries found employment guarding the city gates at Madura as the *Silappatikaram* recounts:

> He entered Madura without alarming the suspicions of the *Yavanas* – the excellent guards with murderous swords who stand at the gate of the city's defences.[261]

Though these Roman mercenaries were distant foreigners, the Tamil rulers trusted them and respected their professional skills. A further account describes a Pandyan prince in his army camp on the eve of battle. He is surrounded by a Roman bodyguard wearing 'foreign' clothing that seemed strange to Tamil observers. The *Mullaippāttu* recalls that the Roman guards were large men dressed in tunics:

> The inner tent has double walls of canvas held firmly by iron chains. It is guarded by powerful *Yavanas* whose stern looks strike terror into every beholder and whose long and loose clothes are fastened at the waist by means of belts.[262]

Tamil literature suggests that the *Yavanas* constructed special machines to help protect the gates of fortified cities. These included mechanical devises that launched spears to cause horrendous injuries to the enemy. This could be a weapon such as the *scorpio* 'dart thrower' used by the Roman legions.[263]

THE CHOLA CHIEFDOM

The Chola dynasty controlled the southeast edge of India beyond the Straits of Palk and their territories included a series of important commercial ports on the Coromandel Coast. The *Periplus* identified three major trade stations in this region listing Puhar, Poduke, and Sopatma. These are described as the 'home ports' for local craft that brought goods from the Malabar settlements to markets on the eastern coasts of India. These ports were also important because they were used by larger Indian vessels that crossed the Bay of Bengal to trade with the Ganges and Malaysia.[264]

Early Tamil literature offers a vivid account of the prosperous city that developed at ancient Puhar. It had a large port complex with quays, storehouses, merchant quarters and customs posts that bore the tiger emblem of the Chola chiefdom.[265] The harbour had lighthouse buildings and an extensive residential area that extended along coastal beaches towards the quarters of local fishermen.[266] Inland, behind the port, was an inner city with prosperous houses, temples, gardens and public meeting places.[267] Busy markets met in the open space between these two parts of the ancient city and business continued into the evening. At night a separate market was convened where girl vendors sold rice cakes and goldsmiths offered their wares lit by lamps suspended from the trade stalls.[268]

Tamil poetry describes the large residences of Roman merchants in the inner district of Puhar. The *Silappatikaram* recalls:

> The sun shines over the open terraces and the warehouses near the harbour. It shines over the turrets that have wide windows like the eyes of a deer. In different places at Puhar the gaze of the observer is attracted by the residences of the *Yavanas*, whose prosperity is without limits. At the harbour there are sailors from distant lands, but in all appearance they live as one community.[269]

Tamil tradition recalls that Puhar was placed under a curse when a Chola prince ignored an important religious festival. Remains have been found on the seabed near the site of the ancient city and this confirms that some great deluge or tidal flood must have engulfed the Tamil port. Even today violent storms along this coast wash up ceramics and other ancient remnants from the sunken city.[270]

North of Puhar was the Tamil trade port of Poduke, which has been identified with the famous archaeological site of Arikamedu. Excavations at the site have revealed further information about the types of Roman goods that were reaching Tamil India. The more unusual finds include sherds from olive oil containers and garum amphorae that would have held popular Roman fish sauces.[271] The early Tamil poetry mentions attractive '*Yavana* lamps' and this could be a reference to olive oil being used as a fuel source that burnt brightly without odour.[272] Fragments of *terra sigillata* were also discovered at Arikamedu and this tableware can be dated on stylistic grounds to the reign of Tiberius.[273] Other finds included pieces of Roman glassware belonging to bulbous *unguentaria* flasks that may have held ink or perfumed oils.[274] These goods are not mentioned in the *Periplus* and might reflect earlier market demands, or perhaps indicate occasional trade commodities.

The Indian pottery sherds found at Arikamedu were inscribed with Tamil-Brahmi script. One fragment bore the name 'Kanan' which also appears on pottery from the Egyptian port of Myos Hormos.[275] Another fragment indicates the involvement of the Tamil elite in this traffic as it bears the phrase *Ko[r]ra Puman*, meaning 'Korra[n] the Chieftain'.[276] Despite much speculation there is currently no conclusive evidence that Roman subjects ever resided at ancient Poduke. The Roman finds so-far discovered at Arikamedu can be best explained as the remains of a Tamil commerce involving Roman goods.

THE FAR EAST

The author of the *Periplus* described the eastern territories of the Deccan Plateau in very vague terms. Although he knew that these regions produced great quantities of cotton garments, he could not name the trade ports where these goods could be acquired. North of these regions there was said to be a land that was home to strange elephants and 'numerous barbaric populations'. These included a race of 'wild men with flattened noses' and a 'horse-faced cannibal people'.[277] Beyond these territories was the Ganges and an important market town that offered malabathrum, spikenard, pearls and the finest muslins to visiting Indian merchants.[278]

The *Periplus* also refers to Indian trade contacts with a distant 'Golden' land called 'Chryse' in Greek. The work states:

> And just across from the Ganges River there is an island in the ocean. It is the last part of the inhabited world in the East and it lies under the rising sun. It is called 'Chryse' and it has the best tortoise-shell of all the places in the Indian Ocean.[279]

This land in the ocean could be part of the Malay Peninsula or even the Adaman Islands. The *Periplus* believed that beyond this location the vast Asian landmass curved north and that somewhere on this outer fringe was China.[280] No Roman ships had ventured this far east and the *Periplus* concluded:

> What lies beyond this region is unclear. Perhaps this is because of extreme storms, bitter cold and difficult terrain. But perhaps these regions have not been explored because some divine power of the gods has prevented it.[281]

Ptolemy used data taken from an advanced trade *Periplus* that was written by a merchant named Alexandros. These details indicate how Roman trade contacts developed after Greco-Roman freighters began sailing around Sri Lanka.[282] Alexandros described Roman trade voyages into the Bay of Bengal as far as the Malay Peninsula where three new trade emporia had opened up on the northeast coast of India. Sophisticated market centres now existed in regions that the *Periplus* had warned were the abode of cannibals.[283] Four new cities had also appeared near the Ganges and the regional market had become a capital. Ptolemy reveals that this information came from later trade accounts when he records, 'in these regions diamonds are found'.[284]

Beyond the Ganges lay Burma, known to the Romans as *India Trans Gangem*, and its coast offered further new market opportunities. When Ptolemy compiled his geography, Roman ships had begun to make trade voyages directly across the Bay of Bengal from eastern India to the Burmese coast.[285] Indian mariners had developed these crossings and the ancient sources suggests that the main commodities they sought on these distant ventures were gold, diamonds, sandalwood, cinnamon and cassia.[286]

Ptolemy mentions at least four cities and two emporia along the Burmese coast. Close to the Malay Peninsula were two further trade ports situated near the Irrawaddy River, which extended far inland into Southeast Asia.[287] Roman merchants must have begun supplying slaves to the courts of the Burmese kings in their dealings with these regions. In AD 121, a Burmese ruler sent an embassy to the Chinese Emperor that contained skilled court entertainers who identified themselves as Roman subjects.[288] Chinese authorities set about questioning these intriguing foreigners to determine their origins. From this information the Han deduced that the Romans had expanded their commercial interests as far as Burma.[289]

In this era, the Malay Peninsula formed a vast geographical barrier confining Roman trade activities to the Indian Ocean. Ptolemy knew the approximate shape of the peninsula, but he had no effective information on the island of Sumatra which lies alongside its southwest coast.[290] This suggests that Roman ships had not sailed east around the headland of the peninsula to reach the Gulf of Thailand.[291]

The ancient Malaysian city of Tamala would have been one of the furthest locations reached by the Roman merchants who sailed the Bay of Bengal. Alexandros knew that Indian traders reaching this city left their ships and began an inland journey across the Kra Isthmus.[292] On the other side of this narrow peninsula lay the Gulf of Thailand and Indian travellers followed the jungle tracks across to this coast. Here they had established trade stations where other ships were prepared and waiting to take them on sailings further into the Far East.[293]

Alexandros described these early Indian trade ventures into the Gulf of Thailand. Leaving the eastern coast of Malaysia, ships sailed along the outer coasts of Thailand and Cambodia. There were two developing metropolises in this region and near the southern tip of Vietnam was a city called Zabai. The Roman traders had been informed that China lay somewhere on the outer limits of the 'Great Bay' formed by these vast coasts.[294]

The route that had been explained to Alexandros did not head north from Vietnam to reach Chinese territory. Instead, Indian ships set out into the open sea bearing southeast to reach a mysterious outpost called Cattigara. Ptolemy's explanation of this route suggests that the Indian ships were sailing to Borneo:

> Alexandros wrote that [beyond the Golden Peninsula] the land curves south and those who sail along it reach the city of Zabai in twenty days. After sailing from Zabai in the

> direction of the south wind, and a little to the left for a number of days, they reach Cattigara.[295]

Alexandros and his informants did not realize that this vast coast was only the outer edge of an enormous unexplored island. Ptolemy therefore imagined that the coast of Borneo was part of the Asian landmass as it curved southward from China to join with east Africa and encircle the entire Indian Ocean.[296]

The Chinese sources suggest that Roman merchants sought contact with Vietnam in order to acquire further supplies of rhinoceros horn, tortoise shell, pearls, ivory and fragrant woods.[297] Only a few decades after Ptolemy completed his geography, Roman ships began to explore beyond the Malay Peninsula.[298] Finally, the Han histories record that Roman subjects reached Chinese territory in AD 166. These exotic foreigners were immediately brought before the Emperor Huan to give an account of themselves and explain their purpose in the Far East. This encounter ought to have marked the beginning of a new international commerce not only in merchandise, but also in ideas and inventions. Yet this was the harbinger of something much more ominous.

THE ANTONINE PLAGUE

A new pandemic called the 'Antonine Plague' devastated the population of the Roman Empire in the period between AD 165 and AD 180. Current estimates suggest that during its epidemic phase, the disease may have killed between 10 per cent and 14 per cent of the entire Roman population.[299] The virus was a highly infectious ancestral form of either smallpox or measles that spread rapidly through the expanding trade networks that connected the ancient world.[300] This pandemic must have caused an immediate decline in Eastern trade and in the long term irreparably damaged the commercial prosperity of the Roman Empire.

The outbreak of various diseases was relatively frequent in antiquity, but the Antonine pandemic was exceptional in its virulence. The infection seems to have started somewhere deep in Central Asia, perhaps when traders or nomadic horsemen came into contact with previously isolated population groups who were carriers of this disease. Distance commerce then provided the chain of infection that brought the disease to the frontier regions of the Chinese and Roman Empires.[301]

The Roman communities most heavily affected by the pandemic were those crucial to the operation of the imperial system. The strongest vectors in the propagation of the disease were the movement of army personnel and the maritime trade connections that sustained Roman prosperity. Individuals, seemingly in good health at embarkation, would fall sick en route and in the confines of a ship quickly communicate the virulent infection to other passengers.[302]

The infection is first attested amongst Roman forces campaigning in Mesopotamia in AD 165. According to classical sources the disease had reached Rome by AD 166 and Jerome records that in AD 168 the illness was devastating communities in the provinces as well as the capital.[303] Academics estimate that the large urban communities associated with Mediterranean commerce could have lost a quarter to a third of their populations in the initial outbreaks. Crowded market environments would create ideal conditions for a continual chain of infection and cities must have been subject to renewed outbreaks as the virus mutated.[304] Viral outbreaks would have been more severe in cities that were densely populated and had hot climates, for instance Alexandria and Antioch.[305] Consequently the retail markets that funded Eastern commerce must have been badly affected.[306] Evidence from Egypt also suggests that people were temporarily fleeing the affected areas to escape possible infection. The movement of refugees from smitten urban populations would have further helped the spread of this horrendous pandemic. Others who had wealth or a suitable level of independence simply withdrew from public life to live in self-imposed isolation.[307]

The Romans who reached China in AD 166 were released to return home after their audience with the Han Emperor. Although the Chinese waited for further contacts, the fleets of Roman ships did not come. From the Antonine period onwards there are far fewer ancient references to Roman involvement in Eastern trade. The coin horde evidence from India suggests that large quantities of Roman coins stopped reaching the distant East in this era. The archaeological evidence from Egypt also suggests a sharp decline in activity at the Red Sea ports.[308] Rome had lost its vibrant Eastern commerce at the very moment of its greatest potential. The evidence suggests that as the Empire descended into financial crisis and civil war, Rome never regained its former prominence in Eastern trade.[309]

3

Rome and the Arabian Trade Routes

In ancient times the African and Arabian coasts around the Gulf of Aden produced valuable aromatics including frankincense and myrrh. Dried lumps of frankincense resin were burnt slowly on hot coals to release a pure, white smoke with a heady astringent aroma. Myrrh was the more costly substance, and was formed from a darker, oily resin with a bittersweet scent.[1] Both substances were so highly prized in the ancient world that they were afforded a value similar to precious metals and gemstones.

Frankincense and myrrh were valued in Greek and Persian society as offerings to the gods, but they were also important components in medical treatments and fragrant perfumes. Encouraged by market demand, the peoples of the Arabian Peninsula developed a thriving commerce that brought great quantities of these aromatic goods north into the Greek Mediterranean and the Parthian Realm. When Augustus overthrew the Ptolemaic regime, the same commercial boom that dramatically increased Roman trade with India also escalated Roman contact with the markets around the Aden Gulf. These developments had a significant impact on Red Sea trade and a series of small Arabian kingdoms became increasingly prosperous through their involvement in this commerce.

It was a feature of the Arabian commerce that goods were brought along interconnected overland and maritime trade networks. The ancient sources indicate a complex interrelated system of commercial routes that defy many modern attempts to generalise about distance trade in antiquity. These trade routes started from the same regions and often led to similar destinations. Small dhow-like vessels sailed from the Yemen north through the Red Sea or Persian Gulf, carrying aromatics destined for the large urban markets of the Mediterranian and Mesopotamia. At the same time, caravans of camels trudged north through the great desert expanse of inner Arabia to converge on these same regions. These trade routes were channelled through the great commercial hub of Petra and desert peoples like the Nabateans grew rich by facilitating this traffic.

THE DISTANT PAST

The ancient evidence for incense trade stretches far back into the distant past and references to the use these aromatics in religious ceremonies are mentioned in the Egyptian *Book of the Dead* and early biblical texts.[2] By about 600 BC, Greek society was familiar with these substances and the female poet Sappho mentions both frankincense and myrrh in her works. In around 500 BC the classical philosopher and mathematician Pythagoras recommended that Greek worshippers burn frankincense as a more attractive alternative to animal sacrifice.[3] The widespread appeal of these substances is suggested by Herodotus, who writes that wealthy Babylonians fumigated themselves with incense before making love and Scythian women used frankincense in an aromatic paste applied to their skin as a beauty treatment.[4]

Herodotus indicates that Gaza, on the Mediterranean coast of ancient Palestine, was a major centre for this early incense traffic. Every year the Arabs at Gaza offered 1,000 Babylonian talents of frankincense as tribute to the Persian king Darius.[5] By the fifth century BC, large quantities of incense were being consumed in the Persian Empire and vast heaps of frankincense burned at Babylon on the golden altar in the temple of Bel.[6] Gaza still dominated this commerce in 332 BC when Alexander the Great captured the city and sent his old tutor Leonidas 500 talents of frankincense and 100 talents of myrrh.[7] When Alexander returned to Babylon from his Indian campaign, he constructed new harbours and dockyards in Persia.[8] These were to house a large fleet that would capture eastern Arabia, but his ambitions were cut short by his early death in 323 BC. The Seleucid dynasty that assumed power in Persia had military interests in the Gulf, but they could not accomplish the Greek conquest of Arabia.[9]

THE NABATEANS

An Arabian people called the Nabateans occupied territories between the Red Sea and the Mediterranean coast. This location gave them an important position as intermediaries in the incense trade and made their developing kingdom extremely wealthy.

Diodorus Siculus suggests that the Nabateans were supplying the eastern Mediterranean with incense as early as the fourth century BC. He reports:

> By custom the Nabateans bring down to the Mediterranean Sea their frankincense and myrrh along with the most valuable kinds of spices. They procure these goods from those who convey them from southern Arabia.[10]

The intermediaries who supplied the Nabateans were a people called the Minaeans who occupied territories north of the Yemen.[11] The scale of this trade is indicated by an event in 312 BC, when a former general of Alexander the Great, named Antigonus, sent an army against the Nabateans. The Greek forces ambushed the Nabateans at their tribal gathering and plundered great quantities of incense and silver bullion.[12]

The Arabian trade routes through the Red Sea and Persian Gulf were travelled by local dhow-like craft. These small ships were very different to the large-hulled Greco-Roman freighters that sailed the Mediterranean. Arab shipbuilders used a sewn-plank technique to construct compact and robust craft that were lightweight, but highly manoeuvrable in treacherous waters.[13] The earliest description of these vessels is given by a Greek historian named Procopius who writes:

> All the local craft that operate in the Indian Ocean are not constructed in the same manner as our ships. They are not smeared with pitch or any other substance. Also, their planks are not fastened together by iron nails, but they are bound together with a kind of cording.[14]

Strabo reports that Arab dhows took seventy days to carry merchandise from southern Arabia to a major Nabatean port called Aila near the head of the Red Sea Gulf.[15] From there it was only a short journey overland by caravan to Gaza and the Mediterranean coast.[16] Under the Ptolemies, Greek-Egyptians began to expand their trade operations into the Red Sea. The Nabateans retaliated by using their dhows to attack Greek shipping.[17] These conflicts culminated when the Ptolemies sent a squadron of *quadrireme* warships to destroy the dhow raiders and sack Nabatean settlements on the coast.[18]

These old rivalries encouraged the Nabateans to assist Octavian in his conflict against Cleopatra. By the Augustan era, Nabatea was a client kingdom of the Roman Empire and the inland city of Petra had developed into an impressive regional capital enriched by the prosperity of trade. The inhabitants of this city carved their famous monumental buildings from the red rock ravines that flanked their growing metropolis.[19] Strabo offers the following vivid account:

> The metropolis of the Nabataeans is Petra which lies on a smooth and level site fortified all round by high rockfaces. The outside parts of the site are precipitous and sheer, but the inside parts have springs in abundance which are used for domestic purposes and for watering public gardens. Outside the circuit of the rock most of the surrounding territory is desert.[20]

Strabo's friend Athenodorus stayed in Petra and reported that there were many foreigners living in the city including Roman citizens, who were probably involved in the incense trade. Strabo writes:

> A philosopher and companion of mine named Athenodorus spent some time in the city of Petra and he used to talk in admiration about their government. He said that there were a large number of Romans and many other foreigners living there.[21]

Strabo also indicates the merchandise that Roman dealers offered at Petra in order to acquire incoming stocks of incense. He writes that the Nabateans were anxious to receive gold, silver, brass, iron, purple cloth, fragrant storax potions and perfumed crocus flowers. The Nabateans also had an interest in decorative pieces created by Roman artisans, including embossed articles, classical paintings, and sculpted artworks.[22]

By the Roman era, a more southerly Red Sea station named Leuke Kome had become the main Nabatean port. It received regular cargoes from southern Arabia and these goods were taken by caravan through Petra to the Mediterranean coast.[23] The harbour at Leuke Kome was substantial and in 26 BC the port was able to accommodate a fleet of up to 130 battle transport vessels which landed close to 10,000 men with supplies and equipment for the Roman invasion of

Arabia.[24] Strabo also stressed the scale of the caravan trade connecting the port to Petra.[25] He writes:

> From Leuce Kome camel traders travel safely and easily on the route to and from Petra, and they move in such numbers of men and camels that they resemble an army.[26]

The *Periplus* confirms that Leuke Kome remained a prominent commercial centre for Arabian trade. The author reports:

> There is a harbour with a fort called Leuce Kome ("The White Village"). From here there is a way inland leading to Petra and to Malichus the Nabatean king. This harbour also functions as a trade port for small craft that arrive loaded with freight from southern Arabia.[27]

Even though Nabatea was a client kingdom of the Empire, the Romans placed their own customs officer at Leuce Kome and supported him with a detachment of soldiers.[28] This officer ensured that the traders who imported their Eastern goods through Nabatea were subject to the same high import tax that was imposed on merchants operating through Egypt. The *Periplus* explains:

> As a security, a customs officer has been dispatched to the port to deal with an import duty of one-fourth on the incoming merchandise. There is also a centurion with a detachment of soldiers.[29]

If this 'security' had not been in place, a large volume of taxable traffic would have shifted from Egypt to the Nabatean kingdom as merchants would have selected the less expensive route. It was logistically practical for Romans to tax the import traffic at Leuce Kome before the goods were dispersed throughout the overland trade routes of the Nabatean kingdom.

Gaza was still an important terminal point for the caravan trade in the Roman era as the city was ideally placed midpoint between Alexandria and Jerusalem.[30] Strabo describes how Eastern goods were also being conveyed by caravan to Mediterranean markets at Rhinocoloura near the Egyptian frontier. He writes:

> Loads of aromatics are conveyed from Leuce Kome to Petra. From Petra they are sent to Rhinocoloura, which is in Phoenicia near Egypt, and from there they are sent to other peoples.[31]

Arab traders also travelled north from Petra to the Decapolis region of Roman Syria on an inland route past the Nabatean city of Bostra. This road connected with a number of regional trade routes that crossed Judaea and took merchants from southern Arabia as far as Damascus.[32] Roman control over these outlying regions had subdued banditry on the Trachonitis Plain between Damascus and the Hauran thus improving the situation for distance trade. Strabo reports:

> The barbarians have been robbing the merchants from Arabia Felix (the Yemen). This is now happening less often because the band of robbers under Zenodorus has been broken up through the good government established by the Romans and through the security maintained by the Roman soldiers that are kept in Syria.[33]

Trade routes also led from Petra across the Arabian Desert to the kingdom of Mesene at the head of the Persian Gulf.[34] Pliny reports:

> There is a city on the banks of the Tigris called Phorath which is subject to the king of Charax. People go there by road from Petra and then they follow the current on a river sailing south to Charax.[35]

These caravan routes brought Eastern goods from Parthia across the desert to the Mediterranean, or supplied Persian markets with aromatics imported through the Red Sea.

THE AXUMITE KINGDOM

The Roman take-over of Egypt greatly increased Mediterranean contacts with Arabia and East Africa. Within only a few years of Roman rule, large fleets were sailing along the coasts of Africa further than ever before in search of new market opportunities.[36] By the late Augustan era, Egypt dominated this expanded commerce and Strabo confidently stated, 'At the present time most aromatics are transported via the Nile to Alexandria.'[37]

The *Periplus* indicates that many Roman ships dealing with markets in Ethiopia sailed from Egypt in September.[38] This meant they left port almost two months after those who made their trade voyages to India.[39] Leaving the Red Sea ports, Roman ships sailed south along bleak coasts inhabited by scattered tribal populations. These coastal peoples lived in basic hut-like dwellings and survived as hunters and gatherers.[40] On sailing south, Roman ships would reach a small trade port called Ptolemais Theron, or 'Ptolemais of the Hunts'. This outpost had been a Ptolemaic military base for the transportation of captured African elephants to Egypt. When these military operations were abandoned, the site was inhabited by local peoples and by the time of the *Periplus*, Ptolemais Theron had no functioning harbour and could only accommodate small ships. There is no mention of Roman exports to Ptolemais Theron and the few commodities available in the local market were mostly the product of native hunting activities. This included small tortoise shells and very occasionally, ivory.[41]

Further south along the African coast was an important trade port called Adulis. Adulis was almost a thousand kilometres distant from Berenice and it was under the control of the rising Ethiopian kingdom of Axum. The settlement at Adulis was a substantial village lying close to a deep coastal bay. This was a major centre for regional trade and received goods from Somalia, as well as the Ethiopian heartlands.[42] Pliny writes:

> Adulis is a place founded by Egyptian runaway slaves. It is the principal market for the Troglodyte (Somali people) and also for the people of Ethiopia. It is five days sail from Ptolemais [Theron].[43]

However, the *Periplus* warns that 'Barbaroi' from the surrounding regions often launched raids on Adulis to attack the visiting ships. For this reason, Roman freighters would anchor offshore in a defensive position near a small local island.[44]

The market at Adulus served an Ethiopian city called Koloe which lay three days inland. Five days travel beyond Koloe was the regional capitol of Axum which the *Periplus* describes as a 'metropolis'.[45] Roman merchants visited Ethiopian markets mainly to acquire large amounts of ivory, tortoise shell, and rhinoceros horn.[46] Big game inhabited the upland regions and the *Periplus* reports that these animals were being slaughtered in large numbers for their horns and tusks.[47] Locals also hunted for turtle shell on nearby sandy islands and collected obsidian rocks from the surrounding bays.[48] Pliny lists other Ethiopian exports including hippopotamus hides and African slaves, suggesting developments in eastern commerce.[49]

Roman traders offered the Ethiopian markets large quantities of fabric that had been produced in the Empire. This included articles of clothing manufactured in Egypt, wraps from Arsinoe and coloured cloaks made from printed fabric.[50] Roman merchants also dealt in cheap decorative items, including numerous types of coloured glass stones and small ornamental objects manufactured at Thebes containing multi-coloured, flower-like patterns.[51] Other Roman goods were more functional in character and included raw metals and brass, which the local people used for ornaments and their chiefs cut up to make coins. Copper pans and drinking vessels from the Empire were also supplied to these ports and the *Periplus* notes with interest that many of the pots were being broken up and worn as armlets and anklets by the local women. There was also a market in Adulis for Roman axes, knives and woodworking tools. Iron was exported to Adulis to make into weaponry for hunting expeditions and armaments for the local conflicts.[52]

Roman merchants and Arabian dealers settled at Adulis to conduct their trade business with the Ethiopian kingdom.[53] Consequently, the *Periplus* records that it was advisable to bring a little Roman money to the settlement for transactions with these resident foreigners. Romans living at the port also asked for Laodicean and Italian wines, as well as fresh supplies of olive oil.[54]

It was possible to travel from Egypt to Axum along arduous overland routes. Later sources suggest it took 30 days for an unencumbered traveller to journey from the Roman frontiers down to the Ethiopian capitol.[55] These routes were not used by merchants from the Empire and at the time of the *Periplus* they had only been surveyed by the Roman military. Pliny explains:

> Among his wars Nero was contemplating an expedition against Ethiopia. So, for the purposes of enquiry, Praetorian troops were dispatched by the Emperor under the command of a tribune. Yet, the expedition brought back word that they had met with nothing but deserts on their route through Ethiopia.[56]

The Roman traders who visited the port of Adulis were on good terms with the local

Ethiopian king, Zoskales. Zoskales ruled from the inland capitol of Axum and he was well known to Roman traders as a shrewd bargainer. But he had an affinity for Hellenic culture and the *Periplus* records:

> Zoskales is astute about his possessions and in his dealings with us he is always holding out for more. In all other respects he is a fine person and he is well versed in Greek reading and writing.[57]

Roman merchants offered the king silverware and goldware that had been 'fashioned in the local manner' as well as moderately priced heavy cloaks, including coloured varieties 'without adornment'. Zoskales was also interested in certain Indian commodities that Roman merchants passed on in their trade dealings with Ethiopia. This included supplies of 'Indian' steel that would have been made into better quality weaponry for Ethiopian troops. Zoskales was also keen to acquire Indian cloth, cotton garments, colourful fabric waistbands and Indian lac dye to produce a red coloration in fabrics.[58] This foreign clothing and specialist dye may have been destined for the Ethiopian court, or the royal army.

Procopius describes how regional craft made leisurely sailings from the Ethiopian ports across to the Arabian side of the Red Sea. He writes, 'The expanse of sea which lies between these lands is crossed in a voyage of five days and nights when a moderately favourable wind is blowing.'[59] Roman merchants who had finished their commercial dealings at Adulis could follow these local craft across the Red Sea to visit an Arabian trade port called Muza. Alternatively, they could continue south along the eastern coast of African to visit markets on the shores of Somalia.

THE 'FAR-SIDE' MARKETS

The African markets on the Somali side of the Aden Gulf are called the 'Far-Side' ports in the *Periplus*. The author describes their inhabitants as 'Barbaroi', though other classical authorities tended to use the name 'Troglodytes'.[60] Merchants planning to trade in the Somali markets were advised to leave Egypt in July at the same time ships bound for India departed on their long voyages east. The Romans were interested in trading with the Far-Side markets mainly because these regions produced large amounts of finer quality incense along with many valuable types of scented wood.[61] Some of the African products cannot be confidently identified, but they were highly sought after ingredients in the lucrative Roman perfume business.[62]

There was frequent traffic between Ethiopia and Somalia. Pliny describes how African rafts made slow sailings across the Aden Gulf to reach ports in southern Arabia. These raft-traders offered African forms of cassia and cinnamon for Arabian 'trinkets' such as cloth, articles of glass, copper, buckles, bracelets, and necklaces.[63] Market conditions in these ports were extremely variable, especially if the commodities on offer were sought after items. As a result, the movement of resources through the various trade contacts was difficult to predict. Roman merchant ships sailing along the African coasts therefore engaged in 'tramp trade' and travelled between markets to pick up whatever commodities might be available. Often they passed on these items at other ports in more profitable exchanges, thereby building up the capital to acquire their final return cargo. The *Periplus* explains, 'Some ships sail principally to these Far-Side ports of trade, but some follow the coast and take on whatever cargoes come their way'.[64]

There were six Far-Side markets along the Horn of Africa. This region began at Avalithes on the Red Sea coast where the *Periplus* warned Roman merchants that the African natives were 'unruly'.[65] From there Roman ships sailed along the northern shores of Somali to visit markets at Malao, Mundu and Mosyllon.[66] These sites were near distinctive coastal features, often promontories, and they offered sheltered bays where ships could lay at anchor while the merchants went ashore to trade.[67] Roman vessels heading for India would sail to the edge of Cape Guardafui before launching into the open sea on direct crossings from Africa to India. Other ships specializing in the Far-Side trade would sail onward around the Horn of Africa, known to the Romans as the 'Spice Promontory'.[68] A large market called the 'Spice Port' existed on the African coast where it began to turn southward away from Arabia. This Spice Port was fully exposed to the Indian Ocean and Roman pilots had to be continually on the alert for any indication of approaching storms. Storm warnings would send ships racing to a nearby sheltered cove to wait out the bad weather as best they could. Beyond the Spice Port was a market called Opone, and this was the most distant African market visited by Roman ships.[69]

The Far-Side markets were each independent and generally under the authority of a local tribal chief.[70] Similar Roman goods could be profitably exchanged at all these African sites. Exports included cheap decorative glass stones and large amounts of used Egyptian clothing that was cleaned and dyed to improve its appearance.[71] Metal exports included copper utensils, low quality ironware and quantities of tin that Alexandrian merchants probably received from Roman Spain.[72] Roman merchants also dealt in foodstuffs including grain and wine, as well as olives from Thebes that were transported in an unripe condition to avoid spoilage during transit.[73] The markets at Malao and Mosyllon offered large stocks of costly incense, so Roman traders brought gold and silver coins to Malao and offered silverwares and precious stones to dealers at Mosyllon.[74] These precious stones could have originated from sites in the Roman Empire, or from the Indian cargoes brought back on Roman trade vessels.[75] Roman ships returning from northern India also offered the Far Side markets stocks of basic Indian produce including grain, rice, ghee, sesame oil, cotton cloth and cane sugar.

The Far Side settlement at Avalithes seems to have had a small market offering limited amounts of fine quality myrrh, ivory and tortoise shell.[76] Malao offered large amounts of myrrh, along with an incense called *duaka*, a fragrant gum resin called *kankamon*, and some form of scented bark called *makeir*.[77] Mundu lay between the myrrh and frankincense growing regions of Somalia and as well as exporting both these incenses, also dealt in an aromatic called *mokrotu*.[78] Mosyllon and the Spice Port offered mainly large quantities of African cassia and fine-grade frankincense.[79] Further supplies of cassia could be sought at Opone which also offered quantities of tortoise shell and African slaves.[80]

The *Periplus* reveals that some Roman merchants specialized in trading with certain Far-Side sites. For example, the traders who visited Mosyllon employed bigger vessels to carry the large amounts of cassia on offer at this market.[81] The *Periplus* also indicates that Arabian traders were frequent visitors to the African ports. They acquired a significant proportion of the incense crop offered at these ports and shipped it across the Aden Gulf to markets on the Arabian coast.[82]

The Roman merchants who reached Opone had sailed more than 3,000 kilometres from their Empire and for most of them it had been more than two months since they had left Egypt.[83] The *Periplus* describes an interesting Arabian trade route that extended a great distance down the eastern coast of Africa to reach a remote trading settlement called Rhapta, close to the northern edge of Zanzibar Island.[84] Rhapta was inhabited by a community descended from Arabian commercial settlers and native African peoples.[85] It offered ivory and rhinoceros horn, as well as tortoise and nautilus shell.[86] Roman merchants did not travel this route because the small profits to be made did not justify the risk, the journey time, or the expense of the voyages. Ptolemy could only name two Roman mariners who had explored the African coast as far as Rhapta. One of these was a merchant named Diogenes who was blown off course on a return crossing from India. Diogenes took the opportunity to sail with the prevailing winds and explore the furthest Arabian trade routes along east Africa. Ptolemy explains:

> Diogenes was one of those people who sailed to India and he was returning for the second time when he was driven back from the Aromatic Lands by the wind. He therefore sailed south far along the African Coast.[87]

Another Roman merchant or pilot called Theophilos also made a voyage from the Horn of Africa south to Rhapta in 20 days, but the details given by Ptolemy suggest that these ventures were exceptional.[88]

The *Periplus* explained that somewhere beyond Rhapta, the coast of the African continent curved west to where the Indian Ocean met with the Atlantic. The author writes:

> Beyond Rhapta lies an unexplored ocean that bends to the west. It extends along southern Africa, beyond Ethiopia and Libya, to join with the western sea.[89]

The *Periplus* was correct about the world oceans being connected, but no Roman merchant ships had reason to explore this treacherous route into the Atlantic.

THE HOMERITE KINGDOM

The *Periplus* describes the dangers of sailing from the Nabatean port of Leuce Kome south along the Arabian coast of the Red Sea. The author reports:

> It is risky to set a course along the coast of Arabia. This region lacks harbours and offers poor anchorage. It has many rocky stretches and the land cannot be entered because of cliffs. It is fearsome in every respect.[90]

The coasts beyond the Nabatean kingdom were inhabited by disparate populations who lived in small clusters of huts near the shore. The *Periplus* warns:

> These coastal people are vicious: they plunder any who stray from a sailing course down the middle of the gulf and they enslave anyone who they rescue from shipwreck. For this reason they are constantly being taken captive by the governors and kings of Arabia.

It seems the Nabatean kings conducted reprisals against these raiders and these expeditions were supported by the governors of the Homerite kingdom on the southwest corner of Arabia.

Some of these Arabian pirates crossed the Red Sea to raid the Ethiopian coasts and Pliny describes a notorious group who operated in the region. He reports:

> Commerce is greatly exposed to the attentions of a piratical tribe of Arabians called the Ascitae who dwell upon the islands. They place two inflated skins of oxen beneath a raft of wood and they conduct their pirate raids with the aid of poisoned arrows.[91]

Consequently the watchmen on the Roman freighters had to be continually vigilant. The attacks took the form of stealthy boarding actions when the crew were off guard or direct assaults to overwhelm isolated vessels. The contingents of mercenary archers onboard Roman ships needed to be on standby when these raiders were sighted.

Roman vessels sailing to southern Arabia set their course down the middle of the Red Sea and used all available sail to speed past the pirate coasts. Once they had reached a landmark called 'Burnt Island' they knew they had arrived at the peaceful shores of the Homerite kingdom.[92] The first trade port they encountered was Muza, which the Romans found crowded with Arabian ships, some of which sailed as far as northwest India. The *Periplus* reports:

> The whole place teams with Arab ship-owners, charterers and sailors. It is busy with commercial activity because they carry on a trade with the 'Far-Side' coast and with Barygaza, sending out their own ships to visit these places.[93]

Muza did not have a harbour, but it was situated in a large sandy bay that offered an excellent offloading site for mooring trade vessels.[94]

Roman merchants found a market at Muza for large quantities of clothing and fabric made in the Empire, especially purple cloth. The Roman territories manufactured this clothing to suit fashion styles in the Arabian markets. Roman exports to the region therefore included Arab-style sleeved clothing, chequered garments, cloaks, waistbands with shaded stripes, and outfits made from fabrics interwoven with gold thread. Also listed are blankets that were offered plain or with patterning that appealed to local styles.[95]

There was also a market at Muza for unguents manufactured in the Empire. These were offered along with more specialized substances including yellow saffron from Asia Minor for dyes, perfumes or medicines. A plant with medicinal properties called cyperus grew in the Yemen, but demand on the Arabian market was so high that Roman merchants exported Egyptian cyperus to Muza.[96]

There were also Roman subjects residing at Muza and the *Periplus* suggested to merchants that they brought a limited amount of Mediterranean grain and wine to the port. Towards the end of this list of trade goods, the *Periplus* advises Roman merchants to bring a considerable amount of money to Muza to conduct their dealings.[97]

The *Periplus* reports that a regional capital called Saue lay three days inland from Muza and the local governor Cholaibos ruled from this city.[98] Nine days further inland from Saue was a metropolis called Saphar where the Homerite king resided.[99] Roman merchants exploited this business opportunity and sent expensive goods to the Homerite courts, including horses and pack mules, goldware, embossed silverware, expensive clothing and copper articles.[100]

In return for these trade goods, Roman merchants visiting Muza would receive large amounts of myrrh along with thick aromatic oils called stacte.[101] Arabian merchants from other territories were also bringing incense to Muza, aware that there was substantial foreign demand at the port.[102] The only other Homerite commodity that was profitable in Roman trade was a regional marble. This was an exceptionally pure white material with a fine crystalline texture that could be easily carved, like alabaster, to make elegant unguent jars.[103] Arabian merchants were engaged in a thriving overseas commerce with Ethiopia and consequently Roman merchants could receive stocks of African merchandise at the busy markets in Muza.[104]

South of Muza, there was a Homerite village and safe harbour called Ocelis near the Straits of Bab-el-Mandeb.[105] At Ocelis, Roman freighters sailing to India took fresh supplies of water onboard in preparation for the voyage through the Aden Gulf and the subsequent ocean crossing. By the time Pliny wrote about Eastern trade, the village of Ocelis had become a market station.[106] Roman vessels sailed on through the straits of Bab-el-Mandeb to enter the Gulf of Aden and from there followed the Arabian coast further eastward.

ADEN

The voyage along the southern Yemen coast took Roman ships past the former city of Aden, known in ancient times as Eudaimon or 'Blessed Arabia'. Aden had once been a major commercial city receiving cargoes from both Egypt and India, but by the time of the *Periplus* it was little more than a village settlement offering passing ships supplies of fresh water.[107] The *Periplus* attributes the decline of Aden to a Roman military attack on the ancient city reporting that, 'not long before our own time, Caesar destroyed it.'[108]

The Roman attack on Aden must be connected with events during the reign of Augustus. In 26 BC the Emperor authorized the invasion of Arabia under the command of Aelius Gallus.[109] The decision to invade was encouraged by the knowledge that a people from the Yemen called the Sabaeans were obtaining large amounts of bullion wealth as profits from the incense trade. They spent this western wealth on beautifully adorned temples and extravagant royal palaces.[110] In this era, the Sabaeans were the main suppliers of incense to the Nabateans and their trade vessels were heavily active in the Red Sea.[111] With the Sabaeans as the target, Augustus hoped that territories as far as the Yemen could be incorporated into the Roman Empire as major new wealth producing provinces.[112] Strabo explains:

> The Emperor's purpose was to win over these Arabians or subjugate them. His considerations were based on the well established reports that the Arabians are very wealthy and that they sell aromatics and the most valuable gemstones for gold and silver, but they never expended the wealth they received from this trade with outsiders. Augustus therefore expected to deal with wealthy friends, or to master wealthy enemies.[113]

Strabo describes how initial preparations for the conquest involved plans to launch a coastal invasion of the Yemen, supported by a fleet of Roman warships. Perhaps this scheme was inspired by reports of Alexander's plans to conquer Arabia using a large military fleet. Preparations for the marine campaign were well advanced before the Roman scheme was abandoned. Gallus had already constructed more than 80 biremes and triremes to fight sea battles against the southern Arabs when the strategy was changed in favour of a land campaign.[114] The sack of Aden must have occurred during this period and was probably carried out by a small exploratory force of Roman soldiers.

The brief, destructive raid on Aden was overshadowed by the large-scale land invasion of Arabia. In 26 BC Gallus led a combined Roman army of about 11,000 troops, on a campaign route from the Nabatean kingdom south into the Arabian Desert.[115] Gallus mounted an assault on the Sabaean territories, but the Roman forces were crippled by disease and the lack of provisions. They were ultimately forced to withdraw before any permanent conquest could be made.[116]

Although the Roman campaign ended in failure, the Homerites exploited the decline of Sabaean power and subjugated their neighbours. Consequently, by the time of the *Periplus*, the Homerite king Charibael was describing himself as the ruler of two nations – the Homerites and the Sabaeans. Charibael also shrewdly portrayed himself as 'a friend of the Emperors' and continually sent embassies and gifts to Rome in order to reinforce his position.[117] By the second century AD, Aden had recovered some of its former prominence and Ptolemy is able to describe the site as an emporium.[118]

THE HADHRAMAUT KINGDOM

Roman merchant ships sailing beyond Aden headed for the edge of the Hadramaut kingdom and the trade port of Qana.[119] Qana served an important inland metropolis called Shabwa where the Hadramaut king Eleazos ruled over the surrounding territories.[120] The Homerite kingdom controlled crops of myrrh, but the Hadramaut tribes of the Dhofar region governed the best frankincense producing territories of Arabia. By the time of the *Periplus* the Hadramaut kings were managing this frankincense crop as a lucrative royal monopoly.

Hadramaut frankincense was collected together at guarded facilities at Qana by royal agents. These supplies were then offered to foreign shipping visiting the port.

Archaeological evidence suggests that Qana was established as a major port in the Augustan era when there was a dramatic increase in Greco-Roman trade sailings into the distant East. The Hadramaut kings must have created the expanded port to facilitate greater trade contacts with the Romans.[121]

The ruins of ancient Qana lie on a barren sandy coast where jagged black volcanic rocks punctuate the shoreline. The ancient settlement stood near a wide sheltered bay below a large, flat-topped volcanic rock that rose as a promontory 140 metres above the port.[122] Roman merchants visiting Qana in the time of the *Periplus* would have seen a range of buildings at the base of this black cliff face, including a large warehouse complex for the storage of frankincense that had been partially built into the hillside.[123] Travellers who climbed the steep and narrow path up the northern slope of the basalt rockface followed stretches of staircase enclosed by stone walls and guarded by square towers.[124] At the summit of the path stood a fortified complex of walls along which were tower-like buildings equipped with large cisterns to collect and preserve rain water. Archaeologists investigating the ruins of this ancient citadel have identified a prominent temple structure that they believe served as a lighthouse to guide incoming ships.[125] From this formidable facility the Hadramaut maintained rigorous controls over the frankincense stocks that were brought to the port.

The *Periplus* explains the operation of the Hadramaut frankincense business. The incense produced in the mountainous Dhofar region was brought overland to Qana along caravan routes, but also shipped by sea using small rafts constructed from inflated animal skins. The *Periplus* reports:

> All the frankincense grown in the land is brought to Qana. It is as though the whole port is a single warehouse. It is brought by camel and by boat. It is also carried on a type of local raft made from leather bags.[126]

The *Periplus* also records how Qana had developed from a government installation to a site where regional merchants came to make exchanges with visiting foreigners. The Arabian traders operating from Qana were also dealing with Far-Side markets, trading with the Persian Gulf ports, and visiting commercial centres in northwest India.[127]

Foreign pottery found at ancient Qana confirms the extent of these early trade connections. Finds have included fragments of green-glazed pottery from Parthian Mesopotamia and coarse 'black and grey' storage vessels from the Persian Gulf. These containers were probably used to transport dates and wine to the Arabian port.[128] A Nabatean connection to Qana is attested by finds of elegant pink-clay tableware that was painted with red patterns, while Indian dealings at the port are suggested by fragmentary pieces of red polished tableware.[129] The significance of foreign commerce is emphasized by the fact that only a quarter of the pottery fragments recovered from early Qana belonged to locally made wares.[130]

Many of the Roman goods sent to Muza were also offered at Qana. The *Periplus* reports that the site received a large volume of printed fabrics and a great quantity of Arabian-style clothing. Roman ships also delivered raw metals to Qana, including copper and tin.[131] Indian contacts with Qana meant that there was a market for Mediterranean coral and fragrant storax potions at the port. The *Periplus* also reveals that Roman merchants offered Mediterranean wines to Qana dealers, along with a limited amount of Egyptian wheat.[132] Archaeology confirms the significance of this wine trade as over half of the pottery fragments recovered at Qana belonged to Roman amphorae.[133] About a fifth of these Roman fragments have black volcanic specks in their composition which would indicate they were manufactured in Campania before the eruption of Vesuvius in AD 79.[134] Some of the amphorae fragments discovered at Qana belong to containers that usually held Roman olive oil or garum fish sauce from Spain.[135]

Large amounts of fine Roman tableware fragments have also been found at Qana. These include Italian styles of *terra sigillata* that were manufactured in the Augustan era.[136] One of these sherds bore the impression of a small stamp in the shape of a man's foot, indicating its manufacture at workshops in eastern Sicily.[137] Finds indicate that Roman traders had switched to exporting *terra sigillata* made in the eastern provinces of their Empire by the late first century AD.[138] Many of the Roman wines and tablewares sent to Qana were sent inland by caravan to supply the Hadramaut metropolis at Shabwa.[139]

At Qana agents of the Hadramaut king supervised the distribution of the frankincense harvest, so Roman merchants had to deal with these officers to gain the precious commodity. The Romans therefore brought expensive articles including embossed silverware and large quantities of imperial money to the port knowing these items would be valued by the Hadramaut kings. King Eleazos was also keen to receive Roman horses, classical statues and the finest quality clothing.[140]

There were only two major exports from the Hadramaut kingdom to interest Roman traders. The *Periplus* reports that Roman merchants visiting Qana sought large amounts of frankincense and considerable quantities of a plant product called 'aloe'. Aloe was an important commodity because it produced cooling juices that were effective in the treatment of skin irritations, burns and abrasive wounds.[141] Qana also offered a range of commodities received from Persia and India. Roman merchants who were not sailing onward to these more distant markets could therefore take advantage of these additional trade opportunities.

The *Periplus* records that Roman merchants supplied Arabian wines to Indian ports and Roman ships must have picked up these cargoes at either Muza, or Qana, on their outbound journeys. However, the local containers used at Qana were large, hand-made vessels that could not have held wines.[142] It has therefore been suggested that Arabian traders refilled used Roman amphoras with their own locally made produce. These repackaged Arabian wines could be offered to any visiting Roman merchants anxious to make further profits in their trade dealings with Indian markets.[143]

This Roman-Arabian wine trade might have alleviated the problem of ballast on Roman voyages to India. Roman ships sailed to the Arabian markets with comparatively heavy cargoes of bulk goods, but they left these ports with much lighter, compacted quantities of valuable incense.[144] Mariners therefore had to stabilize their vessels with increased ballast, so ships sailing on to India could take Arabian wine onboard as a cheap bulk commodity that offered a reasonable profit in more distant markets.

Any Roman vessels not sailing onward to India took onboard rocks to act as ballast for the return journey to Egypt. These rocks were dumped at the Egyptian ports when the ship received its new cargo of outbound Roman goods. This practice explains why there are large heaps of volcanic beach boulders from Arabia at the Egyptian ports of Berenice and Myos Hormos.[145] Samples taken from the ballast debris at Myos Hormos suggest that less than a third of the stones came from Aden, while the remainder came from Qana. It is interesting that all the ballast rocks found at Berenice came from the shores of Qana.[146] This confirms the view that Aden was destroyed in the Augustan era and that Berenice did not begin operating as a harbour for loading Roman ships until the reign of Tiberius.[147]

MOSCHA HARBOUR

In the time of the *Periplus*, Roman merchants operating from Egypt did not sail onwards into the Persian Gulf. After finishing their dealings at Qana, most Roman ships specializing in Arabian trade returned to the Empire. The Persian markets in Mesopotamia were only a few weeks distant from Roman Syria and this allowed people and goods to move easily between these territories. The merchants sailing from Egypt could not profitably intercede in this commerce, so they preferred to concentrate on direct dealings with the Indian and Arabian ports that supplied these Persian Gulf routes.

Roman vessels travelling to India sailed onwards from Qana along the Hadramaut coast. They headed for the great promontory at Ras Fartak where they launched into the open ocean on the long crossing to India. The *Periplus* describes the sailing beyond Qana along the coast of the Dhofar region. Clumps of frankincense grew in the gullies of the limestone highlands and the moisture laden monsoon winds made the atmosphere close and misty.[148] Roman merchants heard stories about how the frankincense was harvested for the Hadramaut king.[149] The *Periplus* reports:

> The frankincense is handled by royal slaves and convicts. These districts are terribly unhealthy. They are harmful to those sailing by and absolutely fatal to anyone who works there. The workers die easily because they lack nourishment.[150]

Near the promontory of Ras Fartak there was a harbour guarded by a fortress of the Hadramaut kingdom. This station served as a storehouse and shipment point for frankincense being conveyed to Qana.[151] Beyond this stretch of coast was another Hadramaut port called Moscha Harbour which operated as a further fortified collection point for the frankincense crop destined for the Qana storerooms.[152]

The Hadramaut station at Moscha was established at about the same time as Qana to manage the increase in direct Roman demand for frankincense.[153] Excavations at Moscha have revealed a substantial settlement with paved streets, houses, temples, shops and at least one open marketplace. Archaeologists estimate that perhaps two hundred Hadramaut people lived and worked within this community. They were protected by heavily-fortified walls and a prominent gate-tower that guarded the main entrance to the town.[154] There are ancient stone-wall structures to the north of

Moscha that may have served as checkpoints to control the caravan traffic bringing the local frankincense crop to the port.[155]

Roman merchant ships had no reason to visit Moscha harbour during their usual trade voyages. Yet sometimes ships returning from India late in the season found that weather conditions had turned against them and it was unwise to continue their journey back to Egypt. In these situations the harbour at Moscha could accommodate foreign shipping and the Hadramaut king allowed Indian and Roman vessels to remain at the port until it was safe to resume their voyages. These merchants came to an agreement with the royal agents at Moscha and exchanged some of their Indian cargo for the incoming frankincense harvests. The *Periplus* reports:

> Ships sailing from Barygaza or the Malabar Coast can pass the winter at Moscha if the season is late. They reach arrangement with the royal agents and take on a cargo of *sachalite* frankincense in return for cotton cloth, grain and oil.[156]

Frankincense could only be removed from Moscha harbour on terms dictated by the royal priests who managed the harvest and this had encouraged stories that the gods were guarding supplies of this precious crop. The *Periplus* reports:

> Frankincense laid out at the harbour facilities can remain there unguarded. This is thanks to some power of the gods who watch over the place. Frankincense cannot be loaded aboard a ship without royal permission. If a grain is taken aboard covertly, the ship cannot sail since it is against the will of the gods.[157]

The royal priests would agree the exchange of frankincense just before the trade winds resumed and any stray Roman ships could then sail back to Egypt with their overdue Indian cargoes. Their precious stocks of fresh frankincense would be some compensation for the difficulties and delay they had experienced on their return journey.

THE INCENSE TRAIL

Such was the Roman demand for frankincense resin that the Hadramaut kings responded by establishing a second harvest. Pliny reports:

> In former times, when they had fewer opportunities for selling it, the Arabians used to harvest their frankincense only once a year. But at present there is a much greater demand for the product, so they now gather a second additional crop.[158]

Under this new arrangement the main summer harvest was gathered in early autumn, while the inferior second crop was collected in spring, months before Roman ships were expected to arrive at Qana.[159] Rather than keep these stockpiles in storage, the Hadramaut kings offered them to other Arabian traders visiting their kingdom. These traders began to organize large caravans to travel from the

Hadramaut kingdom north through the Arabian Desert to reach Roman markets such as Gaza on the Mediterranean Coast.[160]

When Pliny wrote about this 'Incense Trail' it was still a relatively new development; he therefore describes the route in some detail.[161] The trail began in the Dhofar region where the frankincense was gathered and was taken by caravan to the inland capitol of Shabwa.[162] Pliny writes:

> After being collected the incense is carried on camels' backs to Shabwa. In this place a single gate is left open for its admission. The laws have made it a capital offence to deviate from the high road while conveying the frankincense to the city.[163]

This route was a caravan journey of over 640 kilometres that probably took up to 30 days to complete. After entering the vast limestone gates of Shabwa, the incense was taken through the main city streets to the palace of Shaqir and the great temple of the Hadhramaut god Sabis.[164] Temple priests received the deliveries and took for themselves a fixed tithe of the harvest as tax in kind. Pliny explains:

> At Shabwa the priests take a tenth part of the harvest by measure rather than weight. They do this to honour their god who is called Sabis and no one is allowed to dispose of the incense before this has been done.[165]

Once the priests had removed their share, the remaining produce would be sold to visiting merchants. Travellers from distant lands became guests of the priests of Sabis while they waited for the precious incense crop to be made available. Pliny reports:

> The public expenses are defrayed out of the extracted tenth. This is required because the god generously entertains all those strangers who have spent a certain number of days travel coming to the city.[166]

The Hadhramaut kings had an understanding with the rulers of the neighbouring Gebanite kingdom that the caravans would travel west to their capital at Timna.[167] The Gebanite king collected a quarter of all myrrh grown in his kingdom and sold this to his subjects in the city markets.[168] The caravans could therefore load up with myrrh at Timna before heading north towards the Sabaean capital of Marib. From Marib, the caravans made desert crossings onward through Minaean territory to reach Nabatea and the Roman Empire.[169]

Many of the merchants in this frankincense trade were Minaeans as their territory was in a central position to exploit this commerce.[170] Pliny writes:

> The country of the Minaeans is the only transit route for the frankincense which passes along a single narrow road. The Minaeans were the first people to conduct this traffic in frankincense and they still do, to a greater extent than any other people.[171]

Separate caravan routes no doubt led off from Marib toward the Persian Gulf.[172]

The main route from Timna to Gaza ran roughly parallel to the Red Sea coast.

It covered a total distance of over 2,200 kilometres and modern estimates suggest that it could be travelled in 70 to 90 days, provided the caravans met with no serious delays or detours.[173] Pliny describes how the journey was divided into 65 stages with stopping points where caravan travellers could be provisioned by local communities.[174]

All along the caravan route from Timna to Gaza payments had to be made to various agents, guards, and the attendants of local authorities. By the time the caravans reached the Roman frontier they had amassed considerable expenses. Then the Roman customs officers would have been waiting at Gaza to further tax the incoming caravans.[175] Pliny reports:

> All along the route they keep on paying, at one place for water, at another for fodder, at other locations there are charges for lodging at the halts, and again various tolls. Eventually the expenses mount up to 688 denarii per camel and this is before the Mediterranean coast is reached and payment is due to the customs officers of our Empire.[176]

Gaza only became part of the province of Judaea in about AD 70, after the Romans had suppressed a major Jewish uprising.[177] Consequently, Pliny's information on the Incense Trail was contemporary when he wrote his account.

In total, the route from Dhofar to Gaza covered a distance of almost 3,400 kilometres.[178] In terms of journey time it would have taken at least 90 days for the frankincense crop to be trafficked along the overland routes from Dhofar to the Mediterranean coast.[179] This additional frankincense harvest could therefore reach Mediterranean markets before Roman ships had left Egypt to acquire the main crop at Qana.

When Pliny wrote his detailed account of these new caravan contacts, Nabatea was still a client kingdom of the Roman Empire. However, when the reigning Nabatean king died, the Roman government decided to fully subjugate his kingdom and in AD 106 the Emperor Trajan established Nabatea as a new Roman province.[180] This development encouraged greater commercial contacts between Egypt and Nabatea. A year after the Roman annexation, a soldier-secretary stationed at Nabatea reported how merchants were arriving every day from Pelusium in Egypt.[181] In this period Nabatean names also begin to appear on rock graffiti on the caravan routes that crossed the Eastern Desert of Egypt.[182]

TRADE DEVELOPMENTS

Over time the prosperous kingdoms of Arabia established greater authority over the market centres in eastern Africa. This gave them increased control over the African aromatics demanded by Roman markets. Consequently, Pliny talks about a Nabatean colony in east Africa that dealt in precious aromatic gums, including cinnamon and cassia.[183]

Other developments in Arabian commerce affected Roman markets. For example, the Gebanites gained greater authority over the cinnamon markets in northern Somalia. Pliny describes how their king consequently decided the price of cinnamon sold in this region.[184] The Gebanite intrusion into Somalia extended to the cinnamon groves, so when the native peoples were provoked they attacked and burned these Arabian possessions. The consequence was a market shortage in the Roman Empire with a rise in the price of African cinnamon. Pliny explains:

> The price of cinnamon rose by 50 per cent when the groves were set on fire by the barbarians. This was perhaps an act of resentment because some injustice had been exercised by those in power, though its consequences could have been unintentional.[185]

This example indicates how Eastern goods imported into the Roman Empire might fluctuate significantly in price due to distant and unforeseen events.

The *Periplus* recalled a time when Roman ships visited the large island of Socotra lying off the Somali coast. This place had been a traditional meeting point for Eastern traders and was therefore inhabited by a population with a very mixed heritage. The *Periplus* explains:

> The inhabitants of Socotra are few in number and they live on the north side of the island facing the Arabian coast. These settlers are a mixture of Arabs and Indians and even some Greeks who sailed out there to trade.[186]

Roman ships sailing back from India had offered these islanders a range of goods including rice, cotton cloth and female slaves.[187] But by the time of the *Periplus*, the Hadramaut kings who had authority over Socotra had leased out the territory to a consortium of Arab merchants. Consequently, Roman ships were no longer permitted to approach the island for trade purposes. The new managers of Socotra ran the island as a business and supplied its resources to overseas markets. The island produced a valuable resin called cinnabar and it was in the right climate zone to produce aloe and frankincense.[188] Large leopard tortoises also lived on the island and hawksbill turtles could be found around its shores.[189] There was a major Roman fashion in this era for veneered furniture and these large shells were particularly prized.[190] All these resources made Socotra a valuable possession and the merchant consortium running the island maintained a force of private guards to protect their commercial interests.[191]

In the time of the *Periplus*, the Homerite King Charibael had authority over the distant trade station of Rhapta which lay on the eastern coast of Africa. Charibael leased out the station to a merchant oligarchy from Muza who collected taxes from the settlement.[192] By the time Ptolemy compiled his geography, this small mixed community of Arab settlers and African locals had developed their settlement into a trade metropolis.[193]

THE FARASAN COMMAND

Rome also expanded its authority further into these Eastern regions. When the Romans annexed the Nabatean kingdom, they took over responsibility for its security and the well-being of its subjects. The Roman administration therefore inherited the problem of piracy on the eastern coasts of the Red Sea. The Nabatean kings had launched reprisals against these raiders, so the Romans planned similar operations with a new level of organized determination.

Like their Ptolemaic predecessors, the Romans must have maintained a small fleet of military patrol vessels in the northern regions of the Red Sea. There was a strong Roman military presence at the Egyptian port of Berenice, so the fleet probably operated from the restored harbour.[194] The Gallus campaign had equipped the Romans with Red Sea warships, but in the time of the *Periplus*, the remnants of the fleet offered limited protection to merchant vessels sailing the Gulf. The ancient sources stressed the threat of Arabian piracy, but they also indicate that Roman merchant ships managed their own defence with armed mercenaries onboard.

Eutropius suggests that Trajan established a new fleet of Roman warships in the Red Sea in preparation for Eastern wars that he hoped would extend to India.[195] There must have been a change in Roman strategy during this era as the Empire sought greater control over the Red Sea. A Latin inscription from the Farasan Islands reveals that by AD 144 there was a Roman military base on the south-west coast of Arabia.[196] This garrison had a command over the Straits of Bab-el-Mandeb and the entrance to the Red Sea. The text reads:

> For the Emperor Caesar . . . Antoninus Augustus Pius . . . on behalf of the *vexillation* of the Second Legion Traiana Fortis and its auxiliary troops. Castricius Aprinus, son of Publius, prefect of the port of Farasan and of the Sea of Hercules, has made and dedicated [this monument].[197]

The Farasans are a large coral island group positioned on the western side of the Yemen coast about 60 kilometres offshore from Arabia and over 200 kilometres distant from the African shore. In ancient times these islands lay a short distance north of the Homerite trading port at Muza and across the gulf from Adulis in Ethiopia. Archaeological surveys on the main island have recovered sherds of Nabataean tableware, indicating their ancient influence in this area.[198]

Castricius Aprinus, the Roman commander of this Farasan port, must have had authority over military patrol ships. The legionaries were positioned over 1,000 kilometres south of the traditional Roman frontiers in Egypt. As the garrison was from an Egyptian legion, they must have been supplied from the Red Sea ports. No other classical source mentions the 'Sea of Hercules' that Aprinus describes.[199] However, it is likely that the Romans equated the Straits of Bab-el-Mandeb with the so-called 'Pillars of Hercules' at Gibraltar. Both straits had prominent headlands with a similar position in controlling sea-lanes moving from enclosed water into the open sea. The inscription therefore indicates Roman control over any traffic entering the Red Sea. The Farasans are conveniently close to a navigable gap in the reefs that lie alongside the Arabian coast.[200] The Roman garrison was therefore in an ideal position to monitor goods moving between the African and Arabian sides of the Red Sea.

The Roman base on the Farasans might have been established as a launching point for reprisals against pirate raiders on the Arabian coasts. The Romans could also have had an interest in the politics of the Axumite, or Homerite, kingdoms that required a nearby military presence. Another possibility is that the Farasan station was established to collect new tolls and taxes in this distant region.[201]

The Romans could have seized the Farasans from their existing occupants, but another explanation is possible. The Empire might have acquired the Farasans as a commercial grant from the Homerite kings who had already styled themselves as 'friends' of the Emperor and sent regular diplomatic missions to Rome.[202] The Farasans would have been 'given' to Rome, just as the Homerite king had granted Rhapta to an association of Arab merchants. This might resemble the situation on Socotra were the Hadramaut king handed over control of an entire island to an Arab consortium with their own garrison.[203] There was already a precedent for collecting Roman taxes in supposedly 'independent' regions. In the time of the *Periplus*, the Empire had a guard station and a customs post at Luece Kome in Nabatea when it was still a client kingdom.[204]

By the second century AD, Roman military patrols could have been assigned to protect merchant ships sailing through the Red Sea. If this were the case, then the Farasan station would have functioned as an important operational base. The Roman port could also have served as an important supply station for merchant ships passing through the region.[205] It is possible that other distant Roman stations existed on the Red Sea coast, but they still await discovery.[206]

The only other Roman inscription discovered in southwest Arabia consisted of a short bilingual text. The inscription was found at the inland site of Baraqish in an ancient cemetery and it records in Latin and Greek the name Publius Comelius and the word *eques*. This undated funerary piece has been linked to the Gallus expedition with the word *eques* indicating the grave of solider from the Roman cavalry. Yet the *equates* were also an aristocratic social order among the Romans and the presence of imperial troops on the nearby Farasan Islands perhaps suggests other Roman interests in this distant region of Arabia.[207]

Ultimately, it was developments in the Roman markets that led to the decline of the African and Arabian incense trade. Changing consumer fashions and the adoption of different religious observances seem to have reduced the Mediterranean demand for precious aromatics.[208] In the third century, the Empire came under increasingly severe financial pressures and Roman market prosperity declined considerably. In this era, the ancient sources recording Eastern commerce become increasingly scarce and obscure. Consequently, the fate of the Roman soldiers stationed on the distant Farasan Islands remains unrecorded in the records of antiquity.

4

Trade Routes through Asia and the Silk Road Connection

In ancient times, vast overland trade routes stretched across Central Asia bringing Chinese goods into India and the Middle East. Modern scholars often refer to these trade systems as 'The Silk Roads' to emphasize that silk was the most distinctive commodity involved in this commercial traffic.[1] In reality, the Silk 'Road' was formed from several regional trade routes that connected together in Inner Asia to facilitate the movement of goods from India and China into the west. These commercial networks were connected to Roman territory through a number of important trade routes.

Deep within Central Asia, the distant land of Bactria, was connected to the Tarim territories and the outer parts of northwest India. Bactrian trade routes followed the Oxus River northward to the landlocked Caspian Sea and the Eurasian Steppe. Goods arriving in these regions were taken west through passes in the Caucasus Mountains that separated the Caspian from the Black Sea. This was the outer edge of the Roman Empire and Greek communities on the shores of the Black Sea received Eastern goods via these routes. These northern trade networks avoided the core territories of the Parthian Realm, but were controlled by Colchic mountain tribes and steppe populations around the Caspian.

The trade routes of Central Asia were also connected to Parthian Mesopotamia. Caravans conveyed merchandise across the desert plains of Iran along overland trade routes that passed directly through Parthian territory. Hostility between Rome and Parthia discouraged Roman traders from using this route, so only a small number of individuals from the Empire travelled across Iran to reach Bactria. From Bactria, the Silk Roads extended east through the Tarim territories to the edges of China. By using these trails, a few fortunate Romans were able to reach the Chinese Empire.

Eastern goods were also reaching Mesopotamia through the sea routes that connected the Persian Gulf with northwest India. The *Periplus* describes how Chinese goods were being trafficked from Bactria down through the Indus territories to reach markets such as Barbaricon. Arab and Persian ships visited these Indian ports and operated alongside Indian vessels to bring Eastern merchandise to the vast commercial cities of Mesopotamia. A share of these Eastern imports was trafficked northwards from the Persian markets along the Euphrates and Tigris River trade routes into neighbouring Roman Syria. The Syrian city of Palmyra established itself as a pivotal location in these desert trade routes and commemorative inscriptions from the city provide unique detail about caravan ventures south to the Persian Gulf.

EXCHANGES ACROSS THE EURASIAN STEPPE

In antiquity, the vast Eurasian Steppe was inhabited by diverse populations of nomadic pastoralists who were skilled horse-riders. Classical authorities wrote about these wild and warlike horsemen on the Russian Steppe and called them 'Scythians'. In the Far East, the Chinese Empire had to contend with a powerful tribal confederacy called the 'Xiongnu' who occupied the Mongolian Plains. These steppe populations were engaged in exchanges that moved a great range of resources and commodities over enormous distances. To emphasize the significance of this process, some scholars refer to this traffic as the 'Steppe Roads'.

The ancient Chinese records reveal how the early steppe peoples were very different from the settled population of the neighbouring Han Empire. For instance, the *Discourses on Salt and Iron* reports:

> The Xiongnu live in the wilderness and thrive in the land which produces no real food. They have been abandoned by Heaven for being useless. They have no houses to shelter themselves and in their society they make no distinction between men and women. Their villages are the entire wilderness and they use tents for their homes. They wear animal's skins, eat raw meat and drink blood. They travel around to meet others and exchange goods, but they only stay in one place for a while to herd cattle.[2]

Xiongnu horsemen launched destructive raids into the northern Han territories, then retreated back into the vast Mongolian steppe to evade Chinese reprisals. The Han government was therefore forced to develop a range of diplomatic tactics to contain the Xiongnu threat.[3] One of these strategies was to annually offer the Xiongnu vast amounts of Chinese produce as a diplomatic tribute. This outpouring of materials was preferable to the revenue loss caused by destructive Xiongnu raids, or the costs incurred in launching military campaigns against this elusive threat. The Han subversively hoped the Xiongnu population would become economically reliant on Chinese products.[4] A Chinese official warned a Xiongnu ruler:

> Your whole horde scarcely equals the population of a couple of Chinese prefectures. The secret of your strength lies in your independence from China for all your real necessities. Now you have this increasing fondness for Chinese things and the Xiongnu customs are changing. Although the Han Empire sends no more than a fifth of its goods here, it will in the end succeed in controlling the whole Xiongnu nation.[5]

Over time, the Xiongnu became dependent on these Chinese products. Consequently, Chinese 'gifts' of manufactured goods and food were increasingly used to pressurize Xiongnu rulers into political compliance. Xiongnu representatives presented themselves to the Chinese court and demonstrated submission in return for a quantity of gifts that were no longer fixed by prior agreement. Han economic wealth had therefore bought them political authority over people who lived far beyond the Chinese frontiers.[6] Economic exchange had consequently achieved what warfare could not.

Chinese records reveal their escalating involvement in the Xiongnu economy. In 51 BC the Xiongnu were given 20 catties of gold, 200,000 bronze coins, 8,000 pieces of silken fabric, 6,000 catties of silk floss, and an 'enormous quantity' of rice.[7] By the year 1 BC, the annual Han gifts had increased to 30,000 catties of silk floss and 30,000 rolls of silk.[8] This was almost a five-fold increase in the quantity of silk products entering the Steppe territories as Chinese economic assistance.[9] The Chinese therefore used economic production as a political weapon.

The Han also created large border markets where the Xiongnu came to conduct exchanges with Chinese merchants.[10] At these sites, the Xiongnu traded horses and animal furs for agricultural products and manufactured goods such as silk.[11] Huge amounts of traffic reached these frontier markets, as evidenced in AD 135 when steppe raiders held up a Chinese caravan consisting of more than 1,000 ox-drawn carts.[12] The border markets were so important to the Xiongnu that they requested access to these sites in their diplomatic dealings with the Han.[13] The Han government facilitated these exchanges because they appreciated how the markets drew valuable resources away from the Xiongnu territories. The Han also realized that by saturating Xiongnu demands, they could lessen their rapaciousness.[14]

The steppe nomads travelled hundreds of kilometres between their summer and winter pastures and therefore came into contact with a wide range of other transhumant tribes as well as fixed agricultural settlements at the edge of the steppe lands. There is a popular theory that many of the Chinese goods received by the Xiongnu were passed on to other nomadic groups, and through a succession of exchanges, travelled thousands of kilometres across the vast Eurasian steppe. Scholars imagine that these goods would be distributed through various social interactions including gift-giving, tribute extraction, marriage dowries, trade exchanges, mercenary pay and even booty from tribal raids.[15] Grave goods from the Eurasian steppe confirm that this process did occur, but the archaeological evidence cannot reveal the scale of these interactions.[16]

THE SILK ROADS

The Tarim Basin lay west of the Chinese Empire and was enclosed by some of the most forbidding mountain ranges in the world. The region is bordered on the north by the immense terrain of the Tian Shan mountain range which reaches deep into the Eurasian Steppe. Its southern frontiers are defined by the enormous Kunlun Mountains which form the outer edge of the vast Tibetan Plateau. The Tarim Basin is filled by the formidable Taklamakan Desert which stretches over 1,000 kilometres from east to west and is more than 400 kilometres across at its widest point. The vast sandy wastes of the Taklamakan are exceptionally hostile to life and no vegetation or water can be found within its inner reaches. In this desert, the daytime heat beats down across terrain that offers no significant shelter, while at night the temperature plummets well below freezing.[17] The Taklamakan Desert is an immense obstacle to overland travel and in antiquity it greatly limited contacts between China and the distant West.

There were outposts of civilization around the outer edges of the Tarim Basin where melted snow ran down from the surrounding mountain ranges to create small oasis regions. These regions developed into small kingdoms and foreign travellers could circumvent the Taklamakan Desert by journeying along these mountain fringes, receiving supplies and assistance from these far-flung outposts.

The Han Empire had political interests in the Tarim regions and sought to dominate the small independent kingdoms that stretched along its edge. In the first century BC, the Han Empire strengthened its control over the Gansu corridor which connected the Chinese heartland to the outer Tarim territories. The Han military fortified and garrisoned this region, thereby improving conditions for merchant caravans making the journey from China across into the Tarim lands.[18] One of these 'silk roads' followed a northern route around the Tarim Basin, through the oasis kingdoms of Turfan and Kucha to reach Kashgar. The other route skirted the southern regions of the Taklamakan Desert by passing through Niya and Khotan to join the northern route at Kashgar city. From Kashgar, one route headed along the Alai Valley to Balkh and beyond. Another continued around the Pamir mountain range to reach Samarkand in Sogdiana. From Sogdiana, various trade routes followed the Oxus River valley into neighbouring Bactria. Along each of these major caravan routes various smaller courses led off towards other commercial centres that interconnected with regional commerce.[19]

The classical sources confirm that caravan merchants brought large quantities of silk from the Chinese Empire along overland routes into Bactria. The *Periplus* describes how these Bactrian trade routes then conveyed silks down to commercial ports on the northern coasts of India. The author reports:

> There is a very great inland State called Thina (China). From there silk floss, yarn, and cloth are transported by land via Bactria to Barygaza and via the Ganges River to the Malabar Coast.[20]

Growing Roman demand for Chinese commodities was an important factor in the movement of new peoples and ideas into Han China. Around the time of the *Periplus*, Indian peoples began to settle in the Tarim kingdoms and establish a commercial presence in the major Chinese cities. When the Han Emperor Guangwu died in AD 57, Indians were amongst the foreign merchants who established a commemorative shrine at the Chinese capital Luoyang.[21] Buddhist missionaries followed these Indian merchants and by AD 68 the White Horse Monastery had been established in the city.[22]

Chinese merchants also travelled along these caravan trade routes, at least as far as the Tarim kingdoms. When the Han general Ban Chao led a military expedition against the northern Tarim kingdom of Karashahr in AD 94, he was joined in the fighting by several hundred Chinese merchants.[23] While on command in the Tarim territories, Ban Chao also received letters from home sent by his brother Ban Gu, asking him to acquire rare Western goods on his behalf. Ban Gu wanted woollen rugs and he mentions that a Chinese official named Tou Hsien had paid 800,000 in cash to acquire ten of these fashionable items. Tou had also sent out agents with 700 pieces of coloured silk fabric and 300 pieces of plain white silk in order to acquire a range of sought-after Western commodities.[24]

Silk was a comparatively inexpensive commodity in ancient China and could be acquired in the Han markets using stocks of relatively ordinary products.[25] In a similar manner, woollen rugs, even if they were elaborately decorated, would not have been particularly expensive in Central Asia or the Roman Empire. The Sogdians understood the profits of this market situation and they performed an important role in trafficking trade goods across the Tarim territories.[26] Some Sogdian merchants travelled the entire distance from Samarkand to China on their caravan trade ventures.[27] However, most Sogdian dealers probably operated along particular sections of these trade routes using a relay system to receive, then forward, goods to colleagues in more distant territories. Many of the richer Sogdian merchants had ongoing commercial investments at a number of trade centres between Samarkand and China.

The *Sogdian Letters* discovered by Aurel Stein provide the best insight into the operation of these silk route caravans. A Sogdian merchant named Nanai-Vandak from the Chinese town of Jincheng wrote *Letter Two* in this collection. Jincheng was a gateway town in the Gansu corridor that led from the Chinese heartland west to the frontier city of Dunhuang. Nanai was involved in exporting Chinese goods across Central Asia and supplying fellow Sogdians along the silk routes. He wrote *Letter Two* to his business superiors in distant Samarkand to explain how a recent war between China and the Xiongnu had greatly disrupted the movement of caravans. Nanai addressed the envelope:

> Send this letter to Samarkand. And the noble lord Varzakk should receive it complete. Sent by his servant Nanai-Vandak.

In the letter Nanai reveals business arrangements for a consignment of goods and provides instructions on how these items were to be divided amongst his colleagues in the homeland. He writes:

> Under my supervision Wan-razmak has sent 32 vessels of musk to Dunhuang. These belong to Takut and I am delivering them to you. When they are handed over, you should divide them into five shares. Takhsich-Vandak should take three shares, and Pesakk should take one share, and you should also take one share.[28]

Nanai felt demoralized by the escalating war and appalled by the damage it was inflicting on the merchant communities. He feared that his own death was imminent and that he would not see his homeland again. Nanai was adamant that his young son should not follow him into a profession that now carried the threat of a death so far from home. He therefore sent instructions to his business contacts in Samarkand, explaining how funds held on deposit should be invested to ensure that his young son Takhsich-Vandak was financially secure when he reached adulthood. Nanai writes:

> Remind Varzakk that he should withdraw this deposit, and you should both count it, and add interest to the amount. Put the money in a transfer document and give this to Varzakk ... so that this money may increase ... and when Takhsich-Vandak is grown up, give him a wife and do not send him away from yourself ... because from day to day we in China expect only robbery and murder.[29]

The *Sogdian Letters* also indicate the variety of trade goods moving through the caravan routes of Central Asia. The letters refer mainly to small-scale consignments that were low-bulk, but high-value, goods. These commodities were relatively common in their place of production, but unique enough to command high prices in distant markets. Trade goods mentioned in the letters include linen and a kind of unprocessed cloth that may be silk. The Sogdians were bringing goods into China that included Indian pepper, Tibetan musk and a 'white' lead powder that the Chinese aristocracy used as a cosmetic. The Sogdians were also dealing in silver coins to transfer profits.

The author of *Letter Five* was a Sogdian businessman called Fri-Khwataw who was operating in the Chinese frontier city of Guzang in the Gansu corridor. The letter was addressed to the 'Chief Merchant' Aspandhat who was resident at the oasis city of Khotan near the Pamir Mountains. The letter is addressed:

> To the noble lord Aspandhat who is Chief Merchant. Sent by your servant Fri-Khwataw.

In this letter Fri mentions a consignment of goods sent from Central Asia to China, but many of the commodities named are indecipherable. Fri writes:

> In Guzang there are four bundles of 'white' lead powder for dispatch. There are 2,500 measures of pepper for dispatch. There are a double *prasthaka* of *n*[. . .]*t*, and five *prasthakas* of *rysk*, and half a weight of silver.

Fri also had to clarify his involvement in the repayment of a debt due to the Chief Merchant. He was concerned that his superior might think he had stolen some money that was due to be returned. He writes:

> I heard that Kharstrang owed you 20 staters of silver and he promised he would send it. He gave me the silver, but when I weighed it I found there were only four and a half staters. I asked him, if 20 staters were due, then why did he give me only four and a half staters? He said: "Aspandhat found me and I gave him the rest [that I owed]".

Fri was clearly concerned that Kharstrang might claim that he had stolen the money and he therefore wanted to get his explanation to Aspandhat before he received any malicious reports to the contrary.

The Sogdian merchants would have sent regular correspondences back and forth along the Silk Routes and these messages would have informed colleagues about market opportunities that had become available in distant regions. But when Nanai wrote back to his homeland, the opportunities for profit had greatly diminished. He reports:

> It has been three years since [. . .] came from inner China . . . But linen cloth is selling well and anyone who still has not taken his unmade cloth to market can now sell all of it. Sirs, we are the only [Sogdian] survivors in the region from Jincheng up to Dunhuang. If we were to inform you about everything that has happened to China you would be beyond grief. You will not be able to make a profit here.[30]

The letters are describing the collapse of the trade routes, but in doing so they reveal the commercial infrastructure that had been in place before AD 313. Nanai describes how his network of business contacts was disintegrating as large parts of China were overcome by the Xiongnu assault. He writes:

> Sirs, it is eight years since I sent Saghrak and Farn-Aghat into inner China. It has been three years since I last received a message from them saying that they are well. I have not received a reply from them since the last evil event occurred and I do not know how they have fared.[31]

Further passages reveal the anguish felt by Nanai:

> Four years ago I sent Artikhu-Vandak [into inner China]. Wakhushakk also went with the caravan from Guzang, but when they reached Luoyang they found that all the Indians and the Sogdians there had died of starvation.[32]

There was also confusion regarding the situation in inner China:

> Sirs, we do not know whether the remaining Chinese were able to expel the Barbarians from Changan or whether the [enemy] took the country beyond. There are now only a hundred freemen from Samarkand in [. . .] and in Dryn there are only 40 [of our people].[33]

Fri was stockpiling commodities in Guzang that he was supposed to be forwarding to the markets of inner China. The Xiongnu conflict was seriously affecting communications within these regions and Fri was unwilling to risk any delivery. He needed to inform his suppliers about this problem and his letter to the Chief Merchant at Khotan outlined his concerns. The news was worrying. Fri writes:

> Day after day I have received worse news from inner China . . . I am stuck here in Guzang and I have become isolated. I no longer go backwards and forwards [with the caravans]. There are no caravans leaving from here.[34]

Many Sogdians had decided to flee China to escape the hostilities and Fri had recently lost contact with his commercial partner, a man called Ghawtus. The remaining Chinese forces on the frontier were preventing some caravans from leaving the failing empire and Fri could not send goods out to Khotan. He reports:

> When Ghawtus travelled away from Guzang I went after him. I came to Dunhuang, but they prevented me from leaving [China]. If Ghawtus has found a route through then I will send out the 'blacks'. Many Sogdians were ready to leave [China], but they cannot depart . . . I would have remained at Dunhuang, but the Sogdians there are destitute.[35]

Perhaps Fri and Nanai made it safely back to Samarkand before China descended into even greater political and economic chaos. Their letters indicate the complexity of the overland trade ventures that crossed Inner Asia, but they also reveal the human motivations behind these dealings. The surviving classical sources do not offer this level of insight into caravan ventures and this is why the *Sogdian Letters* are so important. They remind modern scholars that the caravans that operated along the great trade routes of the ancient world were formed from numerous individuals, each with their own particular interests that often rose above the immediate concerns of trade and profit.

THE CASPIAN TRADE ROUTES

Ancient trade networks followed the Oxus River as it flowed between Sogdia and Bactria. These trade routes led north into the Caspian region where Eastern commodities could be brought across the Caucasus Mountains. The goods were transported along river valleys and through steep mountain passes to reach Roman territories on the Black Sea coast. Like many other overland trade routes, travel through the Caucasus was seasonally restricted and journeys were not advisable in the harsh winter months.

Most of the traffic crossing the Caucasus Mountains was managed by the disparate hill tribes who occupied this region, especially the Colchic people who controlled territories on the eastern shore of the Black Sea. The geographer Strabo came from the Pontus region and he describes how Indian goods were reaching the nearby Greek communities. From the western shores of the Caspian Sea, travellers followed the Cyrus River inland to a mountain pass deep in the Caucasus. From this remote site, it was a short overland crossing to the Phasis River that led down towards the eastern shores of the Black Sea. Strabo writes:

> The Oxus River divides Bactria from Sogdia. They say it is so navigable that the Indian merchandise packed over the mountains is easily brought along it to the Caspian Sea. From there, the goods are brought by various rivers to the successive regions beyond, as far as the Pontus.[36]

Phasis was in the Colchis region and it was connected to the coastal city of Dioscurias which lay in the mountainous territory to its north. Pliny describes Roman trade at Dioscurias and indicates the difficulties involved in dealing with the Colchis tribes. He writes:

> Dioscurias was once so famous that according to Timosthenes 300 tribes speaking different languages used to go there. Consequently Roman traders had to carry out their business with the help of a staff of 130 interpreters.[37]

Phasis had good communications with the Pontic ports on the southern shore of the Black Sea and the Greek towns of Amisus and Sinope were only two or three days sailing from the port.[38] Indian goods reaching these towns were trafficked overland to cities in Asia Minor. Roman ships also sailed from the Pontic ports through the Bosporus and Hellespont on trade voyages into the Aegean Sea. These trade dealings must have intermixed Indian goods with a wide range of Colchic and Black Sea merchandise.

Roman authorities became interested in these possible routes to India during the Republican era. In 65 BC the Roman general Pompey led his forces to the Caucasus Mountains in pursuit of the Pontic king Mithradites and his tribal allies. Pompey met with the Roman fleet at the port of Phasis on the eastern coast of the Black Sea, but was anxious to know more about this remote territory. Pompey therefore collected intelligence about the Caspian trade routes that lead into India.[39] Colchis was at the very edge of classical civilization and the Roman army found itself in the land of Greek legend. It was here that Jason was believed to have sought the Golden Fleece and the Titan, Prometheus, the fire-bringer, suffered eternal torment chained to a rock somewhere in the furthest recesses of the mountains. Pompey styled himself 'the Great' in admiration of Alexander, so perhaps he hoped to emulate his hero in future campaigns that would take Roman armies deep into India. Pliny summarized this incident:

> Investigation under the leadership of Pompey revealed that the journey from India to Bactria takes seven days with [travellers] reaching a tributary of the Oxus called Bactrus. Indian merchandise can then be conveyed from the Bactrus across the Caspian to the Cyrus River and then carried overland for less than five days to reach the Phasis River leading to the Black Sea.[40]

It seems that some adventurous Greek merchants followed the Caucasus trade routes as far as the Caspian shore. Starting from the Roman port at Phasis, they would travel upstream by small river craft to reach a large mountain fortress called Sarapana. The travellers would then follow an ancient wagon road that wound through the hills to meet with the Cyrus River. The last stage of the journey followed this river down to the coast of the Caspian Sea.[41] Altogether this course covered more than 700 kilometres and goods were moved by river craft, pack animals, wagon, and probably human portage. Strabo confirms this contact route:

> The Phasis is a large river . . . it is navigated upstream as far as a fortress called Sarapana which is capable of admitting the population of a city. From there people travel overland for four days by a wagon-road to reach the Cyrus River.[42]

The route was difficult because of the nature of the terrain and the character of the surrounding hill tribes.[43]

As time progressed, the Roman Empire acquired more extensive control over the Colchis region and extended its authority east over the small kingdom of Iberia on the far side of the Caucasus Mountains.[44] This allowed the Roman army to control the mountain passes that could be used by tribes from the Russian Steppe to invade Armenia. Roman garrisons were placed at strategic points in the Caucasus Mountains including the deep gorge of the Darial Pass which they protected by building a defensive wall.[45] A military inscription found on the eastern side of the mountains reveals that a further Roman detachment was stationed overlooking the shores of the Caspian Sea. This unit guarded a location nearly 1,600 kilometres from its legionary base at Melitene in eastern Asia Minor.[46] The new security arrangements improved conditions for travellers passing through the Caucasus Mountains, but Roman subjects would always remain vulnerable to attack or ambush in such remote and rugged territories.[47]

ROME AND MESOPOTAMIA

The caravan trade routes that crossed from Roman Syria into the Parthian territories of Mesopotamia followed the Euphrates and Tigris river valleys south to reach the great urban centres of ancient Babylonia. The markets of Mesopotamia received Indian and Chinese goods from overland caravan routes that had crossed Iran. They were also supplied with Eastern merchandise by ships bringing trade goods from northwest India into the Persian Gulf.[48] As a consequence of these trade connections, Mesopotamia became one of the major commercial regions of the ancient world.

Strabo describes a journey from Roman Syria down to the great Mesopotamian city of Seleucia. Merchants from the Mediterranean travelled east from the Syrian capital of Antioch to the nearby Roman border on the Upper Euphrates. Strabo indicates that the crossing into Parthian territory was made at Anthemusia near the Roman town of Zeugma.[49] Later, Zuegma became the main border crossing for travellers and Roman customs officials were stationed at the town to tax the movement of commodities across the frontiers. Philostratos repeated a story told about the famous philosopher Apollonius of Tyana. Philostratos writes that Apollonius, a strict moral figure, was questioned by the customs officers who managed the crossing at Zuegma. The tax collector who was in charge led him to the notice board and asked him what he was taking out of the country. Apollonius replied, 'I have nothing to declare but my virtues' and he began to recite a list of his virtues such as Grace, Faith, Charity, Discipline, and so on. The tax collector was immediately interested as he believed these were the names of valuable female concubines who accompanied the philosopher.[50]

After crossing the Euphrates, travellers gathered together into caravans for mutual support and security on the long journey down through northern Mesopotamia. The Parthian rulers did not have extensive control over the various communities that inhabited Upper Mesopotamia and the small city states of this region generally ran their own affairs as vassal subjects. Consequently, passing caravan traffic had to contend with the various local authorities whose territories they wished to traverse.

So it was that the caravans crossing Mesopotamia brought together a broad range of travellers with a diverse variety of destinations and many different purposes for making the journey. Many people would have travelled only a short distance, with the caravan stopping off along the route, while others had business obligations at far-away locations.

Until the reign of the Emperor Vespasian, all Jews were required to pay a temple tax of two shekels to Jerusalem. The large Jewish communities who lived in Mesopotamia were therefore obliged to transport considerable quantities of cash across the Parthian frontiers. Josephus recalls:

> Many tens of thousands of Jews shared in the convoy of these monies because they feared the raids of the Parthians.[51]

In this era, thousands of Mesopotamian Jews visited Jerusalem every year for their religious observances at the Temple. This explains the account in the *Acts of the Apostles* where a miracle in Jerusalem is witnessed by people from Mesopotamia, Media and Elam in southwest Iran.[52] Commercial contacts between these Jewish communities involved goods that would have routinely crossed the frontiers with the religious travellers.

It seems that prominent members of the Jewish community in Mesopotamia and Palestine were active in trafficking and selling imported Chinese silks. Early Jewish texts indicate that Abba, father of Samuel, and Rabbi Judah Ben Bathyra were involved in the silk trade operating through a town called Nisibis in the Upper Euphrates.[53] Rabbi Abba was a silk merchant as the *Midrash* commentary reveals:

> Abba Ben Abba was a dealer in silk. Once Judah Ben Beteirah ordered some silk from him, and Abba laid it aside in his name. But Judah found no opportunity to come for the merchandise for a long time. When he finally arrived, Abba gave him the very silk he had ordered. Judah said: "Why hast thou kept it for me though I did not send thee a deposit?" Abba replied: "Thy word is stronger in my eyes than money".[54]

Towns like Tyre on the Syrian coast were heavily involved in the silk trade and workers at these sites were renowned for their skill at dyeing fabrics. The workshops were particularly well-known for dying purple garments using an expensive locally-produced colourant. Writing in a later era, Procopius reports:

> For many generations the production of silk garments was a staple industry of Beirut and Tyre in Phoenicia. The merchants who handled these goods and the craftsmen and artisans who produced these wares have lived in these places from ancient times and they sent their merchandise from there to every land.[55]

Local caravans regularly criss-crossed the desert tracks between the towns of Upper Mesopotamia, delivering small but precious consignments of foreign imports, as well as more mundane regional goods. The movement of peoples and regional commodities through these territories must have been routine, yet it is barely attested in the surviving evidence. An ancient papyrus recently discovered in this territory reveals how a man from Beth Phouraia in Upper Mesopotamia wrote to his son in AD 240 advising him how to hire camels for an overland journey from the Syrian city of Aleppo to Zeugma.[56]

In the Augustan era, caravans did not take the most direct route from Syria down the Euphrates river valley into Mesopotamia. Instead, they travelled from Edessa into a desert territory occupied by a nomadic tent dwelling people called the Scentae.[57] Pliny describes these pastoral nomads:

> The Scentae have nomadic habits and receive their name from the tents which constitute their dwellings. These are made of goats' hair and they pitch these tents wherever they like.[58]

The route through Scentae territory led to the Balikh tributary and the caravans followed the river down to its confluence with the Euphrates at Nikephorion. This route was longer, but it avoided a stretch of the Upper Euphrates where local communities charged travellers excessively high tolls. By contrast, the Scentae were a generally peaceful people who imposed fewer charges on passing caravans and had established watering points to facilitate Roman travellers. Strabo explains:

> The chieftains who live along both sides of the Euphrates River occupy country which . . . has more resources than that of surrounding lands . . . but they extract considerable tribute.[59]

By contrast:

> The Scentae are peaceful and they take only a moderate amount of tribute from travellers. So merchants avoid the land along the Euphrates River and risk a journey through the desert. Keeping the river to their right, they travel for approximately three days into the wilderness.[60]

By following this diversionary route, the caravans would reach a place called Scenae which was the main settlement of the tent dwelling nomads. This was a long journey and Strabo reports:

> From crossing the Euphrates River the journey to Scenae takes 25 days. On the road there are camel-drivers who keep halting-places which are sometimes well supplied with reservoirs. These are generally cisterns, though in some instances the camel-drivers use waters brought in from other places.[61]

From Scenae, the caravans would then follow the Euphrates river valley south into the lands of Lower Mesopotamia, known to contemporaries as 'Babylonia'.[62] In total it was a journey of perhaps 700 kilometres from Zeugma on the Roman frontier to Seleucia in central Mesopotamia.

The enormous city of Seleucia was a major destination for Roman travellers crossing into Mesopotamia. Seleucia maintained some level of regional independence despite the fact that it was firmly located within the Parthian Realm. The city could resist political interference in its civic business, and Pliny describes its enormous circuit walls that spread out in the shape of an eagle with extended wings.[63] The city was one of the greatest urban centres of the Greek world and contained a vast population drawn from many diverse ancient cultures. Pliny reports that Seleucia had about 600,000 inhabitants and this made it perhaps the third or fourth largest city in the ancient world. The city was founded by the Seleucid dynasty and still preserved its Hellenic character with large sections of its population composed of Macedonians, Greeks, Syrians and Jews.[64] The presence of Greek merchants in Seleucia is mentioned in a Palmyrene inscription dating to AD 19 and these traders were probably involved in the business of supplying Roman markets with Eastern goods.[65]

Seleucia must have been a significant centre for the consumption of Eastern goods as well as an important market for the distribution of these commodities to surrounding regions. The location and character of the city gave the site remarkable advantages in Eastern commerce. Seleucia was located on a canal that connected the Euphrates to the Tigris and this allowed the city to receive traffic from both these major waterways. Eastern goods arriving at ports on the Persian Gulf were shipped north through these river systems to reach the busy commercial markets of the city. From Seleucia, merchants from the Roman Empire could continue south to the small kingdom of Mesene which lay at the head of the Persian Gulf. This area was regularly visited by Eastern merchants who made routine trade voyages to Arabia and northwest India.

The Parthian administrative capital of Ctesiphon was positioned close to Seleucia and lay on the banks of the Tigris only a short distance away. The Parthian king spent the winter at his palaces in Ctesiphon and moved his court to more Eastern cities during the summer months.[66] Pliny describes Ctesiphon as the main capital of the Parthian Realm, but it was also a significant commercial centre for the caravan trade that crossed Iran.

The Ctesiphon markets were stocked by Parthian dealers and Greek merchants were discouraged from travelling east along these Iranian trade routes. Merchants from Seleucia therefore travelled to nearby Ctesiphon to acquire eastern goods at the Parthian bazaars. Strabo reports:

> Ctesiphon is a very large city that lodges a great number of people. It has been equipped with buildings by the Parthians and they provide the city with goods for sale and with arts that are pleasing to them.[67]

Merchants could employ river craft for the journey south from Seleucia along the Euphrates and Tigris river systems to the Persian Gulf. Travellers on the Euphrates route passed through the grandiose remains of ancient Babylon. The Euphrates still flowed through the former capital, past the elaborate riverside quays and abandoned palaces. In the mid first century AD, the Parthian king, Vologaeses, established a new city in the southern vicinity of Babylon and the ancient capital lost more of its dwindling population.[68] The massive circuit walls and huge vaulted hanging gardens still stood, but most districts of the city fell further into disuse and ruin.[69] Pliny explains that over the centuries, most of the population of ancient Babylon had relocated to Seleucia, leaving the older city a marvel of elaborate, but empty, facades.[70]

PALMYRA

The city of Palmyra lay in the Syrian Desert between the Roman Empire and the Parthian Realm. Palmyra was a territorial capital that controlled a large swathe of oasis territory surrounded by a great expanse of desert. Located in the space between the two great regional powers, Palmyra was able to preserve a remarkable level of autonomy. The city authorities raised their own military forces and generally maintained good political relations with both the Roman and Parthian governments. The inhabitants of Palmyra exploited this unique situation to become an important trade intermediary between these two great political entities. As a result, the city developed into a major operational base for distant caravan ventures leading from Syria into Mesopotamia.

There is a vast tax-law inscription from Palmyra which lists tolls on numerous goods coming into the city.[71] This remarkable text indicates how local trade networks conveyed regional produce as well as distantly exotic commodities. It also reveals how Palmyra was itself a consumer and it is likely that the earliest Palmyrene trade ventures into Mesopotamia were to supply their home markets.

The best evidence for Palmyrene caravan trade is provided by the commemorative inscriptions that have been recovered from the desert ruins of the ancient city.[72] These texts offer information about the organization of caravan expeditions by mentioning their main destinations and listing the names of people who had positions of responsibility in these ventures. By way of contrast, the Greek historian Appian provides the only surviving literary reference for Palmyra's position in Eastern trade. His account dates to the mid second century AD and indicates the full development of Palmyrene commerce. Appian reports:

> The Palmyrenes are merchants. They bring the products of India and Arabia from Persia into Roman territory where they distribute them.[73]

Palmyra began developing into an important centre for distance commerce during the first century AD. Strabo does not mention the city in connection with travel routes through Mesopotamia and his sources did not indicate that Palmyra had a significant role in distance trade. The earliest commemorative inscriptions in the city to record distant trade ventures date to AD 19 and AD 24. They mention the presence of Palmyrene merchants at Seleucia and Babylon who must have reached these commercial centres by caravan.[74] Later inscriptions refer to the activities of Palmyrene merchants at Mesopotamian cities closer to the Persian Gulf.[75] It seems that by around AD 70, Palmyrene caravans were travelling down to the head of the Gulf to visit the city of Spasinou Charax in the small kingdom of Mesene.[76] A typical example from AD 81 reads:

> The Palmyrene merchants who have travelled from Charax [dedicate this] to the honour to Zabdibol, the son of Ogeilu, the son of Ammat, the son of A'aqi, the Palmyrene.[77]

Palmyrene trade was not exceptional in the AD 70s when Pliny compiled his encyclopaedic study of the ancient world. When Pliny described Palmyra he noted the agricultural wealth of the oasis city-state, but did not draw attention to Palmyrene commerce. He reports:

> The rich fields of Palmyra are surrounded on every side by a vast circuit of sand and nature has therefore isolated it from the rest of the world. It has its own fate between the two mighty empires of Rome and Parthia.[78]

During this era, the cities of Upper Mesopotamia would have performed a more significant role in distant trade ventures and most Roman travellers continued to follow the courses outlined by Strabo. Overall, there are comparatively few Palmyrene caravan inscriptions dating to the first century AD.

It is not known at what stage Rome assumed full authority over Palmyra and its oasis territories.[79] Pliny was close to imperial government and his testimony suggests that there was still a tendency to regard Palmyra as semi-autonomous during the late first century AD. Even when it was integrated into the Roman Empire, the city councils of Palmyra were still able to exercise their own regional authority and use their initiative to raise and station local forces in the surrounding desert.

By the early second century AD, caravan inscriptions from Palmyra were describing well defined trade routes into Mesopotamia.[80] The caravan trails led from Palmyra across the Syrian Desert to Hit on the mid-Euphrates. This section of the trade route covered a distance of about 470 kilometres and avoided the regions of Upper Mesopotamia which were still controlled by small communities who imposed high tolls on passing caravans.[81] Under Palmyrene direction, caravanserais were established along the desert road to the Euphrates in order to supply and protect merchant travellers. From there, the journey turned south along the Euphrates as far as Charax in Mesene. In total, the attested trade routes from Palmyra to Charax therefore covered a distance of about 1,000 kilometres.[82]

Josephus outlines the position Palmyra held in the region and indicates how the city was connected to the surrounding territories. He writes:

> Palmyra is a distance of two days' journey from Upper Syria and one day's travel from the Euphrates. From the great Babylon the distance is a journey of six days.[83]

These estimates do not represent the steady pace of caravan traffic and modern estimates suggest that it would have taken at least 38 days for ordinary travellers to make the journey from Antioch via Palmyra to Charax.[84]

By AD 108, Palmyrenes were also trading with the newly established Parthian city of Vologesias.[85] Along with Charax, this urban centre formed one of the major destination points for Palmyrene trade ventures into Mesopotamia. Significantly, eight of the surviving caravan inscriptions mention Vologesias, while 16 refer to Charax.[86]

THE PARTHIAN WAR

Palmyra did not rise to full prominence as a distance trade centre until the second century AD. This expansion was connected with a failed Roman campaign to conquer Mesopotamia after the Emperor Trajan invaded Armenia in AD 113. After defeating the Parthians in pitched battle, the Roman forces marched down through Mesopotamia to Mesene. To the Romans, this seemed an easy victory and the Emperor was well received by the small vassal kingdoms of Mesopotamia that had previously been subject to the Parthians.[87]

After completing this dramatic conquest, Trajan travelled down to the shore of the Persian Gulf and inspected the ships that were leaving for India. The Emperor was already in his sixties and perhaps beginning to feel the onset of the illness that would soon claim his life. Dio Cassius writes:

> Then Trajan came to the ocean. When he had learned its nature and had seen a ship sailing to India, he said: "Oh, if only I were still young, then I would certainly have crossed over to India". For he began to think about India and was curious about their affairs. He counted Alexander a lucky man to have been there.[88]

Roman forces immediately began the task of organizing the conquered Mesopotamian territories into new imperial provinces. For local communities, this meant the payment of regular taxes to the Roman State, along with the stricter regulation of regional trade. Small Mesopotamian kingdoms had paid tribute to the Parthians, but had been permitted to collect and manage their own taxes. These new impositions consequently caused outrage and the Mesopotamian city-states were soon in full revolt, either killing, or expelling their new Roman garrisons. Roman reprisals were extreme and the ensuing conflict caused widespread destruction to the urban centres of ancient Mesopotamia. Nisibis was recaptured, but when Roman forces stormed Edessa, the city was sacked and burned. The great capital of Seleucia was also retaken and torched, while Hatra suffered a protracted Roman siege.

The unrest that began in Mesopotamia soon spread into Roman territory. The causes are unknown, but perhaps the Mesopotamian war was drawing too many Roman garrison troops away from the Eastern provinces. Many refugees must have fled the conflict in Mesopotamia and escaped into neighbouring Syria and Palestine where they stirred up long held anti-Roman sentiments. Jewish groups in Egypt and the neighbouring territory of Cyrene also chose this opportunity to revolt.[89] In AD 117, the newly appointed Emperor Hadrian decided that the Mesopotamian conflict should be abandoned. Roman forces were consequently withdrawn from the region, leaving the Parthians to reclaim their former authority over these Eastern communities.

Palmyra and Mesene emerged from this brutal war relatively unscathed. Due to the proximity of the Emperor and his campaigning army, Mesene had not joined the other Mesopotamian communities in revolt against the Roman occupation. The commercial infrastructure that brought Eastern goods into Mesopotamia from the Persian Gulf therefore remained intact.

Palmyra exploited the power vacuum caused by the Roman withdrawal from Mesopotamia. The small city-states on the mid-Euphrates had been weakened by the conflict with Rome, but the Parthians were slow to re-establish their authority over these regions. Uniquely for a Syrian city, Palmyra still maintained its own independent military forces and after the war they began to take greater control over territories around the mid-Euphrates.[90] Palmyrene units were positioned to more effectively control desert traffic and protect caravan travellers. Troops were also arranged to manage river traffic on the Euphrates and used their own craft to better patrol along its length. In this era, Palmyrene units are attested on the islands of Ana and Bijan on the mid-Euphrates.[91] This is significant because river traffic was cheaper than overland haulage and bulky trade goods could often be moved faster and more securely by these means.

As this commerce developed, Palmyrene merchants made more extensive use of river craft to travel the 700 kilometres south from Hit to Charax. The return trade venture involved a sailing upstream where pack animals would be waiting for the crossing back through the desert to Palmyra.[92] This Palmyrene trade route compared favourably with the routes used in Egypt's Eastern commerce. The Palmyrene course must have involved a 16 day overland crossing and perhaps 26 days travelling the length of the Euphrates River. By contrast, Egyptian importers spent up to 12 days on their caravan crossings and a further 12 days on Nile River sailings.[93] The voyage from India to Egypt was a long and dangerous undertaking involving a sailing through the Red Sea that could take up to a month. Importers using the Persian Gulf and the Palmyrene trade routes could therefore reach Mediterranean markets well before their Egyptian competitors.

This increased commerce became a lucrative source of income for the Palmyrenes and their city enjoyed the benefits of greater urban development. As trade expanded, more city resources were redirected to ensure the continuance of commercial traffic. Inscriptions reveal that Palmyrene forces routinely patrolled the desert and the city sent out expeditions to outlying regions to attack bandits and nomad tribes who would threaten the caravans. An example is preserved in the Athena temple at Palmyra revealing how a general from the city named Soados saved a caravan that came under attack from a bandit leader named Abdallat. The text from AD 144 reads:

> The caravan of Palmyrenes who came back from Vologaesias have erected [this monument] because [Soados acted] in a distinguished manner and he advanced with a large force to protect them against Ahdallathos from Eeithe and his robbers . . . For a long time the [robbers] had been lying in wait in order to harm the [caravan but] Soados [intervened and] saved them. Therefore they erected [these statues] to honour him.[94]

A further inscription from this era records how a Palmyrene named Aelius Boras was often selected by the city council to be their *strategoi*, 'commander' on these military operations. Boras is credited with 'establishing peace on the outer boundaries of the city' and although he was not part of the Roman command structure, the inscriptions reveal that two Syrian governors commended his military exploits.[95]

The caravan inscriptions also indicate how Palmyrenes maintained good relations with the Parthian overlords of Mesopotamia. A dedication from AD 131 records how Palmyrene merchants at Charax had officially honoured the Parthian Satrap of Thilouana. Another inscription from AD 138 mentions Palmyrene involvement in an embassy sent to the ruler Orodes of Susa, who was subject to the Parthian High King. The Palmyrenes were especially active at the new Parthian city of Vologesias where they constructed a religious complex dedicated to their chief deity Bel and established an Augustan Temple to acknowledge the cult of the Roman Emperors.[96]

Palmyrene inscriptions confirm the trade increase that occurred within a generation of the Roman-Parthian war. In the century between AD 19 and AD 131 there are six surviving inscriptions recording caravan ventures from Palmyra to the cities of Mesopotamia. By contrast, there are at least 19 inscriptions for the 30 year period from between AD 131 to AD 161.[97] This is also the era when Appian makes his famous statement that the Palmyrenes were merchants engaged in the business of supplying Roman markets with Indian and Arabian merchandise.[98]

The honorary inscriptions reveal how Palmyrene caravans would have been organized for the journey across into Mesopotamia. The caravans are called *synodiai* in the Palmyrene texts and the merchants who formed these companies are referred to as the 'sons of the caravan'. Each *synodiai* was formed from large groups of merchants who appointed a *synodiarchos* or 'caravan leader' and chose a representative who held the position of *archemporos* or 'leading merchant'. The caravan leader dealt with issues relating to the logistics of travel and the leading merchant was concerned with business deals at the destination markets. Together, the caravan members hired armed guards to protect the company from bandit raiders and any interference from outlying nomads.[99] Caravan travellers also contributed funds to pay tolls and protection money to the various communities they would pass on the journey. The caravan leader took charge of these arrangements and ensured safe passage for his company by way of numerous negotiations and payments. The expenses incurred explain references in the inscriptions to individuals bringing back caravans 'at no cost' or 'at their own expense'.[100] On these occasions, wealthy benefactors probably paid the contribution required from each member of the caravan. The frequency of the caravan expeditions is not known, but it seems reasonable to suppose that several ventures were organized every year and that hundreds of merchants travelled in each *synodiai*.

The threats to travellers were real and in some instances the caravan guards would have been involved in serious fighting with bandit raiders.[101] The surviving inscriptions generally acknowledge an individual who performed some extraordinary service to a caravan expedition and most trade ventures must have been completed without incident. Some of the inscriptions do not fully explain the service that a noteworthy individual performed for the *synodiai*. Thus, in AD 135, a caravan returning from Charax erected a statue to a Roman centurion named Julius Maximus, but the reasons for this dedication are not known.[102]

In this era, travellers favoured the Palmyrene trade routes because they were well protected and adequately equipped with supply installations. The traditional routes through the Upper Euphrates crossed a politically fractured landscape where certain communities demanded excessive tolls and there was threat of uncontrolled banditry. The fact that the Palmyrene route was managed by a single strong and accountable authority encouraged the growth of their particular trade course.[103]

As trade contacts developed, Palmyrenes began holding positions of authority in the Mesene kingdom. For example, inscriptions record how the 'Archon of Phorath' and the 'Archon of Mesene' assisted trade ventures between Charax and Palmyra.[104] These men were probably the leaders of Palmyrene communities in Mesene who received their titles from colleagues. It has also been argued that these titles were granted or approved by the local kings of Mesene.[105] From the actions recorded in the Palmyrene inscriptions, it seems that these officials were able to provide considerable assistance to the merchant travellers who entered their districts.[106]

The kingdom of Mesene dominated commercial traffic entering Mesopotamia through the Persian Gulf. Consequently, Palmyrene contacts with the city of Charax would have been particularly significant. Pliny was probably referring to Greek or Roman businessmen when he mentions 'our merchants' at Charax.[107] Mesene is also depicted as a gathering place for Eastern traders in a third century commentary called the *Hymn of the Pearl*.[108] The author recounts:

> I passed through the borders of Mesene which sits on the shore of the sea and is the meeting place for merchants from the East.[109]

Charax was surrounded by large raised embankments to protect its urban districts from the floodwaters of the Tigris. The site had been established as a port, but over generations, alluvial deposits had washed down from the river to extend the coastline far beyond the city.[110] When the Emperor Trajan travelled to this shore, it would have been here that he saw Indian ships and crews from Barygaza, along with Arabian craft from the Yemen.[111]

The caravan inscriptions show that by the mid second century AD, merchants from Palmyra had begun making trade voyages from Mesene to northwest India.[112] These expeditions probably resembled the Egyptian trade dealings documented in the *Periplus*.[113] Like the Roman traders from Egypt, the Palmyrenes referred to northwest India as 'Scythia' and an inscription from AD 157 records:

> The merchants who have returned from Scythia on the ship of Honainu son of Haddudan . . . [dedicate this] to Marcus Ulpius Iarhai, the son of Hairan, the son of Abgar, 'the Patriot'. [They recognize] his honour because he helped and assisted them with great willingness.[114]

In total, the voyage from Charax to Indo-Scythia would have covered more than 2,000 kilometres but on these sailings there must have been detours to outlying ports on the Arab-Persian coasts. Images of ships in Palmyrene funerary art confirm that merchants from the city were involved in ocean trade voyages. The individuals commemorated in these grave sculptures were probably ship-owners who maintained vessels in the Persian Gulf.[115]

The Indian Ocean trade routes were continually evolving, with new commercial ports and market opportunities regularly becoming available to merchant travellers. Pliny offers some interesting information on the expansion of the Persian Gulf trade routes during the Parthian era. One of Pliny's main sources for this region was a study written by a Numidian king named Juba, who died in AD 23. Pliny struggled to make sense of new information that seemed to contradict Juba's early account of the area. Reports reaching Rome from merchants and Arab envoys, suggested that a range of new trade ports had opened up in the Persian Gulf. Pliny writes:

> Juba does not mention the town of the Omani, also called Batrasavave, and the town of Omana . . . and also Homna and Attana. These are towns said by our traders to be the most frequently visited ports in the Persian Gulf.[116]

Omana was a trade port on the southern coast of Iran that is briefly mentioned in the *Periplus*.[117] The other new trade ports of Homna and Attana do not appear in the *Periplus* so they must have rapidly risen to prominence in the decades before Pliny compiled his *Natural History*. The impact that Palmyrene commerce had on the Persian Gulf trade networks can be deduced from the data contained in Ptolemy's *Geography*, but this is another aspect of Eastern commerce that is yet to be fully explored.[118]

ROUTES THROUGH ROMAN TERRITORY

Merchants from Palmyra supplied the Roman markets with a range of exotic goods from Persia, India, Arabia and China. Silks and other elaborate Eastern fabrics were important in this commerce because they were relatively compact and easy to traffic along overland routes.[119] Silk fragments found in Palmyrene tomb-towers verify the significance of this fabric and sculptures from the city show matrons wearing clothing that was fine-formed and multi-layered.[120] Palmyrene traders also dealt in drugs, spices and aromatics that included incense and raw perfumes from Arabia. Pliny suggests that the Persian Gulf was an important supplier of pearls to the Roman Empire and Palmyrene sculptures confirm the popularity of this form of jewellery among the wealthy women of the city.[121]

Palmyrene merchants must have carried a wide range of Roman trade goods to the markets of Lower Mesopotamia. The *Periplus* indicates that visiting Indian merchants were interested in receiving linens, corals, fragrant potions and Roman wines.[122] Arabian traders visiting Charax could be offered purple cloths, saffron, fragrant ointments and gold and silver articles.[123] Palmyrene merchants could also offer Mesopotamian markets a range of food commodities produced in their oasis territories, including wines and dates. These regional products were used to acquire spices and the *Periplus* reveals that there was a significant market in India for Persian dates and Arabian wines.[124] The incident involving Apollonius at the frontier station indicates that specialist Roman slaves were trafficked into Mesopotamia.[125] Palmyrene merchants also dealt in Roman gold coins and a commemorative inscription records that a benefactor gave a larger quantity of older issue aurei to a merchant group.[126]

As the inscriptions from Palmyra mostly acknowledge the Mesopotamian stage of commercial ventures, it is difficult to reconstruct the Palmyrene trade routes through Roman territory. On returning to Palmyra, the merchant caravans would have crossed into Syria or Palestine to deliver their precious Eastern goods to a range of Roman markets. On reaching the relative security of the Roman provinces, the overland trade routes probably became diffuse as the merchants split off into smaller groups to reach their chosen retail destinations.

The Syrian capital of Antioch lay about 300 kilometres from Palmyra and many merchants set out in that direction.[127] One of the caravan inscriptions records how a customs officer from Antioch, who was in charge of taxing Eastern imports, had assisted a group of Palmyrene merchants.[128] The coastal Phoenician ports were also an important destination point for incoming Palmyrene caravans.[129] From these commercial centres, Eastern goods could be picked up by passing trade ships and trafficked across the Mediterranean.[130]

The *New Testament* reveals how Roman trade sailings operated along the Phoenician coast. Eastern goods reaching Phoenician shores through caravan trade must have been loaded into vessels that followed these same commercial sailings. On his last missionary journey, Paul took a cargo ship from Patara in Asia Minor southwards along the shores of Syria, calling at Tyre, Ptolemais and Caesarea.[131] When he was sent for trial in Rome, he was placed on a ship going from Caesarea northwards, calling at Sidon, the island of Cyprus and finally Myra in southern Asia Minor. From there he was transferred to one of the large Alexandrian grain ships bound for Rome.[132]

There is only one piece of literary evidence for Eastern commodities reaching the Phoenician coast. In the mid second century AD, the famous Greek doctor Galen described how he acquired drug specimens on a journey through Palestine. His samples included Indian drugs carried into the area by merchant camel teams. He reports:

> I had the good fortune to get hold of some Indian *lyceum*. The drug had recently been imported to Phoenicia together with some Indian aloe. I received it when I was on my way back from Palestine. I was convinced that the *lyceum* was Indian because it was brought in by camels with a larger cargo and the material is not native to this region.[133]

These Indian drugs came from markets in Mesopotamia and were probably imported by caravan through Palmyra.

RENEWED CONFLICT

In AD 147, after a generation of infighting and division, a ruler named Vologaeses IV came to power in Parthia with plans to reunify the kingdom. Vologaeses began to reinforce Parthian control over its former vassal territories, and in about AD 151 he attacked the kingdom of Mesene and deposed its ruler, Meredates, who had posed a threat to the Parthian succession. An ancient inscription engraved upon a bronze statue of Hercules records these events. The text reads:

> And Vologaeses drove king Meredates out of Mesene. So he himself became the ruler of all Mesene and he brought this bronze statue to this place. And he set it up in the temple of the god Apollo in front of the bronze gates.[134]

Vologaeses now acquired the valuable revenues that this small semi-independent kingdom received from its lucrative Eastern trade.[135]

Palmyrene inscriptions reveal that trade contacts with Mesene continued after Vologaeses had invaded the kingdom. A series of eight caravan inscriptions honouring a Palmyrene named Marcus Ulpius Iarhai all date to the short period between AD 156 and AD 159.[136] This amount of praise is unusual and some scholars speculate that Marcus was some form of Palmyrene 'hero', perhaps lending his support to beleaguered colleagues who were facing increased difficulties in Mesopotamia.[137]

But Mesene was only the beginning of Vologaeses' scheme to restore Parthian authority. In AD 155, Vologaeses invaded the disputed kingdom of Armenia, expelled its king, and put his own nominee on the throne. The Roman military response was ineffective and by AD 161 Parthian forces had invaded Syria, provoking a full scale war with the Empire. The Roman army repelled the invaders and marched east into Mesopotamia, sacking Seleucia and Ctesiphon in the process. The Roman campaign pushed onward into Media, but the outbreak of the Antonine Plague in AD 165 crippled the army's ability to continue with these hostilities.

These events had a severe impact on Palmyrene commerce and from AD 162, for a period of almost 30 years, there are no caravan inscriptions. Although the Palmyrenes protected the Euphrates frontier with their own troops, their soldiers also served as military units in the Roman army. The Parthian forces would have ignored this distinction and destroyed the Palmyrene outposts that guarded the city's Eastern trade routes. The Palmyrene units who remained must have been annihilated by the Parthians. In a short period of time, Palmyrene merchants lost their Messene trade contacts, their vital launching facilities on the Euphrates, and ultimately, the overland security arrangements essential to their eastern businesses.

The campaigning armies must have stripped territories of resources, destroyed urban markets and seized goods in transit. The *Sogdian Letters* offer a vivid account of how merchant lives and livelihoods were affected by prolonged regional conflicts. No merchant caravan letters have survived from this time in Palmyra, but it is easy to appreciate the hardships and distresses these people must have endured. The devastating effect of the Antonine pandemic is another factor in the decline of distance commerce and it must have hampered any quick recovery from the conflict. Palmyrene caravan inscriptions only re-commence after the death of Vologaeses.

PALMYRENES IN EGYPT

The fighting between Rome and Parthia ended in AD 166, but the traditional trade routes through Lower Mesopotamia must have remained unsafe for commercial travel. There was probably a large dispossessed population in the region and the Parthians must have sought retribution as they reclaimed their former territories. Faced with these circumstances, many Palmyrene merchants abandoned their traditional trade routes and chose to head for the friendly territory of Roman Egypt. By avoiding the Persian Gulf and using Egyptian trade routes, these Palmyrenes could continue their livelihoods as merchants who supplied Roman markets with Eastern goods.

An inscription suggests that a company of Palmyrene merchants established a large trade headquarters in Coptos during this period.[138] These wealthy merchants received Eastern cargoes offloaded from Palmyrene ships at the Red Sea ports. The cargoes were brought overland by caravan to Coptos and then shipped downstream to Alexandria on the Mediterranean coast. The Coptos inscription is dedicated to a Palmyrene called Zabdalas who built the trade headquarters from his own funds at great expense. A merchant leader named Zabdalas also appears in earlier caravan inscriptions from Palmyra city.[139] Consequently, some scholars suggest that this could be the same man who had led his merchant colleagues out of danger to build a new livelihood in Egypt.[140] The Coptos dedication reads:

> The merchants of the Red Sea who come from Hadriane Palmyra [made this dedication] to Zabdalas son of Salmanos, also [known as] Aneinas. [Zabdalas] has established the new foundations [of this building] entirely from his own funds. He has set up a monumental gateway and three porticoes along with accompanying chambers. The merchants of Hadriane Palmyra [have set this dedication up] to their companion and colleague to acknowledge his distinguished friendship.[141]

Frescoes decorated the walls of this large building and within its ruins were found twelve *stelai* and two stone altars. The stone slab *stelai* were carved with ornamental images, each one depicting a pair of Palmyrene merchants in the stylised artistic style of their home city.[142]

A fragmentary stone inscription from the Nile city of Dendereh offers further evidence for Palmyrene trade activity in Egypt. The inscription is a dedication in Greek and Palmyrene to a man named Julius Aurelius and it dates to the period between AD 160 and AD 212.[143] Julius was important within the community and the text refers to Palmyrene merchants and *naukleroi* who must be captains, or ship-owners, in the Red Sea commerce.[144]

The Palmyrenes were able to visit new trade ports in southern Arabia as they sailed from Roman Egypt to India. This explains the discovery of a smashed Palmyrene container found by archaeologists on the floor of an excavated storage room in Qana. The fragments of the vessel were carefully reassembled to reveal cursive Palmyrene script drawn on the container before it had been fired. The script read 'Achaea', which was a small Roman territory in Greece, and the container had been painted with a large monogram 'L'.[145] Palmyrene traders were possibly taking orders for merchant colleagues in Greece and these containers would be marked with their Mediterranean destinations.

Palmyrene caravan ventures through Mesopotamia had resumed by the 190s AD. This development offered Palmyrenes even greater opportunities for their trade business as they could offload their Eastern cargoes in either Egypt or Mesopotamia. They could also alternate these destinations to supply Roman Egypt with Persian products as well as Indian goods.[146] This would explain why the second century *Alexandrian Tariff* mentions a range of Persian goods being taxed on entry into Roman Egypt.[147] Among these commodities are Parthian and Babylonian hides, as well as drugs from inner Asia.[148]

In this era the Roman government began stationing units of Palmyrene soldiers in the desert regions of eastern Egypt. An inscription from Coptos dating to AD 216 reveals that Palmyrene archers mounted on camels were garrisoned in the city. These specialist soldiers were deployed in the Eastern Desert to conduct guard patrols and protect important caravans coming from the Red Sea ports.[149] One of these soldiers was a man named Marcus Aurelius Belakabos who left a dedication to the Palmyrene god Hierobolos near his military post.[150]

The Palmyrene troops were an elite desert unit and there is evidence that they had considerable wealth at their disposal. The names of several Palmyrene soldiers appear on elaborate and costly dedications made at sanctuaries in the port of Berenice. The inscriptions acknowledge the Eastern god Hierobolos, but they also recognize the cult of the Roman Emperors.[151] The dedications involved bronze statues and elaborate inscriptions that were beyond the means of an ordinary soldier on a modest military salary. Scholars have therefore suggested that these Palmyrene soldiers could have been in someway profiteering from Eastern commerce. Perhaps they were offering some form of preferential treatment to Palmyrene merchants and in return receiving generous rewards.[152]

The caravan inscriptions from Palmyra continue until the 260s AD when the Palmyrene Queen Zenobia attempted to seize control of the Eastern Roman Empire.[153] By this period, Palmyra had developed a greater role in Eastern politics and Palmyrene troops defended the Roman frontier from the new Sassanid dynasty of Persia. The Emperor Aurelian defeated Zenobia in AD 272 and the captive queen was paraded in a Triumph through the streets of Rome. After a further brief uprising, Palmyra was completely subjugated by Roman forces. In the following era, the city lost much of its distinctive character and became little more than a minor provincial city with a protective Roman garrison.[154]

ROME AND THE SILK ROADS

Centuries before the Parthians came to rule in ancient Iran, the Persian Empire had constructed a major overland highway through the central territories of their realm. The early Parthian kings used this 'Royal Road' to travel from Ctesiphon in Mesopotamia to their summer capitals at Ecbatana and Hyrcania in the eastern reaches of their territory.[155] This thoroughfare also functioned as a major caravan trade route to connect markets in Mesopotamia with urban centres in Central Asia.

Leaving from Mesopotamia, one branch of the caravan routes skirted the southern shores of the Caspian Sea to reach the steppe lands above Iran. These routes were travelled by caravan traders, including Armenians and Medes from the western Parthian Realm. They received Indian and Persian goods from Mesopotamia and travelled to the northern fringes of Parthia to trade with steppe peoples called the Aorsi. The Aorsi controlled the eastern coasts of the Caspian Sea and became wealthy by supplying Indian goods to a vast Sarmation population named the Alani, who lived on the Russian Steppes. Strabo explains:

> The Aorsi rule over much of the Caspian coast and they receive Indian and Babylonian merchandise on camels. They import this merchandise from the Armenians and the Medes and because of this wealth the Aorsi can wear gold ornaments.[156]

Other branches of these caravan routes headed from Mesopotamia across Iran to Bactria and the lands beyond. Large quantities of Roman goods were imported into Mesopotamia, and from cities like Ctesiphon these products would be trafficked along caravan routes to reach Central Asia. The Chinese were aware of this commerce and listed the range of Roman goods arriving in the Tarim regions through

Parthian and Indian trade contacts. The *Hou Hanshu* states:

> *Da Qin* (the Roman Empire) produces plenty of gold, silver, and precious jewels, luminous jade, 'bright moon' pearls, fighting cocks, rhinoceros horn, coral, yellow amber, opaque glass, whitish chalcedony, red cinnabar, green gemstones, decorated gold-threaded and multi-coloured embroideries, woven gold-threaded net, delicate polychrome silks painted with gold, and asbestos cloth.[157]

Many of the goods coming from Roman territory were actually Eastern commodities that had been re-processed in Roman workshops. Merchants from the Empire then re-exported these craft items back into the east through Mesopotamia. An example is Chinese silk that was re-woven by Roman workshops into a finer, gauze-like fabric before being sent back east into the Mesopotamian markets. The *Weilue* collected later Chinese reports of Rome and offers a longer list of Roman goods reaching Central Asia. Sixty-three products are mentioned, including goods from India and Arabia that Roman merchants were re-exporting through overland trade networks.[158]

The Iranian caravan routes that sent these Roman goods into Central Asia would have supplied Mesopotamia with large stocks of Chinese silks. As the profits of this commerce were considerable, the Parthian subjects of Iran denied Roman merchants access to these overland trade routes. If Roman traders wanted to acquire Chinese silks, they travelled no further east than the Parthian bazaars in Ctesiphon. There they met the incoming caravans and received the fabric at a premium price. The *Han Hanshu* records:

> The rulers of Rome have always wanted to send embassies to China. But the Parthians have prevented all contact because they want to trade Chinese silks with the Roman Empire.[159]

The Parthians had political, as well as commercial, reasons for blocking Roman access to the caravan routes of ancient Iran. In the distant East the Parthians faced powerful opponents, such as the Alani and the Kushan, who harboured ambitions to plunder, or conquer, their territories. It was not in the Parthian interest to permit regular channels of communication between these Eastern peoples and the equally ambitious Roman Empire.

There is only one reported instance of a Roman merchant who engaged in an overland trade venture through Parthian Iran to reach Inner Asia. In AD 100 a Macedonian merchant named Maes Titianus managed to send commercial agents along a trade route that reached the outer limits of ancient Bactria. Maes wrote an account of this unique trade venture and Roman geographers were able to use his information to construct improved maps of Inner Asia. The details can be compared with the itinerary collected by Isidore of Charax who describes a similar route through Iran that caravans followed towards the distant East.[160]

Starting from Ctesiphon, the merchants sent by Maes headed northeast across the bleak Zagros Mountains and the Iranian plateau to reach Ecbatana. From there the route ran east through the territories of Media and Hyrcania to the cities of

Hecatompylos and Merv.[161] Ptolemy reports:

> [The route] is through Mesopotamia to the Tigris and from there [the road goes] through the Garamaioi in Assyria and across Media to Ecbatana. From there [the road goes] through the Caspian Gates to Hecatompylos. The Caspian Sea is just a small distance north of this city.[162]

The distances involved in these overland routes were considerable. In total the caravan routes from Seleucia to Merv would have covered more than 1,600 kilometres.[163]

From Merv, the Maes group left Parthian territory and travelled onwards into Bactria. The destination was a 'Scythian' market called the 'Stone Tower' that lay somewhere in the distant Pamir Mountain range. Ptolemy reports:

> From Hecatompylos the road veers north to the city of Hyrcania. The road then leads to Merv [and from there] . . . the road extends east into Bactra . . . and from there onwards towards the Stone Tower.[164]

When the Maes group made their journey, the land of Bactria was part of the Kushan Domain which stretched across Inner Asia to the edge of the Tarim territories. The Stone Tower was probably an ancient site called Tashkurgan which lies midway between Bactria and the Tarim kingdom of Kashgar.[165] This region was a vital meeting point for the main overland trade routes that distributed Indian and Chinese goods across Central Asia.[166] The Maes group planned to intercept this commerce and return to the Roman Empire with valuable packages of Chinese silk.

Traders reaching the remote silk market at Tashkurgan were almost 3,000 kilometres distant from Ctesiphon. The total distance from Ctesiphon to the Chinese capitol Luoyang was over 7,000 kilometres, but few people would ever have travelled this entire route on a single trade venture. The caravan routes through Bactria allowed Parthians to reach the Tarim kingdoms and subsequently these travellers began to arrive in China. In AD 148 a Parthian prince called 'An Shigao' renounced his royal claim in Iran and travelled to Luoyang as a Buddhist missionary. Over the next 20 years he acquired a devoted community of religious followers and translated numerous Buddhist texts from Indian into Chinese. In AD 181 he was joined by a Parthian merchant called 'An Xuan' who contributed to the religious mission.[167]

The Maes expedition was only possible because of unique conditions that were in place for little more than a decade. The venture was made at a time when the Han Empire had just regained its authority over the Tarim kingdoms and Chinese forces were operating near the Pamir Mountains.[168] These Chinese conquests brought a new level of stability to the already well-established overland silk routes.[169] All this occurred when the Kushan Domain was politically secure and there was peace between the Roman Empire and the Parthian Realm.

There cannot have been many other Roman subjects who made the journey across Iran to Tashkurgan. Only a few years after the Maes expedition the Tarim kingdoms rose in full scale revolt against the Chinese Empire.[170] Within a decade Trajan had invaded Mesopotamia and renewed hostilities must have ensured that

1. A group of Romans assembled near a merchant ship to hear a speech by the Emperor Trajan (illustration drawn from Trajan's Column).

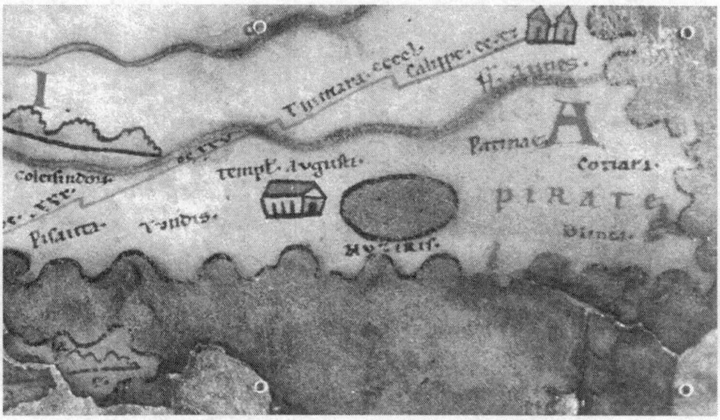

2. Detail from the *Peutinger Map* showing the Roman Temple of Augustus at Muziris in Tamil India.

3. A Palmyrene relief showing wealthy merchants leading a camel.

4. A gold coin of the king Kushan Huvishka. The reverse shows the god Pharro (Hermes-Mercury) holding a purse.

5. A Gandharan sculpture showing the death of the Buddha with a Greco-Roman figure in attendance.

6. A Gandharan carving depicting a scene from the Trojan War.

7. A Roman grave relief from Italy depicting the Peticii merchant family who had business interests in the distant East (Museo dell'Aquila).

8. An Indian statuette found at a house in Pompeii.

9. A Roman mosaic showing how hunters captured tiger cubs (*Hunt Mosaic*, Antioch): 'India produces the tiger which has tremendous swiftness. The hunter lies in wait to seize the tiger cubs, and then escapes on the fastest horse because, as soon as the female finds her lair empty, she springs into pursuit' – Pliny the Elder in his *Natural History*.

10. A classical bust depicting a subject of the Roman Empire who adopted Buddhist beliefs (Museo Nazionale Romano).

no further Roman subjects could have travelled safely through the distant Iranian trade routes.

As far as Ptolemy was aware, the Maes group were the only Romans to have reached Central Asia on an overland trade mission. While they were conducting their dealings at Tashkurgan, they were seized by agents of a mysterious foreign power. The party were taken east across vast unknown territories to a distant capital that Ptolemy located at the edge of the known world. The modern scholar must investigate the diplomatic records of ancient China to understand the significance of this extraordinary encounter.

5

Diplomatic Contacts with the Distant East

The Roman government was aware that there were powerful political regimes in the distant East far beyond their authority. Roman Emperors received embassies sent by the rulers of ancient India and ambassadors from Eastern powers deep in Inner Asia. Reports of these contacts offer an intriguing insight as to how the Romans viewed the ancient world and perceived their political role within it.

There are no 'court records' for the Roman Empire that could concisely explain state 'policy' or reveal the long-term aims of the imperial government. Rome had no extensive 'civil service' or any 'diplomatic core' that could propagate long-term political strategies. Within the Roman government the Emperor and his chosen advisers played a central role in most major political decision-making. Consequently, imperial policy was decided to a large extent by the value systems and personal character of a very small, ruling elite.

Classical accounts describing the arrival of distant emissaries were generally written by authors who were not part of the inner circle of imperial government. This is a concern, because important diplomatic discussions involving the Emperor were generally conducted in private. The consequences of any foreign arrangements were then revealed to the Roman population through large-scale political displays. As honoured guests of Rome, visiting ambassadors from the distant East were invited to attend carefully arranged public events. These stage-managed proceedings were designed to convey political concepts about imperial power and this propaganda influenced how the majority of Roman subjects perceived the distant contacts. Most of the surviving classical accounts do not reveal the business of distant diplomacy. Instead, they reflect the excitement and speculation felt by a population who would simply marvel at the sight of their Emperor in the company of exotic ambassadors from the edge of the known world.

ROME AND THE INDO-SCYTHIANS

The first state-level communication between Roman government and the rulers of ancient India occurred during the reign of Augustus.[1] In the *Res Gestae*, the Emperor records the great achievements of his reign and boasts that he was the first Roman leader to receive Indian ambassadors. He states, 'Embassies from kings in India were frequently sent to me: never before had they been seen with any Roman commander'.[2]

The first diplomatic contacts between Rome and the distant East were initiated by Indo-Scythian kings who ruled eastern territories bordering Parthia. Soon after

Augustus secured Egypt, a new fleet of over a hundred trade ships was constructed by Greco-Roman merchants anxious to reach India.[3] These merchants brought reports to Eastern destinations that described how the Mediterranean kingdoms had been united under a single ruler. The new Emperor had already revealed his ambition for further Eastern conquests by the Roman preparations to conquer Arabia. Indian merchants would have witnessed the Roman attack on the Yemen city of Aden and would have brought news back to their homelands about the Roman battle-fleet being assembled in the Red Sea. At this time there was widespread expectation in the Roman Empire that Augustus was about to launch a military invasion of Parthia in retaliation for the past defeats of Rome.[4] The rulers of northern India recalled the distant history of Alexander the Great who had set the precedent for classical generals to conquer Persia. Anticipating action in the East they therefore sent representatives to meet with Augustus.

The first Indo-Scythian envoys reached Augustus in about 26 BC. The Emperor was in Spain at the time, overseeing the final difficult Roman conquest of this far western region. A century after this event, Suetonius offers an account of this contact that is heavily influenced by Roman propaganda. He reports:

> Augustus gained a reputation for prowess and moderation which led even the Indians and the Scythians to send envoys of their own free will. These were nations previously known to us only through hearsay and now they petitioned for the friendship of Augustus and the Roman people.[5]

An even later account comes from a Roman writer named Paulus Orosius who recalls:

> The ambassadors of the Indians and the Scythians finally met Caesar Augustus in Spain, near a town called Tarracona. They had crossed the whole world and they could not wish for anything more than to praise the Emperor with the glory of Alexander the Great.[6]

This first contact occurred at a time when Augustus was occupied in the west of the Empire, dealing with earlier commitments and consolidating the established Roman territories. His attention was also concentrated on political arrangements he had instigated to secure the stability of the new imperial regime. It was not until 22 BC that Augustus, recently recovered from serious illness, was ready to take personal command in the East and finally deal with the unresolved issue of Parthia.

A second Indian embassy arrived at the Roman frontiers soon after Augustus had reached the eastern Mediterranean and made his presence known in the Greek cities. The embassy was sent by a powerful Saka ruler who commanded numerous small kingdoms around the Indus and Gujarat territories. The Saka court expected that war was imminent between Rome and their common rival, Parthia. They believed that Augustus was about to embark on new Eastern conquests to make himself the equal of Alexander the Great. Consequently, the Saka king wanted to establish an alliance with Rome in the coming war.

The Sakas were already familiar with the Greek legacy in ancient India. They had conquered the Hellenic kingdoms that once ruled the Indus region and Greek was still spoken in their territories.[7] Consequently, the ambassadors of the Saka king astutely carried a letter to Augustus which was written in Greek. The king chose an example from Greek history to indicate his political intentions and declared himself a new 'Porus' in the distant East. This is significant because Porus was the king of the Punjab who made terms with Alexander the Great after his conquest of Persia in 326 BC. Porus fought Alexander's army to a standstill, but in classical tradition the two rulers became firm allies. The Indian king offered his own forces to assist further Greek conquests in the distant East and in return he received grants of territory to add to his own domain.[8] The analogy was a good indication of Saka motives in sending the embassy to Augustus.

There were overland routes through southern Persia where Parthian authority was weak. The Saka group would have travelled these courses to reach the eastern frontiers of Roman Syria. Strabo describes how excited witnesses saw the embassy at Antioch on their way to meet with the Emperor. Strabo reports:

> Nicolaus says that at Antioch, near Daphne, he chanced to meet the Indian ambassadors who had been dispatched to Caesar Augustus. The letter they carried with them plainly indicated that there had been more than three ambassadors, but that only three had survived (whom he says he saw). The rest had died mostly due to the long journey. Their letter was written in Greek on a skin and it plainly declared that 'Porus' was the writer.[9]

The Roman governor at Antioch sent the embassy to meet Augustus on the Greek island of Samos, where the Emperor was holding court in 21 BC. It was here that the ambassadors delivered their message and came to an arrangement with the Emperor that involved a 'treaty of friendship'. Dio writes:

> Augustus returned to Samos . . . where he attended to many matters of business. A great many embassies came to him and the people of India, who had already made overtures, now made a treaty of friendship.[10]

Little is revealed about this treaty, but it probably involved pledges that the Sakas would not oppose Roman forces in their actions against Parthia. The sources also hint at future military co-operation. Strabo writes:

> Although this 'Porus' was ruler of 600 kings, still he was anxious to be a friend to Caesar Augustus, and was ready to allow him a passage through his country, wherever he wished to go. He was also prepared to cooperate with him in anything that was honorable.[11]

Ordinary Roman subjects were not usually informed about the terms of these diplomatic arrangements, but as the Emperor toured the Greek cities, the presence of his Indian visitors created further excited speculation.

Representatives of the Saka king sent prestigious gifts to Augustus that conveyed the power and scope of their Eastern domain. For the Roman people, these exotic wonders represented foreign recognition and demonstrated that the authority of Rome was now acknowledged at the very edges of the world. Augustus displayed his Indian gifts to amazed crowds in the Greek cities, and the offerings were still in the Emperor's possession when he visited the great cultural city of Athens.

One of the Indian gifts was an armless youth that the Greeks proclaimed a 'living Hermes'. Hermes was the Greek deity connected with travel and trade, and therefore the youth embodied ideas of crossing boundaries and establishing distant communications. The Saka king sent him to Augustus precisely because of these associations. Both Nicolaus and Strabo saw the youth:

> Nicolaus says that the gifts brought to Caesar Augustus were presented by eight naked servants who were clad only in loin-cloths besprinkled with sweet-smelling odors. He says that the gifts consisted of a 'Hermes', who is a man who was born without arms, who I myself have seen.[12]

Other gifts included a 'partridge larger than a vulture' that was possibly a brightly coloured monal pheasant from the Himalayan territories.[13] These exotic birds have metallic-coloured feathers of shimmering blue, green, purple, red and copper.[14]

An Indian holy man from Barygaza called Zarmarus also accompanied the Saka ambassadors and remained with the imperial entourage until the Emperor came to Athens. The name 'Zarmarus' is probably a Greek rendition of the Sanskrit term 'shramana', used to describe an ancient Buddhist, or a Jain ascetic. The Athenians believed the holy man was called *Zarmano-chegas* which translates as 'shramana master'. His message of peaceful enlightenment would not have been understood by the Roman crowds and this may explain his subsequent actions. In front of Augustus and the bewildered Athenians, the Buddhist master carefully built a funeral pyre and burned himself alive in the flames. Dio Cassius was perplexed by the event and he writes:

> One of the Indians was named Zarmarus and he belonged to a caste of sages. For some reason he wanted to die . . . perhaps because he wished to make a display for the benefit of Augustus and the Athenians (for Augustus had reached Athens) . . . he therefore threw himself alive into a fire.[15]

Strabo reveals his astonishment at this martyrdom and reports that the cremated remains of Zarmarus were placed in a prominent tomb in Athens. Strabo also describes his death in more dramatic detail:

> His naked body was anointed and wearing only a loin-cloth he leaped upon the lighted pyre with a laugh. The following words were inscribed on his tomb: "Here lies Zarmanochegas, an Indian from Bargaza, who immolated himself in accordance with the ancestral customs of the Indians".[16]

The Greek crowds were shocked by the self-immolation of the Indian holy man, but it was not unprecedented as the event resembled a famous spectacle witnessed by Alexander the Great. An Indian holy man named Calanus, who was accompanying the Greek army, became ill and decided to end his life in the same dramatic fashion.[17] The parallel must have been obvious to the Greek and Roman spectators who now expected war in the East.

Augustus presented his Saka connections as evidence for the extent of Roman political influence under his new regime. Whereas Alexander had travelled to the edges of Persia to gain the acknowledgement of Indian kings, Augustus now received their recognition while in his own Empire. The official message was that the rulers of India now looked to Rome for approval. These carefully presented ideas had a long-term impact on developing perceptions of Roman *imperium* and the possible scope of the Empire.

It could be that Augustus deliberately played upon the image of Alexander the Great in his public displays of the Saka envoys and their diplomatic gifts. The Parthian king Phraates faced political divisions in his own realm and now he had the added concern that Rome had acquired Indian allies in expectation of future Eastern conquests.[18] In the distant East the Saka king awaited the expected reply from Augustus. Perhaps his ambassadors returned from their meeting with the Emperor to confirm that an alliance had been made.

Yet the Roman armies did not march east against the Parthian Realm. In 20 BC Augustus achieved a celebrated diplomatic settlement with Parthia and King Phraates readily agreed to return the standards and soldiers captured in previous conflicts with Rome. Augustus presented this political settlement as a victory achieved simply by coercive threat.[19] In Roman propaganda, Augustus had dictated terms and forced Parthia to be compliant to the point of sending hostages from their royal dynasty to Rome. Augustus could now turn his attention to the Danube and Rhineland territories on the northern limits of Roman authority.

Augustus claimed that he received many Indian ambassadors during the course of his reign and this might have included further Saka envoys. Dio Cassius adds wild tigers to the list of gifts sent by Saka kings and this could be connected with events about 11 BC when Augustus displayed live tigers to astonished Roman crowds. Dio suggests that the Roman population had never seen these ferocious animals before and the account implies that Augustus had once again surpassed the achievements of the ancient Greeks. Dio writes:

> Among their gifts they brought tigers. This was the first time these animals had been seen by the Romans and also I think by the Greeks.[20]

These later Saka contacts would have offered the Romans additional opportunities for gathering intelligence about conditions in the volatile Eastern territories of Parthia. In AD 1 the Romans concluded a further political agreement with the Parthians that verified arrangements for the contested kingdom of Armenia and confirmed the Euphrates as the eastern boundary of the Roman Empire.[21] After this, there is no further indication of direct political contacts between Rome and the Saka kingdoms.

ROME AND THE TAMILS

By the mid 20s BC Roman merchants were arriving at Indian trade ports in the Tamil lands of southern India. Tamil leaders responded by sending emissaries to

Augustus to learn more about Rome and its business in the distant East. These communications seem to have been motivated by curiosity, prestige and trade exchange, rather than military ambition.

The more northerly Chera chiefdom was the first Tamil territory to be reached by Roman merchants. Neighboring Pandyans were envious of these early trade exchanges which supplied their Chera rivals with valuable merchandise, so-called 'gifts' from overseas. The Pandyan leaders were determined to establish their own connections with Rome and sent an embassy laden with precious gifts north to find this distant land intending to establish good terms with its ruler. The group departed on an overland route and arrived at the frontiers of the Roman Empire after an epic four year journey through India and the Middle East. Strabo reports:

> From one Indian king Pandion . . . there came to Caesar Augustus presents and gifts of honor.[22]

The gifts sent to the Emperor included pearls from the fisheries in the Mannar Gulf. This was a shrewd gift if the embassy was sent to encourage the exchange of goods between the Roman Empire and the Pandyan territories.[23] Pearls were admired by Roman society and consumer demand for these jewellery items was already rapidly escalating. Florus writes:

> Ambassadors who sought friendship . . . included the Indians who live immediately beneath the sun. They brought elephants amongst their gifts as well as precious stones and pearls. They regarded their long journey, in the accomplishment of which they had spent four years, as the greatest tribute which they rendered. Indeed their completion proved that they came from beneath another sky.[24]

Other Tamil chiefdoms also sent representatives to meet the Emperor Augustus. Florus connects the Pandyan embassy with the arrival of ambassadors that he calls the *Seres*. Given the context, these other envoys could have come from the Chera chiefdom.[25] The third great Tamil territory was the Chola chiefdom which used the tiger as its emblem. The live tigers that Augustus displayed in 11 BC could have been sent by a ruler of the Chola dynasty.

There were great incentives for the Tamil rulers to control Roman trade and maintain the goodwill of merchants from the Empire. By the time Pliny was writing, over 50 million sesterces of Roman wealth was being exported to India every year and most of this bullion reached the Tamil lands.[26] To place this figure in context, the revenues of the whole of Palestine were about 48 million sesterces per annum.[27] It is therefore not surprising that the Tamil poets recalled epic battles fought between the Pandyan and Chera chiefs over important market ports such as Muziris.[28]

Augustus undoubtedly received enormous prestige when he met with the Tamil representatives. These embassies represented rulers from lands far beyond the limits of Alexander's Eastern conquests. They also brought gifts that suggested impressive new commercial opportunities to be exploited in the distant East and Tamil gemstones quickly became must-have fashion items for many wealthy Romans.

By receiving the Tamil envoys in impressive surroundings, and accepting their diplomatic gifts, the Emperor established goodwill relations that greatly benefited trade. Given the nature of their society, the Tamils probably perceived their early trade associations with Rome in terms of a personal relationship between the Emperor and the Tamil rulers. The Tamil leaders therefore described their initial dealings with Roman merchants as gift exchanges.[29] Roman merchants would not have discouraged this view as it increased their own prestige in the distant East.

The Chera king permitted Roman subjects to build an Augustan temple at Muziris and this structure was probably built by merchants without the direct involvement of imperial government.[30] The temple would have been perceived by the Tamils as the divine Emperor's 'residence' in the Chera chiefdom. The fact that Roman subjects could construct an Augustan temple in Muziris suggests that the Chera had considerable esteem for the Emperor. Imperial figures in this building must have resembled the images depicted on the gold coins sent as 'gifts' from Rome. The Tamil chiefs would have perceived these associations as matters of status and they benefited from good relations with the Romans as trade wealth from the Empire flowed into their territories.

ROME AND THE SINHALESE

The Emperors who succeeded Augustus did not maintain direct diplomatic contact with the Indian kingdoms. The Augustan period had brought about a new era of unprecedented peace and prosperity and Rome was now secure in its international status. There were few external threats that could seriously challenge the Empire and India no longer seemed so extraordinary and remote. Merchants made regular visits to its kingdoms and Eastern products could be seen throughout Rome and the provinces.

By this era, Roman merchants had established good relations with the Indian kings. They frequented the major trade ports of their kingdoms and offered goods to the royal courts of the ruling Indian dynasties. Any state-level arrangements needed for the conduct of Eastern commerce were therefore managed by Roman businessmen operating in India. They could easily gain an audience with the ruling authority and come to their own terms without either the knowledge, or involvement, of the Emperor.[31] For their part, the Indian rulers were keen to engage with prosperous Roman visitors and facilitate their business in whatever way possible. For example, during the time of the *Periplus*, the Saka king Nahapana organized rowing boats to tow Roman vessels through treacherous estuary waters. He also assigned guard ships to protect these freighters from hostile raiders based in a neighbouring territory.[32] Eastern commerce obviously involved a long series of similar dealings and arrangements made for the mutual benefit of Indian rulers and their Roman merchant visitors.

Although Eastern commerce had made India accessible, there were still revelations awaiting the Romans in the distant East. At the time of the *Periplus* there was popular speculation that Sri Lanka was the outer tip of some enormous, savage continent that would equal the Eurasian landmass in its vast extent. However, shortly before the death of Claudius, a Roman freedman who had disappeared on an

Eastern trade voyage, arrived back in Egypt alive and well.[33] He had returned with ambassadors dispatched from the Sinhalese government to seek an audience with the Emperor. This was the first Sinhalese contact with Rome and the information it revealed to Roman businessmen transformed Eastern commerce. Pliny describes how these extraordinary events occurred:

> We gained greater knowledge of Sri Lanka when during the reign of Claudius an embassy actually came from that island. It came about in this way; a freedman of Annius Plocamus who had gained a tax contract for the Red Sea from the Roman treasury, was sailing around Arabia when he was blown off course by the north wind . . . and on the fifteenth day at sea he reached the Sinhalese port of Hippuros.[34]

On reaching Sri Lanka the stranded freedman had been brought before the local authorities and as a tax collector, he must have claimed to be a representative of the Roman administration. He was carrying Roman coins so the Sinhalese recognized that he was someone of significance from a homeland ruled by a sophisticated regime. The freedman was taken to the court of the Sri Lankan king where he remained as a guest. While there, he learned the Sinhalese language and was able to tell the court more about the Roman Empire and its political power in the distant West.

Although the Sinhalese had received Roman goods from Tamil traders, they had not seen denarii before this encounter.[35] At this time, most Indian currencies were heavily debased silver issues that were cast or struck according to a wide variety of different royal standards. By contrast, Roman denarii were almost pure silver and because they were die-struck rather than cast, they had a series of impressive images appearing in sharp-detail on their surface. The Sinhalese court was fascinated by these objects and what they conveyed about Roman power. Pliny explains:

> The freedman was kept by the kind hospitality of the Sinhalese king for six months. After learning their language he spoke to the Sinhalese about the Romans and their Emperor. The king gained admiration for Roman honesty because the denarii which his guest carried were all equal in weight, although their diverse images showed that they were coined by different individuals.[36]

The silver content of most Indian coins fluctuated according to the fortunes of the ruling authority who commissioned them. In contrast, Roman coins had a long series of issues with no discernible decline in silver content. This was significant because it demonstrated to the Sinhalese that Rome had a high level of financial stability. Pliny writes, 'The Sinhalese king, wishing friendship because of this fact, despatched four envoys'.[37]

The four Sinhalese envoys sent to make contact with Rome were led by a chief ambassador whom Pliny names as 'Rachia'. The number of envoys selected for this group could be significant. Buddhist chronicles record that in the third century BC the Sinhalese dispatched a similar party of four ambassadors to the Mauryan kingdom of northern India. This group included a chief minister, a chaplain, a treasurer and another lower-ranked official.[38] It could be that a similar group of authorities were selected for the mission to Rome.

The Romans called the chief Sinhalese ambassador 'Rachia', but this may have been his official title rather than a personnel name.[39] The title *Ratiya* appears in a number of first century Sinhalese inscriptions and describes a district administrator.[40] Rachia could have been selected as leader of this expedition because he already had knowledge of distant overseas travel. Rachia told the Roman court that his father had sailed to the eastern edge of India to trade with a remote and secretive 'silk people' – a population who came from beyond the Himalayas.

The Roman freedman might have informed the Sinhalese court about the true origins of the foreign goods reaching nearby Tamil markets, including the revered red coral that had magical properties in Indian tradition.[41] Perhaps the Sinhalese ambassadors hoped to establish profitable trade contacts with the Roman Empire. The mission could also have had a religious motive with the Sinhalese king asking his ambassadors to bring back an item of special significance from Rome. The early Sinhalese texts record that king Bhatikabhaya was ruling Sri Lanka during the reign of Claudius.[42] They also reveal that Bhatikabhaya received a valuable coral treasure from a distant land and that in an act of great piety he gave this extraordinary artefact to an important Buddhist monastery. This episode is mentioned in two early Sinhalese texts which describe ancient acts of devotion to the Buddhist faith.[43] The *Dipavamsa* records:

> Bhatikabhaya asked that a priceless net be made of corals and the Mahathupa shrine was clothed in this net like a *civara* robe.[44]

The *Mahavansa* simply states, 'Bhatikabhaya had a coral net made and he placed it upon the *cetiya* shrine'.[45] A later historical commentary on the *Mahavamsa* offers further information about this valuable coral gift. The *Vamsatthappakasini* adds:

> Bhatikabhaya had a coral net made. He sent someone beyond the sea to the so-called *Romanukharattha* and had the red coral brought back. He had a great net made out of this coral so that it could be placed all around [the *cetiya* shrine].[46]

Romanukharattha 'beyond the sea' must be the Roman Empire with its red Mediterranean coral. Scholars have therefore suggested that the name *Romanukharattha* is an ancient attempt to render the Latin adjective 'Romanus' into early Sinhalese.[47]

Claudius would also have received considerable prestige from this first diplomatic contact with the Sinhalese. The Emperor had conquered southern Britain and brought Roman authority almost to the western limits of the known world. In classical maps, the Sinhalese landmass appeared at the opposite extreme of the inhabited earth. The arrival of exotic visitors from this unknown region, coming to honour the Emperor, would have been seen as a further indication of the expanding global reach of Roman influence.[48]

Pliny was involved with Roman government during the reign of Vespasian so his account of the Sinhalese embassy remains factual and he does not mention marvellous gifts, or use language that would suggest the envoys were on a mission of personal homage to the Emperor. Details discussed by Pliny in his account of the embassy indicate the type of information that Roman authorities would have been interested in learning from distant emissaries. It seems that the Romans wanted to hear details about Sinhalese government, geography, society and distant trade contacts. This indicates how imperial government had a view of these eastern contacts that was different from the propaganda presented to the Roman population.

Pliny states that his discussion of Sri Lanka included new information obtained from the visiting emissaries. Yet his new account of the island contains a confused fusion of ideas. Rachia must have found it difficult to explain the complex Buddhist principles that governed Sinhalese society. The Roman freedman was probably expected to translate, and he may have had problems rendering these Sinhalese concepts into Latin.

Another distortion is evident in the accounts of Sri Lanka that Pliny had received from friends and colleges in the Roman elite. It was unwise, and often dangerous, to openly criticise the autocratic rule of the Roman Emperors. However, foreign cultures could be used as literary foils and the elite could indirectly criticise their own society by praising the practices of other peoples. For political reasons, members of the Roman elite spread stories about the Sinhalese that reflected how they believed their own government should be managed. These accounts described how the Sinhalese came from a regime where the king was forced to defer to the judgement of a ruling council and the political elite could depose their ruler for serious transgressions, then freely appoint a new head of state. Stories that there was a kingdom in the distant East that was as wealthy as Rome, but maintained elements of 'Republican' style government, promoted the secret hopes of the senatorial elite.[49] Reassurance could be taken from the belief that political reform in Rome was achievable because a precedent existed overseas.

This is the only documented diplomatic exchange between the Sinhalese and Roman governments. It heralded a new era in communications between their subject peoples as further commercial contacts were revealed and explored. The incident marked Sri Lanka's inclusion into the expanding Eastern trade networks of Rome and with the Sinhalese shores now recognized as friendly territory, freighters from the Empire could reach further into the distant East on even more ambitious trade voyages.

ROMAN AGENTS IN THE DISTANT EAST

Roman military commanders realized that certain merchants could travel with ease through the territories of the distant East. They consequently began to use these men as agents in their diplomatic and military designs. Merchants were involved in intelligence gathering and the delivery of dispatches to the courts of Eastern rulers. Agents of Rome were also sent on specific assignments to acquire exotic commodities from territories that were far beyond the Empire.

An important member of the imperial family named Germanicus used Palmyrene agents in his Eastern negotiations with the vassal kings of Parthia. In AD 18, Germanicus was given a military command in the Eastern provinces of the Roman Empire and tasked with reorganizing these frontier territories. Germanicus gave imperial recognition to the rulers of Armenia and reduced the small Eastern kingdoms Cappadocia and Commagene to Roman provincial status.[50] He also opened up communications with a number of vassal kingdoms in the Parthian Realm. One of his agents in these diplomatic dealings was a Palmyrene named Alexandros, probably a merchant with pre-existing, high-level, contacts in these kingdoms.[51] An inscription from Palmyra commemorates an important diplomatic mission led by Alexandros. Unfortunately the text is fragmentary. It reads:

> Alexandros . . . [the] Palmyrene . . . performed . . . and Germanicus sent him to . . . of Mesene and to Orabzes . . . Samsigeram, the Supreme King.[52]

Orabzes ruled the small Parthian vassal kingdom of Mesene at the head of the Persian Gulf. The text also mentions a 'Supreme King' which might indicate official correspondence with the ruler of Parthia. The surviving sources reveal nothing further about the purpose or significance of this diplomatic initiative as Germanicus fell seriously ill and died in suspicious circumstances in late AD 19.

Roman authorities also sent agents eastward to find certain rare articles that could not be obtained through the usual commercial channels. Pliny describes how in the reign of Nero, a Roman *eques* was sent on a mission into the Baltic territories of northern Europe to acquire great stocks of amber for a series of important gladiatorial games.[53] Agents were also sent into the distant East and the sources describe episodes occurring in the third century when these ventures were worthy of notice.

When the Roman Emperor Aurelian reclaimed Egypt in AD 273, he acquired two large elephant tusks from a defeated rival named Firmus. It was reported that Aurelian planned to send representatives to India to acquire more of these exceptional objects. The source claims:

> It is said that Firmus owned two elephant tusks, ten feet in length. Aurelian planned to add two more tusks to make a throne on which he would place a statue of Jupiter made of gold and decked with jewels and clad in a sort of bordered toga. He expected to place this statue in the Temple of the Sun and he asked the advice of the oracle in the Apennines.[54]

Aurelian also received a purple cloak from a Sassanid king of Persia who was said to have acquired the fabric from the furthest regions of India. This prestige item was displayed in the Jupiter Temple on the Capitoline Hill. Later Roman rulers sent agents to acquire more of this material, but each of their missions was unsuccessful. The sources report:

> Aurelian and Probus and later Diocletian ordered a most diligent search for this type of purple dye. They sent out their most able agents, but even so the dye could not be found.[55]

These episodes are recorded in the sources because they represent prominent failures when the Emperors could no longer deliver on expectations, despite their continued claims of 'global' authority. During the height of Empire, when the Eastern trade routes were vibrant, similar Roman missions to acquire special objects or animals were probably completed without difficulty.

Roman commanders also used merchants for serious diplomatic assignments. In AD 58, Rome and Parthia came into conflict over the contested northern kingdom of Armenia. During this crisis the Roman commander Corbulo received diplomats from an important territory called Hyrcania at the eastern edge of the Parthian Realm. Hyrcania had risen in revolt against the Parthian king Vologaeses and was supporting a rival claimant to the kingship. The ensuing conflict distracted Vologaeses from Armenia and the escalating dispute with Rome. Tacitus reports:

> The Roman success against Armenia was easier because the Parthians were distracted by a war against the Hyrcanians. Hyrcanian representatives were sent to the Roman Emperor imploring alliance and drawing attention to the fact that they were detaining Vologaeses as a pledge of amity.[56]

The Hyrcanians hoped that an escalation in the Armenian conflict would further weaken Vologaeses and strengthen their own military position in the East. Vologaeses was therefore facing war on two fronts.

The Romans made special efforts to ensure that the returning Hyrcanian diplomats would not be captured by their Parthian enemies. Tacitus reports:

> When these envoys were on their way home, Corbulo realised that after they crossed the Euphrates they would be intercepted and harmed by their enemies. He therefore gave them an escort and conducted them down to the shores of the Red Sea and, by avoiding Parthian territory, they returned safely to their native lands.[57]

Under Roman guard the Hyrcanians would have been placed aboard a Roman merchant ship leaving Egypt for northwest India. On reaching Indo-Scythia they travelled north via the Indus territories through Bactria to reach Hyrcania.[58] The Hyrcanian incident suggests that territories in Inner Asia were capable of initiating political contacts with Rome and that these efforts involved serious attempts to undermine the political authority of Parthia.

GAN YING'S MISSION TO ROME

In the early 70s AD the Han Empire launched a series of military campaigns to regain control over the Tarim kingdoms. The Tarim states had been largely independent of Chinese rule for almost a century and many of the northern kingdoms had fallen under the dominance of the horse-riding Xiongnu who controlled the Asian steppe. Using a combination of diplomacy and determined military force, the Han general Ban Chao defeated the Xiongnu and brought the Tarim kingdoms back under Chinese authority.

These conquests re-opened Chinese communications with Central Asia and during this period increased rumours about a new formidable power in the distant West began to reach the Han authorities. It was during this period that the Chinese adopted the name *Da Qin*, or 'Great China', for the distant Roman Empire.[59] The name *Da Qin* implies that the Han were aware that the Roman state was a powerful civilization that matched their own empire with its control over territories and resources. The *Hou Hanshu* reports:

> The people of *Da Qin* are all tall and honest. They are very like the people of China and that is why this State is called *Da Qin*.[60]

The Chinese reports suggested that the Roman Empire gathered all the 'precious and rare things' from other foreign kingdoms and that their merchants were honest businessmen.[61] The *Weilue* adds:

> The common people are tall and virtuous like the Chinese, but they wear Western clothes. They have always wanted to communicate with China, but Parthia is jealous of their profits and they will not allow them to pass (through to the Han Empire).[62]

The Chinese were intrigued by these reports and fascinated by the possibility of making contact with another powerful Empire, but between them lay Parthia.

The Han infantry were equipped to overcome the type of mounted steppe armies that the Parthians and the Xiongnu relied upon for their military strength. The Han army had workshops that mass manufactured steel weaponry more durable than anything the Roman Empire could produce. Roman authorities knew about this metal, but did not realize that it was produced by special manufacturing techniques. Instead it was regarded as a foreign resource only available in the distant East, much like silk fabric. In this era, Roman merchants acquired Chinese style steel from Tarim intermediaries, whom the classical sources referred to as the *Seres* or 'Silk People'. Pliny writes:

> Of all the varieties of iron the best is the Seric variety. The *Seres* send us their iron . . . but the second-best quality of iron belongs to Parthia.[63]

The Parthians were receiving supplies of steel from Central Asia and this gave their elite cavalry access to armour and weaponry that was more advanced than their Roman counterparts.

In this era, the Romans had proven military superiority in Western Europe, but their earliest attempt to expand the Empire into Persia had ended in defeat at the hands of a small force of Parthian steppe cavalry. In 53 BC, an ambitious Republican statesman named Crassus tried to invade Mesopotamia with a large Roman army composed of at least 40,000 infantry. In this era the Romans had virtually no experience of steppe warfare.[64] The invading Romans were met on the desert plain of Carrhae by a much smaller force of 10,000 mounted Parthians, mostly equipped as archers. The Parthians quickly overcame the Roman cavalry using their heavily armoured horsemen who were clad in dense armour and equipped with steel tipped lances.[65] They then encircled the legionaries to massacre them with volleys of arrows fired from powerful long-range bows. The legionaries formed *testudo* walls of interlocking shields, but the onslaught was relentless. The Parthian commander had organized relays of camels to deliver new supplies of arrows and these were fired on high trajectories to fall on the legionaries from above. The arrows also lanced into the ranks with such power that men were skewered to their shields, or had their feet nailed to the earth by the missiles.[66] Plutarch writes:

> They fired powerful shots from bows which were large and mighty and curved so as to discharge their missiles with great force . . . The Romans were crowded together and falling upon one another. Men were shot and in convulsive pain, pinned with arrows that they either broke off in their wounds or tried to pull out by force only to find that the barbed heads had pierced veins and torn sinews. Many died and survivors were incapacitated and could not fight.[67]

In total some 10,000 Roman soldiers were slaughtered and the same number were seized at the battle site, or captured in the chaotic retreat back to Syria.[68] The humiliated Roman captives were settled in eastern Parthia near the city of Merv on the edge of the vast Eurasian Steppe.[69]

If the Romans had realized that steel was not a rare eastern material, but a product of manufacturing techniques, and if they had acquired this secret, then their own military workshops could have mass produced the metal. This would have equipped their disciplined legionaries with superior armour and weaponry.[70]

Unlike the Romans, the Han infantry were supplied with powerful crossbows that could outrange the missiles of mounted steppe archers. Greco-Roman crossbows were relatively simple devises largely reserved for hunting game. By contrast, Han crossbows were masterpieces of engineering with sophisticated bronze trigger mechanisms and gridded sighting devises to improve aim and accuracy. These crossbows could be pre-loaded and kept ready to fire when enemy forces came into range. However, Han prohibitions ensured that these weapons were not exported from the Empire to avoid copies being made by foreign, potentially hostile, kingdoms.[71]

The Han also used diplomacy to involve allied steppe forces in their campaigning armies. In the 80s AD, Ban Chao formed a military alliance with the Kushans of Bactria to launch a joint campaign against the Sogdians. By AD 90 the Kushan had broken these agreements and declared hostilities against the Chinese. In the brief ensuing conflict, the Chinese army defeated a large Kushan expeditionary force. The victorious Chinese then re-negotiated their agreements with the Kushan and further strengthened their control over the western Tarim territories.[72] With the Kushan subdued and Chinese forces positioned near the Pamir Mountains, the way was now clear for the Han to explore more distant diplomatic contacts.

When Ban Chao sought new allies in the distant West to help maintain Chinese authority over Central Asia, his thoughts turned to Rome. In AD 97 he sent a chief ambassador named Gan Ying on a challenging overland mission to establish contact with the Roman Empire.[73] Chinese information regarding the overland route to Roman territory was unreliable, but they had reports that Rome lay somewhere to the west of the Indian Ocean.[74] So Gan Ying travelled through the Indus territories and passed incognito through southern Iran where Parthian political influence was weakest.[75] Chinese records tell how, after a long and distressing journey, Gan Ying managed to reach the kingdom of Mesene at the head of the Persian Gulf.[76] The *Hou Hanshu* reports:

> Protector-General Ban Chao sent Gan Ying as an envoy on a mission to the Roman Empire. He arrived in Tiaozhi (Mesene) on the coast of the Great Sea (Indian Ocean).[77]

Gan Ying must have been disheartened to discover that the Persian Gulf was not the western edge of the ocean, but just a vast sea inlet. Yet he was still determined to complete his mission and therefore prepared to make a sea voyage around Arabia to reach Rome. What Gan Ying did not realize was that from Mesene it was only a short overland journey north through Mesopotamia into Roman territory.

Gan Ying, to all appearances a rich and exotic foreigner, approached the sailors at Mesene and asked them to take him around Arabia. The sailors must have seen an opportunity to exploit a traveller who was naïvely unsure about his surroundings and destination. They told Gan Ying that the sailing around Arabia took only a few months, but he would have to hand over a large payment in advance for the ship to be equipped with sufficient provisions for three years. They gave as a reason the unpredictable weather that made massive delays possible. The *Hou Hanshu* reports:

> When he was about to take his passage across the Great Sea, the sailors of the western border of Anxi [Parthia] told him that the sea was very vast. It could be traversed within three months, but with unfavourable winds it might take two years to cross. For this reason those who sail this sea take on board three years worth of provisions.[78]

Their hustle had the opposite effect. Gan Ying was horrified by the prospect of a prolonged and a dangerous voyage into the virtual unknown. He was already feeling homesick and the unfamiliar sight of the sea stirred feelings of dread. The *Hou Hanshu* records the concerns voiced by Gan Ying:

> There is something in this sea which makes a person long for home and many men have lost their lives on it, for a man may surely die from homesickness. Appreciating all this, Gan Ying did not go any further.[79]

Gan Ying returned to Central Asia to report to Ban Chao that Roman territory could only be reached through a treacherous sea crossing. His report suggested that there was no easy overland route of communication between the empires.[80] As a result, Ban Chao was forced to conclude that Rome could not be any assistance to China in its struggle for supremacy in Central Asia. Based on this mistaken belief, no more embassies were dispatched to attempt liaison with Rome.

Had Gan Ying succeeded in his appointed task he would have been brought before the Emperor Trajan during the first year of his reign. Trajan was the great military conqueror who expanded the Roman Empire to its furthest limits and pursued an aggressive war of conquest against the Parthians. If Gan Ying had met the Emperor at this key moment in imperial history, the contact between Rome and China would have brought about a chain of events that might have altered the fortunes of both civilizations forever.

CHINESE CONTACT WITH 'MENG-CHI TOU-LE'

By AD 100, the Han re-conquest of the Tarim kingdoms had placed Chinese forces near the Pamir Mountains contemplating further political expansion. Yet Ban Chao, who had fought for three decades, was now feeling the effects of age and ill health. News that *Da Qin*, the Roman Empire, lay beyond reach, arrived shortly before he made his request to be relieved of his command and return to China.

Ban Chao sent his son to the Han Emperor to deliver his request for retirement. To remind the Han court of his achievements, he also sent foreign representatives from the most distant regions he had reached in his military campaign. Among these exotic foreigners were representatives from a distant land called 'Meng-chi and Tou-le'.[81] The *Hou Hanshu* reports:

> The distant states of Meng-chi Tou-le both came to make their submission by sending envoys to bring tribute.[82]

The Chinese sources record that Meng-chi Tou-le was over 40,000 *li* distant from the Han capital at Luoyang. This suggests contact with a western region that would have been part of the Roman Empire.[83] Scholars have argued that the Chinese words 'Meng-chi' 'Tou-le' could be a phonic fit for 'Macedonia'.[84] Perhaps, but maybe the group were merchants who were following a spoken routine that had seen them safely through Parthia. Ptolemy records that a Macedonian businessman named Maes Titianus sent agents to the Far East and this group must be the 'Meng-chi Toule' reported in the Chinese accounts. Perhaps these merchants repeated that they were sent by someone they called 'Master Maes Titus'. This could have been spoken as 'Maes Chegas Titus', or 'Mengchi Toule'.

According to Ptolemy, Maes sent his agents to trade with a commercial station near the Pamirs called the Stone Tower.[85] But when they reached this distant region, they encountered the 'Silk People' whom Ptolemy calls the *Seres*. The *Seres* took the Roman group on a gruelling seven month trek across a vast expanse of bleak territory wracked by violent storms.[86] Their destination was a distant inland city that Ptolemy calls 'Sera', the 'Silk Capital'. The event was so extraordinary that Maes wrote a book about this venture and later Roman geographers used the information to estimate the possible length of the Asian continent.[87] Ptolemy reports:

> All this became known through an opportunity provided by commerce . . . Maes, also called Titianus, was a Macedonian and a merchant by hereditary profession. He wrote a book giving the measurement of Asia which he had obtained not by visiting the *Seres* in person, but by sending out agents who actually met them.[88]

Intriguing information suggests how the Maes team were able to pass unopposed through Parthian cities such as Ctesiphon and Ecbatana. 'Maes' is a distinctly Syrian name and it is likely that Maes Titianus was 'Macedonian' by ethnic and cultural decent. The name 'Titianus' suggests that his family had received Roman citizenship through the patronage of someone with the Latin name 'Titius'.[89] It has been suggeted that Maes had ancestors who served in Roman government during the late Republic and the early Augustan era. A man named 'M. Titius L.' was consul suffectus in 31 BC and later became governor of Syria in around 13 BC.[90] Strabo reveals that M. Titius helped to conclude the peace settlement agreed between Augustus and the Parthian king Phraates. This M. Titius hosted and attended conferences with the Parthian ambassadors and was also entrusted with the wellbeing of royal princes handed over as hostages into Roman authority.[91] These contacts apparently gave M. Titius and his family lasting influence amongst the Parthian nobility. Decades later, his descendant Maes, was probably able to exploit this family connection to send his agents out through the centre of the Parthian Realm on a mission to find the Stone Tower.

Alexander the Great had settled elements of his Macedonian army in Persian territories as far as Sogdia. The Maes group could have exploited this shared cultural heritage as they passed through these remote outposts on their way to the Pamirs. When the Han first encountered the Macedonian trade party at the Stone Tower, they would have been placed in the custody of armed Chinese escorts and taken to Ban Chao. The general then sent them to accompany his son back to the imperial court. The Macedonian group were shrewd enough to follow Han directions without resistance or protest. This contact occurred at a time when many small previously unknown kingdoms were arriving in the Han capital to formally announce their recognition of the Chinese Empire. The Chinese records therefore present the Meng-chi Tou-le incident as one of these diplomatic receptions.

The Maes group had difficulty communicating with their Chinese hosts and they did not fraudulently misrepresent their trade mission as a diplomatic approach. They must have repeated their origins and their purpose to make an exchange of precious goods on behalf of an authority in their homeland. In the distant East traders were often used to open diplomatic channels between foreign states so if the Han detected the commercial character of the Maes group, this would not have disqualified them from being perceived as possible envoys.

At the Han court, the bewildered Macedonians handed over their trade goods of silk and Roman aurei as 'tribute' to the court of the Chinese Emperor He. The Han Empire did not have a common gold currency and most of their coins were cast in decorative moulds. The Chinese had never seen Roman aurei before and they mistook these gold disks with their imperial portraits as seals belonging to the king of 'Meng-ch Tou-le'. The *Hou Hanshu* therefore states:

> In winter two states from the Western regions named Meng-chi Tou-le sent envoys to submit tribute [to China]. They brought silks and the gold seal of their king.[92]

Chinese diplomatic protocol would have ensured that the Macedonians were richly reimbursed with gifts that demonstrated the wealth and supremacy of the Han Empire.

Maes would have regarded the incident as a commercial enterprise and when his agents returned he kept the exquisite Chinese gifts for himself. Yet this extraordinary story was so unique that Maes felt compelled to write a book on the subject. Unfortunately, this work has not survived, but geographers like Ptolemy knew of Maes and used his information. Other members of the family Maesii Titiani are attested as living in Sicily and Italy in the period between AD 150 and AD 210, but little is known about their activities.[93]

This book written by Maes, would have engaged the interest of other Roman businessmen, and revealed the possibilities of trade with the distant 'Silk Empire'. But Ptolemy knew of no one else who had travelled this far into the distant East. This is unsurprising as any Roman merchants who tried to emulate Maes and reach China must have found their progress blocked. In AD 107 many of the Tarim kingdoms took advantage of the retirement of Ban Chao to expel Chinese officials and reassert their independence in a series of violent revolts.[94] The government of the new Han Emperor An was forced to abandon the Tarim regions and the Chinese retreated back to their former frontiers. The *Hou Hanshu* reports:

> The Imperial Government proclaimed that the post of Protector-General of the Western Regions should be abolished because these remote territories were difficult and dangerous to reach. From this time the Western Regions were abandoned. The northern Xiongnu immediately took control and reclaimed all the kingdoms again. They raided the frontier for more than ten years . . . with much violence and killing.[95]

Chinese communication with Inner Asia was severed. The opportunity to establish direct overland contacts between Rome and China, which had come so tantalisingly close, was now permanently lost.

THE KUSHAN

In AD 101 the Roman army invaded the Transylvanian kingdom of Dacia. After two short wars, the Emperor Trajan conquered the region and established a new Roman province north of the Danube River.[96] Around the same time, Trajan sent orders to Syria that the Arabian client kingdom of Nabatea should be brought into the Empire as a new Eastern province.

Dacia was the first substantial Roman conquest of a new territory since Claudius had ordered the invasion of Britain over sixty years previously. In AD 107, the victorious Trajan returned to Rome to celebrate the Dacian conquest by staging a series of extraordinary spectacles in the Colosseum. These astonishing performances were enacted over many weeks and attracted large numbers of spectators from across the imperial territories. Dio Cassius reports that foreign ambassadors were seated amongst the senators with Indian emissaries prominent amongst these visitors. He writes:

> Upon Trajan's return to Rome many embassies came to him from various barbarians including the Indians. He gave spectacles on 123 days. In the course of these events some 11,000 wild and tame animals were slain and 10,000 gladiators fought . . . At these spectacles the ambassadors who came from the various kings were given seats by Trajan in the senatorial section.[97]

Roman agents might have requested the presence of the Indian emissaries at the

Dacian triumph. An enormous variety of wild and exotic beasts were required for the games and many of these animals must have come from territories in the distant East. For instance, the *Alexandrian Tariff* mentions the Eastern traffic in lions, lionesses, leopards and panthers.[98] The arrival of Roman agents in India demanding exotic animals would have brought news of Trajan's victory to the kings of the distant East, and confirmed the military ambitions of the new Emperor.

Kushan ambassadors were probably prominent among Trajan's guests at the victory celebrations.[99] Like the Romans, the Kushan identified the Parthians as political rivals to be overcome. Knowledge of the Kushan was already spreading through Roman society coinciding with a heightened Roman interest in India.[100] During this era Roman authors, including Curtius Rufus, Plutarch and Arrian, all composed new biographies of Alexander the Great.

By this period, the Kushan had greatly expanded their domain and emerged as one of the major powers of Inner Asia. The Han describe early hostilities between the Kushan and the Parthians when the Kushan tribes were unified under Kujula Kadphises who invaded Parthia and conquered the Kabul region.[101] Josephus refers to this when he describes how the Parthian king Vologaeses rushed to defend his Eastern kingdom from a sudden foreign attack.[102] By the 80s AD, the Kushan were engaged in strategic diplomacy with Chinese generals in the Tarim territories and the two forces conducted coordinated campaigns against common opponents in Sogdia.[103] The Kushan King Vima Kadphises came to power in the 90s AD and he extended Kushan rule into the Indus territories, thereby acquiring incredible wealth.[104] With the retreat of Chinese power from the Tarim territories, the Kushan further strengthened their hold over Central Asia.

The Kushan regarded their king as an equal to the Roman Emperor. Their rulers adopted foreign titles and Kanishka II used the designation *kaisar* to indicate his status as an Eastern 'Caesar'.[105] Cultural influences made the Kushan appealing allies for the Romans. The Kushan commanded territories in Bactria that had once been ruled by the Hellenic successors of Alexander the Great. The Kushan courts were consequently familiar with the Greek language and respected Hellenic traditions. In this era the Kushan heartland of Gandhara had developed its own style of art and architecture that was heavily influenced by classical culture.[106] One Gandhara sculpture shows a scene from the Trojan War with Mediterranean soldiers leading a wheeled horse towards a gateway.[107] Another depicts the death of the Buddha showing foreign figures in attendance, including a Roman subject. This might be evidence of Roman converts to Eastern faiths or simply a further acknowledgement of classical civilization.

Contacts with Rome are evident in the cultural remains of the ancient Kushan domain. Vima was impressed by symbols of Roman authority and he produced gold coins which were closely modelled on imported imperial aurei. These issues show a bearded Vima in traditional Kushan dress, wearing a long-riding coat and a high-domed helmet decorated with ribbons. Indian deities also appear on these coins and the letters that surround these images are a corrupted form of Greek.[108]

The Kushan delegates could communicate in Greek and the crowds of spectators at the Dacian celebrations must have wondered what business their emperor had with these distant and exotic visitors. Some scholars suggest that contacts between

Vima and Trajan may have re-awakened Roman ambitions regarding the conquest of Parthia.[109] The theme of Eastern conquests is raised when Plutarch writes about the final battle between Caesar and Pompey. He muses:

> What Scythian horsemen, Parthian arrows, or Indian riches, could possibly resist 70,000 well-armed Roman soldiers under the command of generals like Pompey or Caesar?[110]

Some scholars suggest that Plutarch is referring to a contemporary debate over the size of the Roman army needed to conquer India.[111] This sort of speculation may have encouraged Trajan to look east for further opportunities to win military fame.

The position of Emperor was an autocratic institution in Roman government and this one individual could determine the principal actions of the state.[112] In AD 113, Trajan deliberately escalated a dispute over Armenia, creating a crisis which gave him the opportunity to fulfil his ambitions for further conquests. Cassius Dio explains that Trajan launched his war against Parthia to 'win military glory' but the profits of Eastern commerce may have been a further incentive. The last major scheme for Eastern conquest had been planned by Augustus who hoped to master the commercial profits of the southern Arabian kingdoms.[113] Since the time of Tiberius the imperial government had been aware that Eastern commerce was transporting Roman wealth into Persia.[114] This trade wealth made Mesopotamia a lucrative target for military glory.

Further Roman motives for Eastern conquest are suggested by the actions of a later Roman Emperor named Caracalla who also planned an unprovoked attack on Parthia. Caracalla wrote to the Parthian king to suggest that their two political territories should be united under a single heir and the account reveals what the Romans hoped to achieve by adding Parthia to their empire. The benefit would be 'a single empire without rival' that could 'easily unite the entire inhabited world under a single authority'.[115] Added to these political ambitions was the expectation of lucrative new trade arrangements between Parthia and the Mediterranean territories. Herodian reports:

> Since the Parthians supply spices and excellent textiles and the Romans produce metals and manufactured articles, these items would no longer be scarce or smuggled by merchants. Instead, when there is one world under one supreme authority, both peoples could enjoy these goods and share them in common.[116]

Trajan is likely to have shared these objectives and sought the enrichment of his new Empire through the free exchange of Eastern trade goods.

The theme of Alexander the Great as world conqueror appears a number of times in the surviving accounts of Trajan's Parthian war. It is likely that the Emperor deliberately played upon these comparisons to emphasize the scope of his ambition and his likelihood of success.[117] Roman ambition for military glory and Eastern wealth converged when the Emperor reached the Persian Gulf. Trajan stood on the shore where 20 years earlier the Chinese envoy Gan Ying had looked out across the sea and despaired of ever reaching Rome. Cassius Dio describes the Emperor watching trade ships leaving for India and dreaming of conquests that would emulate Alexander and take Roman forces to the very edge of Asia. But Trajan died within the year.

Roman ambitions were redefined under the Emperor Hadrian. Nevertheless, Roman government continued to receive emissaries from the distant East. The sources for this period are scant and the surviving records show the influence of rhetorical grandeur. The *Historia Augusta* suggests that several Kushan kings sent representatives to Rome during this era reporting, 'The kings of the Bactrians sent supplicant ambassadors to Hadrian begging for his friendship.'[118]

Diplomatic contacts with the Kushan continued into the reign of Antoninus Pius who ruled from AD 138 to AD 161. Aurelius Victor reports:

> The Indians, the Bactrians and the Hyrcanians all sent ambassadors to Antoninus. They had all heard about the spirit of justice held by this great emperor, justice that was heightened by his handsome and grave countenance, and his slim and vigorous figure.[119]

Scholars suggest that these political dealings were attempts to undermine Parthian authority in the distant East.[120] The Emperors attained great prestige from the reception of distant Kushan emissaries, but the purpose of these meetings remains speculative. In this era, the Kushan continued to value their contacts with Roman government. Images from the Roman Empire appear on the gold coinage of King Huvishka who came to power in about AD 140. His coins include a figure of the Greek-Egyptian god Serapis who also appears on Roman issues. Other Kushan coins represent 'Roma', the personification of Rome, depicted as a classical goddess with the legend 'Riom' recorded in Greek letters.[121] These images perhaps represent trade relations, but they could also signify political contacts and foreign affiliations.

Antoninus was the last Roman Emperor of this era to receive acknowledgement from the Indian kingdoms. The reign of Marcus Aurelius was a traumatic time for the Empire with the outbreak of the Antonine pandemic and the start of extended wars against hostile Germanic tribes who threatened the northern frontiers. In the following era, Rome lost much of its international prestige and as civil wars repeatedly arose within the Roman territories, Emperors paid less attention to distant political issues. The politics of government became increasingly about personal survival in a more violent and uncertain world, while the affairs of the distant East simply fell from notice.

ROMAN KNOWLEDGE OF HAN CHINA

Roman authorities had heard rumours of a significant land in the Far East called 'Sinae' or 'Thina' that lay beyond the Tarim *Seres*. This distant power was the Han Empire, the great political regime that rivalled Rome in its territorial scale and the size of its subject population.

In the Augustan era the Romans believed that the Asian continent ended somewhere just north of the Ganges. From there they thought the Asian landmass must turn northwest to join with the vast Scythian regions of the Eurasian Steppe. In this world view there was no China and the peoples of the Tarim territories lay at the edge of the ancient world. Roman authorities therefore called the Tarim populations the *Seres*, or 'Silk People'. These *Seres* were far beyond the reach of Roman merchants and fanciful rumours began to spread about their great integrity and their ability to live beyond a normal lifespan.[122]

By the time of the *Periplus*, Roman traders had learned about the existence of China, but they did not appreciate the scale of its political domain. The *Periplus* offers the first classical reference to the Han when it reports:

> Beyond these regions, by now at the northernmost part of the earth, where the sea ends, somewhere out there on the outer fringe, there is a very great inland state called Thina.[123]

The *Periplus* was confused about the exact location of China, but was certain about its significance to Eastern commerce. The work records how vast amounts of silk fabric were being trafficked from China into Bactria and then taken down through the Indus and Ganges to reach northern India. These trade routes offered intriguing possibilities for Roman merchants interested in Chinese goods. Yet the *Periplus* warns:

> It is not easy to get to this Thina; only rarely do people come from it and these people are only a few. The area lies right under Ursa Minor and it is said to be linked with the outer parts of the Pontus and the Caspian Sea.[124]

In this early stage of knowledge, the *Periplus* used the relative positions of stellar constellations to locate China. Perhaps Roman merchants were already considering the possibility of direct contacts guided by the stars.

By the time Ptolemy completed his 'Geography', the Romans were aware that the Asian landmass extended beyond the Malay Peninsula as far as the Gulf of Thailand. Using records derived from merchant reports, Ptolemy placed a land called 'Sinai' in a narrow fringe of territory at the very edge of Asia. This must be the 'Thina' mentioned in the *Periplus* and both names seem to be based on Sanskrit words for China.[125] Ptolemy's data indicates that Roman merchants involved in ocean trade had realized the position of China, but did not appreciate its vast extent.

The information that Ptolemy received from the Maes report was vague and difficult to reconstruct into a comprehensive impression of Chinese territory. The Maes group were taken to the capital at Luoyang at a time when the Chinese had just re-claimed the Tarim kingdoms and subjugated their disparate populations. The Romans referred to the Tarim peoples as the *Seres*, so Luoyang was designated as 'Sera', capitol of the *Seres*. Ptolemy did not realize that the *Seres* homeland visited by the Maes merchants was in fact China and the same territory as the 'Sinai' mentioned in the maritime trade reports.

With reports of China remaining vague and confused, it is likely the Roman government took no great political interest in such a distant territory. There is nothing in the classical sources to suggest that the Romans understood the scale, or the political significance, of the Chinese domain. Yet there is an incident in the

Han records that may indicate that one Roman emperor was sufficiently intrigued by rumours of exotic peoples in the Far East to send agents out to make contact with these remote lands.

THE 'ANTUN' EMBASSY

For generations, scholars have been fascinated by a reference in the Han histories to an apparent political contact between the governments of China and Rome. The account describes how in AD 166 Roman delegates reached China and were received by the Han Emperor Huan.[126]

The arrival of these Roman representatives was connected with major upheavals in the distant East. By the 150s AD the so-called Antonine pandemic was spreading slowly through the trade routes of inner Asia towards the Empires of China and Rome. The urban communities of Central Asia must have fallen victim in succession to the infection and this would have interrupted the commercial traffic that formed the silk routes. The decline in caravan traffic reaching Iran probably encouraged Vologaeses to invade Mesene in AD 151, giving the Parthians possession of a maritime trade in Eastern goods that still remained vibrant.

The Saka kingdom of western India supplied Chinese silks to Roman merchants who visited their coastal markets. But, as inland trade communications with Central Asia began to fail, the Sakas would have found that silk supplies reaching their territory greatly diminished. In response the Sakas sent out agents to find new routes to reach China via the still operational maritime networks. The *Hou Hanshu* records that between AD 159 and AD 161 the Han court received its first representatives from the Saka kingdom.[127] These groups probably petitioned for trade relations with the Chinese, recognizing that they had discovered an important new supply route for silks.

In AD 161, the Antonine pandemic reached Han garrisons on the western frontiers of their Empire and in a matter of months this unknown infection was spreading steadily through the wider Chinese population. In AD 162, the Parthians launched their first invasion of Roman territory for almost two centuries. The ensuing war that raged across Mesopotamia must have severed overland communications with the Persian Gulf trade routes. Then in AD 165, Roman forces operating in Mesopotamia began to fall victim to a strange new disease; the pandemic had finally reached the Western world.

With Mesopotamian commerce blocked by campaigning armies, the Red Sea trade routes acquired an even greater significance in supplying Roman markets. From their contact with the Saka courts, Roman merchants would have been intrigued to learn about the new sea-routes to China and see the silks brought back on these missions. On their return to Egypt, these Roman merchants may have prepared their own delegation to establish commercial contact with China.

The Roman merchants sailed around the Malay Peninsula and through the Straits of Malacca to reach the Gulf of Thailand. Sailing north they made landfall on the Vietnamese coast at a district called Rinan. Believing they had reached their destination, they must have exchanged their remaining Roman merchandise for Chinese products available in this region. However, Rinan was a Han military Commandery and once Chinese authorities became aware of their presence, the Romans were seized and taken to the imperial court. Communication must have been extremely difficult and was probably conducted through a series of translators. The group had no valuable Roman gifts to present as diplomatic tribute, so offered the Chinese Emperor the trade goods they had picked-up in Southeast Asia. They confirmed that they were Roman and maintained that they had been sent by a ruler named 'Antun'. According to the *Hou Hanshu*:

> The ruler of the Roman Empire, "Antun", sent envoys from beyond the frontiers to reach us through Rinan. They offered elephant tusks, rhinoceros horn, and turtle shell [as diplomatic gifts]. This was the very first time there was [direct] communication [between our two countries].[128]

'Antun' was the Roman Emperor Marcus Aurelius Antoninus who ruled from AD 161 to AD 180. The Chinese record keepers obviously had difficulty understanding the length of such a name and shortened 'Antoninus' to 'Antun'.[129]

Most scholars believe that these Roman representatives were not sent on an official mission by the Emperor. It is argued that they were simply opportunist merchants who stumbled into contact with Han authorities. This would explain why they had no expensive diplomatic gifts and could only offer the Han Emperor a paltry 'tribute' composed of local goods.[130] Yet Marcus Aurelius was the great philosopher Emperor and he would have approved of an attempt to make contact, especially as popular rumours suggested the virtue of these distant foreigners.[131] Perhaps Rome sought new allies in its conflict against the suddenly resurgent and aggressive Parthia. Even more speculative is the idea that the Kushan had informed the Romans about China and their alliance with Ban Chao.

If the Antun group were sanctioned, then something must have happened to deprive them of their valuable Roman gifts before they reached the Chinese court. When the group were summoned before the court of the Han Emperor, they did not resemble the impressive 'equals of China' that the Han had been led to expect from earlier reports. The Chinese believed the embassy was official and were consequently forced to conclude that previous information about the great wealth of Rome had to be inaccurate. The *Hou Hanshu* comments:

> The tribute they brought was neither precious nor rare, raising suspicion that the accounts [of Rome given by earlier informants] might be exaggerated.[132]

The classical sources that describe the reign of Marcus Aurelius make no mention of any Romans returning from diplomatic dealings in China. If the Antun group successfully returned to Roman territory, they would have found the Empire in crisis as the Antonine pandemic swept through its urban population. Ironically, the communication routes that might have benefited both the Roman and Chinese civilizations now acted as conduits for this devastating disease. Roman merchant communities were unable to capitalize on the trade opportunities offered by any new knowledge of China. As for the Roman authorities, with the army decimated by disease and Germanic tribes threatening to overrun the northern provinces, distant contacts in the Far East could not have been a priority.

Meanwhile the Han government struggled to manage the effects of the pandemic as the virus devastated their military forces and spread unchecked through the vast urban populations of their Empire. Unaware that the same crisis was overwhelming Rome, the Han must have puzzled over the failure of Antun to send further diplomats. For those in government, this would have confirmed the theory that Rome could not have been as powerful as the previous generation of Han officials had believed. No matter how these events are interpreted the Antun mission to China remains one of the most intriguing episodes in the history of both the ancient civilizations involved.

THE DECLINE

As the Antonine pandemic swept through the ancient world, Rome's political relations with the distant East were bound to suffer. Academics refer to the human trait for attributing the origin of virulent new diseases to foreign communities.[133] It is therefore interesting that the Tamil sources mention systematic attacks on Roman shipping during this era with the Chera king Netunceralatan seizing cargoes and taking Roman subjects hostage.[134] According to the *Patirruppattu*:

> Netunceralatan put in chains the rough-speaking *Yavana* and he poured oil upon their heads. Keeping their hands tied behind their backs he seized their precious jewels and their excellent diamonds.[135]

The expectations of Empire changed as the Roman army was decimated by disease and became entrenched in new Germanic wars. Previous military ambitions concerning the distant East became increasingly unrealistic and conquests that once might have seemed achievable were now subjected to ridicule. In this era, Lucian scoffs at stories written about Eastern conquests, and mentions one in particular, where the writer imaged that Vologaeses could be defeated and the Parthian nobility made to fight in the arena for the amusement of the victorious Romans. Lucian reports:

> I have known one writer compile an account of the future. It includes the capture of Vologaeses, the execution of Osroes (he is to be thrown to the lions), and surpassing all of this, our long-deferred triumph. In this prophetic account he sweeps hastily on to the end of his work.[136]

Lucian is even more scathing about an imagined Roman invasion of India to surpass Alexander the Great. He writes:

> This author has also pledged that he will write an account of coming events in India including the circumnavigation of the Outer Ocean and he is halfway finished! The preface to his *India* is already complete: the third Roman legion, the Celtic contingent,

> and a small Moorish division have crossed the Indus in full strength under Cassius. Our most original reporter will soon inform us about their activities, including their method for dealing with elephants. These details will appear in letters marked "Muziris from the Hindu Brahmin".[137]

The existence of these fictions perhaps explains why the report by Maes Titianus about China did not receive widespread recognition.[138] It was probably dismissed by educated Romans as just another improbable fantasy. Maes asked his readers to believe that there was a vast exotic kingdom in the Far East that rivalled the Roman Empire. The party sent by Maes was the only group that had travelled into this distant and strange 'other world'. None were to follow in the succeeding era as the Empire struggled to maintain its northern frontier and the lands that lay between Rome and China descended further into war-torn chaos.

LATER CONTACTS

During the third century AD, Chinese accounts mention three unusual incidents of contact between Roman subjects and Chinese rulers. The evidence suggests that although Eastern commerce declined drastically after the Antonine pandemic, the trade routes into the distant East remained known to some Roman merchants. In this era a few adventurous individuals still dared to venture far into the Indian Ocean, and the seas beyond. These events occurred after the collapse of the Han Empire when the once great Chinese realm had fractured into rival kingdoms, each contending for supremacy, and when civil wars were raging throughout the Roman Empire.

In AD 224 the Persian Sassanid king Ardashir defeated the last Parthian ruler in an epic conflict that was fought across ancient Iran. This Persian war must have paralysed the Iranian silk routes which led to shortages and price rises in Roman markets. Responding to this crisis a Roman merchant named Leon decided to find the sea-route to China and access the silk markets at their distant source.

The *Liang-shu* records that in AD 226, a Roman merchant named 'Da Qin Lun' arrived in eastern China in the territory of the successor Wu State.[139] 'Lun' is probably the Greek name 'Leon' phonically simplified by the ancient Chinese. This Leon was taken to the court of the Wu Emperor Sun Quan and asked to give a full account of his place of origin. The *Liang-shu* reports:

> A merchant of *Da Qin* whose name was Lun came to Tongkin. The prefect of Tongkin named Wu Miao sent him to Sun Quan. The Emperor asked him for details about his native land and its customs. Qin Lun prepared a report in reply.[140]

Leon expressed interest in some small dark-skinned captives that had been brought to the Wu court as a result of a recent conflict. The Emperor Sun Quan gave Leon a gift of 20 of these captives, including ten men and ten women. The Wu government were impressed by this distant foreigner and Sun Quan seized the opportunity to learn more about Rome and its sophisticated civilization. He chose a Chinese officer named Liu Hsien to accompany Leon on his return journey back to the Roman Empire. The *Liang-shu* states:

> Qin Lun saw some small dark skinned captives and he said that in *Da Qin* these men were rarely seen. So Sun Quan gave him ten male and female captives and sent an officer named Liu Hsien of Huiji district to accompany Qin Lun [on his return]. Da Qin Lun returned directly to his native land but Liu Hsien died on the way.[141]

The reference is intriguing because the return journey of Leon and Liu Hsien is not described by the Chinese sources. The classical accounts contain no reports of any silk-laden merchants arriving in the Roman Empire with strange captives from the Far East. It therefore seems likely that Leon did not make it safely back to the Empire.

Emperor Sun Quan must have waited for the return of Leon, for Roman embassies to arrive, for further foreign trade ships to appear. But Liu Hsien did not return and stories that the great sea journey to *Da Qin* brought about illness and insufferable homesickness now assumed a more ominous character. As for Leon, his unexplained disappearance in the Far East must have discouraged other Roman merchants from attempting the journey. One possible explanation for events is that on the return sailing through the treacherous Straits of Malacca, which are subject to paralysing calms, the Roman ship was left stranded at the mercy of coastal pirates. The Straits could have claimed the lives of Leon and his crew and ended the possibilities offered by this extraordinary communication.

By the 260s AD there was a significant recovery in Rome's Eastern commerce. During this period there were improvements made to the Red Sea port of Myos Hormos that involved the construction of a new fortified military base at the site.[142] A Chinese text from this era also notes the reappearance of Roman merchants in the outer regions of Southeast Asia.[143] The *Liang-shu* states:

> Merchants of Rome often visit Fu-nan (Cambodia), Jih-nan and Chiao-chih (Vietnam), but few people from these regions have been to Rome.[144]

A copper coin of the Western Roman Emperor Victorinus was found at U-thong in western Thailand, indicating a contact that had occurred sometime after AD 268.[145]

This trade recovery increased the financial fortunes of merchants from the cities of Alexandria and Palmyra. By this era Britain and Gaul had ceded from Rome and the Western Empire was politically divided. Palmyra had developed into a major military force on the eastern frontier as Rome left the Palmyrenes to counter the threat posed by a resurgent Persian Empire. As Palmyra rose to military and economic dominance in the region, its ruling elite began to question their subservience to Rome. Their Queen Zenobia now seized the opportunity to claim authority over the Eastern Roman Empire.

In Egypt, Alexandrian merchants continued to surrender a large proportion of their eastern trade profits as tax to Roman officials. These taxes went overseas to an Emperor with little interest in their province except as a provider of wealth and grain for Rome. Reacting to this situation, a rich and influential Alexandrian merchant named Firmus sought an alliance with Zenobia to free Egypt from Roman control.

Firmus was originally from Seleucia, but he made his fortune in Egypt conducting trade ventures to India.[146] He was well connected with the Palmyrenes and established important overseas dealings with leading peoples in the Arab and Ethiopian kingdoms. High level contacts in India had also given him impressive ivory trophies. The *Historia Augusta* reports, 'Firmus kept up good relations with the Blemmyae and Saracens, and he often sent merchant vessels to the Indians'.[147] Firmus could also count on a private army of mercenary guards, recruited from his trade business.

In AD 269, Firmus gave his support to Queen Zenobia who sent forces west to take Egypt from Rome. Together, Zenobia and Firmus planned the independence of Egypt and Palmyra, united in a new Eastern empire free from Roman taxation and control.[148] Rome needed Egypt to feed its vast population so the Roman sources were quick to demonize Firmus. They therefore describe him as a monstrous and intimidating character. The *Historia Augusta* reports:

> Firmus was of huge size, his eyes were very prominent, his hair curly, his brow scarred, his face rather swarthy. The rest of his body was white and rough and covered with hair. Many called him a Cyclops.[149]

Stories were also told about his huge wealth and his vast palace-like house fitted with square panels of glass. It seems that he had gathered an enormous collection of papers; perhaps they were contracts or business accounts, or maybe Firmus owned a private library. Alarming stories spread about the great appetite that Firmus displayed in the feasts he organized for leading citizens.

In AD 273 the Roman Emperor Aurelian defeated Zenobia and captured the city of Palmyra. Firmus now stood alone and was forced to use his personal wealth to fund his bid for the independence of Alexandria. Aurelian moved quickly against Egypt.[150] The *Historia Augusta* reports:

> Firmus was a friend and ally of Zenobia. Incited by the madness of the Egyptians, he seized Alexandria and was crushed by the Emperor Aurelian with much good fortune and valour.[151]

Firmus was strangled by the Roman victors as though he was a common criminal.[152] Many of his supporters were taken back to Rome as prisoners with certain Palmyrene leaders who had held high office under Zenobia. The captives were paraded through Rome in a spectacular Triumph to celebrate Aurelian's victory over the Eastern provinces and their distant allies. The prisoners humiliated in this procession through the Roman mobs included Axumites from the African kingdom of Ethiopia, Arabs from the southern Arabian nations, Kushan from Bactria and people from India. Many of these unfortunate individuals were probably business contacts who were captured by the Roman forces when they seized Palmyra and entered Alexandria to find and murder Firmus.[153]

In AD 282, the new Roman Emperor Carus planned an invasion of Persia to attack the ruling Sassanids.[154] Preparations for this campaign must have interrupted Eastern traffic passing from Mesopotamia into the Roman territories. This gave Alexandrian merchants the incentive to find the sea route to China that had been travelled five decades earlier by Leon.

Alexandrian entrepreneurs involved in this new mission to reach China learnt from the example of Firmus and acted in their own interests. The office of Emperor had been undermined by a rapid succession of imperial candidates who were either assassinated, or deposed in repeated rounds of civil war. Furthermore, many of the Alexandrian businessmen involved in this new initiative to contact China would have known Firmus and had commercial dealings with his Palmyrene colleagues. They obviously saw no obligation to make their plans known to the Roman authorities who had mistreated their associates.

The first Roman ship involved in these new explorations arrived in China in AD 282 with its valuable Mediterranean cargo intact. The Chinese marvelled at items such as asbestos cloth that could be scorched clean of stains by the effects of fire. The Chinese records state:

> In this year, (an embassy from) *Da Qin* came to offer tribute and it passed through the Guangxi Circuit. Of the many treasures they offered the strangest was "fire-washed cloth" (asbestos).[155]

Significantly, the account contains no direct mention of traders and no reference to a Roman Emperor dispatching the group. This suggests that the initiative was a private mission by a merchant team trying to open up trade arrangements with the authorities in China.

The Alexandrian team who reached China in AD 282 managed to return to Egypt and inform other merchants about their discoveries. A further Chinese work called the *Nan-fang Tsao-mu Chuang* records that in AD 284 there was another contact with Roman subjects.[156] On this occasion, the Alexandrian merchants offered the Chinese Emperor 30,000 rolls of a scented agarwood called 'honey fragrance paper'. These were commodities from Southeast Asia, but they were valuable in both Chinese and Roman society. The Emperor was impressed by the Roman gift and ordered a senior dignitary to have the Chinese classics written out on these thin wooden scrolls. The brief record for this contact reads:

> In this year *Da Qin* presented 30,000 rolls of honey fragrance paper. The Emperor bestowed 10,000 rolls on the Southern Commander . . . with orders to write out his commentaries and the (Chinese) classics.[157]

In these initial contacts Alexandrian merchants were uncertain about what goods would make the most impressive gifts to Chinese authorities or have the most value in Far Eastern markets. The Roman group must have calculated that they could make more profit from exchanging the agarwood for silk, than they would gain by keeping the product for sale in Alexandria.

These contacts may have been successful, but they came too late to change the fortunes of China and Rome. The Alexandrian entrepreneurs did not have government backing and the incentive was market profit rather than the exchange of knowledge, technologies, or political ideas. The Roman Empire was already developing along economic lines that would soon curb this brief reprisal in Eastern commerce. Faced with continued crises and falling revenues, the Roman government debased the imperial coinage to the extent that market prices began to rapidly escalate. The silver Roman currency that had so impressed Eastern rulers was now reduced to a base metal issue that had only nominal value within the Empire. Finally in AD 301, in a desperate effort to control inflation, the Emperor Diocletian imposed an edict on the Roman population, stating the maximum prices that were to be paid for market goods. Like their Ptolemaic predecessors, the Romans now dictated the prices paid for Eastern merchandise and limited the free market profits that had funded earlier commercial ventures to India.[158] Intrusive politics and economic mismanagement ended the opportunities for profit in the distant East and with it the possibilities for consequential contact between Rome and China.

Ultimately, the two great empires of the ancient world failed to reach out to one another. Their brief, intangible contacts never provided the interchange of ideas and technologies that could have transformed the fortunes of their respective civilizations. Despite these lost opportunities, it is still possible to regard these distant endeavours as fascinating episodes in the history of humanity. Although, like much of world history, the most intriguing thoughts of any scholar are drawn to speculate on what 'might have been'.

6

The Economic Impact on the Roman Empire

The Roman Empire holds a fundamental place in Western notions of identity and civilization. Scholars from Europe and America have therefore placed enormous significance on the history of the Roman state. Yet, in spite of this interest, the operation of the imperial economy remains uncertain. In particular, there is a lack of consensus regarding the revenue system that provided the Roman government with the finances it required to fund its political operations and maintain its professional army.

At the core of this debate is the question of how the early Roman Empire was able to achieve such a remarkable level of economic stability and financial success. The Roman accomplishment seems all the more extraordinary when the economic and political condition of medieval Europe is taken into consideration. Arguably, it is not until the discovery of the Americas that Western Europe had the resources, wealth and opportunities to develop infrastructures comparable to those created by the Roman state. This European revival was connected to expanding commercial interests in the Indian Ocean and the Far East. Yet while this recent aspect of the past is firmly acknowledged, the role Eastern commerce had in Roman civilization has never been comprehensively studied.

EASTERN IMPORTS IN ROMAN SOCIETY

The Roman sources suggest that Alexandria was the major gateway for Eastern imports entering the Mediterranean. Alexandria was a vast cosmopolitan meeting place for a commerce that connected Europe and the Mediterranean world to the Indian Ocean territories of East Africa, Arabia, Persia, India and the Far East. Dio Chrysostom reports:

> Alexandria is situated at the crossroads of the whole world and it serves the world as though it was a market serving a single city. It is connected to the most remote nations and this market brings together into one place all manner of men.[1]

Strabo indicates that Alexandria dominated Eastern trade to the extent that it had a virtual monopoly on these imports. Writing in the Augustan era he states:

> Egypt has monopolies; for Alexandria alone is the main receiver of goods (from India and East Africa) and it is the main source of supply to other Roman territories.[2]

The city dominated Mediterranean commerce, partly because of its control over Eastern imports, but also because it supplied massive quantities of grain to Rome to feed its vast urban population. Dio Chrysostom explains:

> You Alexandrians have a monopoly on the shipping of the entire Mediterranean by reason of the beauty of your harbours, the magnitude of your fleet, and your marketing of abundant products from every land. The outer waters that lie beyond the Mediterranean are within your reach, both the Red Sea and the Indian Ocean, whose name was rarely heard in past times.[3]

Strabo reports that the Roman fleet sailing to India in the early Augustan era numbered at least 120 ships. If each vessel returned with only 300 tons of cargo, then more than 36,000 tons of Eastern goods would be arriving in Alexandria every year.[4] Strabo also talks about large Roman fleets trading with East Africa and records that Egypt dominated Arabian imports into the Mediterranean territories.[5] These further trade ventures would have brought large quantities of additional eastern cargo into Roman markets.[6]

The most obvious place to look for evidence of Eastern commodities entering the Roman Empire is the Egyptian Red Sea ports. The extreme desert environment of Berenice has preserved extensive organic evidence that has been carefully catalogued by archaeobotanists.[7] The volume of spice passing through Berenice was enormous and numerous black peppercorns have been found across the site. During four seasons of excavation, archaeologists recovered almost 1,600 peppercorns within buildings as well as rubbish deposits. This is more than twice the number of lentils found at the site, even though lentils were a staple food at the port. A dump near the Greco-Egyptian temple of Serapis contained a large number of charred peppercorns that must have been the remains of a foreign offering made at the sanctuary.[8] Indians also left their own votive offering to Serapis within the temple confines. Excavations unearthed two large Indian jars embedded into the floor of the Roman courtyard. One of the jars was packed with almost 55 kilograms of black peppercorns and plugged with a wooden stopper.[9]

These excavations at Berenice also uncovered almost 50 specimens of rice in the form of seeds and husks. Rice imports were destined for Roman markets as a component in medical gruels, but visiting Indian traders would also have brought supplies to the port for their own consumption.[10] Coconut oil was used by Indians to preserve the rigging ropes of their ships, but it was also an inexpensive food product brought to Berenice from the distant East. Around 30 fragments of coconut were found in the town, mostly in rubbish deposits. Foreign traders and Roman crews returning from the distant East also brought highly nutritional mung beans to Berenice. The mung plant is cultivated in Southern Asia but dozens of these beans were found in Berenice rubbish deposits. The dried inner remains of Amla fruit also appears at the port. These small fruits are native to the lower Himalayas and being rich in vitamin C they would have been eaten to reduce the risk of scurvy on the long sea voyage back to Egypt.[11]

A list of Eastern goods subject to tax at Alexandria has been preserved in a text called the *Alexander Tariff*. This record indicates the enormous variety of Eastern imports that were reaching Roman markets by the second century AD. It lists many commodities not mentioned in the *Periplus*, including imports arriving from the Persian Gulf. The document records:

> Types of goods liable to *vectigal* (tax): cinnamon; long pepper; white pepper; pentasphaerum leaf; barbary leaf; costum; costamomum; nard; stachys; Tyrian cassia; cassia-wood; myrrh; amomum; ginger; malabrathrum; Indian spice; galbanum; asafoetida; aloe; lycium; Perian gum; Arabian onyx; cardamom; cinnamon-wood; cotton goods; Babylonian hides; Parthian hides; ivory; Indian iron; linen; all sorts of gems – pearls, sardonyx, ceraunium, hyacinth stone, emerald, diamond, sapphire, turquoise, beryl, tortoise stone; Indian or Seric drugs; raw silk, silk or part-silk clothing; dyed cloth; embroidered fine linen; silk thread; Indian eunuchs; lions and lionesses; pards (maneless big cats); leopards; panthers; purple dye; wool; dye; and Indian hair.[12]

There are 56 imports mentioned in the tax. Of the identifiable trade goods, over 30 are Indian products, while several are specific to the Parthian territories. At least 23 of the goods are spices, ten are precious stones, and ten are clothing materials. Almost all these goods leave little or no archaeological trace.[13]

Pliny discusses Eastern products and their uses in Roman society. He also gives prices for over 20 Eastern commodities that probably reflect retail values in Rome.[14] Among the lower-priced Eastern goods were frankincense, sold at three denarii per pound, and pepper, which cost four denarii per pound.[15] This would be several days pay for an ordinary labourer, but these products would still have been affordable to a large section of the Roman population.[16] For most people the purchase of incense and the consumption of spices would be small scale and occasional.[17] Yet the popularity of these products ensured that the accumulative effect of all these small-scale purchases created a vast international commerce.

During the imperial era, pepper became important in the Roman diet and demand for the spice spread across the Mediterranean into Western Europe. The Apicius 'cookbook' is a compilation of early Roman texts on food preparation and it mentions pepper in almost every recipe including those for common dishes.[18] Pepper was sprinkled into sauces offered with sea foods and included in salad dressings.[19] The spice is also mentioned in connection with the preparation of meat and as a flavouring to 'preserve' wine.[20] Pepper could be used in relatively small amounts to greatly enhance flavour and make perishable foods palatable for longer. This would be exploited by the household cook and by urban food sellers who would have added small amounts of spice to improve their stock sales. Pliny was fascinated that Roman society was prepared to send people to the limits of the known world in order to improve the taste of Mediterranean food. He writes, 'Peppers only desirable quality is its pungency, yet for this we bring it all the way from India.'[21] Petronius satirises this situation when he has a businessman send agents to India to collect minute mushroom spores to improve the taste of a Roman feast.[22]

In the Augustan era, spices were sold in stalls around the back streets of Rome near the docks. Horace pictures the area covered with discarded cheap paper that had been used to wrap measures of pepper. He speaks of going, 'Down to the back streets where they sell the spices and everywhere is draped in paper waste'.[23] Academics believe that the Roman government may have seized a quarter of all Eastern goods entering Egypt in a tax called the *tetarte*.[24] The state therefore had access to vast amounts of Eastern produce that it could sell in Alexandria, or stock in Rome for further retail sale.

Eastern products had great significance in classical medicines and Roman religious ceremony. Consequently, it became important for the government to maintain large stocks of these products in a central location. By the time of the Emperor Domitian, enormous spice warehouses called the 'Horrea Piperataria' had been built in the Roman forum near the Colosseum.[25] These facilities were called the 'Pepper Warehouses', but as well as stocking Indian spices, they also stored Arabian incense.[26] The vast depot was divided into multiple modest-sized storerooms, but it also contained a series of high, enclosed courtyards, from which the government sold or distributed its spice supplies. Throughout the complex there were abundant water troughs and cisterns to dampen the oppressive atmosphere caused by the heavy dry aroma of this precious stock.

The importance of the Horrea Piperataria is indicated by the basilica built on the site by the Emperor Maxentius in the late Roman period. The Basilica of Maxentius was the largest enclosed building in the Roman forum and it served as an administrative centre for the entire city.[27] Modern attempts have been made to estimate the grain storage capacity of large Roman warehouses and these studies suggest that the ground floor of the Horrea Piperataria could have stored at least 5,800 tons of spice.[28] To place this figure in context, 5,800 tons of pepper would be worth around 240 million sesterces. If this amount were to be evenly distributed amongst the population of the Empire, then every five people would receive a pound of spice.

Archaeology indicates that pepper reached all regions of the Roman Empire and was enjoyed by people with modest incomes. For example, pepper husks were discovered at the stone quarry of Mons Claudianus in the arid Eastern Desert of Egypt and objects interpreted as pepper pots have been recovered in Gaul and Pompeii.[29] Peppercorns were even discovered in excavations at a Roman army camp in Germany at the very edge of the Empire.[30] Writing tablets found at Vindolanda also provide evidence that consignments of pepper were reaching the soldiers in Britian as far away as Hadrian's Wall.[31]

Eastern products were widely used in medicines. For example Roman apothecaries used myrrh as an ingredient in many of their concoctions. During the crucifixion, Jesus was offered 'wine mingled with myrrh', possibly as an analgesic.[32] A combination of frankincense and myrrh are prescribed in a cream with wax and mistletoe to help sooth backache and muscle pains.[33] A Roman author named Dioscurides produced a handbook on medicines that contains numerous references to Eastern substances as ingredients in remedies. Eastern products are mentioned in the treatment of relatively common medical complaints, suggesting widespread consumption.[34] Spices such as pepper were important ingredients in these medical concoctions, from stimulating tonics believed to cure impotence to potions said to alleviate digestive ailments.[35] The Indians may have begun referring to pepper as 'the passion of the Yavanas' partly because they knew the Romans used the substance in aphrodisiac tonics.[36]

The trade in medical remedies was a significant business within the Roman provinces. Medicines leave some trace in the archaeological record in the form of small bottles or phials that once contained liquid remedies or soothing oils. Myrrh and nard were popular ingredients in eye medicines prepared by specialists who stamped their samples with a personal 'seal' of quality. Hundreds of slate occulist stamps used for imprinting eye salves have been found across northwest Europe, including a single find in Ireland.[37]

The burning of incense and scented woods was also immensely popular throughout the Roman Empire.[38] The crowded public streets of Roman cities would have reeked of body odours, sewage, dung and rotting rubbish. In these densely populated areas incense was placed in lanterns and specially designed burners to mask the foul smell of the streets and improve the atmosphere within public buildings and domestic homes.[39] Due to its importance in classical worship, incense was also burned in copious amounts at temples, during public games, ceremonial processions and at Roman victory celebrations. The burning of frankincense was central to Mithraic ritual at a time when this Iranian cult was spreading through sections of the Roman army in the western provinces. Devotees of Mithras burned incense in large hollow pottery lamps so that light and smoke would pour from complex patterns on the surface of the vessel. This religious practice influenced people from other traditions and the remains of these lamp burners have been found in the temples of Celtic deities.[40] Among the Roman population frankincense was routinely offered to household gods at domestic shrines and burned at feasts, purification rites and wedding ceremonies.

A shopping list recovered from Pompeii indicates the types of goods regularly bought by a relatively ordinary Roman household of three people and a slave. The list covers an eight day period and among the basic goods ordered on one of the days were bread, dates, cheese and a little incense. The incense was the cheapest of these commodities and the small amount bought was worth one-sixteenth of a denarius.[41]

Pliny was aware that these small and frequent offerings collectively created enormous market demand. He also drew attention to a growing fashion at cremation ceremonies for incense to be heaped onto funeral pyres to honour the dead and disguise the stench of burning flesh.[42] Pliny reports:

> Let us take into account the vast number of funerals that are celebrated throughout our world each year and the heaps of incense that are piled on pyres to honour the bodies of the dead. Also consider the vast quantities offered to the gods bit by bit in single grains.[43]

Pliny was concerned that by his era the Roman demand for incense had become more about ostentatious display than honouring the gods. He writes:

> An excess of luxury is displayed even in the paraphernalia of death. Arabia deserves the title 'Fortunate' because we burn with the dead those products originally understood to have been produced for the service of the gods . . . Of all these fragrant substances I would like to know how much really goes to the gods of the heavens and how much is expended on characters in the underworld.[44]

In the Julio-Claudian era, the Roman government amassed vast amounts of Eastern produce from the quarter-tax imposed on imports. These stocks rapidly accumulated if the imperial authorities did not dispose of them in frequent state displays, or sell them on to the Roman public. This explains an incident reported by Pliny, when the Emperor Nero burnt a huge quantity of frankincense to mourn the death of his beloved consort Poppaea.[45] This spectacle involved several thousand tons of incense and Pliny writes:

> Those who are most knowledgeable in this matter assert that Arabia does not produce in a whole year the quantity of perfumes that was burnt by the Emperor Nero at the funeral observances of his consort Poppaea.[46]

This incredible display burned probably several years' worth of government stocks, but the state would have rapidly re-acquired further supplies when the merchant fleets returned from the distant East and were taxed again.

Incense had religious importance to communities subject to Rome and myrrh began to develop great significance in Jewish funerary practices. The *Gospel of John* records:

> Nicodemus came bringing a mixture of myrrh and aloes, about a hundred pounds weight. So they took the body of Jesus and bound it in linen wrappings with the spices, as is the burial custom of the Jews.[47]

Indian products also assumed a greater religious function in Mediterranean society as commerce increased. Nard developed an important ritual purpose in festivity, religious honour, and the ceremonial treatment of the dead. A passage in the *New Testament* describes how Jesus was anointed with costly nard oil in an act that was symbolically linked with preparations for burial.[48]

Roman society had complex attitudes to Eastern products. One of the main issues for Roman moralists was that the same exotic substances that were needed for medicine and demanded by religious practice were being used 'frivolously' for personal display. Nard was important in funerary practices, but Pliny wrote that the product had come to hold the 'principal place' amongst Roman perfumes.[49] Unguents made from myrrh and nard were increasingly used as appealing personal fragrances. Even Roman soldiers began wearing the perfumed oils that previously had been used to anoint their military standards in sacred rituals.[50] Pliny writes:

> The most amazing thing is that this luxurious gratification has even spread to the army camps. The eagles and the standards are dusty and bristling with sharpened points. Yet they are now anointed on festive days . . . and there is therefore a precedent for those who wear unguents beneath their military helmets.[51]

Suetonius records that by this era many Roman troops indulged in excess 'luxuries'. It was widely known that the unpretentious emperor Vespasian disapproved of these practices. Suetonius writes:

> A young officer, reeking of perfume, came to thank the Emperor for a commission he had obtained. Vespasian turned his head away in disgust and cancelled the order, adding the stern reprimand, "I would have preferred if he had stunk of garlic".[52]

A fashion for perfumed hair oil had existed in Republican times, but the practice reached greater popularity under the Emperors.[53] Pliny reveals that a man in hiding was 'smelt out' by his pursuers because of the strength of his perfume.[54] Ovid warned women not to be 'won over' by men with their hair covered in nard ointment.[55] Martial complained about a man whose oily hair could be smelt all over the theatre.[56] It was even said that Nero wore perfumed oils on the very soles of his feet.[57] Pliny was also critical of people who had begun scenting their private rooms with perfumes to disguise other odours.[58]

Pliny considered perfume to be one of the most wasteful items because its effect was soon expended. He writes:

> Some unguents have a price greater than 400 denarii per pound. A vast sum is therefore paid for a luxury that is for the enjoyment others. For the person who wears the perfume is not the one that smells it.[59]

The cost of perfume and its transient nature could be exploited in other ways. A civic official from North Africa tried to disguise part of a large bribe of 200,000 sesterces to a corrupt Roman governor by entering it in his account books under 'perfumes'. He expected that 10,000 sesterces spent on ungents would not arouse suspicion.[60]

It has been established that perfumers, known as *ungentarii*, frequented an area called Seplasia in Capua, but there were perfumers operating in many urban districts of the Roman Empire.[61] Exotic Eastern ingredients became popular in fragrant beauty lotions used by affluent Roman women. Ovid provides a recipe for a 'beauty cream' that women might apply to their faces.[62] Juvenal scathingly refers to Roman women using, 'those imported Indian scents and lotions that she buys with a lover in mind'.[63]

Eastern aromatics also had a pleasing effect when mixed with drinks. It became fashionable to add exotic substances to Roman wine including nard, cinnamon, cassia, ginger, frankincense and myrrh.[64] Pliny comments:

> Nowadays people put perfumes in their drink and the bitterness this produces is highly prized. By this lavishness, perfumes thus gratify two senses at once.[65]

Virgil also indicates that wealthy consumers in Roman society began flavouring their olive oil with cinnamon.[66] An indication of the flavourings available in Roman markets comes from the Pozzino shipwreck. The vessel was a large merchant ship that sank off the north-west coast of Italy sometime in the late first century BC. Underwater archaeologists investigating the sunken cargo retrieved unusual rectangular wooden boxes fitted with sliding lids. They found that these caskets were crammed with numerous carefully arranged tin-lined cases, each packed with three small cylinders sealed with tightly fitted wooden caps. To their amazement when they cracked open the caps, they smelt the powerful aromas of ancient spices including cinnamon, vanilla and cumin. Altogether, the caskets contained 136 cylinders packed with spices from across the ancient world.[67]

The Roman retail trade in perfumes is evidenced by small bottles that were used for scented oils called *unguentarium*. These finds appear among the burial remains of Roman women and they are well attested in Egyptian graves that contain portraits of the deceased on coffin lids.[68] The Romans stored liquid perfumes in delicate alabaster vases such as that used by Mary Magdalene in the *New Testament*.[69] Expensive containers were re-used and had many different contents over time. Consequently, the archaeological evidence can reveal the geographical extent of the market, but can only give an impression of its commercial scale.

There was an enormous demand for Eastern fabrics and jewellery in Roman society and this commerce was driven by fashion. Ancient Chinese silks were relatively dense materials that were rewoven in Roman workshops to create fine lightweight fabrics similar to the silk familiar to modern societies. Roman fabric workers also took this process a stage further and rewove the silk into a translucent, gauze-like material.

At first, silk garments were popular with the more 'disreputable' elements of Roman society. Writing in the Augustan era, Horace contrasts the Roman matron with the prostitute and describes the prostitute standing exposed in her translucent silk clothing. He comments:

> You can see her in her Coan silk as though she is naked. You can inspect her to see if she has a poor leg or an unsightly foot. You can appreciate her whole form with your eye.[70]

Decent Roman women from affluent families were expected to conceal themselves under layers of traditional linen or cotton garments. However, the fashion for easily draped silk fabrics spread to these more respectable classes. Soon sizable sections of the population were wearing lightweight silk fabrics because they were comfortable, and elegant. The use of semi-translucent silks gave respectable women the opportunity to display their figures while still wearing traditionally cut garments.[71] Silk clothing was soon identified with the allure of feminine appeal. Affluent Roman women also developed a desire for fashion accessories including colourful silk parasols made from delicate gauze-like fabrics.[72] Reworked silk would absorb natural dyes to create vibrant colours that often reacted with sunshine to produce deep, shimmering shades of indigo, scarlet and ochre.

A silk market was established at the *Vicus Tuscus* near the centre of Rome and Martial mentions that the finest fabrics were available in this district.[73] The appearance of silk in glamorous and revealing female costumes was one of the most striking visual uses for Eastern imports. As the fabric was costly and exotic, it quickly became a target for traditional moral criticisms.[74] Pliny talks of silks imported, 'to enable the Roman matron to flaunt transparent clothing in public' while Seneca can speak of 'clothes that hide nothing of the matron's body'.[75] Petronius gives the view that brides might as well go naked because their costumes were so revealing and he writes about silk garments, 'like gossamer tissue, transparent as air'.[76] Seneca also offers the following account:

> I see silk clothing – but how can this be called clothing when it offers nothing that could possibly afford protection to the body or provide any modesty? When a woman wears these silks she can scarcely say with a clear conscience that she is not naked. These silks are imported at vast expense from nations unknown to us even through trade. Silk is imported so that our married women can show as much of their bodies to people in the street as they display to their lovers in the bedroom.[77]

Seneca is sensationalising the situation, but female fashion in the Empire encouraged foreign commerce and vast sums of money flowed overseas to acquire the fabric.

A fashion also developed amongst affluent Roman men to wear clothing that had strips of coloured silk incorporated into its design. Unlike female fashion, the fabric on male costumes was fine-spun and opaque, rather than translucent. Soon white linen togas and tunics carried coloured stripes and edgings in this delicate silk fabric. This fashion was regarded with suspicion by traditional Romans and in AD 16, the Roman Senate enacted a law restricting the wearing of silk among the male nobility. This measure was partly an attempt to reduce costly display in senatorial politics, but it also appealed to those who criticised the 'feminising' character of the new fabrics. Tacitus reports:

> A former consul and praetor denounced current extravagance. The use of gold plate for private banquets was prohibited and so was the degenerate silk costume which had been adopted in male clothing.[78]

Measures to restrict fashion trends were unsuccessful, especially when Caligula ignored the prohibition and appeared in public wearing elaborate silks.[79] When Pliny wrote about Roman society, silk was commonplace as the attire of affluent men. Pliny lamented the fact that earlier generations of Romans had been content to wear togas and endure the weight of leather breastplates in the hot summer months. He complained that Romans now preferred clothing that was loose and lightweight and jibes that the next fashion trend amongst Roman men might be the silk dresses worn by Persian eunuchs. He writes:

> Now even men will wear silk clothing in the summer because of its lightness and they do not feel ashamed. Once we used to wear leather cuirasses, but our fashions have become so bizarre that even a toga is now considered to be unnecessarily heavy. Yet we have left Assyrian silk dresses to the women – so far![80]

The Romans also imported vast quantities of Indian cotton, but because Egypt also produced this fabric, the impact of this trade on Mediterranean markets is difficult to assess.[81] Ancient fabrics are only preserved in extreme conditions, but Chinese silks have nevertheless been found at ancient tomb-towers on the outskirts of Palmyra.[82] A tiny delicate fragment of silk was also discovered in an ancient grave at Colchester in Roman Britain.[83] Painted images in rooms unearthed at Pompeii and Herculaneum indicate that fine translucent fabrics were popular amongst wealthy Roman women. The robes and shawls represented in these images are distinguished by a brilliant range of colours and depicted with the particular drape of silk.[84]

Silk commerce also reached the northern frontiers of Britain where refashioned Chinese silks were used in Roman military banners because of their lightweight translucent qualities and bright clear colours. An inscription near Hadrian's Wall commemorates a Palmyrene merchant who was resident in Britain and supplied silk banners to frontier military units.[85]

There was a great fashion in Roman society for Eastern pearls and precious stones for jewellery and other adornments. Martial describes the expensive shops in the Roman Forum where these articles could be purchased. He writes:

> Mamurra complained that some crystal vases had been spoiled by glass. He marked and set aside ten myrrhine cups . . . then counted emeralds set in chased gold, and examined the largest pearl ear-pendants. He looked on every counter for real sardonyxes and questioned the value of some large jaspers.[86]

Throughout this era, Roman fashion was becoming increasingly ostentatious and finding more ingenious ways to display wealth. Consequently, many affluent Roman men began to wear Eastern gemstones often engraved as signet rings.[87] Martial wrote about a friend who wore sardonyxes, emeralds, diamonds, and jaspers on his fingers.[88] The use of Tamil beryls in Roman jewellery became widespread and Propertius writes about the funeral pyre of a courtesan who was cremated with garnet and beryl rings still adorning her fingers.[89]

Pliny also talks about a 'mania' for crystal objects. A gemstone from Iran called fluorspar became popular amongst wealthy Romans who staged extravagant dinner parties.[90] Delicate fluorspar drinking goblets had a rich glassy lustre and the colours ranged from purple and blue, to black and reddish orange. Prized examples included translucent hues with multiple bands of colour or even embedded crystal fragments. Some examples exhibited fluorescence and in a dimly lit environment might glow faintly when subjected to heat.[91] The Romans also infused fluorspar goblets with aromatics such as myrrh to flavour their contents. Pliny indicates the expense of this extravagance when he describes how an ex-consul paid 70,000 sesterces for a single fluorspar cup. The man was greatly enamoured by the object and chewed its rim. Yet despite this damage its value had appreciated due to growing fashion demands.[92] Another ex-consul named Titus Petronius smashed a 300,000 sesterces fluorspar ladle prior to committing suicide on Nero's orders. It seems he wanted to deprive the Emperor of this valuable trophy.[93] This fashion for fluorspar soon spread throughout affluent Roman society as Pliny comments:

> Fluorspar vessels have now passed into everyday use and the material is eagerly sought out for display stands and tableware. This type of extravagance increases daily.[94]

As this fashion developed, gemstones began appearing as decorations to adorn the cups used in Roman banquets. Juvenal observed:

> The cup in Virro's hands is richly encrusted with amber and studded with beryls. No gold is entrusted to you, or if it is, a watcher is posted over it to count the gems and keep an eye on your sharp finger-nails. Pardon his anxiety, but fine jasper is much admired!

> For Virro, like so many others, has transferred gems that should be on his finger rings onto his cups.[95]

Pliny realized that this fashion could not be restrained and he comments, 'We are unable to censure the use of drinking-cups adorned with precious stones and rings that sparkle with gems; these articles are now in common use'.[96]

Amongst Roman woman the fashion for Eastern jewellery attained enormous popularity.[97] Horace described how respectable Roman matrons exhibited rows of emeralds and pearls until they were, 'ornamented with snowy white and green precious stones'.[98] At first the fashion was restricted to the more affluent members of Roman society, but it soon spread to women from more moderate backgrounds. A sense of 'appropriate dress' was also compelling Roman women to follow this fashion. Pliny observes:

> Now even women who are poor have a desire for pearls, and they say that a great pearl is the *lictor* befitting a woman appearing in public.[99]

Pliny suggests that some Roman women were spending more money on their pearl jewellery than many of their other fashionable accessories combined.[100] Wealthy women tried to outdo one another in this display and Pliny writes, 'Our ladies delight in having pearls suspended from their fingers, or two or three of them dangling from their ears'.[101] These multiple pearl earrings came to be known as 'castanet pendants' and Pliny reports that Roman women were, 'easily delighted with the rattling of pearls as they knock against each other'.[102] This ostentatious fashion was also causing discord in early church communities. In the AD 60s the Apostle Paul wrote to Timothy about the Ephesian church in Asia Minor. Paul advises:

> I also want women to dress modestly, with decency and propriety, not with braided hair or gold or pearls or expensive clothes, but with good deeds, appropriate for women who profess to worship God.[103]

Roman writers associated the expense of gems with the declining 'moral' values of their society. In his famous satire, Petronius has his character Trimalchio declare:

> India gives up her pearls; and what does it mean for you? That your wife with sea-spoils decorating her breasts and head, can lie on the couch of a stranger and lift her adulterous legs? The emerald green, the transparent bauble, what does it mean to you? Or the fire of the ruby?[104]

Traditional themes linking luxury with moral decline found new resonance when Seneca appraises female fashion:

> I see pearls – not single ones designed for each ear, but clusters of them. Their ears have been trained to carry these loads. The earrings are joined together in pairs and above each pair still others are fastened. Feminine folly tries to overwhelm men with two or three fortunes hung from each ear![105]

But jewellery conveyed status and made Roman women feel glamorous and attractive. Ovid comments that Roman men were now being 'won over by dress' as appearance began to matter more than traditional female virtues. He cynically states that feminine character was 'concealed by gems and gold' and that 'the actual woman is the least part of herself'.[106] Pliny was also critical of people who had pearls sewn into their footwear to further display their wealth.[107] It is significant that the Emperor Tiberius described the export of Roman wealth to the distant East as occurring for 'the sake of jewels'.[108]

This fashion spread and stone funeral monuments from Palmyra show that rich Syrian women wore pearls and gemstones as part of their elaborate jewellery. Images of jewellery made from pearls and precious stones also appear frequently in painted Egyptian coffin portraits from the Roman era.[109] Pearls were worn on multiple necklaces that ranged from tight chokers to long loops, or fixed to trident earrings with twisted threads of gold wire.[110] The profits to be made by Roman artisans must have been immense.

Pliny supplied one of the best examples of excessive display with his description of Lollia Paulina, consort of the Emperor Caligula. He witnessed her extravagance when he was a young man in Rome and recalls:

> I have seen Lollia Paulina . . . not at some considerable or solemn ceremonial celebration, but at an ordinary betrothal banquet. She was covered with emeralds and pearls interlaced alternatively and shining all over her head, hair, ears, neck and fingers. The sum total of this jewellery was more than 40 million sesterces.[111]

Lollia verified the wealth of her jewellery to interested admirers with the receipts that she had retained. Pliny writes, 'She herself was ready at a moment's notice to give documentary proof of this purchase that had been made at such a great price'.[112]

Taken together, Eastern perfumes, clothing and jewellery combined to create a fashionable 'look' in wealthy Roman society. Martial offers the style summary with the words:

> Let my mistress demand a pound of foliatum perfume or green gems or matching sardonyxes. She may even want the finest silks from Tuscan Street.[113]

Seneca has his female character Phaedra renounce the 'new fashion':

> Send away the scarlet of the Tyrian shell, the silk "webs" which the far-off Seres gather from their trees. Let . . . there be no necklace at my throat, no snow pearls, no gift of the Indian Ocean weigh down my ears, and let my hair hang loose unscented by Assyrian nard.[114]

But many Roman women emulated this fashion and its influence soon became widespread.

The narrator of *The Golden Ass* describes his obsession with women's hair, mentioning how he liked it to be: 'anointed with the lotions of Arabia'.[115] Roman portraits show women with curls and waves styled into their hair using perfumed oils.[116] Elaborate hair-extensions became popular amongst Roman women and the remains of these hairpieces have been found in Egyptian coffins.[117] The *Alexandrian Tariff* reveals that this hair was imported from India and it could have been 'temple hair' donated to the Hindu temples.[118] Martial offers the gift of a gold hairpin with the verse, 'insert a pin to hold up your twisted hair so that your moistened locks may not damage your bright silks.'[119] There was also a fashion for wearing gemstones in hair fasteners and the poet Propertius mentions that the hair of his beloved was, 'tied at the crown with an Indian gemstone.'[120]

Eastern products became synonymous with feminine beauty and Ovid considers the combined effect this fashion produced. He writes:

> You like to scent your hair and change your hairstyle. You like to have your hands ablaze with gems. And round your neck you like to wear great Eastern jewels with stones so large that no ear could take a pair. That's not bad taste: you need to be attractive.[121]

It must be acknowledged that exotic and expensive items from the Eastern trade became a significant and pervasive feature of fashionable Roman society.

Wealthy Romans also had a great desire for expensive craft items made from exotic Eastern materials. The town houses and villas of wealthy Romans were furnished with fashionable ornamental items made from prized woods embellished with tortoiseshell and ivory inlays.[122] Eastern woods such as ebony were used in furniture for beds, sideboards, dining couches and doors, and these luxurious items became synonymous with refined taste.

Martial describes how shoppers in the Roman Forum liked to browse the wares displayed in the expensive retail establishments, even though many of these items were beyond their purchasing means. He describes how Mamurra behaves as a refined Roman gentleman as he inspects imported Eastern goods:

> After walking long and anxiously through the bazaars where golden Rome proudly displays her riches . . . Mamurra uncovers various tables, square ones and round; next he asks to see some rich ivory ornaments, those displayed on the upper shelves. Then, four times he measures a dinner couch for six guests, adorned with tortoise shell.[123]

When Virgil tried to imagine life in an idealized rural setting, he listed the absence of the Eastern products synonymous with urban wealth. Virgil writes:

> There are no doorposts inlaid with beautiful tortoiseshell, no attire of gold brocade, no connoisseur's bronzes. No foreign dyes stain his white fleeces and no exotic spices like cinnamon spoil his olive oil.[124]

Fragments of turtle shell were also used for smaller objects such as combs, brushes, and personal adornments including rings and brooches.[125] Juvenal wrote about Roman men in the public baths who carried items such as oil flasks made from polished rhino horn.[126]

Ivory was popular in the Roman Empire and craftsmen used it extensively for decoration.[127] Tusks from a Roman trade venture to India were the most valuable item recorded in the *Muziris Papyrus*.[128] Ovid talks about 'India yielding carved ivory to charm us' and Martial speaks of Libyan tabletops balanced on Indian tusks.[129] Classical poets also mention that the material was used for couches, fancy cashboxes, medicine chests, birdcages, luxury writing tablets, 'knucklebones' for gaming and even false teeth.[130] Among the debris of the Pozzino shipwreck was a delicately carved ivory hand from an ancient wooden statue.[131]

Some of the expensive ivory ornaments on the high shelves of Roman shops were probably craft items brought back from India, such as the Indian ivory statuette found in the ruins of Pompeii. The statuette is a delicately carved female figure, perhaps a goddess, depicted with two tiny acolytes by her side. This may have been the handle of a mirror, or the leg of a small tripod stool. Perhaps this was the prized possession of some wealthy Roman matron.[132]

Eastern slaves were also imported into the Roman Empire in significant numbers.[133] Wealthy Romans thought it was fashionable and prestigious to have exotic servants and these slaves were selected to wait on invited guests at expensive banquets.[134] The *Alexandrian Tariff* mentions Indian eunuchs and the *Periplus* reports that African slaves were taken from markets in Ethiopia and Somalia.[135] Horace mentions a slave who was named after one of the tributaries of the Indus River and he writes about, 'dark Hydaspes who emerges bearing Caecuban wines'.[136] These exotic slaves were expensive and both Martial and Pliny suggest that eunuchs could be sold at prices over 100,000 sesterces.[137] In an address to the Senate regarding the expense of Roman luxuries, Tiberius identified exotic slaves as a prominent feature of this consumerism. The Emperor is reported to have said:

> Where should I begin my prohibitions and attempt to revert to older standards? Shall I begin with the vast mansions, or the cosmopolitan hordes of slaves? . . . or the (silk) clothing of men that is indistinguishable from women's dress?[138]

The Roman elite also kept Eastern animals as pets for display and entertainment. A favourite was the Indian green parrot which was trained to speak simple sentences in Latin.[139] Ovid wrote a memorial to a pet parrot he had previously given to his mistress Corinna, on hearing that she, clearly distressed, had carefully buried the dead bird under a small marker stone. His poem begins, 'avian imitator from India, has died' and continues, 'the bird is dead, this babbling echo of the human voice, this gift so rare brought from the utmost limits of the world'.[140]

Larger wild animals from the distant East were also brought into the Roman Empire in considerable quantities. Beast fights were frequently staged for public entertainment in the Roman territories and the single-horned rhino from India was pitted against other large animals, including bulls.[141] The *Alexandrian Tariff* lists a range of big cats subject to import duties, including leopards and panthers.[142] Martial wrote a poem to Domitian celebrating spectacular games the Emperor had commissioned involving Indian tigers. He writes:

> The huntsman on the banks of the Ganges . . . never stood in fear to see so many tigers as you now behold in Rome.[143]

Pliny reveals that giant clams up to a metre long were also being brought in from the Indian Ocean to astonish guests at Italian dinner tables.[144] These were called *tridacna* because they took three bites or more to eat. Confirmation of these imports comes from Pompeii were the discarded shells of these large molluscs have been found in archaeological digs.[145]

By the end of the Julio-Claudian era, the Roman elite were spending phenomenal amounts of money on expensive luxuries. The Emperor Galba tried to recover some of the vast wealth Nero had given away in imperial gifts, but found that little of value remained. Tacitus writes:

> Nero squandered 2,200 million sesterces in gifts. It was voted that these individuals should be summoned and that a tenth part of the gifts which Nero had given to them should be returned. But Nero's favourites had hardly one-tenth left, for they had wasted the money on the same extravagances that had depleted their own wealth. The most worthless and depraved had neither lands nor investments, but only the apparatus of their greed.[146]

Competitive spending was a sign of status, and in Rome political advancement had become partly dependent on demonstrations of wealth involving elite consumer goods. The Emperor Vespasian suppressed some of this excessive spending by his widely known disapproval of 'undue' luxury. Yet expensive fashions continued, and Eastern commerce did not diminish during the Flavian era.

EASTERN TRADERS IN ROMAN MARKETS

As a consequence of Eastern commerce, peoples from many distant regions of the ancient world became resident in the Roman Empire. Xenophon of Ephesus tells a story about a wealthy Indian prince who visited Alexandria for sightseeing and trade.[147] Dio Chrysostom also describes foreign spectators at a theatre in Alexandria:

> I see among you not just Greeks and Italians and people from neighbouring Syria, Libya, Cilicia, but also Ethiopians and Arabs from more distant regions, and even Bactrians and Scythians and Persians and a few Indians. All these people help to make up the audience in your theatre and they sit beside you on each occasion.[148]

Nabatean merchants had their own docks and warehouses at Puteoli and Ostia in Italy to distribute incoming Eastern imports.[149] A fragmentary inscription in Latin and Greek indicates that Palmyrene merchants also operated in Rome and had erected a temple dedicated to their god Bel in the city.[150]

Indians also came to Rome and Martial complained about a Roman girl named Caelia who ignored his advances while having relationships with foreigners. Martial was scornful of the fact that Caelia found exotic character and wealth more attractive than Roman status. He writes:

> You are with your Egyptian lover who sails to you from Alexandria, then the dark-skinned Indian one from the Eastern Ocean . . . You are a Roman girl. So why is it you pay no attention to a Roman citizen who is so agreeable to you?[151]

There were Palmyrene businessmen operating in Britain who received shipments of Eastern goods from Syrian colleagues active across the Mediterranean trade routes. An elaborate tombstone found near Hadrian's Wall shows a seated Palmyrene matron dressed in fine fabrics and opening a box of jewellery. The grave belongs to the British wife of a wealthy merchant named Barates who had the following dedication carved in Latin and Palmyrene:

> To the shades of the departed Regina, freedwoman and wife of the Palmyrene Barates, she was a Catuvellaunian by birth, died aged thirty.[152]

Barates supplied silk banners for the nearby garrisons who guarded the Roman frontier and his own tombstone was found at nearby Corbridge.[153]

FINANCING EASTERN COMMERCE

Ancient evidence reveals how an Italian merchant family from Puteoli on the Bay of Naples developed an interest in Eastern trade.[154] In 48 BC, the Roman general Pompey the Great was defeated by Caesar at the battle of Pharsalus in Greece. A humiliated and dishevelled Pompey escaped on a small boat and was rescued by a Roman cargo ship headed for Egypt under the direction of a wheat merchant named Peticius.[155]

In the following decades, Peticius and his sons developed a commercial interest in the Mediterranean wine business and began delivering batches of Italian amphorae to North Africa. An inscription painted on an amphora fragment found at Carthage records the name C. Peticius and dates to about 20 BC. The name Peticius Marsus also appears engraved on a *dolium* wine vat recovered from a shipwreck off the Italian coast.[156]

The following generation of the Peticii family became involved as wine exporters to the distant East. Graffiti on the desert route from Coptos to Berenice records that a C. Peticius visited a rock shelter sacred to the Greek god Pan. Pan was the deity of wild and open spaces, but also a close associate of Bacchus, the god of wine who was said to have led his entourage into India. The young C. Peticius signed his name in both Greek and Latin at the shelter to show his allegiance to this deity.[157]

Further evidence for the Peticii family's interest in Eastern trade exists in the form of a funeral monument found near their Italian home in Apulia. A stone panel depicts a small figure wearing a short tunic leading a heavily laden dromedary camel bearing three wine amphoras. In the foreground are five men from the family in close fitting togas standing next to a female relative.[158] This generation of the family became very wealthy supplying Roman markets with Eastern imports and a costly bronze statute of Hercules dating to the succeeding era records the name 'M. Attius Peticius Marsus' richly inlaid in silver.[159]

A large-scale trade venture to India would have cost over a million sesterces.[160] To place this figure in context, the minimum property qualification for a Roman senator was a million sesterces and this represented the value of a large agricultural estate.[161] Evidence from the late Empire indicates that well connected Roman merchants could secure loans worth the equivalent of around 200,000 sesterces.[162] This suggests that four or five associates working together could raise the funds needed to conduct a large-scale Eastern trade venture.

Papyri contracts confirm that Roman merchants often formed small consortiums of four or five members to finance their trade expeditions. A Ptolemaic loan agreement records that a consortium of five partners arranged finances for an expedition to the 'Spice-Bearing Lands' in Somalia. They secured this loan by arranging to pay back their creditors with the cash they made from the sale of their return trade goods.[163] Philostratus also refers to the pilot of an Egyptian ship who was one of four shareholders in its cargo.[164] Merchants may have formed consortiums to fund trade ventures, but for many businessmen these partnerships were a way to reduce risk. It made better financial sense to invest in quarter shares on a number of trade ships, rather than place all profit expectations on a single vessel. If the venture had several partners, then no one investor would suffer the total loss if a ship was destroyed.

In the Augustan era, a significant number of Alexandrian merchants already had the capital to fund joint ventures to India. Scholars have estimated that a 400 ton cargo of Egyptian grain would have made perhaps 200,000 sesterces of profit when sold in the markets at Rome.[165] Rome needed the equivalent of perhaps 175 transactions on this scale to receive the Egyptian grain it required just to feed its urban population.[166] Consequently, the funds were available in Alexandria to finance numerous Eastern trade ventures.

Eudoxus financed his Indian trade voyage by engaging in regular Mediterranean commerce and amassing the proceeds. Merchants in the Roman era could have followed this example. Strabo reports:

> Eudoxus placed all his property on a ship and he set out to sea. First he put in at Dicaearchia, then at Massilia, and then at the successive points along the coast until he came to Gades. Everywhere he noisily proclaimed his scheme and making money by trafficking he built a great ship and also constructed two tow-boats like those used by pirates. He put music-girls on board, and physicians, and other artisans, and finally he set sail on the high sea on the way to India.[167]

Traders who did not have an extensive Mediterranean business could engage in Eastern trade by hiring out a small amount of cargo space on a Roman Red Sea freighter.[168] They would travel onboard to markets in the distant East and fill their rented cargo space with whatever goods they expected would make a profit back in the Empire. This practice might have allowed dozens of traders with limited funds to participate in commercial expeditions that took them into the distant East.[169]

The largest expense involved in Eastern trade ventures was the 25 per cent import tax that the Roman government charged on goods entering Egypt through the Red Sea ports. This quarter tax was called the *tetarte* and was also imposed on goods entering Nabatea. The *Muziris Papyrus* records that a return Eastern cargo was valued at almost 9 million sesterces, but over 2 million sesterces in tax was owed to the Roman government.[170] Some scholars believe that the Roman government simply took 25 per cent of Eastern imports in goods rather than demand the monetary equivalent. The merchandise could then be sold at Roman markets by imperial agents, or released back to the traders when they could afford to re-purchase the items with their other profits.[171] Alternatively, Roman merchants could have paid the government import tax in cash by taking out loans with financers once they had safely arrived back at the Red Sea ports. This financial agreement could be made by using Eastern goods as security as described in the *Muziris Papyrus*.

After the extraction of the *tetarte*, the eastern cargo documented in the *Muziris Papyrus* was worth almost 7 million sesterces.[172] If this ship had four or five shareholders, then each investor would have received well over a million sesterces from their part of the cargo. They would therefore have had sufficient capital to fund their own separate business ventures to India, providing they were prepared to accept the entire financial risks. They could also act as creditors to merchants who needed start-up capital to finance their own trade ventures to the East, or offer loans to returning merchants who wanted to pay the *tetarte* tax in cash. Successful merchants could expand their Eastern business interests by hiring or purchasing further trade ships and employing additional agents to manage their commercial activities. The Roman businessman Varus owned a number of freighters operating from Berenice which he stocked with his own commodities.[173] The Roman businesswomen Isidora and Olympias owned a 'fleet' of commercial ships and were financial backers as well as merchant managers in the trade.[174]

During the Julio-Claudian era, a new type of entrepreneurial elite began to emerge in Roman society. These self-made millionaires did not have the prestige of aristocracy, but they gained great prominence from their enormous commercial wealth. This new business elite could command vast fortunes that astonished a Roman aristocracy who had traditionally derived most of their wealth from landed estates.[175] Petronius created a fictional character called Trimalchio who demonstrates the attitude of these new entrepreneurs. Trimalchio was a self-publicist who possessed supreme confidence, but he was also a dangerous risk taker. The men typified by Trimalchio often came from undistinguished backgrounds and therefore lacked the social manners that defined the traditional aristocracy. Trimalchio states:

> I got a senator's fortune. But nobody ever gets enough. I wanted to go into business, so I built five ships and loaded them with wine – it was absolute gold at the time – so I sent them to Rome. Every single ship was wrecked – that's a fact, no story! In one single day Neptune swallowed up 30 million sesterces. But do you think I gave up? – No, I did not.[176]

Trimalchio explains how his wife came to his aid:

> I swear this loss just increased my determination. It was as if nothing had happened. I built more boats, bigger and better, and luckier, so nobody could say I wasn't a man of courage. As you know, the greater the ship, the greater the confidence. I loaded them again with wine, bacon, beans, perfumes and slaves. At this point Fortunata did the

> decent thing and sold off all her gold trinkets, all her clothes, and put 10,000 gold pieces in my hand (a million sesterces). This was the least I needed to see my fortune rise again.[177]

Although this is intended to be a satire, the entrepreneurs involved in financing the larger trade ventures to India needed to command capital on the scale indicated by Petronius. Businessmen who came from small provinces soon discovered that their commercial profits could exceed the revenues their homelands paid to the Roman state. Petronius also reveals the ultimate aim of these new entrepreneurs. After succeeding in business, many chose to invest their capital in the security of landed estates and began offering financial loans to lesser businessmen. Trimalchio states:

> In one voyage I gained a good ten million sesterces. I immediately bought back all my old master's estates. I built a house, invested in slaves and in haulage. Whatever I touched grew like a honeycomb. Once I had more money than the entire revenue of my own country, I quit the game! I retired from business and began advancing loans to freedmen.[178]

It is likely that many prosperous entrepreneurs engaged in Eastern commerce would have developed similar ambitions.

The most successful Eastern merchants would have had business agents and commercial contacts working for their interests across the Mediterranean. These representatives and colleagues would have provided them with suitable export commodities. For instance, favoured types of imperial coin had to be removed from circulation and collected in large quantities for export to India and Arabia. In addition cheap Italian wines needed to be sourced and forwarded to the Red Sea ports. These commercial contacts would have been used to distribute Eastern imports across the markets of the Roman Mediterranean.

The activities of an Italian merchant family called the Anni reveals the type of business networks involved in Eastern trade. Annius Plocamus organized Eastern trade ventures, but he also bought contracts to collect taxes for the Roman government. One of his freedmen agents left a Latin inscription in a small natural grotto on the road between Coptos and Berenice in 6 BC.[179] Just after AD 50, another of his freedmen who was assigned to gather the Red Sea taxes was blown off course on a trade sailing to southern Arabia and reached Sri Lanka.[180] The Anni family had further commercial agents working at Puteoli who managed the distribution and retail sale of Eastern goods arriving in Italy. These agents would also have acquired Roman merchandise for export to the distant East. An inscription found at the port mentions a freedman of P. Annius Eros who was a senior business partner. Other early inscriptions record an Annius Maximus who served as a magistrate at Puteoli and another member of the family named P. Annius Seleucius who was conducting business at the port in AD 40.[181]

Marcus Julius Alexander is the most intriguing character referenced in the textual evidence for Eastern trade. Marcus was a rich Jewish resident of Alexandria who held Roman citizenship and was well connected within the cultural and political elite of the city.[182] He was the nephew of a prominent Jewish Greek philosopher named Philo and his father Tiberius Julius Alexander held the position of *arabarch* in charge of Roman custom taxes in the Eastern Desert.[183] Tiberius

Alexander acquired a great fortune from this lucrative position and in AD 36 gave the Judean king Herod Agrippa 200,000 drachmas to help him with his financial difficulties.[184] He also gave an expensive gift of gold-plates to embellish nine gates at the Jewish Temple at Jerusalem.[185] Tiberius Alexander developed close contacts with the Roman imperial household and he was entrusted with the financial affairs of Antonia, who was the mother of the future Emperor Claudius.[186]

Tiberius Alexander used his status, position and finances to establish his son Marcus as an important entrepreneur in Eastern trade.[187] The *Nicanor Archive* reveals that between AD 37 and AD 44, Marcus was operating an extensive business in Egypt that required commercial agents at Coptos and the two main Red Sea ports.[188] Marcus Alexander consequently became extremely wealthy and he married the Jewish princess Berenice who was the daughter of King Herod Agrippa.[189] Marcus probably died in AD 44 as this is the last reference to his business activities in the *Nicanor Archive* and princess Berenice remarried in that same year.[190]

Marcus had an elder brother who was named after his father Tiberius Julius Alexander. In AD 42 the junior Tiberius Alexander held office in the Thebaid district of Egypt at a time when his brother Marcus was operating his trade business at Coptos. After the death of his brother, Tiberius Alexander was appointed procurator of Judaea from about AD 46 until AD 48. Later he served as one of the commanders in the Roman conflict with the Parthians in AD 63. Finally, Tiberius attained high office as the Prefect of Egypt where he served as governor in the months leading up to the civil war of AD 69. Tiberius Alexander backed Vespasian in this civil war and was instrumental in the Flavian victory. In terms of political influence, his status was now only surpassed by the Emperor's son Titus.[191]

THE VALUE OF EASTERN TRADE

Pliny the Elder served in the advisory council of the Emperor Vespasian and it was these contacts that perhaps provided him with figures for the scale of Eastern trade. He indicates the value of Roman bullion exports to the distant East when he declares:

> By the smallest computation, India, the Seres and the Arabian peninsula take 100 million sesterces from our empire every year – so much do our luxuries and our women cost us.[192]

About half of this export figure was spent on Roman commerce with Arabia, while the remainder was exported via the Red Sea to India, which in turn channelled Roman wealth into the land of the 'Seres', or 'Silk People'.[193] Pliny offered information on this commerce when he discussed the development of maritime trade routes between Egypt and India. He reports:

> This is an important matter since India drains more than 50 million sesterces a year from our empire and returns goods which are sold among us at 100 times their prime cost.[194]

A Roman coin hoard found on the Malabar Coast of southwest India could suggest the value of bullion consignments carried aboard Roman trade ships. The Kottayam hoard was buried within a bronze vessel in a sand dune and scholars suggest it was stashed by shipwrecked Romans on their way to the Tamil ports.[195] The find consisted of around 8,000 gold aurei that had monetary value of around 800,000 sesterces. Strabo reports that at least 120 Roman ships sailed from Egypt to India every year.[196] Half of this number, just 60 ships carrying gold consignments the size of the Kottayam hoard, could export 50 million sesterces a year from the Roman Empire.

The Han histories indicate that Roman merchants received a tenfold gain in their trade dealings with India. The *Hou Hanshu* states:

> The Romans trade with Anxi (Parthia) and Tianzhu (northwest India) by sea. The return gain is ten to one.[197]

Evidence from the medieval spice trade confirms that price mark-ups between Indian and Mediterranean markets reached this level in pre-modern economies. In the year 1409, pepper bought at Cochin in southern India was sold in Cairo by the Egyptian Sultans at nine times its Indian price.[198] A Roman ship exporting 800,000 sesterces of gold bullion to India would expect to acquire Indian cargo valued at over 8 million sesterces in Mediterranean markets. Roman exports to the Tamil lands consisted of 'mainly a great amount of money', but also included Mediterranean wines and base metals. These would have increased the value of the returning cargo to around 9 million sesterces.[199]

The *Muziris Papyrus* records that a Roman ship called the Hermapollon brought almost 9 million sesterces worth of Eastern goods back from a trade mission to southern India. This suggests that the entire merchant fleet, consisting of at least 120 Roman ships, would have returned Eastern goods worth about 1,080 million sesterces per annum. The total value of Roman exports to India in bullion and trade goods would therefore have been around 108 million sesterces every year.

Academics estimate that in the first century AD the expense budget of the Roman Empire was 800 million sesterces per annum.[200] They also suggest that the total value of commerce conducted between Rome and the provinces was worth around 1,000 million sesterces per year.[201] The evidence therefore indicates that Eastern trade was an important phenomenon within the Roman economy.

PROCESSING AND PRICE INCREASES

Eastern imports would have been valued at over 1,080 million sesterces when they arrived in Egypt. However, many of these goods would then be re-processed in Alexandria to increase their prices on the Roman market. These activities more than tripled the sales value of many Eastern goods and when the collective imports finally reached retail markets, they would have been worth several billion sesterces.

Large workshops in Alexandria sorted and processed the imported incense destined for Roman retail markets. Pliny was amazed to hear about the tight security that operated in these factories where workers wore protective clothing to ensure that the incense was not contaminated. Apron seals were placed on the garments of workers so employees could not hide the valuable product about their person in order to steal it. Strip-search routines were a further measure to prevent theft. Pliny writes:

> By Hercules! At Alexandria where the incense is processed for sale the workshops can never be guarded with sufficient care. A seal is placed upon the workmen's aprons. A mask and a net with very close mesh is put upon their heads. These people are stripped naked before they are allowed to leave their work.[202]

Workshops in Alexandria also re-wove thick Chinese silk into lightweight and transparent Roman weaves. Lucian imagines how this fabric would look on Cleopatra:

> Her white breasts are splendidly visible through the Sidonian fabric, which is produced as close-textured weave by the skill of the Seres, but the needle of the Nile worker has separated and loosened the warp by stretching out the web.[203]

Pliny also describes this practice:

> To the females of our part of the world the Seres give the twofold task of unravelling their textures and of weaving the threads afresh. Great is the labour and distant are the regions that are exploited to supply a dress through which our Roman ladies may expose their bodies to public display.[204]

The Chinese were also aware that their goods were being reprocessed in Roman manufacturing centres to suit Mediterranean fashions. The *Weilue* reports:

> The colours of Roman fabrics are more brilliant than anything manufactured in the countries of the Indian Ocean. They always make a profit by obtaining the thick plain silk stuffs of China which they split in order to make foreign silk patterned fabrics.[205]

The business of fabric manufacture was highly lucrative and substantially raised the price of imported materials. When Pliny claimed that some Eastern goods received in India were sold among the Romans at, 'one hundred times their prime cost' he is probably referring to these expensive reworked fabrics.[206] Trade with India brought tenfold returns and the reprocessing of certain imports could raise their value by tenfold again. Diocletian's *Price Edict* records that one pound of fine purple-dyed silk was valued at more than twelve times the cost of un-dyed, white silk.[207]

The price increase mentioned by Pliny was also experienced by the Chinese. An official in the Han Empire noted that there was an enormous mark-up in the value of foreign goods between their cost in distant territories and their price in Chinese retail markets. The Han account states:

> Pearls and ivory are produced in Kuei Lin. These places are more than ten thousand li

> distant from Han China. Calculate the labour for farming and silk raising and the costs in material and capital. It will be found that one article of foreign import costs a price one hundred times its actual value.[208]

The Chinese also knew about the production of perfumes in the distant West and described how the Romans made fragrant potions by boiling together certain compounds.[209]

The Roman perfume industry was a substantial business that could create a three to fourfold increase between the cost of raw imports and the sales price of processed unguents. Evidence is provided by the example of balsam which was an expensive resin produced in the Roman Empire under a government monopoly. Balsam was grown in Judaea and Pliny was interested to hear stories of how Jewish rebels had attacked the balsam gardens and Roman troops had fought life and death struggles in defence of the shrubs. The reason for this interest was that balsam produced valuable sustainable revenues for the Roman state. The Roman fiscal authorities sold a *sextarius* of balsam for 300 denarii, but the perfumers who processed the product sold it on for 1,000 denarii.[210]

Roman *ungentarii* would have made higher profits from processing Indian imports like nard. Modern perfumers working with natural substances expect a 6 per cent yield of pure oil from their products. They then dilate this product with 75 per cent essential oils and carrier substances.[211] Pliny records that a pound of nard leaf sold at between 40 to 75 denarii and this would indicate nard perfume prices of between 160 and 300 denarii. This is confirmed by the *New Testament* which gives a price of 300 denarii for pure nard perfume.[212]

Even unprocessed Eastern goods would be subject to a price hike between the markets of Alexandria and Rome. In the twelfth century, merchants from Venice sold spices in Italy for a price 27 times their value in India.[213] The 108 million sesterces of Roman cargo exported to India every year must have created a Mediterranean retail commerce well in excess of 3 billion sesterces per annum. There is also Roman trade with East Africa, Arabia and Persia to consider in the overall appreciation of eastern commerce.

CUSTOMS REVENUES FROM EASTERN TRADE

Roman merchants paid customs tax to bring Eastern goods into Egypt, then paid further tax to export these same commodities from Alexandria into further Mediterranean territories. Roman goods being exported to the distant East were also subject to these 'double duties'. Mediterranean goods were taxed at entry into Alexandria and then taxed again at Coptos before their export to the distant East. Strabo explains:

> At this present time large fleets are sent as far as India and the extremities of Africa. The most valuable cargoes are brought to Egypt and from there they are sent forth again to all other regions. As a consequence, double duties are collected on both imports and exports. In this system, goods that have a high value have a heavy duty imposed on them.[214]

Roman custom taxes on the Eastern frontiers were set at a quarter value.[215] Roman exports to India worth over 108 million sesterces per annum would therefore have generated annual revenues in excess of 27 million sesterces for the Roman government. Returning Eastern imports worth over 1,080 million sesterces would likewise have raised a further 270 million sesterces for the state. In total, the Eastern frontier taxes of Egypt would therefore have generated over 300 million sesterces per annum.

Eastern goods exported from Alexandria into the Mediterranean were subject to further customs taxes called *portoria*, which were generally set at the comparatively low rate of about one-fortieth value. This tax must have added tens of millions to the Roman revenues received from Egypt and when Mediterranean ships leaving Alexandria reached their provincial destination, they had to pay further *portoria* taxes to port authorities. This would have added further millions of sesterces to the Roman finances.[216]

ROMAN REVENUES

The revenues received from taxing Eastern commerce were important because Roman imperialism did not make substantial profits from most of its provinces. The military aspect of the Roman Empire was a profitable business for its subjects, both its citizen class who served in the army and its aristocracy who made great fortunes in overseas commands. Conquest was lucrative because it brought wealth into the Roman economy through war booty and the development of new commercial opportunities. However, once the Empire incorporated an additional territory, it became responsible for the defence and administration of these new lands. This was an expensive undertaking and the return in regional revenues was often not cost-effective. Regional costs tended to consume most provincial revenues until only a small amount of surplus wealth could be forwarded to Rome. From the Augustan era onwards, the Empire also began to incorporate large northern territories that consumed far greater revenues than they produced. Emperors often had a political or strategic reason for subjugating these regions that would justify their expense.

In the Republican era, Asia Minor was probably the only Roman territory that produced significant financial profits for central government. Cicero states:

> The revenues of the other provinces are such that we can scarcely derive enough from them for their own protection. But Asia Minor is so rich and so productive, that in the fertility of its soil, and in the variety of its fruits, and in the vastness of its pasture lands, and in the multitude of all those things that it exports, it is greatly superior to all other countries.[217]

The Augustan conquest of the Danube and Rhineland territories undoubtedly brought greater security to the Mediterranean core of the Roman Empire. But these regions were revenue-deficit territories and required large sums of cash from central government to meet their military costs. This was a long-term situation as Appian writes:

> Though the Romans lose money on some of their subject nations, they are ashamed to set them aside even though they are detrimental.[218]

In the Augustan era, Strabo had thought that Britain should not be incorporated into the Roman Empire because of the risks involved and the inevitable revenue deficit it would create for the imperial finances. It seems the Romans obtained more cash revenue from taxing trade goods moving between Britain and Gaul, than it could expect from conquest and direct taxation. Strabo writes:

> At present more revenue is derived from the custom duties imposed on their commerce than the tribute could bring in, given the expense of the garrison needed to guard the island and to collect the tribute from it.[219]

The eventual conquest of Britain was politically motivated and created a further deficit territory. As Appian reports on the Roman annexation of Britain:

> The Romans have taken possession of the larger and better part of Britain and they do not care for the remainder. The part they do hold is not very profitable to them.[220]

In provinces where military costs were comparatively low, the Roman government spent excess revenues on regional projects such as building works to improve the local infrastructure. Philostratus suggests that the revenues collected from 500 cities in Asia Minor were spent on the construction of a single aqueduct costing 28 million sesterces.[221] Most Roman provinces probably sent a small token amount of revenue to central government, largely as a symbolic act of tribute. Caligula is supposed to have spent 10 million sesterces on a single banquet, which Seneca calls the 'tribute-money from three provinces'.[222] The fictional character Trimalcio lampoons this situation when he boasts that the income from his commercial dealings was greater than the revenues his home province offered to Rome.

The Romans considered their system 'reasonable' because the state demanded revenues that were then overwhelmingly spent locally on necessities such as defence. Tacitus has a Roman commander deliver the following speech to some defeated rebels in northern Gaul:

> We have imposed upon you by right of conquest only this one demand: that you pay the costs of keeping peace here . . . Perhaps you think that you can equip armies to repel the Germans and the Britons for less tribute than you now pay us?[223]

When Roman authorities increased taxes in the provinces, the effort was in part an attempt to make regional revenues meet provincial costs.

The ancient sources reveal how Rome came to depend on Eastern commerce to meet its imperial financial commitments. After Pompey's triumph in 61 BC, the total revenues of the Republican State were about 340 million sesterces per annum. Plutarch states:

> It was demonstrated on written tablets that the new taxes amounted to 50 million denarii

> and with the amount that Pompey had added to the State, the Republic now received 85 million denarii.[224]

A further major conquest of the Republic was Caesar's annexation of Gaul which brought in initial revenues worth around 40 million sesterces. This would have raised the revenue of the Roman Republic to over 380 million sesterces per annum. Suetonius reports:

> Those parts of Gaul . . . Caesar then reduced to the status of a province and imposed upon them a yearly tribute of 40 million sesterces.[225]

The economy of Egypt was in serious disrepair when Augustus secured the territory. Egypt initially produced revenues of only 40 million sesterces per annum for the new regime. This would have brought the total annual revenues of the Roman Empire to somewhere in excess of 420 million sesterces. Velleius states:

> Augustus made Egypt tributary thereby contributing nearly as much revenue to the treasury as Caesar had brought in from the Gauls.[226]

In this era, the expanded Empire was financially unsustainable and the Roman commander Agrippa informed Augustus that the new regime did not have the revenues to pay for its long-term costs. Augustus was told:

> You will need to procure a large supply of money from all sources. Our present revenues are not sufficient to support the troops, not to mention our other expenses.[227]

Augustus was advised to overhaul the existing tax system and draw funds from every possible source of revenue.[228] Plans were made for the conquest of Arabia and schemes drawn up for an expansionist war against the prosperous Parthian Realm.

Augustus and his advisors had not foreseen the rapid growth in Eastern commerce that was to transform the finances of the new Empire. Within only five years of Roman rule, the merchant fleet sailing from Egypt to India had increased more than sixfold.[229] The taxation of this new commerce and the economic restoration of Egypt rapidly increased the revenues available to the Roman State. Under Augustus, the Egyptian revenues soon began to exceed the amounts received by the Ptolemaic king Auletes who had ruled Egypt in the early first century BC, before its economic decline. Strabo writes:

> Cicero tells us about the revenues of Egypt in a certain speech. He says that Auletes, who was the father of Cleopatra, received annual revenues of 12,500 talents (300 million sesterces). If this man who administered the kingdom in the worst and most careless way obtained so much revenue, then what should we think of the present circumstances? Now that the revenues are managed with so much diligence, and now commerce with the Indians and the Africans has been increased to such a great extent?[230]

With the restored Egyptian revenues reaching almost 300 million sesterces per annum, the total annual income of the Empire must have exceeded 680 million sesterces. The trade wealth of Africa and India had therefore saved the Roman Empire from impending financial crisis.

This foreign trade wealth helped transform the new Roman Empire into a regime that had unprecedented economic prosperity. Augustus initiated major reforms in the Roman army and created a large professional well-paid military to protect and control the provinces. The Empire now extended its direct rule further into northern Europe and established secure boundaries that could be effectively consolidated. Academics estimate that with these reforms, the expenses of the Roman state would have approached 600 million sesterces per annum.[231] Shortly before his death Augustus warned his successors to avoid conquests that would further stretch the resources of the Roman state.[232]

Eastern trade expanded during the reign of Tiberius and customs taxes began to deliver even larger amounts of revenue into the funds of central government.[233] Soon the cash received by the Roman state surpassed its traditional expenses. When the reclusive Emperor Tiberius died in AD 41, his successor Caligula spent the enormous wealth that had accumulated in the Roman treasuries. Suetonius reports:

> Vast sums of money, including the 2,700 million sesterces which Tiberius Caesar had amassed, were squandered by Caligula in less than the revolution of a year.[234]

To have acquired this amount of wealth, the Roman government must have been receiving an annual revenue surplus of more than 120 million sesterces per annum during the reign of Tiberius. The new wealth of the Empire encouraged financial leniency and Caligula restored several client kingdoms in the Eastern empire, refunding the tribute they had paid to previous Roman governments.[235] Strabo had advised against conquering Britain because of its poor revenue prospects, but in AD 43 the annexation of southwest Britain was achieved by the Emperor Claudius. The Emperor had a complex range of political motives for this conquest, but his scheme benefited from the long-term pacification of the now well-established Roman provinces and was financed by wealth produced by Eastern commerce.

By the Flavian era, the revenues produced by Egypt must have been more than 600 million sesterces per annum. At the height of the Ptolemaic era, Egypt produced 300 million sesterces in revenues from taxes imposed on its internal agriculture, resident population, occupational dues and its indigenous Mediterranean commerce.[236] The Roman regime matched this revenue figure and added a further 300 million sesterces derived from taxing Eastern commerce. Josephus confirms that by AD 66 the Romans were receiving an enormous quantity of revenue from Egypt. On the eve of a revolt, the Jewish king Agrippa addressed his people to warn them of the hopelessness of any rebellion against Rome. He reportedly said:

> Look at Roman power in our nearest neighbour Egypt. Egypt stretches as far as Ethiopia and Arabia Felix; it is the port for India . . . what a stimulus to revolt Egypt has in Alexandria with its great size, its population and its wealth! A city three-and-a-half miles long and over a mile wide, which pays Rome every month more tribute than you pay in a year, and annually sends Rome enough corn for four months use.[237]

In another passage of his work Josephus records that Palestine produced revenues of about 48 million sesterces per annum.[238] Egypt would therefore have supplied Rome annually with more than 576 million sesterces in cash revenues.[239]

Academics estimate that by this era the expense budget of the Roman Empire was between 800 and 900 million sesterces per annum.[240] Around 600 million sesterces of this figure would have come from Egyptian revenues, with a further 380 million sesterces being collected and spent as provincial revenue funds. About a third of the imperial finances were therefore funded by the tax profits of Eastern trade. Apart from the Egyptian revenues, there was no other large scale transfer of provincial taxes to the Roman capital.

Possession of Egypt meant control over two-thirds of the imperial cash revenues and a third of the grain that was needed annually to feed the population of Rome.[241] The danger posed by the city of Alexandria was that a claimant to the imperial throne might establish himself in the region and place an economic stranglehold over the Empire. The importance of Egypt to Roman finances was one of several factors that led Augustus to impose and maintain severe political restrictions on the province. Under the Roman regime, the governor of Egypt held equestrian rank and no senators were allowed to visit the region. Furthermore, no Alexandrian could become a senator and the city was not allowed an administrative council.[242] One of the reasons why the general Vespasian was the strongest claimant in the Roman civil war of AD 69 was because the governor of Egypt, Tiberius Julius Alexander, declared in his favour.[243]

ROMAN FINANCES

During the reign of the Emperors, Rome continued to exploit extremely productive silver and gold mines in its conquered provinces. These resources produced enormous wealth for the Roman government and must have contributed to the revenue surplus that was already occurring in the time of Tiberius. One of the most significant producers of this bullion was Roman Spain. During the height of production, the principal mines in Spain were producing annual wealth equivalent to about 40 million sesterces of silver and 90 million sesterces of gold.[244]

The Roman economy was not consciously designed for stability, but circumstances had converged to ensure that, in the short term, the system was financially stable. The Roman government minted coinage from its stocks of newly mined bullion and this money was sent to armies in the frontier provinces to pay military wages. This process continually introduced large quantities of new coins into circulation and compensated for the coined wealth, lost to the Empire through Eastern exports.[245] In their trade dealings with Rome, the Arabs sought silver bullion and the Tamils had a preference for gold. Consequently, by the time of Pliny, the Roman economy was exporting perhaps 50 million sesterces of silver and up to 50 million sesterces of gold every year to the distant East.[246] As long as mining operations continued to produce large volumes of new bullion, the Roman economy would be unimpaired by the eastward drain of precious metals.

Bullion values in India had a reciprocal effect on the Roman monetary system.

The northern Indian kingdoms valued silver more highly than the Romans and they favoured a ratio of about 10 quantities of silver to 1 quantity of gold.[247] The Roman monetary system formalised by Augustus fixed a different value on precious metals and effectively undervalued silver. Denarii and aurei from this era represented a value of about 12 quantities of silver to 1 quantity of gold. Contact with India affected bullion prices within the Roman territories and as Eastern trade developed, the Augustan monetary system became less representative of actual bullion values on the Roman market.

Nero had a number of reasons to 'reform' the Roman coinage in AD 64, but Eastern trade and its effect on bullion values, possibly encouraged this readjustment of the imperial currency. Nero's reforms debased silver denarii so that in terms of bullion, Roman money was valued at 11 quantities of silver to 1 quantity of gold.[248] Trajan later re-adjusted the gold to silver ratios of imperial coinage to a level that more closely resembled the Indian appreciation of these precious metals.

THE ROMAN ECONOMY

The Roman military success in conquering the Mediterranean gave the Empire possession of a vast and vibrant trade network. Then Augustus, by annexing Egypt, opened up the Indian Ocean to Mediterranean trade. Eastern commerce gave the Mediterranean system a new intensity and Rome was soon presiding over an unprecedented commercial economy.[249] The Roman system was now distinct from the preceding Hellenic or Classical Greek economies.[250] The new prosperity and security instigated by Rome transformed Western Europe and the population of the Empire increased from 45 to 60 million people between the Augustan and the Antonine era.[251]

Roman trade with the distant East intensified production in the Mediterranean economy. For example, wine surplus from Italy found markets in India and Egyptian workshops manufactured Arabian style clothing to be traded at distant Eastern bazaars.[252] The developing commerce also had an impact on Mediterranean resources as the Roman provinces were stripped of their natural reserves for trade items. Pliny records the effect Indian fashions were having on delicate coral producing habitats in the Mediterranean Sea. He writes:

> The Gauls used to ornament their swords, shields and helmets with coral. But this was before the Indian love of this material became known. Since coral became profitable merchandise there has been a shortage of it, and now it is very rarely seen in its natural habitat.[253]

These comments express an awareness that Roman subjects had developed from communities that once produced simple military decoration into a society that increasingly valued competitive fashion-driven consumerism. Juvenal talked of gemstones once used to decorate military trophies, being worn on the fingers of wealthy men, and then debased into decorating tableware.[254] Pliny also wrote about campaign body-armour being replaced by togas, and then discarded for fashionable silk clothing.[255] This Roman consumerism had a devastating effect on a valuable North African plant called silphium. Silphium had antiseptic properties, but its premium market value encouraged overexploitation and the plant rapidly became extinct. Pliny reports that the final stalk was sent as a curiosity to the Emperor Nero.[256]

By the time Pliny wrote his *Natural History* Roman commerce had completely transformed classical civilization. Pliny writes:

> We should be struck with wonder and admiration, that coming from a primitive state, we are now cleaving the mountains apart for their marbles, reaching the Seres to obtain our clothing, seeking the pearl in the abysses of the Indian Ocean, and the emerald in the very depth of the earth. And we should also be amazed that people have taken up the notion of piercing their ears for these adornments. It is no longer enough to wear these gems in necklaces and tiaras, so people have chosen to insert them in their own flesh.[257]

The busy retail markets and bazaars of Rome were the engine for this commercial economy. Rome was a prime destination for Alexandrian trade ventures that brought new Eastern goods into the Mediterranean markets. Rome was also the most densely populated city in the ancient world with close to a million inhabitants. As such, it required vast amounts of basic consumer products, as well as supporting an enormous trade in luxury imports.[258]

At the time of Pliny, Rome had become far more than a centre of consumption. The city operated as a massive centrally placed market that facilitated the sale and distribution of commodities throughout the Empire. In the ancient world, market information only moved as fast as supplies and cargo. Environmental conditions meant that there would be food deficits in some regions of the Empire, while there could be surplus in other territories.[259] Rome was the meeting place where traders with excess would go to make a profitable sale and merchants coming from regions with markets deficits would be assured of finding the goods they were seeking. The higher prices paid in the markets at Rome drew in commerce from across the Roman Empire.[260]

It is significant that people from the provinces saw Rome's great wealth in terms of its commerce, especially in the distribution of Eastern goods. The author of *Revelations* singled out Eastern luxuries to typify the losses incurred after the great fire of AD 64. He writes:

> The merchants of the earth weep and mourn over her, for no man buys her merchandise any more; merchandise of gold, silver, jewels, pearls and fine linen, purple, silk and scarlet, all kinds of scented wood, ivory, articles of costly wood, bronze, iron and marble, cinnamon, spice, incense, myrrh and frankincense, wine, oil, fine flour and wheat, cattle and sheep, horses and chariots, and slaves.[261]

Of the first twenty commodities listed in this passage, nine are costly products indigenous to the Empire and eleven are valuable imports from the distant East.

To observers, it seemed as though Rome owed its prosperity to a vast international commerce in exotic goods. In a rhetorical speech Aristides indicates the significance of Rome as an enormous market for the consumption and distribution of Eastern imports. He describes Rome:

> So many merchant ships arrive here, conveying every kind of goods at every hour of every day that the city is like a factory common to the whole earth. It is possible to see so many cargoes from India and Arabia Felix that you may imagine that their trees are left bare and they must come here to beg for their own produce if they need anything. Here there can be seen clothing from Babylon and ornaments from the barbarian world beyond.[262]

Every year merchant fleets sailed to Rome from Alexandria with enough Egyptian grain to feed the city for four months. They also carried a vast range of unique and exotic Eastern commodities worth billions of sesterces. These Eastern goods were not available within the Roman Empire, so there was a guaranteed market for this merchandise. However, after selling these commodities in the markets at Rome, Alexandrian merchants could not find equivalent cargoes for the return voyage. Strabo reports:

> The exports from Alexandria are larger than the imports. Anyone can judge this by seeing the merchant vessels at either Alexandria or Puteoli. They can observe how ships on arrival are heavy and vessels on departure are much lighter.[263]

Alexandrian merchants would therefore have returned to Egypt with a large proportion of their trade profits in cash and this had significance for the Roman economy.[264] Every year central government was removing up to 600 million sesterces of revenue cash from Egypt, yet Eastern trade created conditions that allowed Egypt to re-acquire this cash as commercial profits. This ensured that in the long-term, Roman revenues would never exhaust the coined wealth reserves of Egypt.[265]

Egypt maintained its own regional coinage, so merchants returning to the province from the markets at Rome converted their cash profits back into their local currency.[266] The Roman state taxed this conversion of Roman coin into Egyptian issues and must have maintained a large fund of both coin types for this purpose. This vast reserve of money allowed the government to convert provincial tax revenues raised in Egypt into imperial coin for dispatch back to Rome.

Egypt could produce revenues on this scale because of market conditions across the Roman Empire. Alexandrian merchants paid the Roman government large tax dividends to bring Eastern imports into Egypt. They then recouped the cost of these impositions by increasing the retail price of their goods in Rome and other Mediterranean markets. This system meant that the wider Roman population effectively paid the customs revenues of Egypt. Through Eastern trade, Rome was taxing merchant profit and therefore indirectly taxing communities across the Empire who had sufficient surplus to spend on desirable Eastern products.[267] The Roman soldier who bought pepper in northern Britain was funding a commercial system that paid money into the Egyptian revenues. Eastern trade consequently drew profits from all parts of the Empire, as Roman subjects aspired to popular new fashions and willingly offered up their wealth to purchase these desirable imports.

More than half of the revenues produced by Roman Egypt were generated by taxing Eastern commerce. This meant that Egyptian revenues were proportional to the value of Eastern imports. The retail value of Eastern imports also determined the amounts of cash returning to Egypt as market profits. There was therefore a direct relationship between distance trade and state finances, with revenues proportional to a commerce which also determined the profits returning from overseas sales. This tax-trade system had an equilibrium that created long-term stability within the Roman economy. As long as Eastern trade existed, Egypt could produce enormous tax revenues for central government, but Eastern trade also gave the province the means to replenish this lost coinage as commercial profits from Rome.

In this era, the Roman Empire derived much of its wealth from what was essentially an incentive-based system. As Roman commerce expanded, substantial new revenues were acquired by the government without the state having to resort to greater coercion of its subjects. In this system, merchants who were compelled by profit sought out territories in the Roman provinces where there was surplus prosperity, then obtained this wealth by exploiting local demand for Eastern commodities. The Roman government sent coinage out to its deficit provinces to pay these military regions in wealth gained from Egyptian tax and new bullion. These funds ensured that Roman forces on the frontiers regularly received at least part of their pay in coin. The availability of this money attracted traders to the frontier provinces with merchandise and supplies to sell to the Roman armies. Merchants therefore created an infrastructure that supplied and equipped the frontier military.[268]

Eastern commerce could raise vast revenues with a minimal amount of state infrastructure. The Roman government only needed to control a few Red Sea customs points and their outlying districts to gather the enormous revenues of this commerce. A relatively small investment of military personnel could collect more than a third of the total imperial finances. This minimal bureaucracy reduced the potential for extortion in provincial administration and allowed a greater proportion of taxed wealth to reach the Roman treasury. This financial system meant that, in many subject provinces, the Romans could afford to leave local administration largely in the hands of the traditional ruling elite. As the local elite were the most obvious candidates for inducing wider dissent against Rome, central government benefited from their compliance.[269] The Roman system was so successful that few contemporaries could have foreseen how this prosperity would end.

THE CHALLENGE TO EMPIRE

The Roman Empire had developed an economic system that was highly resistant to disruption. For two centuries the Emperors of Rome ruled over a politically stable regime funded by a prosperous economy producing enormous financial revenues. These finances were heavily dependent on the successful management of commercial wealth drawn from Egypt, India and the distant East.

Alexandria and Rome were at the economic centre of the Roman financial system. These two commercial cities were connected by the pacified Mediterranean Sea which acted as a major conduit for trade communications. A buffer zone of large provinces protected this economic core of the Empire and on the frontiers a well-equipped professional army countered any external threat. The city of Alexandria was a market supplier and intermediary between the Western and Eastern worlds. Rome was the crucial retail market that enabled this commerce to be profitable. Bullion producing provinces such as Spain and Dacia sustained imperial wealth with their extensive mining operations. To maintain continued prosperity, the Empire had to retain control over the Egyptian economy and ensure that the commercial markets of Rome were free from disturbance. Prosperity was also dependent on the government having access to large supplies of fresh bullion to replenish the precious metals expended in Eastern commerce. Natural disasters such as the eruption of Vesuvius or bush fires in Somalia damaged aspects of Eastern commerce. However, international trade was so extensive that these events did not cause lasting harm, and the commerce quickly recovered.

By the mid second century AD the commercial and financial prosperity of the Roman Empire was formidable. When Antoninus Pius died in AD 161, the revenue surplus allowed him to leave his successor Marcus Aurelius with 2,700 million sesterces in the Roman treasury.[270] Provincial revolt and foreign incursions could disrupt the outlying provinces, but Rome did not depend on their finances for its overall operations.[271] Central Roman government had both the income and the military resources to deal with any possible domestic insurrection or foreign invasion with devastating force. Civil war was a threat to the stability of the system, but these conflicts were ultimately brief because the military faction that held Egypt controlled the finances of the Roman state. No single enemy was strong enough to defeat the Roman Empire and its position within the ancient world seemed unassailable. In the Far East, the vast armies of the Han Empire matched the Roman state in size and organization, but the distance was too great to constitute a meaningful military threat. Imperial propagandists therefore confidently imagined the eternal rule of a universal Roman Empire.

The crisis that incapacitated the Roman Empire in the second century AD, and fatally damaged its supremacy, was not caused by a human enemy, but by a lethal microscopic virus. This invisible threat originated in Central Asia where it was released into the expanding population of the ancient world. Disease was the one assailant that the vast empires of Rome and China could not overcome with the force of their armies or the massive resources commanded by their imperial governments. When the spreading pandemic reached the Far East in AD 161 it began to inflict horrendous casualties on the population of the Han Empire. On the military frontiers the Chinese forces lost between 30 and 40 per cent of their numbers as soldiers were either killed or debilitated by the first deadly outbreaks of this infection.[272] The crisis was unprecedented and confidence in the government began to fail as the demoralized Chinese population came to realize that their rulers were ineffective against this new threat. After a generation of decline, the Han Empire entered an era of political turmoil which ended with the state fracturing into rival kingdoms.

The virus brought the same devastation to the fortified Roman frontiers, and inflicted greater casualties amongst the legions, than any barbarian hoard could have hoped to achieve.[273] The pandemic also spread its infection through the

Mediterranean core of the Empire, transmitted in the crowded Roman bazaars where people congregated to conduct their business.

The fortunes of Rome changed dramatically in the aftermath of the Antonine pandemic. Augustus had appreciated that the expanded Empire could not be sustained by the tax system that Rome had traditionally imposed on its subject populations. Yet bolstered by the revenues of Eastern commerce succeeding Emperors had annexed further deficit territories and increased state expenditure on the military. By the second century AD, Rome was therefore dependent on the high revenues it derived from Eastern trade. When the pandemic destroyed the commercial profits of the Roman financial system, the government found that it could no longer pay its full military costs from the revenues it received from the provinces. For the first time since the Augustan era there was a serious shortfall in state finances, and the Empire now faced a sustained series of disasters that threatened to overwhelm the regime.

The Germanic peoples who lived beyond the northern frontiers were not so heavily affected by the pandemic. Their disparate societies lacked the densely populated urban centres of the Mediterranean and their warriors were not barracked in closely-knit communities like the Roman garrisons. When the Roman military on the frontiers became overcome by disease, the Germanic hoards, led by the Marcomanni tribe, launched a ferocious assault on the weakened Empire. Eutropius recalls:

> The Marcomannic war was formidable because whole armies had been lost through disease . . . the destructive pestilence spread from Rome throughout Italy and the provinces. The greater part of the population and almost all the troops contracted the disease.[274]

The threat was so great that later sources compared the conflict to the Punic war fought between Carthage and Rome when barbarian armies had overrun large parts of Italy. It was generally perceived that the Germanic invasion had to be halted or the supremacy of the Empire would be lost.

The Emperor in this era was the stoic philosopher Marcus Aurelius. Aurelius rallied the shattered Roman forces to overcome the invaders and pull the Empire back from the brink of destruction. Ancient accounts recall the extraordinary measures the Emperor took to restore the Roman army and successfully pursue his war. The sources state:

> Since the pestilence was still raging, he trained slaves for military service . . . he also armed gladiators. He recruited the bandits of Dalmatia and Dardania as soldiers. He armed the city vigilantes and even hired auxiliaries from among the Germans to fight against their own people.[275]

Throughout this campaign against the Germans the Roman institutions had to fight against the debilitating effects of disease. The sources recall:

> The Marcomannic war was greater than any conflict in memory. The Emperor waged

war with great valour at a time when a terrible disease was regularly killing thousands of civilians and soldiers.[276]

Aurelius funded the war effort with the finances of the Roman treasury, drawing upon the vast store of wealth that had accumulated over previous generations. But when finances became scarce, the Emperor began to sell the imperial treasures to raise badly needed funds. The sources record:

> When the Emperor had drained the treasury for this war, he could not bring himself to impose extra taxes on the provincials. He therefore held a public sale in Trajan's Forum where he sold the imperial furnishings including crystal and gold goblets, royal cups, gold-embroidered silk robes belonging to his wife, and Hadrian's jewels.[277]

Under the charismatic leadership of Marcus Aurelius the Empire halted the Germanic invasion, restored its northern frontiers, and retained its past integrity. But in AD 180, exhausted by these campaigns, the Emperor himself succumbed to the disease. In his final hours, Aurelius ordered his son Commodus to leave his company in case he too contracted the infection and when he saw the distress of his councillors mused, 'Why do you weep for me? Instead think about the disease and death which is common to all of us'.[278]

Dio remarks that after the death of Aurelian, Roman history descended from 'a realm of gold' to one of 'iron and rust'.[279] The 'Golden Age' of the Roman Empire was effectively over. Imperial politics would no longer be sustained by the profits of consumerism, but decided by military force in a world of failing grandeur. Many of the problems that the Roman state faced in the third century AD are symptomatic of its revenue decline.[280] The Empire could not restore its vital commercial contacts with the distant East and over time the financial crisis only worsened.

The Han Empire had collapsed, but the Roman state endured far longer, due to the cohesion of its military institutions. As the revenue crisis continued, the legions were forced to intervene in the affairs of central government to ensure that their financial needs were met from the reduced imperial income. Civil wars became more frequent as the regional armies supported their own generals for the position of Emperor. Once in power these generals soon realized that they could not manage the financial system to ensure that all legionary armies received sufficient long-term pay.[281] Neglecting certain military regions only led to renewed rounds of civil war as further challengers were sent to claim the position of Emperor. Roman government now faced the threat of its own armies and political supremacy was increasingly determined by force of arms. This was the 'kingdom of iron' described by Dio.

The Emperors who succeeded responded to the shortfall in revenues by debasing the Roman coinage in a desperate attempt to create more money from insufficient funds. The first large-scale debasement of the silver coinage occurred in AD 194 and this practice soon became commonplace.[282] Throughout the third century AD, economic deterioration was inexorable as imperial revenues failed to meet required expenditure and the military were offered progressively devalued pay. The frontier military needed effective cash to purchase food supplies and other market essentials. But as military pay became increasingly debased, merchants from the more productive provinces were less inclined to bring their goods to the frontier forces. As these essential trade systems failed, the military were compelled to adopt more oppressive measures and forcefully extract required supplies from beleaguered local communities.

A century after the Antonine pandemic, the Roman silver currency was so debased that it had little more than notational value. The third century Emperors eventually introduced so much devalued coin into circulation that they caused price inflation and there was a steep rise in the retail cost of commodities. Finally, the Emperor Diocletian instigated a series of reforms to restructure the revenue system of the Roman Empire and try to restore the integrity of the imperial currency. The Roman administration now formally adopted a greater role in supplying the military with basic essentials. This required the creation of a more extensive state bureaucracy that needed to be financed from increased taxes. Greater bureaucracy also introduced an increased likelihood of administrative corruption and this became a persistent feature of the later Empire. The reforms of the early fourth century should be seen as attempts to make the Roman Empire operate almost entirely on the basis of its internal economy and the taxable production of this closed system.

The growth in bureaucracy meant that the Roman state became too large to be effectively administered by a single government. In this era the Roman administration was formally divided between the Greek East and the Latin West.[283] The Greek East remained prosperous because many of its territories had once existed as wealthy independent kingdoms populated by significant urban communities. By contrast the Western state was more structurally and financially vulnerable. The Western empire had been built around the conquest of large regions with relatively basic agricultural territories. In the Golden Age of the Roman Empire many of the northern provinces were revenue deficient regions that had a large part of their military expenses paid for by central government. These territories had undergone significant economic development under Roman rule, but the possibility remains that they never produced a substantial amount of revenue surplus for the imperial regime.

The relentless civil wars of the third century AD devastated the veteran legions that had distinguished the Empire from its foreign rivals. The Roman armies that emerged in the following era did not have the training, discipline and equipment of their predecessors. With limited finances and a depreciated military, the Roman Emperors were forced to make greater use of barbarian allies in their wars against rival candidates and foreign invaders. Previous Roman regimes had used barbarian forces as allies, but these foreign groups had been quickly integrated into the provincial population through settlement and military service. This process was not possible in the late Empire as Rome now lacked the military institutions to overcome or assimilate these foreign populations.[284]

Rome came to rely on the service of Germanic allies to conclude its civil wars and repel further barbarian migrations into the Empire. In the fourth and fifth centuries this dependence reached a new intensity when a steppe people called the Huns began to make serious inroads into Europe. Germanic society had retained its martial prowess, so entire German populations were settled within the Empire in return for pledges of military service. This further diminished the taxable resources available to the Roman government and placed large, integral communities within the Empire who retained their own cultural allegiances. The imperial army recruited so heavily from these populations that the division between 'Roman' and 'German' became indistinct.

The final generations of the Western Empire found themselves dependent on Germanic generals who were legitimised by Rome, but increasingly followed their own agenda. These German leaders took advantage of factional intrigue among the traditional Roman elite to impose their own rule. Europe was now divided into Germanic kingdoms engaged in a series of conflicts that culminated in the fall of the Western Roman Empire.

To have endured this crisis, the Latin West would have required substantial assistance from the more prosperous Greek East. This help was not forthcoming; and under the Germanic kingdoms, the European territories sank back into an economic and social situation similar to circumstances before the rise of the Roman Empire. Western Europe now discovered that it could not sustain complex institutions without the finances of the Eastern world.

Rome left its former territories in Europe with an affinity for classical art, architecture and learning. Under the name 'Byzantium' the Greek East of the Roman Empire survived the Latin West by almost 1,000 years. When the last remains of the Byzantine state fell in the fifteenth century, Christian scholars from Constantinople fled to Italy with the remnants of classical learning that would ignite the Renaissance.

The map projections of Ptolemy were studied by a new generation of European explorers who sought lucrative trade opportunities in the distant East. Thus began the so-called Age of Discovery, when the lure of Eastern commerce compelled Europeans on their first major voyages of exploration to discover western routes to India. When these expeditions brought the first Europeans to the American continents, the explorers carried mutated versions of the measles and smallpox infections that had devastated the Roman and Han Empires. Through generations of suffering and death the Europeans had developed an ancestral resistance to these diseases, but the new peoples of America were as vulnerable as the Antonine Romans had once been. As the native populations of America were decimated by pandemics, the European settlers extended their control over the immense new resources of the American continents. Vast reserves of bullion extracted from America transformed the economy of Western Europe and gave fresh impetus for the development of a new form of aggressive Eastern trade. Thus commenced the era of European colonialism.

By the Victorian era, the history of the Roman Empire had been re-written as a European achievement that ignored the contribution of Eastern civilizations. The success and prosperity of Rome became a character-driven story that celebrated European ingenuity. This history focused on the dealings of an aristocratic elite that included generals, politicians and Emperors. There was no longer any significance placed on the multi-racial merchants who had haggled at distant bazaars. Rome and its culture became the justification for European hegemony and the doctrines taught in educational institutions promoted and harboured these social views down through the subsequent generations.

We now live in an era when governments direct their societies and manage their economies in a global context. The factors that created and destroyed the Roman Empire are paramount concerns of the twenty-first century. Modern governments must find effective ways to deal with economic inter-dependence, to manage global commerce, control mass population movement and integrate foreign cultures. The consequences of war, natural disasters, depleting resources and the continued threat of global pandemic, are a renewed concern in our modern times. Perhaps new lessons can be learnt from the ancient world.

The time has come to write another history of the ancient world that fully acknowledges the contribution of Eastern civilizations to the development of early Europe. The Roman accomplishment was extraordinary because its Empire presided over an economic system that extracted productive materials from India and the distant East without the need to conquer or oppress these vast foreign territories. Eastern peoples profited from Roman wealth and the Roman government gained from a foreign trade that drew together the collective prosperity of its subject peoples. A comprehensive understanding of the Roman Empire must acknowledge its global economic setting within the ancient world. Placing Rome in its ancient context makes the reach and achievements of classical civilization far more complex and extraordinary than most modern scholars have realized.

APPENDIX A

The Products of the Roman Empire

This table lists the products of the Roman Empire according to the Chinese *Weilue*.[1]

Gold	Orpiment
Silver	Nephrite
Copper	Multicoloured jade or gemstone
Iron	Twelve sorts of wool rugs: yellow, white, black, green, purple, fiery red, deep red, dark blue, golden yellow, light blue, black, and yellow
Lead	Finely patterned multicoloured wool carpets
Tin	Nine colours of multicoloured lower quality wool carpets
Tortoises used for divination	Gold-threaded embroidery
White horses with red manes	Polychrome fine silk
Fighting cocks	Woven gold cloth
Rhinoceroses	Purple *chi* cloth
Sea turtle shell	*Falu* cloth
Black bears	Purple *chiqu* cloth
Product of red hornless dragons (cinnabar resin = 'dragons blood')	Asbestos fire-proof cloth
Mongooses	Fine silk gauze cloth
Large cowries	Shot silk
Mother-of-pearl	*Dudai* cloth
Carnelian	Cotton-wool cloth
'Southern gold'	Multicoloured *tao* cloth
Kingfisher feathers	Crimson curtains woven with gold
Ivory	Multicoloured 'spiral curtains'
Coloured veined jade	*Yiwei*
'Bright Moon' pearls	Myrrh
Large diamonds	Storax
Genuine white pearls	*Diti*
Yellow amber	Rosemary

Red coral	Incense resin
Ten varieties of glass: red, white, black, green, yellow, blue-green, dark blue, light blue, fiery red, and purple	*Bai fuzi*
A magnificent jade	Frankincense
White carnelian	Turmeric: saffron or tulips
Rock crystal or transparent glass	Rue oil
Various semi-precious gems	Oriental lovage
Realgar	

APPENDIX B

Eastern imports into the Roman Empire

This table lists Eastern products subject to customs tax on import into Alexandria.[1]

Cinnamon	Linen
Long pepper	All sorts of gems
White pepper	Pearls
Pentasphaerum leaf	Sardonyx
Barbary leaf	Ceraunium (bloodstone)
Costum	Hyacinth stone (blue gems)
Costamomum	Emerald
Nard	Diamond
Tyrian cassia	Sapphire
Cassia-wood	Turquoise
Myrrh	Beryl
Amomum	Tortoise stone
Ginger	Indian or Seric drugs
Malabrathrum	Raw silk
Indian spice	Silk or part-silk clothing
Galbanum	Dyed cloth
Asafoetida	Embroidered fine linen
Aloe	Silk thread
Lycium	Indian eunuchs
Perian gum	Lions
Arabian onyx	Lionesses
Cardamom	Pards (maneless big cats)
Cinnamon-wood	Leopards
Cotton goods	Panthers
Babylonian hides	Purple dye
Parthian hides	Wool
Ivory	Dye
Indian iron	Indian hair

APPENDIX C

The Prices of Eastern Goods

This table lists Pliny's prices for Eastern goods in Roman markets (1 denarius is worth 4 sesterces).[1]

Commodity	*Price in Denarii per Roman Pound (12 oz)*
Frankincense (best variety)	6–10 denarii
Frankincense (second grade)	5 denarii
Frankincense (third grade)	3 denarii
Myrrh (Stacte variety)	3–50 denarii
Myrrh (Somali variety)	16.5 denarii
Myrrh (Erythraean variety)	16 denarii
Myrrh (perfume variety)	12 denarii
Myrrh (cultivated variety)	11 denarii
Pepper, long	15 denarii
Pepper, white	7 denarii
Pepper, black (common pepper)	4 denarii
Nard	100 denarii
Nard leaf (three varieties)	40–75 denarii
Nard (Ganges variety)	3 denarii
Cinnamon	1,500 denarii[2]
Cinnamon (Daphnis variety)	300 denarii
Cinnamon wood	10 denarii
Amomum	48–60 denarii
Costus	5.5 denarii
Caredamon	12 denarii
Ammoniacum	2 denarii
Styrax	17 denarii
Sweet Flag	1 denarii
Sweet Rush	5 denarii
Bdellium	3 denarii
Cardamom (best variety)	3 denarii
Cassia	5–50 denarii
Ginger	6 denarii
Ladanum	2.5 denarii

Notes

Notes to Chapter 1: Ancient Evidence for Eastern Contacts

1 Herodotus, 3.89–96.
2 Pliny, *Natural History*, 6.21.
3 Pliny, *N.H.* 6.26.
4 Suetonius, *Julius Caesar*, 25.
5 Strabo, *Geography*, 16.23.
6 Seneca, *Natural Questions*, preface 1.11.
7 Seneca's book 'De Situ Indiae'. See Pliny, *N.H.* 6.21; Servius, *Commentary on Virgil*, 1.9.30.
8 Seneca, *N.Q.* 5.18.11.
9 Chi I, *Hsin Shu*, 4.41.
10 Huan Kuan, *Yan Tie Lun* (*Discourses on Salt and Iron*), 2.14.
11 Tacitus, *Annals*, 3.53.
12 Seneca, *De Beneficiis*, 7.9.
13 Pliny, *N.H.* 12.41.
14 Mela: "Hipparchus suggests Sri Lanka may be the first part of another world. Hipparchus is probably right because the landmass is inhabited yet no one is reported to have sailed around it." Mela, 3.70.
15 Seneca, *N.Q.* 5.18.4.
16 On Ireland: 'The approaches to its harbours are well known to us through trade and the activities of our entrepreneurs'. Tacitus, *Agricola*, 24.
17 See De Romanis, (1997) 17; 37.
18 The original Chinese name for the Far West was *Li-jian*. *Weilue*: 'The kingdom of *Da Qin* (Rome) is also called *Li-jian*.' (*Weilue*, 11). *Li-jian* is possibly an abbreviation of 'Alexander', 'A-li-jian-der'. The Chinese name would mean 'the land of Alexander' i.e. the 'classical world'. Discussed: Pulleyblank, (1999) 74; 76.
19 See Leslie & Gardiner, (1996) 4.
20 See Casson, (1989) 10.
21 See Cimino, (1994) 8–9.
22 Ball, (2000) 123; Casson, (1989) 7–8.
23 De Romanis, (1997) 14–5; Casson, (1984) 211.
24 See Robin, (1997) 42; Cimino, (1994) 8.
25 *CIS*. 2.161. See Young (2001) 6; De Romanis, (1997) 15; Casson, (1989) 7.
26 'Panjtar Inscription'. See Robin, (1997) 44; Cribb, (1992) 133; (1998) 177.
27 Manbanos = Nahapana. Based on phonic resemblance, distribution of inscriptions and coin finds in the Gujarat region. See Casson, (1989) 197–8.
28 *Periplus Maris Erythraei* = *P.M.E.* Nahapana is mentioned *P.M.E.* 41. See also 52.
29 Identifying the Saka era with the reign of Gondophares (beginning c. AD 20). See Cribb, (1998) 172–3; 177.
30 Pliny, *N.H.* 6.84–5.
31 See Ball, (2000) 126; Casson, (1991b) 8–11; Miller, (1969) 16–20; Warmington, (1928) 43; Wheeler, (1954) 141–52.
32 Dueck, (2000) 75; 180–6; Clarke, (1997) 193; 203.

33 Dueck, (2000) 69–75.
34 Strabo, *Geog.* 12.3.15; 12.3.39. Dueck, (2000) 1–2; Clarke, (1997) 92–110.
35 Dueck, (2000) 4; 7–8.
36 Strabo, *Geog.* 2.5.11–12. See Dueck, (2000) 8; 21; 85; 87; 101.
37 *Ibid.* 2–3; 85.
38 *Ibid.* 53; 87; 96. Strabo's ideas on the study of geography: see Dueck, (2000) 163–4; 168.
39 See *Ibid.* 136; 144; 156.
40 For instance: Strabo, *Geog.* 15.1.57.
41 Strabo, *Geog.* 15.1.4.
42 Pliny: 'tales invented for the purpose of enhancing the prices of these commodities' ('winged serpents' said to guard cinnamon groves). See Pliny, *Natural History,* 12.42.
43 See Strabo's account of whales chasing Roman ships sailing to India (they had to be scared away with trumpets). Strabo, *Geog.* 15.2.13.
44 Strabo, *Geog.* 15.1.4–5.
45 Exact measurements: 0.37 by 6.75 metres. See Cimino, (1994) 10.
46 *Peutinger Map*, segment 11. See Ball, (2000) 123.
47 See Talbert, (2004) 126–8.
48 Discussed: Young, (2001) 22; 187; 198; Millar, (1998) 120–1.
49 See Young, (2001) 140–1; 147; Ball, (2000) 133.
50 Discussed: Millar, (1998) 120.
51 *Ibid.*
52 Isidore, 1.4. See Mattern, (1999) 34.
53 Pliny, *N.H.* 6.31 (events 1 BC).
54 Dionysius as Isidore see Mattern, (1999) 34.
55 Latest dateable details are 26 BC. See *Ibid.* 34–5.
56 Pliny's life: see Healy, (1999) 1; Beagon, (1992) 2. Ancient sources: three letters of his nephew Pliny the Younger (3.5; 6.16; 6.20), a summary biography attributed to Suetonius, what can be inferred from brief remarks in the *N.H.* See Murphy, (2004) 2.
57 Career: see Healy, (1999) 1–22, esp. 4–7; Beagon, (1992) 1–10.
58 Pliny possibly served in Africa or Gaul. See Pliny, *N.H.*, 25.76; 35.48; 18.51 (Africa); 3.5 (Gaul). Pliny, *Letters,* 3.5. Discussed: Healy, (1999) 6–9.
59 Pliny, *Letters,* 3.5. Suetonius, *Vespasian,* 21. Discussion of duties see Healy, (1999) 7; 32.
60 See Pliny, *Letters,* 6.16. See Healy, (1999) 8; Beagon, (1992) 6.
61 Healy, (1999) 33; Murphy, (2004) 3.
62 Pliny also wrote a thirty-book history of Rome, completed a six-volume work on the education of an orator and an eight-volume grammatical treatise. Pliny, *Letters,* 3.5. See Beagon, (1992) 3.
63 Discussed: Murphy, (2004) 5–6; 10; Beagon, (1992) 24.
64 Murphy: 'it owes its shape more to whimsical gigantism than designing intelligence'. See Murphy, (2004) 30; 34.
65 See Healy, (1999) 39–41; 63–70.
66 'Scientific method': see Isager, (1991) 43. 'Critical method': Murphy, (2004) 5; 33. Moral codes: Healy, (1999) 3; 29; Beagon, (1992) 14.
67 Pliny: 'According to Arab envoys and our own traders who have come from the place'. Pliny, *N.H.* 6.31. Military expedition to Ethiopia: Pliny, *N.H.* 6.35. Dionysius of Charax: Pliny, *N.H.*, 6.31.
68 Discussed: Murphy, (2004) 5.
69 Pliny, *N.H.* Preface.
70 Discussed: Murphy, (2004) 34; Healy, (1999) 62; 109; Beagon, (1992) 24.
71 Berggren & Jones, (2000) 3.
72 *Ibid.* 26–7.
73 Bagnall, (2000) 3; Adams, (2007) 226.
74 Significance discussed: Bagnal, (2000) 9–10, 15–6; Adams, (2007) 227.

75 Bagnall, (2000) BE 38.
76 Discussed: Bagnall, (2000) 16.
77 Discussed: Adams, (2007) 227.
78 Details see Fuks, (1951) 207–16; Sidebottom, (1989) 83–92; Young, (2001) 64–5.
79 See Adams, (2007) 222–5 (*O. Petr.* 245).
80 See Fuks, (1951) 209.
81 *Coptos Tariff*: *OGIS* 674. Discussed: Adams, (2007) 132–3; Sidebotham, (2008) 187.
82 Discussed: Sidebotham, (2008) 192.
83 *P. Vindob. G* 40822 = SB 8.13167. Discussed: Adams, (2007) 229.
84 See Millar, (1998) 133.
85 Discussed: Franck & Brownstone, (1986) 140.
86 See Young, (2001) 139; 168; Gawlikowski, (1994) 32–3.
87 Discussed: Millar, (1998) 131. Inscriptions listed in Gawlikowski, (1994) 27–33.
88 *CIS* 2.3.3913. Discussed: Elton, (1996) 94; Millar, (1998) 171.
89 Details: Turner, (1989) esp. 5–16.
90 See Ball, (2000) 127; 132; Whittaker, (2004) 164.
91 Discussed: Tomber, (2008) 120.
92 See Thapar, (2002) 266–7.
93 *Ibid.* 260.
94 Discussion: De Romanis, (1997) 16–7. Sceptical: Ball, (2000) 126–7.
95 See Ball, (2001) 126.
96 See Zvelebil, (1992) 12.
97 See Champakalakshmi, (1996) 175–7.
98 Discussed: Strauss, (2007) 253.
99 Parker, (1992) 1077.
100 Considered in Strauss, (2007) 253.
101 Near modern Pattanam. See Tomber, (2008) 140–3.
102 Discussed: Rajan, (1996) 100; Champakalakshmi, (1996) 117; 127.
103 Investigation of site: Tomber, (2008) 138.
104 See Waugh, (2004) 1.
105 *Ibid.* 1–3.
106 *Hou Hanshu*, 88. Discussed: Leslie & Gardiner, (1996) xviii.
107 Discussed: *Ibid.* 22.
108 King Meredates was ruling in Mesene and the territory around Dura-Europos was still under Parthian control. Discussed: Leslie & Gardiner, (1996) 4; 7–10; 20–2. Hill, *Weilue: About the text* (2004).

Notes to Chapter 2: Roman Egypt and the Sea Routes to India

1 Discussed: Sidebotham, (2008) 152–6.
2 Darius, *Suez Inscription.*
3 Herodotus, 4.44. Discussed: Ray, (1994) 52.
4 Nearchus: Arrian, *Campaigns of Alexander,* 8.20–33; Strabo, *Geography.* 15.2.14; 16.3.2; Pliny, *Natural History*, 6.26.96–100.
5 See Strabo, *Geog.* 15.2.9.
6 An inscription from the Nile Delta known as the 'Pithom Stele' documents these initiatives. Discussed: Sidebotham, (1989) 486; (2008) 164; Tomber, (2008) 64.
7 Ptolemaic finds discussed: Sidebotham, (2008) 162–4.
8 Ivory: *IG* 11.2.163,aa7 (279 BC); 203.a71 (269 BC); 287.a118 (250 BC). Discussed: Sidebotham, (2008) 162–4.
9 *SB* 3.7169 (c.200–150 BC). See Adams, (2007) 233.
10 Details: Whittaker, (2004) 163.

11 Discussed: Tchernia, (1997) 260.
12 Agatharchides, 5.105. See also Diodorus Siculus, 3.47.
13 Strabo, *Geog.* 2.3.4–5.
14 Strabo, *Geog.* 2.3.4. Discussed: Singer, (2007) 18; Tchernia, (1997) 259.
15 Strabo, *Geog.* 2.3.4.
16 *Periplus Maris Erythraei*, 26.
17 Strabo, *Geog.* 17.1.13.
18 Strabo, *Geog.* 2.5.12. Discussed: Sidebotham, (1986a) 49.
19 Bernand, (1972) no. 72. Details: Sidebottom, (1986a) 2; Ray (1994) 57.
20 Dio Cassius, 51.7; Plutarch, *Antony*, 69.
21 Suetonius, *Julius Caesar*, 52; *Augustus*, 17.
22 Plutarch, *Antony*, 81.
23 Strabo, *Geog.* 17.1.12–13. Evidence considered: Adams, (2007) 166.
24 Josephus, *Jewish War*, 2.16.14. Discussed: Rickman, (1980); Adams, (2007) 159–160.
25 Resources and infrastructure in the Eastern Desert: see Sidebotham, (2008) 61–94 (stone quarries); 213–26 (gold mining); 277–302 (gemstone mines).
26 See Sidebotham, (1986a) 62–3; (1988) 493.
27 Sidebotham, (1996a) 292; Adams, (2007) 22.
28 Discussed: Adams, (2007) esp. 197.
29 *Hydreumata* and desert travel see Sidebotham, (1986a) 63; Adams, (2007) 24; 38; 45; 52–3.
30 Strabo, *Geog.* 17.1.45.
31 Discussed: Sidebotham, (1986a) 59; 64; (1988) 492.
32 Strabo, *Geog.* 16.4.23.
33 Strabo, *Geog.* 2.5.12.
34 Strabo, *Geog.* 17.1.13. Discussed: De Romanis, (1997) 84; Raschke, (1978) 662; Whittaker, (2004) 164; 168; Sidebotham, (2008) 177.
35 Strabo, *Geog.* 17.1.13. See Sidebotham, (1986a) 49.
36 Paulus Orosius: 'Augustus conquered Alexandria, by far the richest and greatest of all cities. It's riches so enhanced Rome's wealth that the abundance of money raised the value of property and other saleable goods to double what they had been up to this time.' Paulus Orosius, 6.19.
37 Suetonius: 'Augustus brought the treasures of the Ptolemies to Rome for his Alexandrian triumph. So much cash passed into private hands that the interest rate on loans dropped sharply, while real estate values soured.' Suetonius, *Augustus*, 41.
38 Dio Cassius: 'Augustus gave gifts to the soldiers and distributed 400 sesterces to the Roman citizens . . . So vast an amount of money circulated through all parts of Rome that the price of goods rose and loans for which the borrower had been glad to pay 12 per cent could now be had for one third that rate.' Dio Cassius, 51.21. Discussed: De Romanis (1997) 83–4.
39 See Sidebotham, (1989) 486; (1996) 289.
40 See Whittaker, (2004) 163.
41 Modern estimates suggest that it cost less than 400,000 sesterces to construct a large Roman freighter (400 tons). See Hopkins, (1983) 92–4. The *Muziris Papyrus* records that a single Eastern cargo was worth almost 9 million sesterces (before tax). *P. Vindob. G* 40822, verso, 29.
42 Pliny: 'Pearls came into common use at Rome after the reduction of Alexandria under our sway'. (Pliny, *N.H.* 9.59). Tacitus: 'Extravagant consumption of edible luxuries reached fantastic heights in the century between the close of the Actian war and the struggle which placed Servius Galba on the throne.' (Tacitus, *Annals*, 3.55). Discussed: De Romanis, (1997) 82–3; Tchernia, (1997) 261.
43 Strabo, *Geog.* 15.1.4. Discussed: De Romanis, (1997) 84.
44 Strabo, *Geog.* 17.1.45; Pliny, *N.H.* 6.26.102–3. Discussed: Sidebotham, (1986a) 81–2.
45 *OGIS* 674.

46 Myos Hormos: Strabo, *Geog.* 2.5.12. Berenice: 16.4.5; 16.4.24; 17.1.45; Pliny, *N.H.* 6.26.102–3. Discussed: Sidebottom, (1986a) 49–53. Adams, (2007) 35–6.
47 Strabo, *Geog.* 17.1.45. Average travel in the Eastern Desert was 30 km per day. See Adams, (2007) 45.
48 Pliny, *N.H.* 6.26.102. Discussed: Sidebotham, (2008) 159; De Romanis, (1997) 166.
49 See Adams, (2007) 83; 207; 223.
50 Details: *Ibid.* 225.
51 *Syriac Acts of Thomas*, 1–3. Tradition discussed in Thorley, (1979) 188.
52 For instance: 'The bowl of the lamp was held in the hands of the statue of beautiful workmanship that had been made by the *Yavanas*.' *Manimekalai*, 19.1.45. Discussed: Ray, (1995) 79.
53 Gallus left with 130 transport ships but many were wrecked. Strabo, *Geog.* 16.4.23–24. See Tomber, (2008) 57.
54 Discussed: Sidebotham, (1986a) 49; (1988) 488; (2008) 170.
55 Strabo, *Geog.* 16.4.5.
56 See Sidebotham, (1986a) 52.
57 Strabo, *Geog.* 7.1.45.
58 *Ibid.*
59 Details: Whitewright, (2007) 85–7. Discussed: Tomber, (2008) 63.
60 See Sidebotham, (1986a) 52–3.
61 *Ibid.* 54; 81.
62 Details: Adams, (2007) 226.
63 For instance: wine 48 vessels (*BE* 39); 1 jar sweet Rodian wine and beets (*BE* 87); onions (*BE* 78). See Bagnall, (2000) 15.
64 *Pharmakoi*: *O. Petr.* 275, 283.
65 Quince (*BE* 4). Discussed: Bagnall, (2000) 22.
66 Pliny, *N.H.* 6.26.102–4. Details: Sidebotham, (1986a) 60–1.
67 Details: Adams, (2007) 210; 213.
68 Discussed: Fuks, (1951) 214; Sidebottom, (1986a) 49–51; Casson, (1989) 13.
69 Fuks, (1951) 211.
70 *P.M.E.* 1.
71 Details: Sidebotham, (2008) 170; Tomber, (2008) 57–8; 60.
72 Blue, (2002) 38.
73 Details: Tomber, (2008) 60.
74 Discussed: Sidebotham, (1986a) 55–6; (1988) 490; Peacock & Blue, (2006) 5–6; Tomber, (2008) 59.
75 Details: Blue, (2002) 9.
76 See Sidebotham, (2002) 233; Tomber (2008) 62.
77 Sidebotham, (2008) 192.
78 *Ibid.* 165; 174.
79 Ptolemy, *Geog.* 4.5. Previous history of canal: Pliny, *N.H.* 6.33. Discussed: Young, (2001) 75–8.
80 Lucian, *Alexander the False Prophet*, 44.
81 Discussed: Sidebotham, (1989) 487; Sidebotham, (1996a) 290. Sceptical: Adams, (2007) 35.
82 Details: Sidebotham, (1989) 487.
83 Attested by *P. Vindob. G* 40822, recto, 1–15 (Second century AD).
84 See Fuks, (1951) 209–10.
85 Details: *Ibid.* 211.
86 *IGRR* 1.1172. Details: Fuks, (1951) 211. Discussed: Sidebotham, (1986a) 84.
87 *P. Lond.* 2.260.1.42. Discussed: Ray, (1994) 64; Adams, (2007) 233.
88 *IGRR* 1.1172. Details: Sidebotham, (1986a) 99. Discussed: 84; 88–9. See also *O.Petr.* No. 287.

89 For instance: Tiberius Claudius Agathocles (*O. Petr.* Nos. 275, 276), Gaius Julius Bacchylus (*O. Petr.* Nos 228; 291), and Gaius Norbanus (*O. Petr.* Nos. 244, 257). Roman citizens who may have owned firms: Popilius Mamilius Andromachus (*O. Petr.* No. 271), Tiberius Claudius Castor (*O. Petr.* No. 275), Claudius Demetrius (*O. Petr.* No. 275) and Tiberius Claudius Theodorus (*O. Petr.* No. 276). Discussed: Sidebotham, (1986a) 85–6.
90 See Bagnall, (2000) 26–7 (further *ostraca* to be published).
91 Anduros: *BE* 52–3. Discussed: Sidebotham, (1986a) 66–7; 86; (2008) 186; 192 (Eros).
92 Italian wine trade discussed: Bagnall, (2000) 20; Tomber, (2008) 59.
93 For instance: L. Titus Primus, L. Piso and Ti. Cl. Serenus. Details: Sidebotham, (1986a) 86; 89.
94 For instance: *O. Petr.* Nos. 244, 257. Discussed: Sidebotham, (1986a) 84.
95 Bagnall, (2000) *BE* 71.
96 *SB* 7539.
97 Discussed: Sidebotham, (1986a) 86–8.
98 Himyaritic from the Homerite kingdom. Details: Sidebotham, (1986a) 86–8 (1989) sherds: 490; graffiti: 497.
99 *RES* 2771; 3022. Details: Sidebotham, (1986a) 99–100.
100 Dio Chrysostom, 32.40. Discussed: Sidebotham, (1989) 497–8.
101 Sidebotham, (2008) 181.
102 Details: Sidebotham, (2008) 195.
103 Bernand, (1972) no. 38. See Sidebotham, (1986a) 100–1.
104 Discussed: Ray, (1994) 66.
105 Details: Sidebotham, (1989) 490; 497. Discussed: Champakalakshmi, (1996) 117; Rajan, (1996) 97.
106 Philostratus, *Life of Apollonius of Tyana*, 3.35.
107 Freighters of 500 tons: see Casson, (1991) 10; Whittaker, (2004) 178 fn. 53. Quseir shipwreck (33 metres long) suggesting a cargo capacity exceeding 300 tons (ships in this era were 'smaller vessels', see *P.M.E.* 57). English ships trading with India in the 18th century had an average size of 440 tons burden. Roman ship size and cargo capacity in the Mediterranean see Hopkins, (1983) 98–9.
108 See Blue, (2002) 27.
109 Discussion: Casson, (1991) 10.
110 See Cappers, (1989) 59; Blue, (2002) 81; Sidebotham, (2008) 181–2.
111 See *P.M.E.* 36. Copper alloy nails were used in shipbuilding.
112 *OGIS* 674.
113 Details: Blue, (2002) 9; 38; 82.
114 See Sidebotham, (2008) 165.
115 Philostratus, *Life of Apollonius of Tyana*, 3.35. The 'bolts' are mortise-and-tenon joints.
116 Mediterranean merchant ships see Casson, (1971) 157–68.
117 Small craft used to escape a sinking grain freighter: see *New Testament*, *Acts*, 27. An Italian freighter sends out a small craft to rescue the Roman general Pompey: see Plutarch, *Pompey*, 73.
118 Discussed: Ray, (1995) 79.
119 *Perumpanarruppatai*, 316–18.
120 Lucian, *The Ship*. 5.
121 For instance: *Manimekalai*, 19.1.45 (Yavana built pavilion: 19.1.108).
122 Discussed: Casson, (1991) 10.
123 Details: Sidebotham, (2008) 195.
124 Brailing rings range from 37 to 88 millimetres (diameter). Details: Blue, (2002) 8; 78; 81. Coils of thick rope recovered near the ancient shore used to secure ocean-going merchant ships. See Whitcomb (1982): 37–42.
125 Identification issues discussed: Tomber, (2008) 73.
126 *P. Vindob. G 40822*, verso, 28.

127 Details: Sidebotham, (2008) 195.
128 Details and discussion: Adams, (2007) 41.
129 Philostratus, *Life of Apollonius of Tyana,* 3.35.
130 *OGIS* 674.
131 Strabo, *Geog.* 2.3.4.
132 Theories: Young, (2001) 55–8.
133 Philostratus, *Life of Apollonius of Tyana,* Books 2–3.
134 Lucian, *Alexander the False Prophet,* 44.
135 Thebes in Egypt. Palladius, *On the Races of India and the Brahmans,* 1.3–10. Discussed: Weerakkody, (1997) 165.
136 See *P.M.E.* 20.
137 Philostratus, *Life of Apollonius of Tyana,* 3.35.
138 Pliny, *N.H.* 6.26.101. Discussed: Sidebotham, (1989) 492.
139 *P. Vindob. G* 40822, verso, 29 (after quarter tax).
140 Plus auxiliary support (1st century AD). See Duncan-Jones, (1994) 34.
141 See *P.M.E.* 39. Details of sailing timetables and seasonal conditions: Casson, (1991) 8.
142 Pliny, *N.H.* 6.26.104.
143 The *Periplus* explains: 'in the past, smaller vessels sailed along the coast from Qana and Aden [to India] following the coastal route'. *P.M.E.* 57.
144 Discussed: Tchernia, (1997) 257.
145 See *P.M.E.* 57. Discussed: Tchernia, (1997) 252–3.
146 Profit motives see De Romanis, (1997) 85; 88.
147 Pliny, *N.H.* 6.26.101. Discussed: Tchernia, (1997) 251.
148 Pliny's information on the voyage to India dated to the period between AD 49–52 (based on details given about the Roman and Egyptian calendars). See Tchernia, (1997) 252.
149 See *P.M.E.* 57. Discussed: Tchernia, (1997) 252–3.
150 About three weeks visiting markets around the Gulf of Aden, then a two week ocean crossing to India. Pliny, *N.H.* 6.26.104. Discussed: Tchernia, (1997) 251.
151 Speed and journey time discussed: Casson, (1980), 32–3.
152 Wind velocity over open waters averaging 22–33 knots with gusts frequently rising to gale force 34–47 knots. Details: Casson, (1991) 9.
153 Details: *Ibid.* 10.
154 See *P.M.E.* 39.
155 See Casson, (1991) 9.
156 See *P.M.E.* 38.
157 Pliny, *N.H.* 32.11.
158 Buddhabhatta, *Ratnapariksa*, 250–2 (date uncertain). Discussed: De Romanis, (1997) 190; 229.
159 Details: Tomber, (2008) 117–51.
160 See *P.M.E.* 39.
161 See *Hou Hanshu*, 88.15.
162 Archaeologists excavating the ancient Kushan palace at Begram in Afghanistan found classical bronzes and Roman glassware, including bowls, goblets and brightly painted vases (exported around AD 100). Vases were decorated with colourful episodes from Greek myth and showed scenes from the Empire, including gladiatorial combat and a view of the Pharos lighthouse at Alexandria. Details: Tomber, (2008) 123–4. Discussed: Ray, (1994) 77; Thapar, (2002) 238.
163 See *P.M.E.* 41.
164 See *P.M.E.* 40.
165 See *P.M.E.* 40.
166 See *P.M.E.* 43.
167 See *P.M.E.* 48.
168 Paithana: 20 days distant, Ter: a further 10 days distant (*P.M.E.* 51). Indian texts mention

caravans carrying 500 carts of merchandise (*Apannaka-Jataka*, 1). Discussed: Prasad, (1984) 127.

169 See *P.M.E.* 36; 51; 54. Discussed: Tomber, (2008) 125; Thapar, (2002) 236.
170 See *P.M.E.* 41.
171 See *P.M.E.* 41.
172 See *P.M.E.* 49.
173 Lucian, *Nigrinus*, 5. Influenced by Dionysus and Bacchus myth-traditions, but more than barbarian *topos*. Discussed: Dalby, (2000) 192–3.
174 See Strauss, (2007) 253.
175 Realgar is arsenic sulphide.
176 Indian texts suggest that perfume manufacture was an important industry. Discussed: Prasad, (1984) 120; 128.
177 See *P.M.E.* 49. Discussed: (1989) 157–8. Significance: Macdowell, (1990) 61.
178 Indo-Greek legacy is another factor. Discussed: Varadpande, (1987) 129. Early Jain religious texts confirm that Indian courts had foreign female attendants. Stage directions: Yavani attendant: 'Enters with a bow in her hand' (Kalidasa, *Vikramorvasiyam*, 5). Discussed: Gupta, (1997) 8.
179 Details: Cappers, (1989) 56.
180 *Periplus*: 'All over India there are these rivers that have extreme ebb and flood tides. These tides come in at the time of the new and the full moon and they can last up to three days. At Barygaza they are more extreme than anywhere else.' See *P.M.E.* 45.
181 See *P.M.E.* 45. The author of the *Periplus* may have witnessed a tsuami style event.
182 See *P.M.E.* 45.
183 See *P.M.E.* 46.
184 See *P.M.E.* 50.
185 The cache contained a statuette of Poseidon (Third century BC). Details: Tomber, (2008) 130–3.
186 Discussed: Ray, (1994) 72–3. (1995) 93.
187 *Periplus*: 'Kalliena was a port of trade where everything went. [But no longer] because now Sandanes has occupied it there is great hindrance [to trade].' See *P.M.E.* 52. Discussed: Casson, (1989) 215.
188 Cribb, (1998) 177.
189 See *P.M.E.* 50–1.
190 Date: 1st–2nd century AD. Details: Thapar, (1997) 34–5; (2002) 260.
191 Discussed: *Ibid.*
192 See Thapar, (2002) 243.
193 Interpretation: Ball, (2000) 126 (interpretation problematic).
194 Significance: Thapar, (1997) 34–5; Ray, (1995) 80.
195 Nasik Cave 17. Hall with a votive *stupa* and stone cisterns (dated after AD 110). Details: *Ibid.*
196 Discussed: Tomber, (2008) 132. A *Yavana* 'doctor': see Ray, (1995) 80.
197 Discussed: Ball, (2000) 401.
198 See *P.M.E.* 51.
199 Pliny, *N.H.* 6.21.
200 See *Purananuru*, 17.9–13. *Akananuru*, 10.8–13 (fishing community at Tyndis). Discussed: De Romanis, (1997) 92.
201 Pirates: *P.M.E.* 53; Pliny, *N.H.* 6.26.104; Ptolemy, *Geography.* 7.1; Discussed: Casson, (1989) 217. The *Peutinger Table* displays the words 'PIRATE' in bold red letters near the southern part of India. See *Peutinger Map,* Segment 11.
202 See *P.M.E.* 55.
203 See *P.M.E.* 54.
204 See *P.M.E.* 54; Pliny, *N.H.* 6.26.104–5.
205 See *Akananuru,* 149.7–11. Discussed: De Romanis, (1997) 98.

206 *Purananuru*, 343.1–10. Discussed: De Romanis, (1997) 95; 136–7; Gupta, (1997) 5.
207 *Peutinger Map*, Segment 11.
208 An Augustan Temple in Parthian Mesopotamia (founded c. AD 150). See Palmyrene inscription: *CIS* 2.3917. Discussed: Young, (2001) 144.
209 Eusebius, *Church History*, 5.10.
210 *Periplus*: 'Grain in sufficient amount for those involved with shipping, because the [local] merchants do not use it.' *P.M.E.* 56. Discussed: Casson, (1989) 85; 221.
211 Pliny, *N.H.* 6.26.104–5.
212 *Akananuru*, 57.14–17. Discussed: De Romanis, (1997) 108.
213 See *Akananuru*, 149.7–13.
214 Maturaikkanci, 75–88 (large ships at Nelcynda bringing gold) See De Romanis, (1997) 107–8; 144.
215 See *P.M.E.* 56.
216 See *P.M.E.* 56.
217 See De Romanis, (1997) 98; 139.
218 See *P.M.E.* 56.
219 Pliny, *N.H.* 34.48.
220 *Periplus*: 'wine – limited quantities, as much as goes to Barygaza'. (Perhaps only 'limited' compared to other exports). See *P.M.E.* 56.
221 Italian wine vessels in Coan style containers. Details: Will, (1991), (1996), (2004) 435; 438. Discussed: Rauh, (2003) 98; Whittaker, (2004) 164 n.17.
222 Rauh, (2003) 99.
223 Persius, *Satires*, 5.53–5 (mid 1st century AD).
224 *Purananuru*, 56.18–21. See Begley, (1996) 23.
225 Details: Williams, (2004) 438; 441; 449–50.
226 *Periplus*: 'Ships in these ports of trade carry full loads because of the volume and quantity of pepper and malabathron.' *P.M.E.* 56.
227 Details: De Romanis, (1997) 100; Gupta, (1991) 128.
228 Details: Casson, (1989) 222.
229 See *P.M.E.* 56.
230 Details: Rajan, (1996) 103; Rajan, (1996) 103. The best beryls had the greenness of pure seawater. See Pliny, *N.H.* 37.20.
231 See Casson, (1989) 223.
232 See *P.M.E.* 56.
233 See *Maturaikkanci*, 75–88.
234 These details indicate that Nelcynda was the main port for heavy cargoes like pepper and malabathrum (ships were still relatively light after leaving Muziris).
235 See *P.M.E.* 55. Discussed: Casson, (1989) 220.
236 Pliny, *N.H.* 6.26.105–6.
237 Details: *P.M.E.* 56; Pliny, *N.H.* 6.26.104–6; Ptolemy, *Geog.* 7.1.
238 See *P.M.E.* 51; 59. Discussed: Casson, (1989) 226; 228.
239 See *P.M.E.* 59.
240 Pliny, *N.H.* 6.26.106. Sailing timetables were partly determined by seasonal harvests. Black pepper was picked in October and November. After a few days drying in the sunshine, it could be packed into sacks and brought to the waiting Roman merchants. Details: Casson, (1989) 220.
241 *Silappatikaram*, 14.104–12. Discussed: Champakalakshmi, (1996) 187.
242 See *P.M.E.* 57.
243 In Roman terms these Indian craft had a cargo capacity of around 3,000 amphorae. See Pliny, *N.H.* 6.24.82–3. Discussed: De Romanis, (1997) 108.
244 *Periplus*: '*Sangara* are large dugout canoes held together by a yoke. The very large *kolandiophonta* sail across to Chryse and the Ganges region'. *P.M.E.* 60.
245 See *P.M.E.* 60.

246 Pliny: 'To get pearls the Indians go to the islands . . . the most productive is Sri Lanka.' Pliny, *N.H.* 9.54.
247 See *P.M.E.* 61. Strabo: 'They say Sri Lanka sends great amounts of ivory, tortoise-shell and other merchandise to the markets of India'. Strabo, *Geog.* 2.1.14.
248 Strabo: 'Sri Lanka is a large island to the south of India. It stretches lengthwise in the direction of Ethiopia for more than 5000 *stadia* [c. 800 kilometres]'. Strabo, *Geog.* 2.1.14.
249 *Periplus*: 'There is an island called Sri Lanka that projects west across the ocean . . . it extends almost up to that part of East Africa that lies opposite . . . the parts of it that lie towards the north are civilized'. *P.M.E.* 61.
250 See Pliny, *N.H.* 6.24.84–6.
251 Ptolemy: 'among these rice, honey, ginger, beryl, amethyst, also gold, silver, and other metals are found'. See Ptolemy, *Geog.* 7.4.
252 Ptolemy's maps portray the general shape of Sri Lanka but he exaggerated the size of the island (to fit with classical tradition). Discussed: Weerakkody, (1997) 89; 97.
253 See Warmington, (1928) 124–5.
254 Details: Weerakkody, (1997) 54. The Chera trade port of Naura had become an emporium and Tyndis had developed into a coastal city. See Ptolemy, *Geog.* 7.1.
255 Details: Ptolemy, *Geog.* 7.1. Tamil literature: *Pattinappalai,* 184–93. Discussed: De Romanis, (1997) 115; Zvelebil, (1974) 22.
256 Pliny, *N.H.* 6.26.105.
257 See *Maturaikkanci,* 331–669. Discussed: Champakalakshmi, (1996) 122.
258 Dio Chrysostom, 35.22.
259 The Roman merchant fleet was composed of at least 120 ships and assuming that each ship carried just 20 professional guards, then well over 2,000 mercenaries could be arriving in India every year.
260 Discussed: De Romanis, (1997) 104–5.
261 *Silappatikaram,* 14.66–7.
262 *Mullaippattu,* 59–62.
263 *Silappatikaram,* 15.207–16. Romans called their heavy artillery 'scorpions' but the Tamils may have invented other imaginative names. 'Machines invented by the *Yavanas* made with the help of their intelligence'; 'The hundred-killer'; 'Mechanical bows that shoot their own arrows'; 'Human statues and figures of swans that spit out red flames' (Greek fire?); 'Mechanical owls, beams that crushed heads' (Swing-beam cranes or clawed grappling hooks? Archimedes claw?). See *Sivakasindamani,* 1.101–4.
264 See *P.M.E.* 60.
265 See *Purananuru,* 30; *Maduraikkanci,* 54. Discussed in Champakalakshmi, (1996) 181.
266 Lighthouses: *Kalam karai ilangu cudar* or 'the light that beckons the ship'. See *Perumpanarruppatai,* 349–51.
267 *Manimekalai,* 1.72; 3.45; 19.54; *Silappatikaram,* 5.117; 5.213; 6.127; 10.31.
268 *Akananuru,* 73.10; *Silappadikaram,* 5.63. Discussed: Champakalakshmi, (1996) 104; 127; Prasad, (1984) 129–30.
269 See *Silappatikaram,* 5.9–12. Discussed: De Romanis, (1997) 116–7; 151; Champakalakshmi, (1996) 105.
270 Details: Rajan, (1996) 100; Champakalakshmi (1996) 117; 127; Tomber, (2008) 138.
271 Garum 'unappetising' for Tamils see Will, (2004) 438–9.
272 Roman lamps: 'The beautiful lamp seen on the statue made by the *Yavanas*'. *Perungadai,* 1.17.15.
273 See Whittaker, (2004) 164; Slane, (1996) 351–68; Begley, (1983) 461–81.
274 *Unguentaria*: See Slane, (1996) 367. Sand 'coating' on amphorae: Sidebotham, (1996b) 110. Significance of finds: Sidebotham, (1986a) 26; Wheeler, (1946) 41–5; Johnson & Whitcomb, (1979) 68–70; Whitcomb, (1982) 64; 67; 69. Tomber, (2008) 148–50.
275 See Begley, (1996) 23–4; Champakalakshmi, (1996) 135.
276 Mahadevan, (1996) 291.

277 See *P.M.E.* 62.
278 See *P.M.E.* 63.
279 See *P.M.E.* 63.
280 See *P.M.E.* 64.
281 See *P.M.E.* 66. Discussed: Casson, (1989) 238.
282 Discussed: Berggren & Jones, (2000) 26–7; 74.
283 Ptolemy, *Geog.* 7.1.
284 Ptolemy, *Geog.* 7.1 (diamonds); 7.2 (Ganges).
285 Paloura was a launching point for Roman ships sailing straight across the sea to Burma. Ptolemy reports: 'The sail across from Paloura to Sada is 13,000 *stades* in the direction of the equatorial sunrise (due east)' (Ptolemy, *Geog.* 1.13). Ships also made crossings from the nearby emporium of Alosygni, a port used by: 'those who sail and navigate the bay'. Ptolemy, *Geog.* 7.1.
286 Indian trade contact with an overseas 'Golden' land. See: *Jatakas*, 3.360; 4.442; *Arthasastra*, 2.11.59. Discussed: Prasad, (1984) 143; Casson, (1984) 237; Glover, (1996a) 130. Thapar, (2002) 243.
287 See Ptolemy, *Geog.* 7.2.
288 The Roman slaves exported to Burma would have included musicians similar to the servants sent to the Saka courts (*P.M.E.* 49). The group seen by the Chinese included conjurors and jugglers. See *Hou Hanshu,* 5.
289 They told the Chinese they came from: 'West of the Sea' and the Chinese concluded: 'West of the sea is in fact Rome. To the south-west, the State of Shan [in Burma] communicates with Rome'. *Hou Hanshu,* 5. Discussed: Leslie & Gardiner, (1996) 150–1.
290 Ptolemy, *Geog.* 1.14.
291 Discussed: Warmington, (1928) 128–9.
292 Ptolemy: '[Alexandros] records that after this they traverse from Tamala over the Golden Peninsula. This crossing is 1,600 *stades*, in the direction of the winter sunrise (due East)'. Ptolemy, *Geog.* 1.14. Discussed: Berggren & Jones, (2000) 75 fn. 5.
293 The Roman trade routes described by Alexandros are measured in Greek *stadia*, but the information he received from Indian traders only reported the number of days travelled.
294 Ptolemy, *Geog.* 7.3.
295 Ptolemy, *Geog.* 1.14. No Sumatra; unless Labadius, 'Barley Island' is Sumatra. Ptolemy: 'Labadius is said to be fruitful and produces much gold'. Also islands in area inhabited by 'Satyrs' and cannibals (Ptolemy, *Geog.* 7.3). See Warmington, (1928) 128–9.
296 Ptolemy, *Geog.* 1.14; 7.3. Discussed: Warmington, (1928)129–30; Ferguson, (1978) 584–5; Young, (2001) 34.
297 See *Hou Hanshu,* 88.12; *Huai-nan Tzu,* 18.21. Discussed: Yu, (1967) 182.
298 Objects said to be 'gold medallions' (possibly aurei) of Marcus Aurelius and Antoninus Pius have been found at Oc-eo in southern Vietnam. Details: Ray, (1994) 212.
299 Plague: 'There was such a pestilence that the dead were removed in carts and wagons . . . Thousands were carried off by the disease, including many nobles'. *Historia Augusta, Marcus Aurelius*, 13. Pandemic spread to Rhine and Gaul: See Ammianus, *Roman History*, 23.6.24. Discussed: Potter & Mattingly, (1999) 105–6.
300 Details: McNeill, (1976) 116; Duncan-Jones, (1996) 108–9.
301 Details: McNeill, (1976) 107–9; Duncan-Jones, (1996) 117–8; 136;
302 See McNeill, (1976) 107–8.
303 See Jerome, *Chronicle,* 236th Olympiad = AD 168.
304 See McNeill, (1976) 116; Duncan-Jones, (1996) 118–20.
305 See McNeill, (1976) 117; 136; Duncan-Jones, (1996) 135.
306 Duncan-Jones, (1996) 116–7; 121. An association of traders at the Italian port of Puteoli petitioned for help in AD 174 because their group had lost so many members. *OGIS* 595.
307 Details: Bagnall, (2000) 188–92.

308 Details: Berghaus, (1991) 110; Sidebotham, (1989) 499; (2008) 181–2; Thapar, (1997) 39.
309 Discussed: Young, (2001) 82; Tomber, (2008) 130.

Notes to Chapter 3: Rome and the Arabian Trade Routes

1 Details: Singer, (2007) 6.
2 For instance: *Egyptian Book of the Dead, Papyrus of Nu*, sheet 21, chapter 30, rubric 2.7. ('Anoint the mouth of the body with myrrh unguent and recite the following words of magical power'); *Papyrus of Ani*, plate 5 (servant carrying myrrh and unguent pots). Also: *Old Testament, Song of Solomon*, 3. Era discussed: Singer (2007) 24–5; Peacock, (2006) 1.
3 For instance: Sappho, *To Aphrodite*; Diogenes Laertius, *Life of Pythagoras*, 8.8. Full details: Crone, (1987) 17.
4 Scythian women: Herodotus, 4.75. Babylonian use: 1.198. Discussed: Singer, (2007) 6.
5 Herodotus, 1.183. Babylonian talents: over 30 tons. Also see Pliny, *Natural History*, 12.80.
6 See Herodotus, 1.183.
7 Greek talents: over 13 tons frankincense and over 2 tons of myrrh. See Plutarch, *Alexander*, 25; Pliny, *N.H.* 12.32.62–3.
8 Arrian, *Campaigns of Alexander*, 7.9; 7.19.
9 Seleucid military interests in the Persian Gulf: see Salles, (1996a) 260; 262.
10 Diodorus Siculus, 19.94. Discussed: Crone, (1987) 18.
11 Diodorus Siculus: 'The Gerrhaeans and Minaeans convey all the frankincense and the other aromatic wares that they bring in from southern Arabia to Nabatea and then on to Palestine'. (Diodorus Siculus, 3.42. See also Strabo, *Geography.* 16.4.18). The coffin of a Minaean frankincense merchant named Zayd'il was found at Memphis in Egypt (Late 2nd to early 1st century BC). See Singer, (2007) 13. Dedications from the sanctuary of Artemis on Delos record that Minaean and Hadramaut merchants were visiting the Greek island (Mid 2nd century BC). See Sedov, (2007) 101.
12 Diodorus Siculus, 19.95–6.
13 Discussed: Ray, (1994) 173.
14 Procopius, *Persian Wars,* 1.19.23–4 (6th century AD).
15 Strabo: 'Frankincense and myrrh and other aromatics are bartered between merchants. They arrive in seventy days at Aila which is a city on the furthest recesses of the Red Sea, close to Gaza'. Strabo, *Geog.* 16.4.4. Information possibly derived from Eratosthenes (c. 275–194 BC). See Crone, (1987) 18.
16 Nabateans also travelled to the Yemen. A Sabaean inscription mentions a Nabatean residing in this region presumably for trade. (1st century BC). *RES* 4153. See Sidebotham, (1986a) 93. Communities of Nabateans were also living in Egypt. For instance: fragmentary Ptolemaic inscription records a lease made between a Nabatean priest and a Palmyrene. See Littman and Meredith (1953) no. 81. Discussed: Sidebotham, (1986a) 96.
17 Diodorus Siculus: 'When the Ptolemaic kings in Alexandria opened the [Red Sea] waters to their merchants, the Arabs not only attacked the shipwrecked, but fitting out pirate vessels they preyed upon the voyagers . . . But later they were caught on the high seas by some *quadrireme* warships and punished just as they deserved'. Dio Cassius, 3.43.
18 Strabo: 'The Nabataeans had been peaceful, but then they launched small ships to plunder the vessels of people sailing from Egypt. They paid the penalty when a fleet went over and sacked their country'. Strabo, *Geog.* 16.4.4.
19 See Pliny, *Natural History,* 6.32.144.
20 Strabo, *Geog.* 16.4.21.
21 *Ibid.*
22 Strabo, *Geog.* 16.4.26.
23 The northerlies of the Red Sea Gulf made sailings to Aila difficult and time-consuming. Details: Whitewright, (2007) 85–7.

24 Strabo, *Geog.* 16.4.23 (many ships lost on crossing).
25 *Ibid.*
26 Strabo, *Geog.* 16.4.23. Discussed: Stoneman, (1992) 35; Sidebotham, (2008) 169.
27 *Periplus Maris Erythraei,* 19. Discussed: Millar, (1998) 124.
28 Debate: Young, (2001) 95–6. Conflicting views: Millar, (1998) 124.
29 See *P.M.E.* 19.
30 See Strabo, *Geog.* 16.4.21; 16.2.30–1; Pliny, *N.H.* 6.32.144–6.
31 Strabo, *Geog.* 16.4.24.
32 Discussed: Millar, (1998) 124.
33 Strabo, *Geog.* 16.2.20. Discussed: Millar, (1998) 125.
34 Roads extended from Petra as far as Palmyra. See Pliny, *N.H.* 6.32.
35 Pliny, *N.H.* 6.32. Discussed: Millar, (1998) 126. See: Potts, (1988) 127–62.
36 Strabo, *Geog.* 17.1.13. See Sidebotham, (1986a) 49.
37 Strabo, *Geog.* 16.4.24.
38 Voyages were made from January to September (September favoured). See *P.M.E.* 26.
39 See *P.M.E.* 49.
40 See *P.M.E.* 2.
41 See *P.M.E.* 3.
42 Discussed: Munro, (1996) 406.
43 Pliny, *N.H.* 6.32.145. See also Ptolemy, *Geography* 4.7.
44 Previous merchant visitors had encamped on a nearby headland but barbarian raiders could overrun this site via a causeway. See *P.M.E.* 4.
45 See *P.M.E.* 4.
46 See *P.M.E.* 6.
47 See *P.M.E.* 4.
48 See *P.M.E.* 5.
49 Pliny may be using Juba as a source. He reports: 'The [Ethiopians and Somali peoples] bring ivory in large quantities to Adulis along with rhinoceros horns, hippopotamus hides, tortoise-shell, hawkmoths and slaves'. Hawkmoths are giant colourful insects, possibly a delicacy. See Pliny, *N.H.* 6.34 (Some translations: 'shell', 'apes', and 'slaves').
50 Including linens and double-fringed items, perhaps square scarves or throws. Discussed: Casson, (1989) 111.
51 See *P.M.E.* 6.
52 *Ibid.*
53 Discussed: Casson, (1989) 112.
54 See *P.M.E.* 6.
55 Procopius, *Persian Wars,* 1.19.27–8.
56 Pliny, *N.H.* 6.35.180–1. The team of explorers included centurions (Seneca, *Natural Questions*, 6.8.3–4). See also: Dio Cassius, 63.8.
57 See *P.M.E.* 5.
58 See *P.M.E.* 6.
59 Procopius, *Persian Wars,* 1.19.17–19.
60 See Pliny, *N.H.* 6.34.
61 For instance: see Pliny, *N.H.* 12.69.
62 Casson, (1989) 122–6. African 'cinnamon', see Pliny, *N.H.* 12.42. Discussed: Crone, (1987) 36; 253–63.
63 Pliny, *N.H.* 2.42.88–9.
64 See *P.M.E.* 14.
65 See *P.M.E.* 7.
66 Mundu dealers had a reputation for being 'hard bargainers'. See *P.M.E.* 9.
67 See *P.M.E.* 7–18. Locations discussed: Casson, (1989) 127–30.
68 *P.M.E.* 30. See also: Strabo, *Geog.* 16.4.14; Ptolemy, Geog. 1.9 (the 'Aromatic Lands'). Discussed: Casson, (1989) 129.

69 See Casson, (1989) 132.
70 See *P.M.E.* 14; 16.
71 *P.M.E.* 7–10. Including tunics and inexpensive woollen cloaks from the Arsinoe district of Egypt. See *P.M.E.* 8.
72 See Casson, (1989) 118.
73 See *P.M.E.* 7.
74 See *P.M.E.* 8–10.
75 See *P.M.E.* 14. Roman gemstones: see Casson, (1989) 128.
76 See *P.M.E.* 7.
77 See *P.M.E.* 8.
78 See *P.M.E.* 9.
79 See *P.M.E.* 12–13.
80 See *P.M.E.* 13. Slaves were available at Malao but rarely offered. See *P.M.E.* 8. Somali markets shipped captives in local craft to Ethiopia. See Pliny, *N.H.* 6.34.173–4.
81 See *P.M.E.* 10.
82 See *P.M.E.* 8; 21.
83 See Casson (1989) 287. Estimate: 30 days sailing Red Sea. Pliny indicates ships bound for India spent 26 days visiting markets in the Aden Gulf (the ocean crossing to India took 14 days making it a 40 day sailing from Ocelis to Muziris). See Pliny, *N.H.* 6.26.84; 6.26.104.
84 Rhapta, meaning 'sewn', received its name from the Arabian ships that frequented the port. See *P.M.E.* 15–16. Discussed: Casson, (1989) 134–6; 140–2.
85 The native peoples in the regions surrounding Rhapta lived in large family groups. *Periplus*: 'Large men inhabit this region and they till the soil. Each one has his own place and behaves like a chief' and 'Through continual intercourse and intermarriage Arab skippers and agents have become familiar with the area and its language.' *P.M.E.* 16.
86 See *P.M.E.* 17.
87 Ptolemy, *Geog.* 1.9.
88 *Ibid.* Discussed: Berggren & Jones, (2000) 68.
89 See *P.M.E.* 18.
90 See *P.M.E.* 20.
91 Pliny, *N.H.* 6.34.175–6 (information possibly from Juba).
92 See *P.M.E.* 20.
93 See *P.M.E.* 21.
94 See *P.M.E.* 24.
95 See *P.M.E.* 24.
96 Discussed: Casson, (1989) 153.
97 See *P.M.E.* 24.
98 See *P.M.E.* 22.
99 See *P.M.E.* 23.
100 See *P.M.E.* 24.
101 Stacte was made by crushing and pressing myrrh and mixing the resulting oil with further aromatic ingredients.
102 For instance: *P.M.E.* 31.
103 Details: Casson, (1989) 156.
104 See *P.M.E.* 24.
105 See *P.M.E.* 25.
106 Pliny: 'those sailing to India find that Ocelis is a very convenient place for departure'. Pliny, *N.H.* 6.26.104. Discussed: Casson, (1989) 158.
107 See *P.M.E.* 26. Details: Casson, (1989) 159.
108 Theories discussed: Casson, (1989) 160; Seland, (2005) 60–4. Writing about the Yemen Pliny reports: 'Only Aelius Gallus of the equestrian order has sent Roman forces into this region'. Pliny, *N.H.* 6.32.160.
109 Augustus, *Res Gestae*, 5.26. Campaign described: Strabo, *Geog.* 16.4.22–4. Mentioned:

Pliny, N.H. 6.32.160–1, Josephus, *Jewish Antiquities*, 15.9.3; Dio Cassius, 53.29. Discussed: Sidebotham, (1986a) 590–4; Seland, (2005) 61.

110 Strabo: 'From their trafficking of incense the Sabaeans and the Gerraeans have become richest of all the Arabians. They consequently have a vast store of both gold and silver articles including couches, tripods, bowls, and drinking-vessels. They have very costly houses with doors, walls and ceilings decorated with ivory, gold and silver, and set with precious stones.' Strabo *Geog.* 16.4.19. See also: Pliny, *N.H.* 6.32.162. Discussed: Singer, (2007) 10.

111 Strabo: 'The Sabaeans are a very large tribe in whose country myrrh, frankincense and cinnamon are produced' and 'From the Sabaeans the Arabs who live close to one another receive in continuous succession the loads of aromatics and deliver them to their neighbours as far as Syria and Mesopotamia.' Also: 'The Sabaean people engage partly in farming and partly in the traffic of aromatics, including both local [Arabian] goods and goods from Ethiopia. To get the latter they sail across the [Red Sea] straits in leather boats.' Strabo, *Geog.* 16.4.19. Discussed: Crone, (1987) 23; Groom, (1981) 243.

112 Sabaeans as the military objective. See Horace, *Odes*, 1.29. Frankincense and myrrh were connected with kingship and divinity. See *Matthew*, 2.11.

113 Strabo, *Geog.* 16.4.22.

114 Strabo: 'Gallus built more than eighty boats, biremes and triremes at Clysma . . . before he realized that he had been thoroughly deceived.' Strabo, *Geog.* 16.4.23.

115 Roman army (10,000 troops). Nabateans allies (1,000 soldiers commanded by a vizier named Syllaeus). King Herod of Judaea also sent a contingent of 500 Jewish troops. Strabo, *Geog.* 16.4.23. Discussed: Sidebotham, (1989) 493–4.

116 See Strabo, *Geog.* 16.4.24; Dio Cassius, 53.29. Discussed: Sidebotham, (1989) 493–4.

117 See *P.M.E.* 23. Pliny refers to 'the ambassadors that have come from Arabia in my own lifetime'. They possibly offered diplomatic gifts that included whole branches from the myrrh tree. See Pliny, *N.H.* 12.31.

118 Ptolemy, *Geography*. 6.7. Discussed: Casson, (1989) 159. A Greek temple inscription from Coptos records that a resident from Aden was visiting Egypt in AD 70, probably for trade purposes (*IGRR*. 1.1172). Details: Sidebotham, (1986a) 99.

119 Discussed: Sedov, (1996) 23–4; (2007) 100.

120 See Tomber, (2008) 105; Singer, (2007) 22; 25.

121 See Sedov, (1996) 12.

122 The black rock with its ominous ruins has become known in modern times as Husn al-Ghurab or 'Fortress of the Crows'. Discussed: Sedov, (2007) 71; 101; Singer, (2007) 24.

123 Sometime in antiquity a violent fire destroyed the incense storerooms, carbonising large amounts of their precious contents. Amongst the debris archaeologists found the remains of large palm baskets and woven bags used to carry and store the collected frankincense crop. Details of site see Sedov, (2007) 74; 76; 90–1.

124 Details: Tomber, (2008) 103; Sedov, (2007) 73–4; 101.

125 See Sedov, (2007) 74; 91–2; Singer, (2007) 24.

126 See *P.M.E.* 27. See Casson, (1989) 163; Singer, (2007) 23.

127 See *P.M.E.* 27; 36. See Sedov, (2007) 99.

128 Discussed: Sedov, (2007) 60; 78; 102.

129 See Sedov, (1996) 25; (2007) 78.

130 Sedov, (2007) 76; 78; 102. Pottery evidence can only be suggestive. Some merchants favoured perishable containers; others re-used foreign vessels for moving local produce.

131 See *P.M.E.* 28.

132 Wheat intended for Roman subjects resident at the port or for limited market exchange.

133 Mostly Coan-style amphorae produced in Italy, Egypt and the Greek east (Late 1st century BC – Mid 2nd century AD). See Sedov, (2007) 78. Some of the Roman amphorae may have carried wheat. See Sedov, (1996) 24; (2007) 101–2.

134 Details: Sedov, (1996) 12; 15; (2007) 76; 78; 101.

135 Discussed: Singer, (2007) 23; Tomber, (2008) 104.
136 Manufactured from 15 BC to 15 AD. See Sedov, (1996) 15; 60.
137 The stamp impression 'AGATE' would identify the manufacturer as AGATHEMERUS (NAEVI) who owned workshops in and around Catania. See Sedov, (1996) 60.
138 Details: Sedov, (2007) 78.
139 Details: Tomber, (2008) 105.
140 See *P.M.E.* 28. See Dalby, (2000) 195.
141 See Casson, (1989) 164–5.
142 Local pottery of Qana known as *zirs* probably used to store food produce. See Sedov, (2007) 76; 102.
143 See Sedov, (1996) 25.
144 Peacock, (2006) 28; 62.
145 Details: *Ibid.* 30–1
146 Details: *Ibid.* 29; 59; 62.
147 By the time Berenice began functioning as a loading harbour Qana had replaced Aden as the centre for incense trade.
148 See *P.M.E.* 29. Discussed: Singer, (2007) 8.
149 A different account is offered by Pliny, *N.H.* 12.30 (information possibly received from Juba, c. 48 BC–AD 23). See information in *N.H.* 12.31. Discussed: Singer, (2007) 10.
150 See *P.M.E.* 29.
151 See *P.M.E.* 27; 30.
152 *Ibid.*
153 Details: Tomber, (2008) 106.
154 Details: Singer, (2007) 23.
155 Discussed: Sedov, (1996) 24.
156 See *P.M.E.* 32. Indian goods destined for Far Side markets on return sailings to Egypt. See *P.M.E.* 14.
157 See *P.M.E.* 32.
158 Pliny, *N.H.* 12.32.58.
159 Details: Singer, (2007) 22.
160 Merchants from the Yemen were visiting Syria in the Augustan era, but the ventures that were taking them into this region are not described. They may have been mostly maritime (via the Red Sea then overland through Petra). See Strabo, *Geog.* 16.2.20; 16.4.4.
161 Strabo did not know about direct routes into the Yemen. Gallus was surprised to find the journey from Sabaean territory to the Nabatean kingdom could be completed in only 60 days (See Strabo, *Geog.* 16.4.24). The *Periplus* was unaware of the incense trail and does not mention a second frankincense harvest.
162 See Singer, (2007) 22.
163 Pliny, *N.H.* 12.32.63. Discussed: Crone, (1987) 19.
164 Details: Singer, (2007) 12.
165 Pliny, *N.H.* 12.32.63–4.
166 *Ibid.*
167 Pliny: 'Frankincense can only be exported through the country of the Gebanitae (Qataban) and accordingly a tax is paid to the king of that people.' (Pliny, *N.H.* 6.32.64). Timna was a large city that had 65 large temples within its districts (see Pliny, *N.H.* 6.32.153–4). Roman finds at Timna include Italian and Syrian *sigillata* (Augustan era), glazed wares from Egypt and Asia Minor. Details: Tomber, (2008) 105. Discussed: Singer, (2007) 25.
168 Pliny: 'The growers of myrrh pay a fourth part of their stocks to the Gebanitae (Qataban) king. Myrrh is bought indiscriminately by the common people and packed into bags which are later sorted out by our perfumers.' See Pliny, *N.H.* 12.35.
169 Details: Singer, (2007) 15–6.
170 See Singer, (2007) 13.
171 Pliny, *N.H.* 12.30.

172 Discussed: Singer, (2007) 16. Gerrha connection (Persian Gulf; Hellenic era): Dio Siculus, 3.42; Strabo, *Geog.* 16.4.18. Petra connection: Pliny, *N.H.* 6.32.144–6.
173 Estimate: 69–88 days travel. See Groom, (1981) 213. Discussed: Millar, (1998) 123–4; Stoneman, (1992) 35.
174 Pliny: 'Timna is 1,485 miles distant from the town of Gaza in Judea on the Mediterranean coast. The journey is divided into 65 stages with halts for camels. The king's secretaries, and the guards, and their attendants, and the gate-keepers and even the servants, all take a portion of this incense.' See Pliny, *N.H.* 12.32.65.
175 Discussed: Millar, (1998) 125–6; Crone, (1987) 19.
176 Pliny, *N.H.* 12.32.65.
177 See Millar, (1998) 124.
178 See Sedov, (2007) 94. Caravan routes from Petra to the Persian Gulf covered a distance of at least 1,300 kilometres. Discussed: Millar, (1998) 126.
179 See Peacock, (2006) 62.
180 Discussed: Bennet, (1997) 58; Young, (2001) 117–120; Stoneman, (1992) 38.
181 Julius Apollinaris a secretary of Cyrenaica III. See *P. Mich.* 466. Discussed: Elton, (1996) 80. Perhaps similar to the Rhinocoloura route mentioned by Strabo. See Strabo, *Geog.* 16.24.
182 Details: Sidebotham, (1986a) 93–5; (1988) 497.
183 The Nabatean 'Troglodytes'. See Pliny, *N.H.* 12.44.
184 Pliny: 'The right of regulating the sale of the cinnamon belongs solely to the king of the Gebanites (Qataban) who opens the market for it by public proclamation'. See Pliny, *N.H.* 12.32.93.
185 Pliny, *N.H.* 12.32.93–4.
186 See *P.M.E.* 30.
187 *Periplus*: 'Trade with Socotra used to be carried on by some of the shippers from Muza and also by ships that chanced upon the island on the return sailing from Barygaza and the Malabar Coast'. *P.M.E.* 31.
188 Possible stonewall boundary divisions between commercial plantations. Details: Sedov, (2007) 100.
189 See *P.M.E.* 30–1.
190 Details: Casson, (1989) 168–9.
191 See *P.M.E.* 31. Discussed: Casson, (1989) 169.
192 *Periplus:* 'The region is under the rule of a governor called Mapharitis and by ancient right it is subject to the [Homerite] kingdom of Arabia. Merchants from Muza have been given Rhapta as a grant from the king and they collect taxes from it'. *P.M.E.* 16. Discussed: Casson, (1989) 140–2.
193 Ptolemy, *Geog.* 4.8.
194 Centurions stationed outpost near Berenice (Nicanor made deliveries to a military granary). See *O. Petr.* No. 245 (AD 62). Details: Sidebotham, (2008) 189–90; (1986a) 55; Adams, (2008) 224. (Also note *ostraca*: *BE* 50). Naval station at Myos Hormos (Augustan era). See Strabo, *Geog.* 17.1.45. An ostraca from Myos Hormos mentions a man named Satornilus Tessararius who was possibly a military helmsman. Details: Sidebotham, (1986a) 69.
195 Eutropius: 'Trajan fitted out a fleet for the Erythraean Sea so that he might use it to lay waste to the coasts of India'. Eutropius, 8.3. Discussed: Adams, (2007) 35.
196 Carved on a rectangular block of calcareous stone from a small to medium sized monument. Exact modern location: Site of Gharrain, located west of Farasan town. Details: Phillips, (2004) 245.
197 See Phillips, (2004) 244.
198 Details: *Ibid.*
199 Explanations for the 'Hercules' command: legends of the region (See Agatharchides, 5.97) or the emblem of the garrison (see Phillips, (2004) 248).
200 See Phillips, (2004) 247.
201 Pliny reports that Annius Plocamus, 'gained a tax contract for the Red Sea from the Roman

treasury' (See Pliny, 6.26.84). In a list of income received by the Roman treasury Statius refers to wealth 'gathered by the divers who search the eastern seas' (Statius, *Silvae*, 3.3.89). This could be a reference to Roman controlled pearl fisheries in the Red Sea (See Millar, (2003) 69–70). The Farasan Command could have been established to protect this lucrative state business.

202 See *P.M.E.* 23.

203 See *P.M.E.* 16; 31.

204 See *P.M.E.* 19.

205 For the significance of nearby Ocelis: *P.M.E.* 25; Pliny, *N.H.* 6.104.

206 Possibility of other Roman 'relay' stations, see Phillips, (2004) 246.

207 Discussed: Phillips, (2004) 239; 248. Theory that Cornelius was connected with the Gallus campaign, see Bowersock, (1983) 148–53.

208 Decline discussed: Crone, (1987) 24; 27–8; Young, (2001) 123–35.

Notes to Chapter 4: Trade Routes through Asia and the Silk Road Connection

1 The German phrase 'Die Seidenstrassen' was first used in the 19th century by a geographer named Baron Ferdinand von Richthofen (1833–1905). Ferdinand von Richthofen was a relative of the notorious German fighter ace 'The Red Barron'. See Christian, (2000) 2.

2 Huan Kuan, *Yan Tie Lun (Discourses on Salt and Iron)*, 14.70 (an early stage in the development of Xiongnu society). Quoted and discussed: Yu, (1967) 40. (This passage of the *Yan Tie Lun* is not available in all translations).

3 Details: Yu, (1967) 41–2.

4 Discussed: *Ibid.* 36; 46.

5 Sima Qian, *Shiji* (*Records of the Grand Historian*) 110.8 (170 BC).

6 Discussed: Yu, (1967) 11; 13–4; 37; 43–4; 46. Some Xiongnu forces who surrendered to the Chinese were subsequently incorporated into the Han army (*Ibid.* 14).

7 Fan Ye, *Han Shu* (*History of the Former Han Dynasty*) 94.2. Details: Yu, (1967) 45–7.

8 See table in Yu, (1967) 47. Discussed: Raschke, (1978) 615; 617–8.

9 Fed by Han subsidies and sustained by Chinese trade, the southern Xiongnu population rapidly increased (60,000 in the mid 1st century BC increased to 237,300 by AD 90). See *Hou Hanshu,* 199.6. Discussed: Yu, (1967) 50–1.

10 Suggested Han policy: 'We should immediately open up many large-sized border markets in locations of strategic importance. In each of these market places sufficient military forces must be stationed for our self protection.' Chi I, *Hsin Shu,* 4.41.

11 Huan Kuan, *Yan Tie Lun* (*Discourses on Salt and Iron*), 2.14. They also smuggled supplies of contraband items (Chinese iron). Details: Lui, (1988) 14; Yu, (1967) 121–3; 191.

12 See *Hou Hanshu,* 120.2 (Wuhuan barbarians from the northwest frontiers). Details: Yu, (1967) 31.

13 Han: 'The Xiongnu need the border markets and they have sought desperately to obtain them from us, even resorting to force'. Chi I, *Hsin Shu,* 4.41 (see: 4.5). Quoted in Sinor, (1990) 119.

14 See Yu, (1967) 100. Discussed: Franck & Brownstone, (1986) 107. Markets used for control: 'Our markets beneath the wall will surely swarm with the Xiongnu. If their kings and generals try to force the population to return to the north, the people will turn and attack their rulers'. Jia Yi, *Hsin Shu,* 4.41.

15 Theories: Raschke (1978) 622–3; Ball, (2000) 138–9.

16 'Sycthic' motifs in archaeological finds, see Christian, (2000) 15.

17 The modern name 'Taklamakan' is derived from the Uigur language meaning: 'Go in and you'll never come out'.

18 See Franck & Brownstone, (1986) 92; 101; Lui, (1988) 16.

19 See Thapar, (2002) 238; Yu, (1967) 151.

20 See *Periplus Maris Erythraei*, 64.
21 *Tung-kuan Han-chi,* 143. Yu, (1967) 212.
22 See details and discussion in Thapar, (2002) 255.
23 *Hou Hanshu,* 77.4. See Yu, (1967) 138.
24 *Chuan Hou-Han Wen,* 25.4 (events in the late 1st century AD). Discussed: Yu, (1967) 195; Lui, (1988) 16.
25 See Yu, (1967) 151.
26 See Waugh, (2004) 1.
27 Distances Sogdia to China: outer Han frontiers (at least 2,500 kilometres); the Han capitol Luoyang (perhaps 4,000 kilometres). The Arabian caravan trail from Dhofar to Gaza covered a distance of at least 3,000 kilometres.
28 *Sogdian Ancient Letter,* no. 2.
29 *Ibid.*
30 *Ibid.* Discussed: Waugh, (2004) 1.
31 *Sogdian Ancient Letter,* no. 2.
32 *Ibid.*
33 *Ibid.*
34 *Ibid.*
35 *Sogdian Ancient Letter,* No. 5.
36 Strabo, *Geography.* 2.1.15.
37 Pliny, *Natural History* 6.5.
38 Strabo, *Geog.* 11.12.17.
39 Discussed: Charlesworth, (1924) 104.
40 Pliny, *N.H.* 6.19. Myth in region: anchor of the Argo on display at Phasis. See Arrian, *Periplus of the Black Sea*, 9.2–3.
41 Caspian ships were not comparable to the Greco-Roman freighters that plied the busy sea-lanes of the Mediterranean and Black Sea. Strabo: 'The Caspian Sea has received little attention because the governors of this region are barbarians and all of the neighbouring country is full of brigands and nomads who occupy deserted regions'. See Strabo, *Geog.* 11.7.2. Discussed: Warmington, (1928) 28.
42 Strabo, *Geog.* 11.2.1.
43 Strabo: 'The Colchic tribes all speak different languages because of their stubbornness and ferocity. They live in scattered groups and do not communicate much with one another'. See Strabo, *Geog.* 11.2.1. Discussed: Warmington, (1928) 26–7.
44 The Roman governor Arrian reports that a 'secure fort with war engines' was maintained at Phasis (2nd century AD). See Arrian, *Periplus of the Black Sea*: '400 select troops are quartered for the safety of those who sail' (9.3); settlement of veterans at Phasis (9.5); further garrison at Dioscurias (Sebastopolis) (10.3).
45 *ILS* 8795.
46 Caspian rock inscription (Azerbaijan): *AE* 1951 263 (Dating to the reign of Domitian, AD 81–96). Details: Whittaker, (2000) 309.
47 The Roman garrisons would have demanded regular provisions and this required secure communication routes.
48 Significance of the Syrian routes into Mesopotamia discussed in Millar, (1998) 129–30; 136; Young, (2001) 187; 194.
49 Discussed: Charlesworth, (1924) 100–1; Young, (2001) 187.
50 See Philostratus, *Life of Apollonius of Tyana,* 1.20. Discussed: Elton, (1996) 89.
51 Josephus, *Jewish Antiquities,* 18.9.1. Discussed: Elton, (1996) 99.
52 *New Testament, Acts,* 2.9.
53 Samuel's home city was Nehardea near Babylon, but he was sent to Nisibis to be educated. Judah Ben Bathyra was an adult before the destruction of the Jewish Temple in AD 70 and Samuel Ben Abba was still alive in the mid second century AD. Discussed: Young, (2001) 190.

54 *Midrash Samuel*, 10. Translation: Newman, (1945) 204.
55 Procopius, *Secret History*, 25.14–5.
56 Cotton and Cockle, (1995) no. 33. Details: Millar, (1998) 129.
57 Discussed: *Ibid.* 126.
58 Pliny, *N.H.* 6.32.143–4.
59 Strabo, *Geog.* 16.1.27.
60 *Ibid.*
61 *Ibid.*
62 Discussed: Millar, (1998) 126–7. Isidore suggests other routes in his *Parthian Stations*. See Isidore, 1. Discussed: Charlesworth, (1924) 101. Routes used by Trajan in his Parthian campaign, see Dio Cassius, 68.21–2; 68.26.
63 Pliny, *N.H.* 6.30.122–3.
64 *Ibid.*
65 *Inv.* 9.6. Details: Young, (2001) 190.
66 Strabo: 'The Parthian kings are accustomed to spend the winters at Ctesiphon because of the good climate, but because of ancient tradition they spend their summers at Ecbatana and Hyrcania.' See Strabo, *Geog.* 16.1.16.
67 *Ibid.*
68 Pliny, *N.H.* 6.30.122–3.
69 Strabo, *Geog.* 16.1.5; 16.1.16.
70 Pliny, *N.H.* 6.30.123.
71 *CIS* 2.3913 (Dated AD 137). Discussed: Millar, (1998) 171; Matthews, (1984) 157–80.
72 Discussed in Young, (2001) 139; 149–57; 168; Gawlikowski, (1994) 32–3.
73 Appian, *Civil Wars*, 5.9. Discussed: Young, (2001) 136; Gawlikowski, (1994) 27; Stoneman, (1992) 31; Millar, (1998) 131.
74 *Inv.* 9.6 (Seleucia: AD 19); *Inv.* 9.11 (Babylon: AD 24). Discussed: Young, (2001) 140; Stoneman, (1992) 45.
75 See Young, (2001) 139.
76 See Stoneman, (1992) 45.
77 *Inv.* 10.40. Discussed: Young (2001) 140.
78 Pliny, *N.H.* 5.21.88.
79 Discussed: Young, (2001) 136–7; 143; Elton, (1996) 90–2.
80 Discussed: Stoneman, (1992) 45.
81 Palmyran trade routes, see Young, (2001) 148; Gawlikowski, (1994) 31.
82 Compare: Samarkand to China (over 2,500 kilometres); Arabian trail from Dhofar to Gaza (at least 3,000 kilometres); Egyptian route from Coptos to Berenice (370 kilometres).
83 Josephus, *Jewish Antiquities*, 8.6.1.
84 Estimates: eight days journey from Antioch to Palmyra. Then six days from Palmyra to Dura-Europos (closest town on the Euphrates). Then 12 days from Dura to Bablyon. See Millar, (1998) 130–1.
85 For instance: *CIS* 2.3917. See Stoneman, (1992) 45.
86 In the catalogues consulted by Young, (2001) 140.
87 Dio Cassius: 'Trajan easily subdued the land of Mesene on the Tigris River and won over their king Athambelus . . . Athambelus remained loyal to Trajan even though he was ordered to pay tribute and the inhabitants of Charax received the Emperor kindly'. See Dio Cassius, 68.28. Discussed: Young, (2001) 145–6.
88 Dio Cassius, 68.29.
89 See *Ibid.* 68.29–32.
90 See *CIS* 2.3973; *CIL* 2.3934. Details: Elton, (1996) 91–3. A detachment of Palmyrene soldiers appears at the strategic city of Dura-Europos (*Dura*, 7–8, no. 909). Details: Elton, (1996) 91–3. An inscription refers to a Nabatean cavalryman serving with Palmyrene troops at Hit (AD 132) (See *CIS* 2.3973). Details: Young, (2001) 158–9.
91 Details: Gawlikowski, (1985) 15–26; Elton, (1996) 93.

92 Details: Young, (2001) 149.
93 Route from Antioch via Palmyra to Mesopotamia. Egyptian route: see Pliny, *N.H.* 6.26.101–4.
94 Quoted and discussed: Millar, (1998) 133.
95 *SEG* 7.138. Discussed: Young, (2001) 161; Elton, (1996) 93.
96 Thilouana: *Inv.* 10.38; Orodes: *Inv.* 10.114; Augustan Temple: *CIS* 2.3917. Discussed: Elton, (1996) 94.
97 In catalogues consulted by Young, (2001) 144.
98 See Appian, *Civil Wars,* 5.9.
99 Discussed: Elton, (1996) 91–2. Theories examined: Young, (2001) 154–6.
100 For instance: *CIS* 2.3948 (AD 193). Details: Millar, (1998) 132.
101 See *Ibid.* 137.
102 *Inv.* 10.81. Discussed: Elton, (1996) 91–3.
103 Strabo suggests the Scentae shepherds could become 'brigands' when pastures failed (*Geog.* 16.1.26). Strabo: '[Upper Euphrates:] it is hard to travel among communities who are strong willed. It is hard to establish a common standard of tribute that is advantageous for the merchant' (*Geog.* 16.1.27).
104 See: *Inv.* 10.38 (Phorath); *Inv.* 10.112 (Mesene). Discussed: Stoneman, (1992) 45.
105 Theories: Young, (2001) 144–5.
106 Details: *Ibid.*
107 Pliny, *N.H.* 6.32.146. Discussed: Young, (2001) 189.
108 Description of Charax see Stoneman: 'One may imagine an imposing commercial quarter, like Corporation Square at Ostia, the port of Rome, with offices of all the merchants surrounding a courtyard where cameleers, retailers, armed escorts, and the gaudy-robed merchants themselves would jostle and bargain among their bales of raw, dyed, and woven wares'. Stoneman, (1992) 45.
109 *The Hymn of the Pearl* which appears in the Syriac *Acts of Thomas*, 109. Discussed: Stoneman, (1992) 45; Millar, (1998) 128.
110 Pliny, *N.H.* 6.31.139–40.
111 Dio Cassius, 68.29.1. Discussed: Millar, (1998) 128.
112 Discussed: *Ibid.* 136; Salles, (1995) 140.
113 There is currently no evidence that the Palmyrenes extended their trade ventures south to reach markets in the Deccan Plateau or the Tamil lands.
114 *Inv.* 10.96. See Elton, (1996) 91–2.
115 See Colledge, (1976) 76, pl. 103.
116 Pliny, *N.H.* 6.32.149.
117 See *P.M.E.* 36. Discussed: Casson, (1989) 180–1.
118 Persian Gulf and Parthian territories see: Ptolemy, *Geog.* 6.1–5.
118 Views: Stoneman, (1992) 39; Young, (2001) 142.
119 Discussed: Stauffer, (1996) 425–30.
120 See Pliny, *N.H.* 6.32.148.
121 See *P.M.E.* 39; 49.
122 See *P.M.E.* 24; 28.
123 See *P.M.E.* 36.
124 An expense of 300 'old gold' aurei (AD 193). See *Inv.* 3.28.
125 Persian Gulf exports to India and Arabia. See *Periplus*: 'Persian pearls, purple cloth, native clothing, wine, large amounts of dates, gold, slaves' (*P.M.E.* 36). Roman slaves trafficked into Mesopotamia: see Philostratus, *Life of Apollonius of Tyana*, 1.20.
125 Views: Young, (2001) 193.
126 *Inv.* 10.29 (AD 161). Discussed: Young, (2001) 149.
127 Possible significance of Edessa, see Young, (2001) 149; 193–4. Tyre cloth-dying industry, see Strabo, *Geog.* 16.2.22–3; Pliny, *N.H.* 5.16.76–7.
128 Discussed: Millar, (1998) 134.

129 *Acts,* 21.1–8.
130 *Acts,* 27.1–6.
131 Galen, *On the mixtures and properties of simple drugs,* 12.215. Quoted with discussion: Millar, (1998) 134.
132 Quoted and discussed: Young, (2001) 146.
133 See Potts, (1996) 280.
134 According to catalogues consulted by Young, (2001) 147.
135 Views: Young, (2001) 147.
136 Inscription dating from mid to late 2nd century AD. Details: Sidebotham, (1986a) 95; Young, (2001) 80–1; 142; Stoneman, (1992) 45.
137 See *OGIS* 663 (AD 154–5). Zabdalas or a relative (theory tenuous).
138 Theories: Sidebotham, (1986a) 95–6; Young, (2001) 80–1.
139 Quoted and discussed: Young, (2001) 80–1.
140 Details: Sidebotham, (1986a) 95–6.
141 Details: *CIS* 3.3910.
142 Discussed: Sidebotham, (1989) 497.
143 See Sedov, (1996) 15.
144 The Chinese *Weilue* describes voyages around Arabia (in the era between AD 116 and AD 164). The author writes: 'From the city of Angu (Gerrha), on the frontier of Anxi (Parthia), you take a boat and go directly across to Haixi (Egypt). With favourable winds it takes two months'. See *Weilue,* 11 (account perhaps influenced by *Hou Hanshu,* 88.10).
145 See *Justinian Digest,* 39.4.16.7. A rock inscription from a coronation site near Shabwa in southern Arabia indicates that Palmyrenes, Indians and Babylonians were visiting the area in 235 AD (*RES* 2771; 3022). Discussed: Hoyland, (2001) 94.
146 By this era, the Nabateans were subjects of the Roman Empire. Their trade voyages into the Persian Gulf were 'Roman'. The *Weilue* writes: '*Da Qin* (the Roman Empire) trades with Anxi (Parthia) across the middle of the sea (Indian Ocean)'. See *Weilue,* 12.
147 Discussed: Sidebotham, (1986a) 66.
148 See *OGIS* 639. Details: Sidebotham, (1986a) 95–6; (1996a) 198.
149 See *Ibid.*
150 Theories: Sidebotham, (2008) 191–2.
151 Caravan ventures resumed by c. AD 188–9 (*Inv.* 10.18); definitely by AD 193 (*CIS* 2.3948). The last securely dated caravan inscription is AD 257/8. Details: Millar, (1998) 131.
152 Details: Elton, (1996) 95.
153 Persian Royal Road: Herodotus, 5.52–4; 8.98. Parthian use: see Strabo, *Geog.* 16.1.16.
154 *Ibid.* 11.5.8.
155 *Hou Hanshu,* 88.12.
156 See Appendix A. *Weilue,* 12 (information dating AD 116–164).
157 *Hou Hanshu,* 88.12. Discussed: Hill, *Notes to the Hou Hanshu* (2003). Account possibly received from Roman merchants who visited China in AD 166. Views: Thorley, (1969) 214; Ferguson, (1978) 594.
158 Discussed: Young, (2001) 101; 136; Berggren & Jones, (2000) 27; Millar, (1998) 120–1.
159 See Isidore, 2–13. Views: Charlesworth, (1924) 102–3; Miller, (1969) 120–4; 136; Ferguson, (1978) 587.
160 Ptolemy, *Geography* 1.11.
161 Compare: Palmyra to Charax (over 1,000 kilometres); Dhofar to Gaza (over 3,000 kilometres).
162 Ptolemy, *Geog.* 1.11; 6.13.
163 Possibly midpoint between Ferghana and Kashghar. Discussed: Warmington, (1928) 23; Charlesworth, (1924) 104; Miller, (1969) 127–31; Ferguson, (1978) 594; Ball, (2000) 134.
164 See *P.M.E.* 39; 64.
165 See details and discussion in Kumar, (2005) 50–2.
166 See Pulleyblank, (1999) 71.

167 See Thorley, (1971) 80.
168 See *Hou Hanshu,* 88.1.

Notes to Chapter 5: Diplomatic Contacts with the Distant East

1 Discussed: Warmington, (1928) 35–6.
2 Augustus, *Res Gestae*, 31.
3 Strabo, *Geography.* 2.5.12.
4 Propertius, 2.27.5 ('If we march on Parthia'); 3.5.47–8 ('War is gratifying, bring Crassus' standards home'); 3.4 ('Bring Parthian trophies to the Temple of Jupiter. Avenge the disaster of Crassus. Fulfil Roman destiny!'); 4.3.67 ('When the land of the Parthian brood is conquered'). Discussed: Mattern, (1999) 186.
5 Suetonius, *Augustus*, 21.
6 Paulus Orosius, 6.21.19 (5th century AD).
7 See Warmington, (1928) 36. Greek legacy in northern India, see *Periplus Maris Erythraei*, 41; 47.
8 See Arrian, *Campaigns of Alexander,* 5.18–22; 5.24.
9 Strabo, *Geog.* 15.1.73.
10 Dio Cassius, 54.9. Discussed: Warmington, (1928) 36.
11 Strabo, *Geog.* 15.1.73.
12 Strabo, *ibid.* Dio Cassius: 'They gave Augustus a boy who, like our statues of Hermes, had no shoulders or arms'. See Dio Cassius, 54.9.
13 Strabo: 'The gifts included large vipers, a serpent ten cubits in length, and a river tortoise three cubits in length, and a partridge larger than a vulture'. See Strabo, *Geog.* 15.1.73.
14 Stories of the phoenix connected with India. See Philostratus, 3.49.
15 Dio Cassius, 54.9.
16 Strabo, *Geog.* 15.1.73.
17 Strabo: 'Gifts of honour were given to Caesar Augustus and an Indian sophist burnt himself up at Athens, just as Calanus had done when he made a similar spectacular display before Alexander'. Strabo, *Geog.* 15.1.4.
18 Rome's eastern ambitions: Horace, *Odes*, 1.12.53–6 (Parthia and beyond); Virgil, *Georgics*, 2.172 (India). Impact of imperial propaganda: Horace, *Carmen Saeculare*, 55–56 ('Now the Indo-Scythians and the proud Indians seek his rulings'); Propertius, 2.10.15 ('Emperor, India bows its head to your triumph'); 3.4.1 ('Our god Caesar Augustus plots war against rich India'); 2.9.29 ('What if I was a solider to be sent to India?').
19 Augustus: 'I *forced* the Parthians to return to me the spoils and standards of three Roman armies and to seek as supplicants the friendship of the Roman people'. See Augustus, *Res Gestae*, 29. Impact of propaganda: Horace, *Odes*, 3.5.4 ('Parthians bow before his throne').
20 Dio Cassius, 54.9. See also: Pliny, *Natural History,* 8.25; Suetonius, *Augustus*, 43.
21 Details: Campbell, (1995) 6.
22 Strabo, *Geog.* 15.1.4. Discussed: Warmington, (1928) 36.
23 Views: Warmington, (1928) 60.
24 Florus, 2.34–62. Discussed: Warmington, (1928) 36.
25 Florus: 'Ambassadors who sought friendship included the Seres' (Florus, *Roman History*, 2.34.62). The soft 'ch' occurring in the name 'Chera' could have been confused with the similar sounding 'Seres'. Argument: Warmington, (1928) 37.
26 See Pliny, *N.H.* 6.26.101–2. *P.M.E.* 49; 56.
27 See Josephus, *Jewish Antiquities*, 19.8.2.
28 Details: De Romanis, (1997) 107–8.
29 For instance: 'The "gifts" of gold brought by the large ships . . . Kuttuvan presents to visitors, the rare products'. See *Purananuru*, 343.1–10.
30 *Peutinger Map,* Segment 11. A caravan inscription from Palmyra records how a wealthy

businessman used his own initiative and finances to found an Augustan temple in the Parthian city of Vologesias. See *CIS* 2.3917. Discussed: Elton, (1996) 94.

31 Roman merchant contact with the Saka court, see *P.M.E.* 49.

32 See *P.M.E.* 43; 52.

33 See Pliny, *N.H.* 6.24.84–91. Some of Pliny's information on trade voyages to India dates to this contact (AD 48–52). See *N.H.* 6.26.101–6. Details: De Romanis, (1997) 201.

34 Pliny, *N.H.* 6.24.84.

35 Sinhalese unfamiliar with denarii further suggesting that Roman coin exports to the Tamil lands was mainly in gold bullion.

36 Pliny, *N.H.* 6.24.84–5.

37 *Ibid.*

38 *Mahavamsa*, 11.20. Details: Weerakkody, (1997) 57–8.

39 Pliny, *N.H.* 6.24.85.

40 Theories: Weerakkody, (1997) 57.

41 Also see: Pliny, *N.H.* 32.11.

42 Bhatikabhaya ruled AD 38–66. Details: De Romanis, (1997) 192; Weerakkody, (1997) 53.

43 Details: De Romanis, (1997) 189; 201.

44 *Dipavamsa,* 21.13.

45 *Mahavamsa,* 34.47.

46 *Vamsatthappakasini*, 104–11 (7th to 13th century AD). Details: De Romanis, (1997) 190.

47 Details: De Romanis, (1997) 227–8.

48 See Strabo, *Geog.* 2.5.32. Pliny describes Sri Lanka: 'banished by nature beyond the confines of the world'. See Pliny, *N.H.* 6.24.89.

49 Pliny: 'the Sinhalese told us there was greater wealth in their own country than in ours'. Pliny, *N.H.* 6.24.89. Issues discussed: Weerakkody, (1997) 59–63; De Romanis, (1997) 201.

50 Discussed: Mattern, (1999) 174–5.

51 Theories: Richmond, (1963) 44.

52 Quoted and discussed: Matthews, (1984) 164.

53 See Pliny, *N.H.* 37.11.45–6.

54 *Historia Augusta, Firmus,* 3.

55 *Historia Augusta, Aurelian,* 28–9.

56 Tacitus, *Annals*, 14.25.

57 *Ibid.*

58 Views: Schmitthenner, (1979) 102.

59 A 'counter-China' at the western end of the known world. See Pulleyblank, (1999) 71.

60 *Hou Hanshu,* 88.11.

61 *Hou Hanshu,* 88.12.

62 *Weilue,* 11.

63 Pliny, *N.H.* 34.41. Discussed: Leslie & Gardiner, (1996) 121–4. Steel available via Indian markets. See *Justinian Digest*, 39.4.16.7 ('Indian iron').

64 Plutarch: 'Crassus led the army through the midst of plains that had no trees, no water, and no limit anywhere within sight . . . only billows of desert that might envelope an army' (Plutarch, *Crassus,* 22). An Armenian advisor quipped: 'Romans you are not in Campania now'.

65 Parthian steel: 'Suddenly the enemy dropped their coverings and exposed their armour. Shining helmets and breastplates, their steel weapons glittering and their horses clad in plates of bronze and steel'. (Plutarch, *Crassus,* 24). 'The Roman thrust attacks were done with small and feeble spears against leather and steel breastplates.' (*Ibid.* 25); 'The spears which the Parthians thrust into the Roman cavalry were heavy with steel, and they had the force to pierce through two men at once.' (*Ibid.* 27).

66 Plutarch: 'When urged to charge the mail-clad horsemen of the enemy, the Romans showed that their hands were pined to their shields by the arrows and their feet nailed to

the ground. They were helpless either for flight or for self-defence'. Plutarch, *Crassus,* 25. (Connotations of crucifixion: a criminal's death). Battle discussed: Man, (2008) 160.

67 Plutarch, *Crassus,* 25. Dio Cassius: 'The arrows hitting them from all sides, killed many men and left many others useless for battle. Men were struck in their eyes by these missiles, arrows pierced their hands and punched through their armour into their bodies'. Dio Cassius, 40.21.

68 See Plutarch, *Crassus*, 28–31; Dio Cassius, 40.25–8.

69 See Pliny, *N.H.* 6.18.47. Many of the captives from the first two Parthian wars were returned to Augustus as part of the political settlement with Phraates. Yet the Parthians were unable to repatriate all the former soldiers. A significant number had escaped east to 'remote locations' and could not be tracked. Dio reports: 'Phraates returned the standards and all the prisoners of war, except for those who had taken their own lives out of shame and those who had managed to escape detection and had hidden themselves in rural places.' Dio Cassius, 54.8. Discussed: Sampson, (2008) 183.

70 Ferghana and the Tarim kingdoms learned Chinese techniques for making cast-iron and steel from captured Han prisoners. Details: Yu, (1967) 167–9.

71 Details: Needham & Yates, (1994) 144–5; 152–3.

72 Details: Benjamin, (2007) 103.

73 See *Hou Hanshu,* 88.10.

74 See *Wei-shu,* 102. See Ferguson, (1978) 594.

75 Hill suggests that the Chinese account indicates a route south from Gandhara along the Indus into Sind and then west to Kandahar and Herat, before heading southwest to Susa and Mesene. See Hill, (2003) Appendix D.

76 Discussed: Raschke, (1978) 618–9.

77 *Hou Hanshu,* 88.10.

78 *Ibid.*

79 *Hou Hanshu,* 88.10. Other interpretations: Charlesworth, (1924) 108–9; Warmington, (1928) 149; Miller, (1969) 133–6; Ferguson, (1978) 594; Franck & Brownstone, (1986) 126–7; Stoneman, (1992) 44; Young, (2001) 195.

80 The *Weilue* states: 'In early times only the maritime routes to *Da Qin* were discussed because we did not know there were overland routes'. *Weilue,* 13.

81 *Hou Hanshu*, 4.14; 88.1.

82 *Hou Hanshu*, 88.1.

83 Distance: 40,000 *li* = c. 16,000 km (c. 10,000 miles).

84 The Chinese text reads: 'Meng-chi Tou-le both'. Views: Leslie & Gardiner, (1996) 149. Disagreement: Pullybank, (1999) 27.

85 Ptolemy, *Geography*, 1.11. Discussed: Leslie & Gardiner, (1996) 149.

86 Ptolemy: 'From the Stone Tower to Sera, the metropolis of the Seres, is a seven-month journey or 6,3200 *stadia*'. Ptolemy, *Geog.* 1.12; 6.16 (Serica). See Millar, (1998) 136.

87 The Stone Tower must have been about 3,600 kilometres from the Mediterranean seaboard. See Cary, (1956) 131.

88 Ptolemy, *Geog.* 1.11. Views: Young, (2001) 195–8; 276.

89 See Cary, (1956) 130–2.

90 Dio Cassius, 48.30; 49.17; 50.13. Further details see: Cary, (1956) 132.

91 Strabo: 'Phraates was so eager for friendship with Caesar Augustus that . . . he called Titius the Praefect of Syria to a conference and he gave into his care, four of his legitimate sons as hostages'. Strabo, *Geog.* 16.1.28. Discussed: Cary, (1956) 132. The hostages also included the grandchildren of the Parthian king.

92 *Hou Hanshu*, 4 (November, AD 100). Discussed: Leslie & Gardiner, (1996) 148.

93 Details: Cary, (1956) 132.

94 See Yu, (1967) 150.

95 *Hou Hanshu*, 88.1.

96 Political significance: Campbell, (1995) 6.

97 Dio Cassius, 68.15.
98 *Justinian Digest,* 39.4.16.7.
99 Views: Warmington, (1928) 95; Thorley, (1979) 189.
100 Kushans (Bactrians) in Alexandria: 'they are known to be excellent at horsemanship – for they cultivate this skill for the defence of their empire and independence'. In Rome: 'Here in your city are people . . . wearing the turbans and trousers of Persians and Bactrians'. Dio Chrysostom, 32.43; 72.3.
101 See *Hou Hanshu*, 88.13.
102 Josephus refers to the Kushans as the 'Sacae': 'That very night Vologaeses received letters revealing that a great band of Dahae and Sacae despised him and because he was such a long journey from home, they had sent an expedition to lay waste to Parthia. Vologaeses was forced to return immediately'. Josephus, *Jewish Antiquities*, 20.4.2. (c. AD 55).
103 Prasad, (1984) 150. Military strength of the Kushan nation: *Hou Hanshu*, 88.13.
104 Chinese accounts: 'Vima defeated Tianzhu (Northwest India) and installed a general to supervise and lead it. The Kushan then became extremely rich'. *Hou Hanshu*, 88.13.
105 Attock inscription (Indus region). Details: Thorley, (1979) 186.
106 These issues are discussed with references in Tomber, (2008) 123.
107 The woman dressed as an Indian princess could be Helen or Cassandra. Dio Chrysostom: 'It is said that Homer's poetry is sung even in India, where people have translated it into their own language and dialect'. Dio Chrysostom, 53.6. See also: Aelian, *Varius History*, 12.48. Discussed: Parker, (2008) 110–11.
108 Details: *Ibid.* 184.
109 Theories: Warmington, (1928) 96; Thorley, (1979) 189.
110 See Plutarch, *Pompey,* 70.
111 Views: Whittaker, (2004) 152.
112 Discussed: Mattern, (1999) 121–2; Campbell, (1995) 216.
113 Trajan's motives: Dio Cassius, 68.7; 68.17. Strabo (concerning Augustus): 'His considerations were based on the well established reports that the Arabians are very wealthy and that they sold aromatics and the most valuable gemstones for gold and silver'. See Strabo, *Geog.* 16.4.22.
114 Tiberius: 'Our wealth is transported to alien and hostile countries'. Tacitus, *Annals,* 3.53.
115 Herodian: 'Caracalla pointed out that the Roman and the Parthian Empires were the largest in the world. If they were united by marriage then the result would be a single empire without rival'. And 'The rest of the barbarian nations not subject to our authority could easily be reduced as they are only governed by tribes and confederacies . . . By waging war together, we could easily unite the entire inhabited world under a single authority'. Herodian, 4.10.
116 *Ibid.*
117 For instance: Dio Cassius, 68.29–30.
118 *Historia Augusta, Hadrian,* 21.
119 Aurelius Victor, *Roman History,* 15.4. Discussed: Ball, (2000) 400.
120 Views: Harmatta, (1999) 474.
121 Details: Warmington, (1928) 299.
122 Mela: 'The Seres are . . . a race eminent for integrity'. (Mela, 3.59). Strabo: 'Some say that the Seres live longer than 130 years'. (Strabo, *Geog.* 15.1.34).
123 See *P.M.E.* 64.
124 *Ibid.* Discussed: Casson, (1989) 239–41.
125 Ch'in – the name of the dynasty that unified China (221–206 BC). Details: Casson, (1989) 238. Ptolemy, *Geog.* 6.16 (Serica); 7.3 (Sinae).
126 The Antun group arrived between the 12th October and the 10th November, AD 166. Details: Leslie & Gardiner, (1996) 153.
127 The *Hou Hanshu* reports that the Saka: 'came repeatedly with tribute from beyond the frontier of Jih-nan'. (*Hou Hanshu,* 88.15). Discussed: Leslie & Gardiner, (1996) 137; 153.

128 *Hou Hanshu*, 88.12.
129 Views: Hill, *Notes to the Hou Hanshu* (2003) for *Hou Hanshu*, 88.12.
130 Views of Hirth, (1885) 173–8. Discussed: Young, (2001) 33; Mattern, (1999) 33; Ferguson, (1978) 594; Charlesworth, (1924) 72; Warmington, (1928) 131, 394. Sceptical: Leslie & Gardiner, (1996) 176.
131 For instance: Mela, 3.59.
132 *Hou Hanshu*, 88.12.
133 See McNeill, (1976) 107.
134 Netunceralatan ruled from c. AD 174–196. Details: De Romanis, (1997) 104–5.
135 *Patirruppattu*, 2.7–10.
136 Lucian, *How to write history*, 31.
137 *Ibid.* Views: Mclynn, (2009) 154–5.
138 The Roman literary elite were sceptical about merchant reports. Many regarded merchants as social inferiors. Ptolemy: 'Marinos did not trust merchant accounts'. See Ptolemy, 1.11.
139 'Roman Leon' or *Da Qin Lun* (abbreviated to *Qin Lun*). The Greek name Leon appears at Coptos and sites in the Eastern Desert connected with the god Pan. See Bagnall, (2000) 24.
140 Yao Silian, *Liang-shu*, 48. Discussed: Leslie & Gardiner, (1996) 100–1.
141 *Ibid.*
142 Details: Sidebotham, (1986a) 50–1; (1988) 499 fn. 11.
143 Yao Silian, *Liang-shu*, 54 (events 3rd century AD). Discussed Leslie & Gardiner, (1996) 159; Yu, (1967) 175–6.
144 Yao Silian, *Liang-shu*, 54.
145 Details: Ray, (1994) 112; Glover, (1996b) 373; (1998) 135.
146 Discussed: Sidebotham, (1986a) 163; Young, (2001) 82.
147 *Historia Augusta*, *Firmus*, 3.
148 Details: 'Firmus laid claim to Egypt but without the imperial insignia, as though he planned to make it into a free state'. *Historia Augusta, Aurelian,* 32.
149 *Historia Augusta, Firmus,* 4.
150 Details: 'Firmus now seized the imperial power in opposition to Aurelian with the purpose of defending the remainer of Zenobia's party'. *Historia Augusta*, *Firmus*, 5.
151 *Historia Augusta*, *Firmus*, 3. Discussed: Sidebotham, (1989) 499.
152 Reports suggested that Firmus or his supporters were tortured. His Indian trophies were taken by the imperial household. See *Historia Augusta*, *Firmus*, 3; 5.
153 The account reads: 'There were Blemmyes, Axumites, Arabs from Arabia Felix, Indians, and Bactrians . . .' and 'among them there were men from Palmyra, who had survived its fall. These were the foremost men of their state and they were accompanied by Egyptians who had also rebelled'. See *Historia Augusta, Aurelian,* 33.
154 Significance discussed: Leslie & Gardiner, (1996) 159.
155 *I-wen Lei-chu,* 76 (year AD 281–282). Discussed: Leslie & Gardiner, (1996) 160.
156 The Emperors Probus (AD 276–282) and Diocletian (AD 285–305) sent agents out to 'furthest India' to try to locate the source of a valuable purple dye (see *Historia Augusta*, *Aurelian*, 29). Perhaps these men reached China.
157 *Nan-fang Tsao-mu Chuang*, 9 (5th year Tai-kang era AD 184/5). Views: Leslie & Gardiner, (1996) 159–60.
158 The *Edict on Maximum Prices* may have set unrealistically low prices for Eastern goods. Edict: a pound of Troglodytic myrrh equivalent to 1.8 grams gold (32.1.83). Pliny: a pound of Troglodytic myrrh equivalent to 4.7 grams gold (Pliny, *Natural History*, 12.35). Details: Rathbone, (2000) 47. (See also nard leaf prices: *Edict*, 32.1.36; *N.H.* 12.26).

Notes to Chapter 6: The Economic Impact on the Roman Empire

1 Dio Chrysostom, 32.36.
2 Strabo, *Geography.* 17.1.13.
3 Dio Chrysostom, 32.36.
4 This figure includes Arabian and African goods that were picked up on route to India. It also includes Far Eastern goods shipped through Indian markets. A commodity weighting at least 140 tons was removed from the Hermapollon (perhaps pepper or malabathron). See *P. Vindob. G* 40822, verso. Details: Rathbone, (2000) 43; 46. The cargo figure of 500 tons has been used in other reconstructions. See Whittaker, (2004) 178 n. 53. *Periplus*: 'Ships in these ports carry full loads'. See *Periplus Maris Erythraei*, 56.
5 Strabo, *Geog.* 16.4.25; 17.1.3.
6 Pre-modern economies operated on a substantial scale. Chinese records suggest at least 4 million bolts of silk fabric were stored in the capital Luoyang (early 4th century AD). Details Lui, (1988) 70. During periods of the Tang era (AD 618–907) the Chinese were sending up to a million bolts of silk into the Uighur steppe territories per annum. Details: Lui, (2001) 169. At the beginning of the 16th century southern Asia was exporting around 10,000 tons of spice per year (including 7,000 tons of pepper). Details: Kratoska, (2001) 116–7. By 1622, Western Europe was consuming 3,500 tons of pepper per annum. Details: Attman, (1981) 31–2.
7 Details: Tomber, (2008) 76.
8 Details: *Ibid.* 55.
9 Discussed: Sidebotham, (2008) 172.
10 Details: Cappers, (1999) 56–7.
11 Details: *Ibid.* 58–9.
12 *Justinian Digest*, 39.4.16.7. Details: Young, (2001) 209.
13 Discussed: Elton, (1996) 85.
14 See Appendix B. Views: Groom, (1981) 154–5; Whittaker, (2004) 169.
15 Discussed: Harl, (1996) 300. See also Young, (2001) 222–3.
16 Estimates: 4 sesterces (a denarius) a day a generous 'living wage' for a labourer (300 denarii or 1,200 sesterces per year). Details: Mattern, (1999) 28; Alston, (1995) 105–8; Harl, (1996) 275–9.
17 Eastern goods were cheaper and more accessible in the Roman era. A Ptolemaic papyrus places a price restriction on the sale of frankincense – equivalent to 40 sesterces (per mina). Pliny indicates that frankincense sold in Roman markets at a price equivalent to 32 sesterces per mina (Pliny, *N.H.* 12.32.65). Papyrus details: *P. Tebt.* 1:35. Discussed: Bagnall, & Derow, (1981) 197.
18 Discussed: Sidebotham, (1986a) 34; Stoneman, (1992) 34; Whittaker, (2004) 172–3; Dalby, (2000) 195.
19 For instance: Apicius, 1.29 (spiced salts); 2.2.55 (pepper gravy); 3.17.110 (spiced salad dressing); 9.10.420 (peppered sardines). Discussed: Singer, (2007) 20.
20 Apicius: 'spiced honey wine which keeps forever is given to people on a journey' (2 pints wine, 4 ounces pepper). See Apicius, 1.2.
21 Pliny, *N.H.* 12.14.
22 Petronius, *Satyricon*, 38.
23 Horace, *Epistles,* 2.1.270.
24 Details: Rathbone, (2000) 47.
25 North of the Horrea Vespasiani, the large warehouses of Vespasian (completed: AD 81–96). See Jerome, *Chronicle*, 217th Olympiad. Eusebius, *Chronicle*, AD 354.
26 The Spice Warehouses were destroyed by fire in AD 192. Dio writes: 'The fire spread to the storehouses of Egyptian and Arabian wares. From there the flames were borne aloft and reaching the palace, they consumed very extensive portions of it and nearly all the state records were destroyed'. Dio Cassius, 72.24.

27 Area of basilica (length: 100 meters, width: 65 meters). Details: Rickman, (1971) 104–6; Whittaker, (2004) 156.
28 Details grain warehouses: Hermansen, (1982) Chapter 7; 230–1. Rickman, (1971) 104–6.
29 Details: Veen, (1998) 101–5. Silver pepper pots modelled to resemble tiny amphora. See Warmington, (1928) 183–4; Strong, (1966) 154, 178–9.
30 A *castrum* at Oberaden on the Lippe River in Germany (abandoned c. 8 BC). Details: De Romanis, (1997) 100; Whittaker, (2004) 172.
31 See Bowman, (1994) 69.
32 *Mark*, 15.23.
33 For instance: Celsus, *De Medicina*, 5.18.6–7 (muscle pain); 5.25.3 (menstrual pains). Galen, *De Antidoto*, 2.10 (myrrh would healant).
34 For instance: Dioscurides, *De Materia Medica*, 1.24 (Indian resin remedy for toothache); 5.57 (pepper remedies). Discussed: Harris, (1993) 13.
35 Discussed: Singer, (2007) 20.
36 '*Yavanapriya*' and '*Yavanestha*', see De Romanis, (1997) 100; Gupta, (1991) 128.
37 See Raftery, (1994) 218. Ingredients in eye salves, example: Celsus, *De Medicina*, 6.6.24 (salve invented by Hermon).
38 Discussed: Bird, (2007) 122. Frankincense and myrrh connected to kingship and divinity. See *Matthew*, 2.11.
39 Discussed: Singer, (2007) 21.
40 Details: Bird, (2007) 127.
41 The list reads: 'bread: 4 asses; dates: 1 ass; cheese: 2 asses and incense: 1 ass'. Details: Etienne, (1992) 184–5.
42 See also Martial: 'That lavender and myrrh stinking of funerals, half-burned frankincense and cinnamon snatched from the midst of pyres'. Martial, *Epigrams*, 11.54. Discussed: Singer, (2007) 21.
43 Pliny, *N.H.* 12.41.
44 *Ibid.*
45 Discussed: Singer, (2007) 21.
46 Pliny, *N.H.* 12.41.
47 *John*, 19.39–40.
48 *Mark*, 14.3–9. See also *Matthew*, 26.6–13; *John*, 12.1–8; *Luke*, 7.36–50. Discussed: Dalby, (2000) 197.
49 Pliny, *N.H.* 12.26. The Hermapollon was carrying 60 boxes of Gangetic nard individually priced at 4,500 dracma per container. See *P. Vindob. G* 40822, verso, 2–3. Details: Rathbone, (2000) 43.
50 Discussed: Dalby, (2000) 196.
51 Pliny, *N.H.* 13.4.
52 Suetonius, *Vespasian*, 8.
53 Cicero referred to devious men who had: 'carefully combed hair, thick with perfumed oil'. Cicero, *Catiline*, 2.22.
54 Lucius Plautius Plancus (43 BC). Valerius: 'they sniffed out the secret room to which he had fled' (Valerius Maximus, 6.8.5). (Martial, 9.59). Pliny: 'The smell of his perfume was a disgrace greater than his criminal guilt'. (Pliny, *N.H.* 13.5)
55 Ovid, *Art of Love*, 3.10.
56 See Martial, *Epigrams*, 2.29.
57 Pliny: 'How could a perfume be perceptible, productive or pleasurable, when applied to that part of the body?' Pliny, *N.H.* 13.4. Discussed: Croom, (2000) 68; Dalby, (2000) 196.
58 Pliny: 'I have heard also of a person giving orders for his private bath-room to be fragranced with unguents.' Pliny, *N.H.* 13.4.
59 Pliny, *N.H.* 13.4.
60 Leptis Magna in North Africa. See Pliny, *Letters*, 2.11.23. Potter, (2002) 168.
61 See *CIL* 1.1594; *CIL* 10.3968.

62 Ovid, *The Loves*, 3.15.83–98.
63 Juvenal, 6.462–9. Perfume types and manufacture centres discussed in Athenaeus, *Deipnosophists*, 15.38.688.
64 Discussed: Singer, (2007) 20.
65 Pliny, *N.H.* 13.5.
66 Virgil, *Georgics*, 2.466. Nard flavoured wine: see Martial, *Epigrams*, 4.13.
67 Details: Strauss, (2007) 247.
68 Details: Roberts, (2008) 61.
69 Luke, 7.37. Unguents best preserved in alabaster containers. See Pliny, *N.H.* 13.3.
70 Horace, *Satires*, 1.2.101–3. Coan silk: an inferior form of the fabric produced from the cocoons of 'wild' insects on the Mediterranean island of Cos. The cocoons were chewed through by the pupa leaving damaged and weakened threads (Pliny, *N.H.* 11.27). Coan silk was difficult to dye and had a coarser less-appealing texture. (With Chinese silk the pupae was killed by scalding or inserting a needle into the cocoon leaving the delicate threads intact). Chinese silk drove Coan silk 'off the market'. Details: Raschke, (1978) 623–5.
71 Discussed: Croom, (2000) 123–4.
72 In the *Golden Ass* Triton protects Venus from sunburn with a silk parasol (Apuleius, *Golden Ass*, 4.31). Parasols: Martial, *Epigrams*, 14.28; Ovid, *Fasti*, 2.209; Juvenal, 9.50 (green parasols). Discussed: Croom, (2000) 107–8.
73 Martial, *Epigrams*, 11.27.
74 Discussed: Dalby, (2000) 200; Stoneman, (1992) 42.
75 Pliny, *N.H.* 6.20; Seneca, *Debates*, 2.5.7. Discussed: Croom, (2000) 123–4.
76 Petronius, *Satyricon*, 55.
77 Seneca, *De Beneficiis*, 7.9.
78 Tacitus, *Annals*, 2.33. 'Tiberius forbade any man to wear silk clothing'. Cassius Dio, 57.15.
79 Suetonius: 'Caligula often made public appearances in a cloak covered with embroidery and encrusted with precious stones, a long-sleeved tunic and bracelets; or in silks which men were forbidden by law to wear'. Suetonius, *Caligula*, 52.
80 Pliny, *N.H.* 11.27.
81 Discussed: Wild, (1997) 287–98.
82 Details: Stauffer, (1996) 425–30; Young, (2001) 142.
83 Colchester Museum.
84 Multi-coloured robes and shawls that would have: 'shone in the bright Mediterranean sunshine'. See Wilkinson, (2003) 28. Pastel colours: see Croom, (2000) 80–1.
85 Details: Salway, (1965) 25; 60–2; 228; 256.
86 Martial, *Epigrams*, 9.59.
87 See Pliny, *N.H.* 37.6.
88 Martial, *Epigrams*, 5.11.
89 Propertius: 'Her garment charred against her side: The fire consumed the beryl ring from her finger'. Propertius, 4.7.18–19.
90 Pliny, *N.H.* 37.7. Discussed: Singer, (2007) 20.
91 Pliny, *N.H.* 37.8.
92 *Ibid.* 37.7.
93 Pliny: 'Petronius broke the ladle to deprive the Emperor Nero of this prize for his dining table. However, the Emperor then outdid everyone by paying a million sesterces for a single bowl'. Pliny, *N.H.* 37.7.
94 *Ibid.*
95 Juvenal, 5.67–74.
96 Pliny, *N.H.* 37.6.
97 Pliny: 'Pearls the most prized of all jewels'. See Pliny, *N.H.* 9.54.
98 Horace, *Satires*, 1.2.80.
99 Pliny, *N.H.* 9.56.
100 Large supplies of Indian pearls: see Pliny, *N.H.* 9.54; values: 9.58.

101 Pliny, *N.H.* 9.5.6.
102 *Ibid.*
103 *Timothy,* 1.2.9–10.
104 Petronius, *Satyricon,* 55.
105 Seneca, *De Beneficiis*, 7.9.
106 Ovid, *Cures for Love,* 5.53–4.
107 Pliny: 'They put pearls on their feet, not just on the laces of their sandals, but all over their footwear. It is not enough to wear pearls; that they must tread upon them as well?' Pliny, *N.H.* 37.6.
108 Tacitus, *Annals,* 3.53.
109 Details: Croom, (2000) 98–105.
110 Discussed: Croom, (2000) 117–8; Roberts, (2008) 61.
111 Pliny, *N.H.* 9.35. Compare this to early Gallic tribute (40 million sesterces) and the revenues of Palestine (48 million sesterces). Suetonius, *Julius Caesar,* 25; Josephus, *Jewish Antiquities,* 19.352. Augustus donated 50 million sesterces worth of pearls and precious stones to the Temple of Jupiter Capitolinus. See Suetonius, *Augustus,* 30.
112 Pliny, *N.H.* 9.58.
113 Martial, *Epigrams*, 11.27. Foliatum was a popular exotic perfume that included nard and myrrh. See Pliny, *N.H.* 13.2.15.
114 Seneca, *Tragedies,* 1.387–91.
115 Apuleius, *Golden Ass*, 2.9.8.
116 See Croom, (2000) 105–6.
117 Details: Roberts, (2008) 61.
118 Tax imposed on imports of 'Indian hair'. *Justinian Digest,* 39.4.16.7.
119 Martial, *Epigrams*, 14.24.
120 Propertius, 2.22.
121 Ovid, *The Loves*, 3.15.24–8.
122 Value of precious woods: Pliny, *N.H.* 37.58. Use discussed: Singer, (2007) 20.
123 Martial, *Epigrams*, 9.59.
124 Virgil, *Georgics,* 2.463–6.
125 For instance: Martial, *Epigrams*, 9.59. Also: 14.87–8 (furniture inlaid with shell); *P.M.E.* 30 (shell for small items). Discussed: Casson (1989), 101–2.
126 Juvenal, 7.130–1.
127 Discussed: Dalby, (2000) 194.
128 The Hermapollon carried 45 talents-weight of ivory valued at 85 talents 5,157 dracmas (around 515,000 sesterces). This may have been over 100 complete pairs of tusks and 17 pairs composed of fragments (total weight: c. 4 tons). *P. Vindob. G* 40822, verso, 4–26. Details: Rathbone, (2000) 43; 46.
129 Ovid, *Cosmetics for Women*, 1.20. Martial, *Epigrams*, 14.3. See also: Virgil, *Georgics*, 1.57.
130 Martial, *Epigrams*, 14.5 (ivory tables); 14.12 (ivory cashboxes for gold); 14.14 (gaming dice); 14.77 (ivory birdcage); 14.78 (medicine chest). See also Petronius, *Satyricon*, 135; Pliny, *N.H.* 12.2 (statues and images of gods).
131 Details: Strauss, (2007) 247.
132 Indian statuette found at a home on the Via dell'Abbondanza. There is a hole drilled partially down through the centre of the object. Details: Sidebotham, (1986a) 23; Wilkinson, (2003) 13; Butterworth & Laurence, (2005) 62.
133 Indian eunuchs and prostitutes a familiar sight in Rome. Views: Whittaker, (2004) 151; Dalby, (2000) 191.
134 See Juvenal, 5.67–74.
135 *Justinian Digest,* 39.4.16.7; *P.M.E.* 8; 13; 31. Pliny, *N.H.* 6.34. Human cargo: Roman slaves to the Saka courts (see *P.M.E.* 49).
136 Horace, *Satires,* 2.8.14–5. Discussed: Parker, (2008) 157.
137 See Pliny, *N.H.* 7.39 (exceptional prices); Martial, *Epigrams*, 3.62; 11.70 (costly slaves).

Perhaps 500 dracma for an ordinary slave (Horace, *Satires*, 2.7.43). In Egypt female slaves sold at 1,200–1,500 dracma (= sesterces). Details: Westermann, (1955) 100–1.

138 Tacitus, *Annals,* 3.53.

139 See Aelian, *Nature of Animals*, 16.2; Martial, *Epigrams*, 14.73 (a parrot trained to say 'Hail Caesar!'); Statius, *Silvae*, 2.4 (memorial ode); Pliny, *N.H.* 10.58 (green parrots trained to speak Latin). Discussed: Dalby, (2000) 193.

140 Ovid: 'Your wings made the green of emeralds look dull and your beak was coloured as though it was stained by Tyrian purple. No bird could better mimic a human voice than you: you spoke back the words perfectly, but with a fetching lisp.' Ovid, *The Loves*, 2.6.21–4.

141 Martial: 'That terrible anger when the rhino lowered its head and charged forward! With its horn it threw the bull into the air as though it were a toy.' Martial, *Spectacles,* 9. Rhinos from India and East Africa see Dalby, (2000) 179.

142 *Justinian Digest,* 39.4.16.7. Indian animals depicted in a Roman mosaic: Casale at Piazza Armerina in Sicily (4th century AD).

143 Martial, *Spectacles*, 8.26.

144 Pliny, *N.H.* 32.21.

145 Details: Butterworth & Laurence, (2005) 62.

146 Tacitus, *Histories,* 1.20.

147 Xenophon of Ephesus, *Ephesian Tale*, book 3 ('Psammis': a wealthy merchant from India). Discussed: Whittaker, (2004) 156-7.

148 Dio Chrysostom, 32.40.

149 See inscriptions: *CIS* 2.1.158; *CIL* 10.2644; *CIL* 10.2935. Discussed: Sidebotham, (1986a) 93.

150 *ILS* 4334. Details: Elton, (1996) 94.

151 Martial, *Epigrams*, 7.30. Discussed: Parker, (2008) 157.

152 *RIB* 1065. The Catuvellaunian were a tribal confederacy near Londinium.

153 Discussed: Salway, (1965) 25; 60–2; 228; 256; Elton, (1996) 94.

154 Discussed: Tchernta, (1997).

155 Plutarch, *Pompey,* 73.

156 Details: Tchernta, (1997) 241.

157 Tiberian era (AD 14–37). Details: *Ibid.* 241–3; 147.

158 *CIL* 8.22640, 65 (late 1st century BC). Discussed: Adams, (2007) 233.

159 See Tchernta, (1997) 245; 247.

160 Eastern cargo worth 9 million sesterces (*P. Vindob. G* 40822, verso, 29). Tenfold return on outbound investments (*Hou Hanshu,* 88.12).

161 See Pliny, *Letters*, 3.19.7.

162 See Rufinus, *Historia Monachorum*, 16; John Moschus, *Pratum Spirituale*, 193; Palladius, *Historia Lausiaca*, 14. Discussed: Whittaker, (2004) 169–70; Jones, (1964) 870–1.

163 *Papyrus SB 7169.* A further papyrus records a trade venture where four investors each put up eight talents to charter a Mediterranean ship. *P. Vindob. G* 19792 (= *SB* 6.9571). Details: Whittaker, (2004) 169; Young, (2001) 54–5.

164 Philostratus, *Life of Apollonius of Tyana,* 3.24 (Mediterranean).

165 Grain worth 185,000 sesterces in Egypt and 400,000 sesterces in Rome. Details: Hopkins, (1983) 95; Rathbone, (2002) 211.

166 Egypt supplied perhaps 70,000 tons of grain to Rome per annum (equivalent to 175 ships with cargo capacities of 400 tons). Details: Hopkins, (1983) 101; Harris, (2000) 717; Rickman, (1980) 67–71; Potter & Mattingly (1999) 192–200.

167 See Strabo, *Geog.* 2.3.4.

168 Theories: Casson, (1989) 34–5; (1992) 11; Young, (2001) 55–8.

169 Views: Bagnall, (2000) 15.

170 *P. Vindob. G* 40822, verso, 29 (value); 6; 12 (quarter-tax). After deduction of quarter-tax: 6,936,852 sesterces. Details: Rathbone, (2000) 48.

171 Views: Rathbone, (2000) 43; Adams, (2007) 226–8.

172 *P. Vindob. G* 40822, verso, 29.

173 See Bagnall, (2000) *BE* 68–79.
174 *SB* 7539.
175 The Senator Pliny the Younger owned estates and finances worth 17 million sesterces. His income may have been around one million sesterces per annum. Details: Duncan-Jones, (1974) 17–32; Mattern, (1999) 123; Hopkins, (2002) 206–7.
176 Petronius, *Satyricon,* 76.
177 *Ibid.*
178 *Ibid.* Discussed: De Romanis, (1997) 120.
179 Annius Eros (*CIL* 10.2389). Further details: Sidebotham, (1986a) 32–3; 67; (2008) 192; Adams, (2007) 233.
180 Pliny, *N.H.* 6.24.84.
181 Details: De'Arms, (1981) 166.
182 Discussed: Fuks, (1951) 214; Adams, (2007) 223.
183 Josephus, *Jewish Antiquities,* 18.8.1; 205.5.20. Discussed: Sidebotham, (1986a) 85; Fuks, (1951) 215.
184 Josephus, *Jewish Antiquities,* 18.6.3.
185 Josephus, *Jewish War,* 5.8.5.
186 Josephus, *Jewish Antiquities*, 19.5.1.
187 Discussed: Sidebottom, (1986a) 84–5; 102–3.
188 *Nicanor Archive*. See *O. Petr.* 266 (AD 43); 267 (AD 43); 268 (AD 44); 271 (AD 43/44).
189 Josephus, *Jewish Antiquities,* 19.5.1. Discussed: Fuks, (1951) 214–5.
190 Josephus, *Jewish Antiquities,* 19.5.1. Discussed: Sidebotham, (1986a) 84–5.
191 Procurator Judea: Josephus, *Jewish Antiquities*, 20.5.2. Parthian war: Tacitus, *Annals*, 15.28; Civil war: Josephus, *Jewish War*, 4.10.5; Tacitus, *History*, 2.7.9; Suetonius, *Vespasian*, 6.3. Status: *Jewish War*, 5.1.6. See Fuks, (1951) 215–6; Sidebotham, (1986a) 84–5.
192 Pliny, *N.H.* 12.41.
193 Theories: Groom, (1981) 156–61. In Rome 50 million sesterces could buy up to 2,000 tons of low grade frankincense, or almost 560 tons of the least expensive myrrh. Modern authorities estimate that around 5,500 tons of frankincense is currently produced every year in the Yemen and Somalia (Arabia alone: 3,300 tons). It is possible that 10 times this amount is produced but undeclared. Details: Shackley, (2006) 21; 141.
194 Pliny, *N.H.* 6.26.101–2. Figures 'suspiciously rounded', see De Romanis, (1997) 120–2. Discussed: Stoneman, (1992) 34; Tchernia, (1997) 271; Adams, (2007) 228–30.
195 Details: Turner, (1989) 8–9; 62–3.
196 Strabo, *Geog.* 2.5.12. Trade ships increased in size. See *P.M.E.* 57.
197 *Hou Hanshu,* 88.12. Information probably obtained by Han court officials who questioned merchant members of the Antun delegation.
198 Details: Carter, (1972) 269.
199 See *P.M.E.* 56.
200 Details: Duncan-Jones, (1994) 33–46 esp. 45.
201 Details: Hopkins, (2002) 199; 210.
202 Pliny, *N.H.* 12.32.59–60.
203 Lucan, *Pharsalia,* 10.169–71.
204 Pliny, *N.H.* 6.20.
205 *Weilue*, 12. Discussed: Leslie & Gardiner, (1996) 72.
206 Pliny, *N.H.* 6.26.101–2.
207 *Price Edict,* 23.1.1 and 24.1.1. Discussed: Harl, (1996) 301; 467.
208 Huan Kuan, *Yan Tie Lun* (*Discourses on Salt and Iron*), 2.15–16. (10,000 *li* = c. 4,100 kilometres). Discussed: Yu, (1967) 193.
209 Possible Chinese interest in Roman storax perfume: see *Hou Hanshu*, 88.12.
210 Pliny, *N.H.* 12.54.
211 Details: Shackley, (2006) 144; 146.
212 *John,* 12.3–5.

213 A hundredweight of pepper cost 3 ducats in India and was sold in European markets at a price of 80 ducats (Details: Reid, (1994) 27). Medieval era: A kilogram of pepper cost 1–2 grams in India; 10–14 grams at Alexandria; 20–30 grams in northwest Europe (Details: Braudel, (1982) 405).
214 Strabo, *Geog.* 17.1.13.
215 *P. Vindob. G* 40822, verso, 6; 12; *P.M.E.* 19. Discussed: Young, (2001) 52; 57; 67; 209; Sidebotham, (1986a) 102–10; Adams, (2007) 226.
216 The *Alexandrian Tariff* might be an additional levy devised by the state to raise further income from Eastern commerce. The tax is linked to Commodus who was said to have devised new customs tariffs. See Herodian, 2.4.7. Different view: Young, (2001) 208–9.
217 Cicero, *For Manilia*, 14.
218 Appian, *History, preface,* 7.
219 *Strabo, Geog.* 2.5.8. See also: 4.5.3 *(*AD 21). Cost of a legion about 12 million sesterces. See Duncan-Jones, (1994) 34.
220 Appian, *Praef.* 5.
221 Philostratus, *Life of the Sophists,* 548.
222 Seneca: 'Caligula dined one day at a cost of 10 million sesterces. Though everybody used their ingenuity to help him, he found it difficult to spend the tribute-money from three provinces on one dinner'. Seneca, *Ad Helviam matrem,* 10.4. Discussed: Mattern, (1999) 136.
223 Batavian revolt, Germania Inferior. Tacitus, *Histories*, 4.74 (AD 70).
224 Plutarch, *Pompey,* 45.
225 Suetonius, *Julius Caesar,* 25.
226 Velleius, 2.39.
227 Dio Cassius, 52.6.
228 Dio Cassius. 52.28. Discussed: Mattern, (1999) 129.
229 Strabo, *Geog.* 2.5.12.
230 *Ibid.* 17.1.13.
231 Military costs alone could have totalled more than 400 million sesterces per annum. Details: Duncan-Jones, (1994) 33–46, esp. 45; Campbell, (1984) 161–9; Mattern, (1999) 127; 129; Hopkins, (2002) 199.
232 Tacitus, *Annals,* 1.11. Following severe military defeats in Germany (AD 9).
233 Trade increase discussed: Whittaker, (2004) 164. In this era the aristocratic elite began to consume vast quantities of exotic goods in competition for prestige and political status. See Tacitus, *Annals,* 3.52–5.
234 Suetonius, *Caligula,* 16.3. Dio gives the figure of 2,300 million sesterces (according to some reports: 3,300 million). See Dio Cassius, 59.2. Discussed: Mattern, (1999) 136.
235 These Eastern princes had been Nero's companions in the imperial court. These decisions were not purely 'financial' but they were enabled by imperial wealth.
236 See Strabo, *Geog.* 17.1.13. Sceptical: Duncan-Jones, (1994) 53, 254.
237 Josephus, *Jewish War,* 2.16.4. Grain supply estimates discussed: Harris, (2000) 717; Rickman, (1980) 67–71.
238 Revenues extracted from Palestine by Herod Agrippa (AD 41–44). Josephus: 'The revenues that Herod Agrippa received from his territories were very great, no less than 12 million drachme'. Josephus, *Jewish Antiquities,* 19.8.2. Discussed: Duncan-Jones, (1994) 254.
239 Sceptical: Duncan-Jones, (1994) 254; Hopkins, (2002) 210.
240 Details: Duncan-Jones, (1994) 33–46, esp. 45; Hopkins, (2002) 200.
241 Much of this revenue was derived from customs taxes. The governors of Egypt therefore had access to enormous reserves of disposable cash.
242 See Dio Cassius, 51.17. Discussed: Goodman, (1997) 110; Morgan, (2006) 187.
243 Money was the 'sinews of the civil war'. See Tacitus, *Histories,* 2.84.
244 Different eras represented. See Pliny, *N.H.* 33.21 (gold); 33.31 (silver). Details discussed: Wilson, (2007) 113.

245 It is possible that new amounts of silver entering the Roman economy were not enough to replace quantities exported in trade dealings with the distant East (in particular Arabia). Dio Chrysostom talks of silver leaving the Empire in large amounts through trade dealings with 'Indians, Iberians, Arabs and Babylonians'. See Dio Chrysostom, *On Wealth,* 79.5 (early 2nd century AD). The bullion loss may have been detrimental.

246 Pliny's export figure of 100 million sesterces was possibly composed of roughly equal amounts of silver and gold (Pliny, *N.H.* 12.41). Northern India received gold and silver Roman money (*P.M.E.* 38; 49). Arabians received silver (Diodorus Siculus, 19.95; Agarchides, 5.104; *P.M.E.* 28. Silver denarii: Pliny, *N.H.* 6.24.84–5); silver and gold (Strabo, *Geog.* 16.4.19; 16.4.22; 16.4.26; *P.M.E.* 24). Ethiopians received Roman silver and goldware (*P.M.E.* 6). East Africans received silver (*P.M.E.* 8–10 and gold: *P.M.E.* 8).

247 Details: Macdowell, (1991) 151.

248 See Pliny, *N.H.* 33.13.

249 Dio Chrysostom: 'The Indian Ocean, whose name was rarely heard in past times'. Dio Chrysostom, 32.36.

250 Pliny: 'It used to be customary to gather all one's ingredients at home and there was no demand for Indian pepper and the other luxuries that we now import from overseas'. Pliny, *N.H.* 19.19.58.

251 Details: Potter & Mattingly, (1999) 105–6.

252 For instance: *P.M.E.* 24; 28.

253 Pliny, *N.H.* 32.21, 23. Discussed: De Romanis, (1997) 190.

254 Juvenal, 5.56–65.

255 Pliny, *N.H.* 11.27.

256 See Pliny, *N.H.* 19.15.

257 *Ibid.* 12.1.

258 Details: Frier, (2000) 811–6.

259 Details: Horden & Purcell, (2000) 175–231.

260 *Revelations*: 'That great city, wherein all who had ships in the sea were made rich by reason of her costliness'. (*Revelations*, 18.19.) Aelius Aristides: 'Rome, the common trading centre of mankind and the common market for the produce of the earth' (*Orations*, 26.7).

261 Rome is personified as 'Babylon' evoking the image that even Rome could one-day become a city of ruins like the grandiose but largely derelict Babylon.

262 Aelius Aristides, *Oration*, 26.11–12.

263 Strabo, *Geog.* 17.1.7. Guilds provided these ships with ballast for the return journey to Alexandria. See *CIL* 14.102 (2nd century AD). Discussed: Warmington, (1928) 272–3.

264 Alexandria needed Italian wines for trade ventures to Arabia and India.

265 Egyptian revenues greater than 600 million sesterces (Eastern imports worth more than 1,000 million sesterces).

266 Details: Harl, (1996) 117–24. Roman coins were also needed for trade exports to Arabia, Somalia and India.

267 The wealth of powerful estates was released back into the wider Roman economy through elite expenditure. This was important as the Roman aristocracy traditionally favoured ideas of autarky.

268 Roman army supplies and equipment received from market exchanges and private workshops. Discussed: Harris, (1993) 17.

269 Military expenditure was needed to subdue indigenous dissent as well as defend against external threats. Exploitation did occur, for instance the financial events leading up to the Boudicca revolt of AD 60. See Tacitus, *Annals,* 14.31; Dio Cassius, 62.2.

270 See Dio Cassius, 74.8. The figure suggests that during the reign of Antoninus Pius the Roman Empire was receiving revenues that were on average more than 100 million sesterces greater than state expenses.

271 For instance: Nero temporarily 'liberated' Greece from the tribute taxes it paid to Rome (c. AD 67). See *ILS* 8794.

272 See details and discussion in McNeill, (1976) 128.
273 The Empire may have lost: 30–40 per cent of its frontier military; 30 per cent of its revenues, 25 per cent of its urban inhabitants; 14 per cent of its total population. Jerome: 'There was such a plague throughout the whole world that the Roman army was reduced almost to extinction.' Jerome, *Chronicle,* 236th Olympiad = AD 168.
274 Eutropius, 8. 12. Roman military commitment to the Parthian war was another factor in the success of the Germanic invasion.
275 *Historia Augusta, Marcus Aurelius,* 21.
276 *Ibid.* 17.
277 *Ibid.*
278 *Ibid.* 27–8.
279 Dio Cassius, 72.36.
280 Crisis discussed: Duncan-Jones, (2004) 20–52.
281 On his deathbed the emperor Severus advised his successors: 'Get along, pay the soldiers and disregard everyone else.' See Dio, 76.15.
282 Details: Mattern, (1999) 137; Duncan-Jones, (1994) 223–31.
283 Collapse of the Western Roman Empire. Recent views: Ward-Perkins, (2005) 40–1. Developments in Germanic society: Heather, (2005) esp. 444; 459. Bureaucratic corruption, administrative failure, civil wars: Goldsworthy, (2009).
284 For instance: In the reign of Nero the Roman governor of Moesia, a man named Tiberius Plautius Silvanus, halted a major European migration. He defeated Sarmation forces and settled 100,000 'trans-Danubians' in the outer Roman provinces. He also took hostages and established treaty arrangements. This type of operation could be successfully concluded during early empire because Rome maintained a well-financed professional army. See *ILS* 986. Details: Mattern (1999) 162–3.

Notes to Appendix A: The Products of the Roman Empire

1 *Weilue,* 12 (information AD 116–164).

Notes to Appendix B: Eastern imports into the Roman Empire

1 *Justinian Digest,* 39.4.16.7.

Notes to Appendix C: The Prices of Eastern Goods

1 See Pliny, *Natural History,* Book 12. Details: Groom, (1981) 154–5; Young, (2001) 222.
2 This price may be a 'copyist error'. Details: Sidebotham, (1986a) 35.

Concerning the Ancient Sources

Most classical texts referenced in this study are available online, in their original language and in modern translations. The reader may also wish to consult:

Casson, L. (1989), *The Periplus Maris Erythraei: Text with Introduction, Translation, and Commentary*. Princeton: Princeton University Press.

And for a translation of the *Muziris Papyrus*:

Rathbone, D. (2001), 'The 'Muziris' papyrus (SB XVIII 13167): financing Roman trade with India', in *Alexandrian Studies II in Honour of Mostafa el Abbadi*, (full details available from the British Library), pp. 39–50.

Casson, L. (1990), 'New light on maritime loans: P. Vindob. G 40822', *Zeitschrift für Papyrologie und Epigraphik*, 84, pp. 195–206.

Details about the ancient Chinese texts, including translations of crucial passages can be found in:

Hill, J. E. (2009), *Through the Jade Gate to Rome: A Study of the Silk Routes during the Later Han Dynasty 1st to 2nd Centuries CE*. Seattle: BookSurge Publishing.

Leslie, D. D. and Gardiner, K. H. J. (1996), *The Roman Empire in Chinese Sources*. Rome: Bardi.

Yu, Y. (1967), *Trade and Expansion in Han China: A Study in the Structure of Sino-barbarian Economic Relations*. Cambridge, Cambridge University Press.

The *Sogdian Letters* that describe ancient business deals on the silk routes can be found in:

Waugh, N. S. (2004), *The Sogdian Ancient Letters*. Washington University: Seattle Silk Road Project.

The main Tamil texts describing Roman contacts are referenced and translated in:

De Romanis, F. (1997), 'Rome and the notia of India: relations between Rome and southern India from 30 BC to the Flavian period', in De Romanis, F. and Tchernia, A. (eds), (1997), *Crossings: Early Mediterranean Contacts with India*. New Delhi: Manohar Publishers & Distributors, pp. 80–160.

Zvelebil, K. (1956), 'The Yavanas in old Tamil literature', in *Charisteria Orientalia praecipue ad Persiam pertinentia*. Prague: Nakladatelství Ceskoslovenské Akademie Ved, pp. 401–9.

The ancient Sinhalese texts and the classical accounts referring to Sri Lanka are referenced and translated in:

Weerakkody, D. P. M. (1997), *Taprobane: Ancient Sri Lanka as known to Greeks and Romans*. Turnhout: Brepols.

Select Bibliography

Adams, C. (2007), *Land Transport in Roman Egypt*. Oxford: Oxford University Press.

Alston, R. (1995), *Soldier and Society in Roman Egypt: A Social History*. London: Routledge.

Attman, A. (1981), *The Bullion Flow between Europe and the East 1000–1750*. Göteborg: Kungl. vetenskaps- och vitterhets-samhället.

Bagnall, R. S. and Derow, P. (1981), *The Hellenistic Period: Historical Sources in Translation*. Oxford: Blackwell.

Bagnall, R. S. and Helms, C. and Verhoogt, A. M. F. W. (2000), *Documents from Berenike 1: Greek Ostraka from the 1996–1998 Seasons*. Bruxelles: Fondation Égyptologique Reine Élisabeth.

Balasubramanian, C. (1980), *A Study of the Literature of the Cera Country up to 11th Century AD*. Madras: University of Madras.

Ball, W. (2000), *Rome in the East: The Transformation of an Empire*. London: Routledge.

Barber, E. W. (1999), *The Mummies of Urumchi*. New York: W.W. Norton & Company.

Beagon, M. (1992), *Roman Nature: The Thought of Pliny the Elder*. Oxford: Clarendon Press.

Begley, V. (1983), 'Arikamedu reconsidered'. *American Journal of Archaeology*, 87, 461–81.

Begley, V. and Francis, P. and Mahadevan, I. (eds), (1996), *The Ancient Port of Arikamedu: New Investigations and Researches 1989–1992*. Pondicherry: Centre d'histoire et d'archéologie, École française d'Extrême-Orient.

Begley, V. and Francis, P. and Karashima, N. and Raman K. V. (eds), (2004), *The Ancient Port of Arikamedu: New Excavations and Researches 1989–1992*. Paris: Centre d'histoire et d'archéologie, École française d'Extrême-Orient.

Benjamin, C. G. R. (2007), *The Yuezhi: Origin, Migration and the Conquest of Northern Bactria*. Turnhout: Brepols.

Bennet, J. (1997), *Trajan, Optimus Princeps: A Life and Times*. Bloomington: Indiana University Press.

Bentley. J. H. (2000), *Old World Encounters: Cross-cultural Contacts and Exchanges in Pre-modern Times*. Oxford: Oxford University Press.

Berggren, J. L. and Jones, A. (2000), *Ptolemy's Geography: An Annotated Translation of the Theoretical Chapters*. New York: Princeton University Press.

Berghaus, P. (1991), 'Roman coins from India and their imitations', in Jha, A. K. (ed.), *Coinage Trade and Economy*. Bombay: Indian Institute of Research in Numismatic Studies, pp. 108–21.

Berghaus, P. (1992), 'Three denari of Tiberius from Arikamedu', in Macdowall, D. W. and Sharma, S. (eds), *Indian Numismatic, History, Art, Culture* New Delhi: Agam Indological series. pp. 95–8.

Bernand, A. (1972), *Le Paneion d'El-Kanaïs: les inscriptions grecques*. Leiden: E. J. Brill.

Bird, D. G. (1972), 'Roman gold mining in north-west Spain'. *Journal of Roman Studies*, 62, pp. 59–74.

Blue, L. (2002), 'Myos Hormos – Quseir al-Qadim: A Roman and Islamic port on the Red

Sea coast of Egypt – a maritime perspective'. *Proceedings of the Seminar for Arabian Studies*. London: Seminar for Arabian Studies, pp. 139–50.

Blue, L. (2006), 'The sedimentary history of the harbour area', in Peacock, D. and Blue, (eds), *Myos Hormos – Quseir al-Qadim: Roman and Islamic Ports on the Red Sea, Survey and Excavations 1999–2003*. Oxford: Oxbow.

Bopearachchi, O. (1996), *Seafaring in the Indian Ocean: Archaeological Evidence from Sri Lanka in Tradition and Archaeology*. Turnhout: Brepols.

Bowersock, G. W. (1973), 'Syria under Vespasian'. *Journal of Roman Studies*, 63, pp. 133–40.

Bowersock, G. W. (1994), *Roman Arabia*. London: Harvard University Press.

Bowman, A. K. (1994), *The Vindolanda Writing Tablets*. London: British Museum Press.

Bowman, A. and Wilson, A. (2009), *Quantifying the Roman Economy: Methods and Problems*. Oxford: Oxford University Press.

Butterworth, A. and Laurence, R. (2005), *Pompeii the Living City*. London: Weidenfeld & Nicolson.

Braudel, F. (1981), *Civilization and Capitalism 15th–18th Century, Volume 2: The Wheels of Commerce*. London: Collins.

Campbell, B. (1984), *The Emperor and the Roman Army, 31 BC–AD 235*. Oxford: Clarendon.

Campbell, B. (1995), 'War and diplomacy: Rome and Parthia, 31 BC–AD 235', in Rich, J. and Shipley, G. (eds), *War and Society in the Roman World*. London: Routledge, pp. 213–39.

Campbell, B. (2001), 'Diplomacy in the Roman world (c. 500 BC–AD 235)', *Diplomacy & Statecraft*, 12, (1), pp. 1–22.

Cappers, R. T. J. (1999), 'Archaeobotanical evidence of Roman trade with India'. In *Archaeology of Seafaring: The Indian Ocean in the Ancient Period*, Himanshu Prabha Ray (ed.). Delhi: Indian Council of Historical Research, pp. 51–69.

Cary, M. (1956), 'Maes, qui et Titianus'. *Classical Quarterly*, 6, pp. 130–4.

Casson, L. (1971), *Ships and Seamanship in the Ancient World*. Princeton: Princeton University Press.

Casson, L. (1980), *Transactions and Proceedings of the American Philological Association*, 110, pp. 32–3.

Casson, L. (1984), *Ancient Trade*. Detroit: Wayne State University Press.

Casson, L. (1986), 'P. Vindob. G40822 and the Shipping of Goods from India'. *Bulletin of the American Society of Papyrologists*, 23, pp. 73–9.

Casson, L. (1988), 'Rome's maritime trade with the Far East'. *The American Neptune*, 48, pp. 149–53.

Casson, L. (1989), *The Periplus Maris Erythraei: Text with Introduction, Translation, and Commentary*. Princeton: Princeton University Press.

Casson, L. (1990), 'New light on maritime loans: P. Vindob. G 40822', *Zeitschrift für Papyrologie und Epigraphik*, 84, pp. 195–206.

Casson, L. (1991a), *The Ancient Mariners, Seafarers and Sea Fighters of the Mediterranean in Ancient Times*. Princeton: Princeton University Press.

Casson, L. (1991b), 'Ancient naval technology and the route to India', in Begley, V. and De Puma, R. D. (eds), *Rome and India: The Ancient Sea Trade*. Madison: University of Wisconsin Press, pp. (full details available from the British Library).

Champakalakshmi, R. (1996), *Trade, Ideology and Urbanisation: South India 300 BC to AD 1300*. Delhi: Oxford University Press.

Champion, C. B. (2004), *Roman Imperialism: Readings and Sources*. Oxford: Blackwell Publishers.

Charlesworth, M. P. (1924), *Trade Routes and Commerce of the Roman Empire*. Cambridge: Cambridge University Press.

Chaumont, M. L. and Gawlikowski, M. (1984), 'Etudes d'histoire Parthe V – La Route Royale des Parthes de Zeugma a Seleucie du Tigre d'apres l'itineraire de Charax', in *Syria*, 61, pp. 63–107.

Christian, D. (2000), 'Silk roads or steppe roads? The Silk roads in world history', *Journal of World History*, 11.1, pp. 1–26.

Cimino, R. M. (ed.), (1994), *Ancient Rome and India: Commercial and Cultural Contacts between the Roman World and India*. New Delhi, Munshiram Manoharlal Publishers.

Clarke, K. (1997), 'In search of the author of Strabo's Geography', in *the Journal of Roman Studies*, 87, pp. 92–110.

Colledge, M. A. R. (1976), *The Art of Palmyra*. London, Thames and Hudson.

Cotton, H. M. and Cockle, W. E. H. (1995), 'The Papyrology of the Roman Near East: a Survey', *Journal of Roman Studies*, 85, pp. 214–35.

Cribb, J. (1992), 'Numismatic evidence for the date of the "Periplus"', in Macdowall, D. W. and Sharma, S. (eds), *Indian Numismatic, History, Art and Culture*. India: Agam Kala Prakasha, pp. 131–45.

Cribb, J. (1998), 'Western satraps and Satavahanas: old and new ideas of chronology', in Jha, A. K. and Garg, S. (eds), *Ex Moneta: Essays on Numismatics, History, and Archaeology in Honour of Dr David W. MacDowall*. New Delhi: Harman Publishing House.

Crone, P. (1987), *Meccan Trade and the Rise of Islam*. Princeton: Princeton University Press.

Croom, A. T. (2000), *Roman Clothing and Fashion*. Stroud: Tempus.

D'Arms, J. H. (1981), *Commerce and Social Standing in Ancient Rome*. Harvard: Harvard University Press.

Dalby, A. (2000), *Empire of Pleasures: Luxury and Indulgence in the Roman World*. London: Routledge.

De Romanis, F. (1997), 'Romanukharattha and Taprobane: relations between Rome and Sri Lanka in the first century AD', in De Romanis, F. and Tchernia, A. (eds), (1997), *Crossings: Early Mediterranean Contacts with India*. New Delhi: Manohar Publishers & Distributors, pp. 161–237.

De Romanis, F. (1997), 'Rome and the notia of India: relations between Rome and southern India from 30 BC to the Flavian period', in De Romanis, F. and Tchernia, A. (eds), (1997), *Crossings: Early Mediterranean Contacts with India*. New Delhi: Manohar Publishers & Distributors, pp. 80–160.

De Romanis, F. and Tchernia, A. (eds), (1997), *Crossings: Early Mediterranean Contacts with India*. New Delhi: Manohar Publishers & Distributors.

Drexhage, R. (1988), *Untersuchungen zum Romischen Osthandel*. Bonn: Habelt.

Dubs, H. (1941), 'An ancient military contact between Romans and Chinese', *American Journal of Philology*, 42, pp. 322–30.

Dubs, H. (1943), 'A Roman influence upon Chinese painting', *Classical Philology*, 38, (1), pp. 13–9.

Dubs, H. (1957), *A Roman City in Ancient China*. London: The China Society.

Dueck, D. (2000), *Strabo of Amasia: A Greek Man of Letters in Augustan Rome*. London: Routlege.

Duncan-Jones, R. (1974), *The Economy of the Roman Empire: Quantative Studies*. London: Cambridge University Press.

Duncan-Jones, R. (1990), *Structure and Scale in the Roman Economy*. Cambridge, Cambridge University Press.

Duncan-Jones, R. (1994), *Money and Government in the Roman Empire*. Cambridge: Cambridge University Press.

Duncan-Jones, R. (1996), 'The impact of the Antonine plague', *Journal of Roman Archaeology*, 9, pp. 108–136.

Duncan-Jones, R. (2004), 'Economic change and the transition to late antiquity', in Swain, S. and Edwards, M. (eds), *Approaching Late Antiquity: The Transformation from Early to Late Empire*. Oxford: Oxford University Press.

Elton, H. (1996), *Frontiers of the Roman Empire*. London: Batsford.

Etienne, R. (1992), *Pompeii: The Day a City Died*. London, Thames & Hudson.

Ferguson, J. (1978), 'China and Rome'. *Aufstieg und Niedergang der Römischen Welt*, 2.9.2, pp. 581–603.

Franck, I. M. and Brownstone, D. M. (1986), *The Silk Road: A History*. Oxford: Facts on File.

Fraser, P. M. *Ptolemaic Alexandria*. Oxford: Clarendon Press.

Frier, B. W. (2000), 'Population', in Bowman, A. and Garnsey, P. and Rathbone, D. (eds), *The Cambridge Ancient History (Volume 11): The High Empire AD 70–192*. Cambridge: Cambridge University Press, pp. 811–6.

Fuks, A. (1951), 'Notes on the archive of Nicanor'. *Journal of Juristic Papyrology*, pp. 207–16.

Gawlikowski, M. (1983), 'The Roman frontier on the Euphrates'. *Mesopotania*, 22, pp. 77–80.

Gawlikowski, M. (1994), 'Palmyra as a trading centre'. *Iraq*, 56, pp. 27–33.

Glover, I. C. (1996a), 'Recent archaeological evidence for early maritime contacts between India and South-East Asia', in Ray, H. P. and Salles J. (eds.), *Tradition and Archaeology Early: Maritime Contacts in the Indian Ocean*. New Delhi: Manohar Publishers and Distributors, pp. 128–80.

Glover, I. C. (1996b), 'The archaeological evidence for early trade between India and Southeast Asia', in Reade, J. (ed.), *The Indian Ocean in Antiquity*. London: Kegan Paul International in association with the British Museum, pp. 373–78.

Goldsworthy, A. (2009), *How Rome Fell*. New York: Yale University Press.

Goodman, M. (1997), *The Roman World 44 BC–AD 180*. London: Routledge.

Graf, D. T. (1996), 'The Roman East from the Chinese perspective', *Les Annales Archéologiques Arabes Syriennes. Revue d'Archéologie*, 42, pp. 199–216.

Graf, D. T. (1997), *Rome and the Arabian Frontier: From the Nabataeans to the Saracens*. Aldershot: Ashgate.

Griffin, M. (2000), 'Trajan', in Bowman, A. and Garnsey, P. and Rathbone, D. (eds), *The Cambridge Ancient History (Volume 11): The High Empire AD 70–192*. Cambridge: Cambridge University Press, pp. 96–131.

Groom, N. (1981), *Frankincense and Myrrh: A Study of the Arabian Incense Trade*. London: Longman.

Groom, N. (1995), 'The Periplus, Pliny and Arabia'. *Arabian Archaeology and Epigraphy*, 6, pp. 180–95.

Gupta, S. (1997) *Roman Egypt to Peninsular India: Archaeological Patterns of Trade, 1st century BC–3rd Century AD*. Pune: PhD thesis, Deccan College.

Gupta, P. L. (1991), 'Coins in Rome's Eastern Indian trade', in Jha, A. K. (ed.), *Coinage, Trade and Economy*. Bombay: Indian Institute of Research in Numismatic Studies, pp. 122–37.

Gurukkal, R. and Whittaker, C. R. (2001), 'In search of Muziris'. *Journal of Roman Archaeology*, pp. 333–50.

Harl, K. W. (1996), *Coinage in the Roman Economy, 300 BC to AD 700*. London: Johns Hopkins University Press.

Harmatta, J. (1999), *History of Civilizations of Central Asia (Volume 2)*. Delhi: Motilal Banarsidass.

Harris, W. V. (1993), 'Between archaic and modern', in Harris, W. V. (ed.), *The Inscribed Economy: Production and Distribution in the Roman Empire in the Light of Instrumentum Domesticum*. Ann Arbor: University of Michigan.

Harris, W. V. (2000), 'Trade', in Bowman, A. and Garnsey, P. and Rathbone, D. (eds), *The Cambridge Ancient History (Volume 11): The High Empire* AD *70–192*. Cambridge: Cambridge University Press, pp. 710–40.

Healy, J. F. (1999), *Pliny the Elder on Science and Technology*. Oxford: Oxford University Press.

Heather, P. J. (2005), *The Fall of the Roman Empire*. London: Pan Books.

Hermansen, G. (1981), *Ostia: Aspects of Roman City Life*. Edmonton: University of Alberta Press.

Hill, J. E. (2003), *Notes to the Hou Hanshu*. Washington University: Silk Road Seattle.

Hill, J. E. (2004), *Weilue: About the Text*. Washington University: Silk Road Seattle.

Hill, J. E. (2009), *Through the Jade Gate to Rome: A Study of the Silk Routes during the Later Han Dynasty 1st to 2nd Centuries CE*. Seattle: BookSurge Publishing.

Hirth, F. (1885), *China and the Roman Orient: Researches into their Ancient and Mediaeval Relations as Represented in Old Chinese Records*. Chicago: Ares (reprint: 1975).

Hopkins, K. (1983), 'Models, ships and staples', in Garnsey, P. and Whittaker, C. R. (eds), *Trade and Famine in Classical Antiquity*. Cambridgeshire: Cambridge Philological Society, pp. 84–109.

Hopkins, K. (2002), 'Rome, taxes, rents and trade', in Scheidel, W. and Von Reden, S. *The Ancient Economy*. Edinburgh: Edinburgh University Press, pp. 190–232.

Horden, P. and Purcell, N. (2000), *The Corrupting Sea: A Study of Mediterranean History*. Oxford: Blackwell Publishers.

Hoyland, R. G. (2001), *Arabia and the Arabs*. London: Routledge.

Huntingford, G. W. B. (translator) (1980), *The Periplus of the Erythraean Sea by an Unknown Author: with some Extracts from Agatharkhides 'On the Erythraean Sea'*. London: Hakluyt Society.

Isaac, B. H. (1990), *The Limits of Empire: The Roman Army in the East*. Oxford: Clarendon Press.

Isager, J. (1991), *The Elder Pliny's Chapters on the History of Art*. Odense: Odense University Press.

Johnson, W. R. and Whitcomb, D. S. (1979), 'Pottery: Roman pottery – Islamic pottery', in Johnson, W. R. and Whitcomb, D. S. (eds), *Quseir al-Qadim: Preliminary Report*. Cairo: American Research Centre in Egypt, pp. 64–143.

Jones, A. H. M. (1964), *The Later Roman Empire 284–602: A Social, Economic and Administrative Survey*. Oklahoma: University of Oklahoma Press.

Kratoska, P. H. (2001), *South East Asia: Colonial History*. London: Routledge.

Krishnamurthy, R. (1998), 'Imitation Roman gold coins from Tirukoilur hoard, Tamilnadu', in Jha, A. K. and Garg, S. (eds), *Ex Moneta: Essays on Numismatics, History, and Archaeology in Honour of Dr David W. MacDowall*. New Delhi: Harman Publishing House.

Kumar, Y. (2005), *A History of Sino-Indian Relations: 1st century* AD *to 7th century* AD. New Delhi: APH Publishing.

Leslie, D. D. and Gardiner, K. H. J. (1996), *The Roman Empire in Chinese Sources*. Rome: Bardi.

Levi, A. and Levi, M. (1967), *Interaria Picta: Contributo Alla Studio della Tabula Peutingeriana*. Roma, 'L'Erma' di Bretschneider.

Levi, A. (1978), *La Tabula Peutingeriana*. Bologna: Edizioni Edison.

Littmann, E. and Meredith, D. (1953), 'Nabataean Inscriptions from Egypt', *Bulletin of the School of Oriental & African Studies*, 15, pp. 1–28.

Liu, X. (1988), *Ancient India and Ancient China*. Oxford: Oxford University Press.

Liu, X. (2001), 'The Silk Road: Overland Trade and Cultural Interaction in Eurasia' in Adas, M. (ed.) *Agricultural and Pastoral Societies in Ancient and Classical History*. United States: Temple University Press, pp. 151–81.

MacDowall, T. C. L. (1998), 'The defacement of Roman aurei exported to India', in Jha, A. K. (ed.), *Coinage Trade and Economy*. Bombay: Indian Institute of Research in Numismatic Studies.
Macdowell, D. W. (1990), 'Finds of Roman coins in southern Asia: Problems of interpretation'. *Ancient Ceylon*, 9, pp. 49–73.
Macdowell, D. W. (1991), 'Indian imports of Roman silver coins', in Jha, A. K. (ed.), *Coinage Trade and Economy*. Bombay: Indian Institute of Research in Numismatic Studies.
Macdowell, D. W. (1996), 'The evidence of the Gazetteer of Roman artefacts in India', in Ray, H. P. and Salles, J. (eds), *Tradition and Archaeology: Early Maritime Contacts in the Indian Ocean*. New Delhi: Manohar Publishers and Distributors, pp. 79–94.
Mahadevan, I. (1996), 'Pottery inscriptions in Brahmi and Tamil-Brahmi', in Begley, V. and Francis, P. and Mahadevan, I. (eds), *The Ancient Port of Arikamedu: New Investigations and Researches 1989–1992*. Pondicherry: Centre d'histoire et d'archéologie, École française d'Extrême-Orient, pp. 287–315.
Mallory, J. P. and Victor, H. M. (2000), *The Tarim Mummies: Ancient China and the Mystery of the Earliest Peoples from the West*. London: Thames & Hudson.
Man, J. (2008), *The Great Wall*. London: Bantam.
Mattern, S. P. (1999), *Rome and the Enemy: Imperial Strategy in the Principate*. Berkeley: University of California Press.
Matthews, J. F. (1984), 'The tax law of Palmyra: evidence for economic history in a city of the Roman East'. *Journal of Roman Studies*, 74, pp. 157–80.
McLynn, F. (2009), *Marcus Aurelius: Warrior, Philosopher, Emperor*. London, Bodley Head.
McNeill, W. H. (1976), *Plagues and Peoples*. New York: Anchor Press.
Meredith, D. (1953), 'Annius Plocamus: two inscriptions from the Berenice road'. *Journal of Roman Studies*, 43, pp. 38–40.
Millar, F. (1977), *The Emperor in the Roman World (31 BC–AD 337)*. London: Duckworth.
Millar, F. (1993), *The Roman Near East 31 BC–AD 337*. Cambridge: Mass.
Millar, F. (1998), 'Caravan cities: the Roman Near East and long-distance trade by land', in Austin, M. and Harries, J. and Smith, C (eds), *Modus Operandi: Essays in Honour of Geoffrey Rickman*. London: Institute of Classical Studies, pp. 122–37.
Millar, F. (2003), *Rome, the Greek World, and the East: Volume 2: Government, Society, and Culture in the Roman Empire*. North Carolina, University of North Carolina Press.
Miller, J. I. (1969), *The Spice Trade of the Roman Empire, 29 BC to AD 641*. Clarendon Press, Oxford.
Morgan, G. (2006), *69 AD the Year of Four Emperors*. Oxford: Oxford University Press.
Moriyasu, T. (1999), 'The west Uighur kingdom and Tun-huang around the 10th–11th centuries', in *Berichte und Abhandlungen*, 8, pp. 337–70.
Munro, S. C. H. (1996), 'Aksumite overseas interests', in Reade, J. (ed.), *The Indian Ocean in Antiquity*. London: Kegan Paul International in association with the British Museum.
Murphy, T. M. (2004), *Pliny the Elder's Natural History: The Empire in Encyclopaedia*. Oxford: Oxford University Press.
Needham, J. and Yates, R. D. S. (1994) *Science and Civilisation in China (Volume 6)*. Cambridge: Cambridge University Press.
Newman, L. I. (ed.), (1945), *The Talmudic Anthology*. New York: Behrman House.
Nicolet, C. N. (1996), *Financial Documents and Geographical Knowledge in the Roman World*. Oxford: Leopard's Head Press.
Parker, A. J. (1992), *Ancient Shipwrecks of the Mediterranean and the Roman Provinces*. Oxford: Tempus Reparatum.
Parker, G. (2008), *The Making of Roman India*. Cambridge: Cambridge University Press.

Peacock, D. and Williams, D. (eds), (2006), *Food for the Gods: New Light on the Ancient Incense Trade*. Oxford: Oxbow.

Phillips, C. and Villeneuve, F. and Facey, W. (2004), 'A Latin inscription from South Arabia', *Proceedings of the Seminar for Arabian Studies*, 34, pp. 85–100.

Potter, D. S. and Mattingly, D. J. (eds), (1999), *Life, Death and Entertainment in the Roman Empire*. Ann Arbor: University of Michigan Press.

Potts, D. T. (1988), 'Arabia and the kingdom of Characene', in Potts, D. T. (ed.), *Araby the Blest*. Copenhagen: Carsten Niebuhr Institute of Ancient Near Eastern Studies. University of Copenhagen: Museum Tusculanum Press. pp. 137–67.

Potts, D. T. (1990), *The Arabian Gulf in Antiquity*. Oxford: Clarendon.

Potts, D. T. (1996), 'The Parthian presence in the Arabian Gulf', in Reade, J. (ed.), *The Indian Ocean in Antiquity*. London: Kegan Paul International in association with the British Museum. (full details available from the British Library).

Potter, D. S. (2002), 'Odor and power in the Roman Empire' in Porter, J. I. *Constructions of the Classical Body*. Michigan: Ann Arbor.

Potts, D. T. (ed.), (1988), *Araby the Blest*. Copenhagen: Carsten Niebuhr Institute of Ancient Near Eastern Studies. University of Copenhagen: Museum Tusculanum Press.

Prasad, K. (1984), *Cities, Crafts and Commerce under the Kusanas*. Delhi: Agam Kala Prakashan.

Pulleyblank, E. G. (1981), 'Han China in Central Asia'. *International History Review*, 3, pp. 278–86.

Pulleyblank, E. G. (1999), 'The Roman Empire as known to Han China'. *Journal of the American Oriental Society*, 119, pp. 71–9.

Raftery, B. (1994), *Pagan Celtic Ireland: The Enigma of the Irish Iron Age*. London: Thames and Hudson.

Rajan, K. (1996), 'Early maritime activities of the Tamils', in Ray, H. P. and Salles J. (eds), *Tradition and Archaeology Early: Maritime Contacts in the Indian Ocean*. New Delhi: Manohar Publishers and Distributors, pp (full details available from the British Library).

Raschke, M. G. (1978), 'New studies in Roman commerce with the East', *Aufstieg und Niedergang der Römischen Welt*, 2:9.2, pp. 604–1378.

Rathbone, D. (1996), 'The imperial finances', in Bowman, A. and Garnsey, P. and Rathbone, D. (eds), *The Cambridge Ancient History (Volume 11): The High Empire* AD *70–192*. Cambridge, Cambridge University Press, pp. 309–23.

Rathbone, D. (2001), 'The 'Muziris' papyrus (SB XVIII 13167): financing Roman trade with India', in *Alexandrian Studies II in Honour of Mostafa el Abbadi*, (full details available from the British Library), pp. 39–50.

Rathbone, D. (2003), 'The financing of maritime commerce in the Roman Empire, I–II AD', in Lo Cascio, E. (ed.), *Credito e moneta nel mondo romano: atti degli Incontri capresi di storia dell'economia antica*. Bari: Edipuglia, pp. 197–229.

Rathbone, D. W. (2002), 'The ancient economy and Graeco-Roman Egypt', in Scheidel W. and Reden, S. (eds), *The Ancient Economy.* Edinburgh, Edinburgh University Press, pp. 155–67.

Rauh, N. K. (2003), *Merchants, Sailors and Pirates in the Roman World*. Stroud: Tempus.

Ray, H. P. (1994), *The Winds of Change: Buddhism and Maritime Links of Early South Asia*. Oxford: Oxford University Press.

Ray, H. P. (1995), 'A resurvey of 'Roman' contacts with the East', in Boussac, M. and Salles, J. (eds), *Athens, Aden, Arikamedu: Essays on the Interrelations between India, Arabia and the Eastern Mediterranean*. Manohar: Centre de Sciences, pp. 97–114.

Reid, S. (1994), *The Silk and Spice Routes: Exploration by Sea*. London: Belitha.

Richmond, I. A. (1963), 'Palmyra under the aegis of Rome'. *Journal of Roman Studies*, 53, pp. 43–54.

Rickman, G. (1971), *Roman Granaries and Store Buildings*. Cambridge: Cambridge University Press.

Rickman, G. (1980), *The Corn Supply of Ancient Rome*. Oxford: Oxford University Press.

Roberts, P. (2008), *Mummy Portraits from Roman Egypt*. London: British Museum Press.

Robin, C. (1997), 'The date of the Periplus of the Erythraean Sea in the light of South Arabian evidence', in De Romanis, F. and Tchernia, A. (eds), (1997) *Crossings: Early Mediterranean Contacts with India*. New Delhi: Manohar Publishers & Distributors, pp. 41–65.

Romm, J. S. (1992), *The Edges of the Earth in Ancient Thought*. Princeton: Princeton University Press.

Salles, J. (1995), 'The Periplus of the Erythraean Sea and the Arab-Persian Gulf', in Boussac, M. and Salles, J. (eds), *Athens, Aden, Arikamedu: Essays on the Interrelations between India, Arabia and the Eastern Mediterranean*. Manohar: Centre de Sciences, pp. 115–46.

Salles, J. (1996a), 'Achaemenid and Hellenistic trade in the Indian Ocean', in Reade, J. (ed.), *The Indian Ocean in Antiquity*. London: Kegan Paul International in association with the British Museum, pp. 251–67.

Salles, J. (1996b), 'Hellenistic seafaring in the Indian Ocean', in Ray, H. P. and Salles J. (eds), *Tradition and Archaeology Early: Maritime Contacts in the Indian Ocean*. New Delhi: Manohar Publishers and Distributors, pp. 293–309.

Salway, P. (1965), *The Frontier People of Roman Britain*. Cambridge: University Press.

Sampson, G. C. (2008), *The Defeat of Rome: Crassus, Carrhae and the Invasion of the East*. Barnsley: Pen & Sword Military.

Schmitthenner, W. (1979), 'Rome and India: aspects of universal history', *Journal of Roman Studies*, 69, pp. 90–106.

Schoff, W. H. (translator), (1912), *The Periplus of the Erythraean Sea*. New York: Green & Co.

Schoff, W. H. (translator), (1914), *Parthian Stations by Isidore of Charax*. Philadelphia: Commercial Museum.

Sedov, A. V. (1996), 'Qana (Yemen) and the Indian Ocean: the archaeological evidence', in Ray, H. P. and Salles J. (eds,), *Tradition and Archaeology Early: Maritime Contacts in the Indian Ocean*. New Delhi: Manohar Publishers and Distributors, pp. 128–80.

Sedov, A. V. (2007), 'The Port of Qana and the Incense Trade', in Peacock, D. and Williams, D. (eds), (2007), *Food for the Gods: New Light on the Ancient Incense Trade*. Oxford: Oxbow.

Seland, E. L. (2005), '"The Periplus", report of a Roman attack on Aden: an unintended result of successful propaganda?', *Symbolac Osloenses*, 80.1, pp. 60–7.

Seray, H. M. B. (1993), *The Arabian Gulf from the 3rd century B.C. to the 1st/2nd century A.D.*, Manchester, Manchester University.

Shackley, M. (2006), 'Frankincense and Myrrh today', Peacock, D. and Williams, D. (eds), *Food for the Gods: New Light on the Ancient Incense Trade*. Oxford: Oxbow.

Sidebotham, S. E. (1986a), *Roman Economic Policy in the Erythra Thalassa 30 BC–AD 217*. Leiden: E. J. Brill.

Sidebotham, S. E. (1986b), 'Ports of the Red Sea and the Arabia-India trade', *Münstersche Beiträge zur Antiken Handelsgeschichte*, 5, (2), pp. 16–36.

Sidebotham, S. E. (1986c), 'Aelius Gallus and Arabia'. *Latomus*, 45, pp. 590–602.

Sidebotham, S. E. (1989), 'Ports of the Red Sea and the Arabia-India trade', in French, D. H. and Lightfoot, C. S. (eds), *The Eastern Frontier of the Roman Empire: Proceedings of a Colloquium held at Ankara in September 1988*. Oxford: British Archaeological Reports, pp. 485–509.

Sidebotham, S. E. (1991), 'Ports of the Red Sea and the Arabia-India Trade', in Begley, V. and De Puma, R. D. (eds), *Rome and India: The Ancient Sea Trade*. Oxford: Oxford University Press.

Sidebotham, S. E. and Wendrich, W. Z. (eds), (1995a), *Berenike 1994: Preliminary Report of the 1994 Excavations at Berenike (Egyptian Red Sea Coast) and the Survey of the Eastern Desert*. Leiden, Research School CNWS.

Sidebotham, S. E. and Wendrich. W. Z. (eds), (1995b), 'Berenike Port of Elephants and Pearls'. *Egypt Today*, December, pp. 144–5.

Sidebotham, S. E. and Webdrich, W. Z. (eds), (1996a), *Berenike '95 Preliminary Report of the 1995 Excavations at Berenike and the Survey of the Egyptian Eastern Desert, including Excavations at Shenshef*. Leiden: Netherlands, Research School (CNWS).

Sidebotham, S. E. (1996b), 'Excavations', in Begley, V. and Francis, P. and Mahadevan, I. (eds), *The Ancient Port of Arikamedu: New Investigations and Researches 1989–1992*. Pondicherry: Centre d'histoire et d'archéologie, École française d'Extrême-Orient, pp. (full details available from the British Library).

Sidebotham S. E. and Wendrich. W. Z. (eds), (1996c), 'Berenike: Roman Egypt's maritime gateway to Arabia and India'. *Egyptian Archaeology*, 8, pp. 15–8.

Sidebotham, S. E. (1996d), 'Roman interests in the Red Sea and Indian Ocean', in Reade, J. (ed.), *The Indian Ocean in Antiquity*. London: Kegan Paul International in association with the British Museum, pp. (full details available from the British Library).

Sidebotham, S. E. and Webdrich, W. Z. (eds), (1998), *Berenike '96 Report of the Excavations at Berenike (Egyptian Red Sea Coast) and Survey of the Eastern Desert*. Leiden, Research School (CNWS).

Sidebotham, S. E. and Webdrich, W. Z. (eds), (1999a), *Report of the 1997 Excavations at Berenike and the Survey of the Egyptian Eastern Desert, including Excavations at Shenshef*. Leiden: Research School (CNWS).

Sidebotham, S. E. and Wendrich, W. Z. (eds), (1999b), 'Berenike: an ancient emporium at the cross-roads of the Mediterranean-Red Sea-Indian Ocean trade', *The Indian Ocean Review*, 12, (16), (full details available from the British Library).

Sidebotham, S. E. and Wendrich, W. Z. (eds), (2000), *Report of the 1998 Excavations at Berenike and the Survey of the Egyptian Eastern Desert including Excavations in Wadi Kalalat*. Leiden: Research School CNWS.

Sidebotham, S. E. (2002), 'Late Roman Berenike', *Journal of the American Research Centre in Egypt*, 39, pp. 217–40.

Sidebotham, S. E. and Wendrich, W. Z. (eds), (2006), *Berenike 1999–2000: Report on the Excavations at Berenike, including Excavations in Wadi Kalalat and Siket, and the Survey of the Mons Smaragdus Region*. Cotsen Institute of Archaeology at University of California Los Angeles.

Sidebotham, S. E. (2008), *The Red Land: The Illustrated Archaeology of Egypt's Eastern Desert*. New York: American University in Cairo Press.

Singer, C. (2007), 'An outline history of the South Arabian incense trade', in Peacock, D. and Williams, D. (eds), *Food for the Gods: New Light on the Ancient Incense Trade*. Oxford: Oxbow.

Singh, A. K. (1988), *Indo-Roman Trade: An Archaeological Perspective*. New Delhi: South Asia Books.

Sinor, D. (ed.) (1990), *Cambridge History of Early Inner Asia*. Cambridge: Cambridge University Press.

Slane, K. W. (1996), 'Other ancient ceramics imported from the Mediterranean', in Begley, V. and Francis, P. and Mahadevan, I. (eds), *The Ancient Port of Arikamedu: New Investigations and Researches 1989–1992*. Pondicherry: Centre d'histoire et d'archéologie, École française d'Extrême-Orient, pp. 351–68.

Stauffer, A. (1996), 'Textiles from Palmyra: local production and the import and imitation of Chinese silk weavings', *International Colloquium on Palmyra and the Silk Road*, 42, pp. 425–30.

Stoneman, R. (1992), *Palmyra and its Empire: Zenobia's Revolt against Rome*. Ann Arbor: University of Michigan Press.

Strauss, J. E. (2007), *Roman Cargoes: Underwater Evidence from the Eastern Mediterranean*. London: Thesis (PhD), University of London.

Strong, D. E. (1966), *Greek and Roman Gold and Silver Plate*. London: Methuen.

Suresh, S. (1992), *Roman Antiquities in Tamilnadu*. Madras: C. P. Ramaswami Aiyar Institute of Indological Research, C. P. Ramaswami Aiyar Foundation.

Tainter, J. A. (1995), 'Sustainability of complex societies'. *Futures*, 27, pp. 397–407.

Talbert, R. J. A. (ed.), (2000), *Barrington Atlas of the Greek and Roman World*. Princeton: Princeton University Press.

Talbert, R. J. A. and Brodersen, K. (eds), (2004), *Space in the Roman World: Its Perception and Presentation*. New York: Distributed in North America by Transaction Publishers.

Tchernia, A. (1997), 'The dromedary of the Peticii and trade with the East' in De Romanis, F. and Tchernia, A. (eds), (1997), *Crossings: Early Mediterranean Contacts with India*. New Delhi: Manohar Publishers & Distributors, pp. 238–49.

Tchernia, (1997), 'Winds and coins: from the supposed discovery of the monsoon to the denarii of Tiberius' in De Romanis, F. and Tchernia, A. (eds), (1997), *Crossings: Early Mediterranean Contacts with India*. New Delhi: Manohar Publishers & Distributors, pp. 250–76.

Thapar, R. (1997), 'Early Mediterranean contacts with India: an overview', in De Romanis, F. and Tchernia, A. *Crossings: Early Mediterranean Contacts with India*. New Delhi: Manohar Publishers & Distributors, Preface.

Thapar, R. (2002), *Early India: From the Origins to AD 1300*. Berkeley: University of California Press.

Thorley, J. (1969), 'The development of trade between the Roman Empire and the East under Augustus', *Greece and Rome*, 16, pp. 209–23.

Thorley, J. (1971), 'The silk trade between China and the Roman Empire at its height, circa AD 90–130'. *Greece and Rome*, 18, pp. 71–80.

Thorley, J. (1979), 'The Roman Empire and the Kushans'. *Greece and Rome*, 26, (2), pp. 181–90.

Tomber, R. (2004), 'Rome and South Arabia: new artefactual evidence from the Red Sea'. *Proceedings of the Seminar for Arabian Studies*, 34, pp. (full details available from the British Library).

Tomber, R. (2008), *Indo-Roman Trade: From Pots to Pepper*. London: Duckworth.

Turner, P. J. (1989), *Roman Coins from India*. London: Royal Numismatic Society.

Turner, P. J. and Cribb, J. (1996), 'Numismatic evidence for the Roman trade with ancient India', in Reade, J. (ed.), *The Indian Ocean in Antiquity*. London: Kegan Paul International in association with the British Museum, pp. (full details available from the British Library).

Ustinova, Y. (2000), 'New Latin and Greek rock-inscriptions from Uzbekistan'. *Hephaistos*, 18, pp. 169–79.

Varadpande, M. L. (1987), *History of Indian Theatre*. New Delhi: Abhinav.

Veen, M. (1998), 'A life of luxury in the desert? The food and fodder supply to Mons Claudianus'. *Journal of Roman Archaeology*, 11, pp. 101–5.

Vogel, A. (1984), 'L'ethnographie de Srabon: ideologie ou tradition?', in Prontera, F. (ed.), *Strabone, contributi allo studio della personalita e dell'opera*. Perugia: Universita degli Studi di Perugia, pp. 29–86.

Ward-Perkins, B. (2005), *The Fall of Rome and the End of Civilisation*. Oxford: Oxford University Press.

Warmington, E. H. (1928), *The Commerce between the Roman Empire and India*. London: Curson Press.

Watson, B. (1961), *Records of the Grand Historian of China, Translated from the Shih chi of Ssu-ma Ch'ien (Volume 2)*. New York: Columbia University Press.

Waugh, N. S. (2004), *The Sogdian Ancient Letters*. Washington University: Seattle Silk Road Project.

Weerakkody, D. P. M. (1997), *Taprobane: Ancient Sri Lanka as known to Greeks and Romans*. Turnhout: Brepols.

Wheeler, R. E. M. (1946), 'Arikamedu: an Indo-Roman trading station on the east coast of India', *Ancient India*, 2, pp. 17–124.

Wheeler, R. E. M. (1954), *Rome beyond the Imperial Frontiers*. London: Bell.

Westermann, W. L. (1955), *The Slave Systems of Greek and Roman Antiquity*. Philadelphia: American Philosophical Society.

Whitcomb, D. S. and Johnson, J. H. (1982), *Quseir al-Qadim 1980: Preliminary Report*. Malibu: American Research Centre in Egypt Reports.

Whitewright, J. (2007), 'How fast is fast? Technology, trade and speed under sail in the Roman Red Sea', in Starkey, J. and Starkey, P. and Wilkinson, T. (eds), *Natural Resources and Cultural Connections of the Red Sea*. Oxford: Archaeopress, pp. 77–87.

Whitfield, S. (2004), *Aurel Stein in the Silk Road*. London: British Museum.

Whittaker, C. R. (2000), 'Frontiers', in Bowman, A. and Garnsey, P. and Rathbone, D. (eds), *The Cambridge Ancient History (Volume 11): The High Empire AD 70–192*. Cambridge: Cambridge University Press, pp. 293–319.

Whittaker, C. R. (2004), *Rome and its Frontiers: The Dynamics of Empire*. London: Routledge.

Wild, J. 'Cotton in Roman Egypt: some problems of origin'. *Al-Rafidan*, 18, pp. 287–98.

Wilkinson, P. (2003), *Pompeii: the Last Day*. London: BBC Books.

Will, E. L. (1991), 'The Roman shipping amphoras from Arikamedu', in Begley, V. and De Puma, R. D. (eds), *Rome and India: The Ancient Sea Trade*. Madison: University of Wisconsin Press, pp. 151–6.

Will, E. L. (1996), 'Mediterranean shipping amphoras from the 1941–50 excavations', in Begley, V. and De Puma, R. D. (eds), *Rome and India: The Ancient Sea Trade*. Madison: University of Wisconsin Press, pp. 317–49.

Will, E. L. (2003), 'From Italy to India: Mediterranean amphoras and Roman economic history'. *Amphora*, 2, (2), pp. 16–8.

Will, E. L. (2004) 'Mediterranean amphoras in India', in Eiring J. and Lund J. (eds), *Transport Amphorae and Trade in the Eastern Mediterranean*. Aarhus: Aarhus University Press, pp. 433–40.

Williams, D. F. (2004), 'The eruption of Vesuvius and its implications for the early Roman amphora trade with India', in Eiring J. and Lund J. (eds), *Transport Amphorae and Trade in the Eastern Mediterranean*. Aarhus: Aarhus University Press, pp. 441–50.

Wilson, A. (2007), 'The metal supply of the Roman Empire', in Papi, E. (ed.), *Supplying Rome and the Empire*. Portsmouth: *Journal of Roman Archaeology*, pp. 109–25.

Young, G. K. (2001), *Rome's Eastern Trade: International Commerce and Imperial Policy, 31 BC–AD 305*. London: Routledge.

Yu, Y. (1967), *Trade and Expansion in Han China: A Study in the Structure of Sino-barbarian Economic Relations*. Cambridge, Cambridge University Press.

Zvelebil, K. (1956), 'The Yavanas in old Tamil literature', in *Charisteria Orientalia praecipue ad Persiam pertinentia*. Prague: Nakladatelství Ceskoslovenské Akademie Ved, pp. 401–9.

Zvelebil, K. (1974), *Tamil literature*. Wiesbaden: Harrassowitz.

Zvelebil, K. (1992), *Companion Studies to the History of Tamil Literature*. New York: Brill.

Index